LEGAL ANALYSIS: 100 EXERCISES FOR MASTERY

Practice for Every Law Student

LEGAL ANALYSIS: 100 EXERCISES FOR MASTERY

Practice for Every Law Student

Cassandra L. Hill
Director of Legal Writing and
Assistant Professor of Law
Texas Southern University
Thurgood Marshall School of Law

Katherine T. Vukadin
Assistant Professor of Law
Texas Southern University
Thurgood Marshall School of Law

ISBN: 978-1-4224-8324-4

NOTE TO USERS

To ensure that you are using the latest materials available in this area, please be sure to periodically check the LexisNexis Law School web site for downloadable updates and supplements at www.lexisnexis.com/lawschool.

Editorial Offices
121 Chanlon Rd, New Providence, NJ 07974 (908) 464-6800
201 Mission St., San Francisco, CA 94105-1831 (415) 908-3200
www.lexisnexis.com

MATTHEW◆BENDER   (2012–Pub.3320)

DEDICATION

The authors dedicate this book to their late fathers,

Joshua Hill, Sr., who always displayed a passion for family, education, teaching, and community and who continues to inspire his children to be true visionaries and always to aim for excellence,

and

Alan Traverse, whose example taught excellence, whose intellect encouraged careful logic at the kitchen table and beyond, and whose confidence in his daughters inspires us still.

ABOUT THE AUTHORS

Cassandra L. Hill is the Director of Legal Writing and an Assistant Professor of Law at Texas Southern University Thurgood Marshall School of Law (TMSL), where she teaches legal analysis and writing. Professor Hill began her teaching career at UCLA School of Law and practiced in the areas of tax and employee benefits law at Baker Botts LLP. She also served as a federal law clerk for the Honorable Vanessa D. Gilmore, United States District Court Judge. As a law professor, Professor Hill provides students with an engaging and dynamic academic environment that serves the needs of students with different learning styles. She teaches students practice-oriented lawyering skills using a variety of subject matters and a process-based approach to skill development.

Professor Hill's research interests include legal education and assessment, legal writing pedagogy, learning theory, and employment law matters. Her article, *Peer Editing: A Comprehensive Pedagogical Approach to Maximize Assessment Opportunities, Integrate Collaborative Learning, and Achieve Desired Outcomes*, was published in the *Nevada Law Journal* (Spring 2011). In addition, her article (co-authored with Katherine Vukadin), *Now I See: Redefining the Post-Grade Conference as Process and Substance Assessment*, was the lead article in volume 45 of the *Howard Law Journal*. Professor Hill also has written several essays on law school and legal writing pedagogy.

Professor Hill is a member of the Legal Writing Institute (LWI) and the Association of Legal Writing Directors. In addition, Professor Hill is the Managing Editor for the *LWI Monograph Series*. She has served on the Program Committee for the AALS Section on Legal Writing, Reasoning, and Research and the AALS Section on Teaching Methods. She is the Secretary for the Diversity Committee of the AALS Section on Legal Writing, Reasoning, and Research. Professor Hill is the founder of Prep for Law, a law school preparation consulting company.

Katherine T. Vukadin is an Assistant Professor of Law at Thurgood Marshall School of Law, where she teaches legal analysis and writing. She began her legal career as an associate in the trial department at Baker Botts L.L.P.

Professor Vukadin first taught legal writing as a third-year law student at The University of Texas School of Law, later teaching at the University of Houston Law Center and now at Thurgood Marshall School of Law. Her research interests include legal education, legal writing pedagogy, and healthcare regulation.

Her article (co-authored with Professor Hill), *Now I See: Redefining the Post-Grade Conference as Process and Substance Assessment*, was the lead article in volume 45 of the *Howard Law Journal*, and her article on healthcare regulation, *Delayed and Denied: Toward an Effective Remedy for the Improper Processing of Healthcare Claims,* appeared in the Yale Journal of Health Policy, Law & Ethics in the summer of 2011.

Professor Vukadin specializes in using innovative teaching techniques to make legal writing compelling and accessible to all law students. Through her work with foreign law students seeking an American L.LM degree as well as remedial legal writing students and mainstream first-year students, Professor Vukadin has learned that with commitment, practice, and patience, all law students can master the essentials of legal writing.

To contact the authors, access additional helpful information about this book, or read helpful tips about legal analysis and writing, visit their blog site at www. legalwritinginbrief.com.

ACKNOWLEDGMENTS

This book could not have been written without the assistance and support of our national and institutional colleagues, students, and families.

Our heartfelt thanks go to our colleagues, Shaundra Kellam Lewis, Lydia Johnson, Laura Cisneros, and Teri McMurtry-Chubb, for ideas, materials, and thoughtful suggestions; to Walter Champion for his expert guidance; and to the faculty at Thurgood Marshall School of Law, for constant support and encouragement.

We also would like to thank our research assistants, Lauren Dahlstein, Jana Lewis, Colleen Lowry, Venessa Smithwick, and Theresa Thomas; our faculty assistant, Gertrude Florent; and our IT support team, Paul Stein, Tarius Anderson, and Trina Leach. We also are greatly indebted to our legal writing colleague, Professor Tobi Tabor of the University of Houston Law Center, for her thoughtful edits and encouragement. We also would like to recognize our students, who have taught us so much over the years and served as the impetus for writing this book. We also acknowledge with much gratitude the generous support of our school, Texas Southern University Thurgood Marshall School of Law, in investing in our project with research grants, assistance, and supportive mentoring.

And to our wonderful family and friends: Cassandra Hill thanks her husband, William Grogan, for his love and support, creative contribution, inspiration, and unwavering patience; her mother, Etta M. Hill, for her steadfast support, prayers, and words of wisdom; and her many family members and friends for their kind thoughts and constant encouragement.

Katherine Vukadin thanks her husband, Davor Vukadin, for his abiding love and support; her mother, Anne Traverse, whose love of words and ability to juggle three energetic grandchildren made Katherine's work on this book possible; her children, Chris, Sophie, and Nick, who are her joy and who inspired more than one of these exercises, and her family and friends who encouraged and supported this project.

Lastly, the authors are thankful for this opportunity to continue their collaborative work and efforts. They have learned so much from each other through the brainstorming sessions, edits, revisions, suggestions, and late-night texts, and they wholeheartedly appreciate the benefits, synergies, and hearty laughter gained from collaboration.

PREFACE

Each year, over 45,000 students enter law school. In the first year, students are introduced to the skill of legal analysis—the identification of relevant legal issues and law and the application of law to fact that forms the foundation of legal reasoning. At the end of their first year, law students should be proficient in the process of legal analysis. A fortunate few do accomplish this goal, but many do not. For the latter group, legal analysis remains a code they never quite crack. These students' law school days become frustrating, they fail to thrive in their development of key lawyering skills, and their bar passage is in doubt.

Legal employers agree that law school graduates' analysis skills need work. A "Special Report on Law Schools" (dated April 2009 in the *New York Law Journal*[1]) reported law firm attorneys' frustrations over new lawyers' inability to organize facts and principles in a crisp and logical way—essentially, their poor legal analysis and argument structure skills. Likewise, the American Bar Association's (ABA) 1992 MacCrate report[2] on narrowing the gap between law school and practice mandates that law graduates should have mastered two skills that are the conceptual foundations for virtually all aspects of legal practice: problem-solving and legal analysis.

The premise of this book is that all law students could master the process of legal analysis, if only they had more practice. Now practice is available. This book provides a variety of practice exercises and fills the legal analysis gap between mystery and mastery. By beginning with critical thinking exercises, moving on to rule-based and analogical reasoning problems, and finishing with statutory interpretation drills, students will deepen their understanding of the legal reasoning process. Our purpose is to provide a practical, easy-to-use workbook rather than to teach any particular subject matter or substantive law. For pedagogical reasons, some exercises may use edited case opinions; others may require students to apply rules of law adapted from several jurisdictions. Given that the law is ever-changing, students should not use this workbook to learn and memorize substantive law, but they should expect each completed exercise to transform them from novice legal thinkers to expert problem-solvers.

Furthermore, this book encourages students to organize their written answers in a widely-accepted and familiar legal writing structure but does not set out to teach another format or paradigm for legal writing. Students can use the 100 distinct exercise opportunities in this book to practice the specific paradigm they have learned in law school. Thus, this book is perfect for first-year legal writing students and complements any legal writing textbook. The book equally benefits

---

[1] *What Law Firms Want in New Recruits,* THE NEW YORK LAW JOURNAL, Apr. 27, 2009.

[2] American Bar Association, Legal Education and Professional Development—An Educational Continuum, Report of the Task Force on Law Schools & Profession: Narrowing the Gap (1992) (hereinafter the "MacCrate Report").

students in any other course that teaches legal reasoning and writing. Law students can find the extra help they need, using the alternately-answered exercises to check their own progress. Pre-law students and remedial writing students can find a paced and reassuring introduction to legal reasoning and analysis.

GOALS OF THIS BOOK

This book benefits both students and professors by providing an array of legal analysis drills designed to achieve key learning outcomes and objectives and to offer multiple assessment opportunities.

Student Learning Outcomes and Objectives

This book first aims to provide pre-law students and law students varied practice with legal analysis, argument structure, and written analysis. By completing the exercises in this book, students will learn and practice a number of key lawyering skills. In particular, students will be able to develop and achieve the following proficiencies[3]:

Critical Reading and Thinking

- Read, understand, and evaluate cases by:

    o Dissecting a case and identifying key components of the opinion; and

    o Synthesizing related cases; and

- Read, understand, and evaluate statutes and regulations.

Legal Problem Solving

- Identify legal issues presented by the facts;

- Determine the relevant controlling authority for the issue;

- Use interpretation of pertinent authority to predict outcomes;

- Describe possible solutions to reach a client's objective; and

- Outline unanswered legal questions and incomplete fact issues.

---

[3] These Student Learning Outcomes were developed using the following resources: MICHAEL HUNTER SCHWARTZ, SOPHIE SPARROW & GERALD HESS, TEACHING LAW BY DESIGN: ENGAGING STUDENTS FROM THE SYLLABUS TO THE FINAL EXAM 37-85, 135-163, 191-205, 247-255 (2009); GREGORY S. MUNRO, OUTCOMES ASSESSMENT FOR LAW SCHOOLS (Inst. for L. Sch. Teaching 2000); Lisa G. Lerman, *Teaching Legal Analysis: An Inventory of Skills, in* GERALD F. HESS & STEVEN I. FRIEDLAND, TECHNIQUES FOR TEACHING LAW 32-37 (Carolina Academic Press 1999); Nelson P. Miller, *Mapping Lawyer Competencies onto the Law School Curriculum to Confirm that the Curriculum Prepares Graduates for Practice*, http://law. du.edu/documents/assessment-conference/Miller-Curriculum-Mapping.pdf; MacCrate Report, *supra* note 2, at 138-221; National Conference of Bar Examiners, *Skills Tested by the MPT*, http://www. ncbex.org/multistate-tests/mpt/mpt-faqs/skills-tested/ (September 27, 2011); ROY STUCKEY AND OTHERS, BEST PRACTICES FOR LEGAL EDUCATION: A VISION AND A ROADMAP (Clinical Legal Education Association 2007); B.S. BLOOM, ET. AL, ED., TAXONOMY OF EDUCATIONAL OBJECTIVES: THE CLASSIFICATION OF EDUCATIONAL GOALS (1956).

Legal Analysis

- Identify the legal issues presented by the facts;

- Identify the relevant facts and applicable authority (cases, statutes, and/or regulations);

- Develop and assess legal theories relevant to a client's situation;

- Accurately derive rules and apply authority to a client's situation;

- Strengthen a client's position by analogizing to similar or favorable facts, reasoning, and policy in authority;

- Overcome weaknesses in a client's situation by distinguishing dissimilar or unfavorable facts, reasoning, and policy in authority;

- Articulate clear inferences for factual support; and

- Identify components of statutory interpretation and analysis (legislative history and canons of interpretation) relevant to the client's position.

Legal Drafting

- Communicate their analysis and position effectively and appropriately in writing to intended audience (colleagues, clients, opposing counsel, or court); and

- Organize and explain ideas clearly using appropriate conventions.

Formative and Summative Assessment

In addition to achieving these student learning outcomes and objectives, this book aims to provide professors with a wide selection of formative and summative assessment opportunities for use in class or as homework. As the American Bar Association shifts its focus from input measures to outcome assessment,[4] many law professors will need not only to develop clear learning outcomes for their courses but also to identify whether the teaching strategies being used in their courses help them achieve the desired outcomes. Further, many law professors will also need to add new teaching strategies and skills and writing exercises to their courses to monitor their students' development effectively throughout the course. By utilizing the exercises in this book, professors will be able to integrate multiple faculty-, peer-, and self-assessment opportunities that allow them to track their students' proficiencies in legal analysis, argument structure, and legal writing.

---

[4] Donald J. Polden, Chair, *Statement of Principles of Accreditation and Fundamental Goals of a Sound Program of Legal Education*, Standards Review Committee, Am. Bar. Ass'n (May 6, 2009) (on file with authors), available at http://www.abanet.org/legaled/committees/Standards%20Review%20docu-ments/Principles%20and%20Goals%20Accreditation%205%206%2009.pdf; Steve Bahls, Chair, *Key Issues Considered by the Student learning Outcomes Subcommittee*, Student Learning Outcomes Subcommittee of the Standards Review Committee, Am. Bar Ass'n (Dec. 15, 2009) (on file with authors), available at www.abanet.org/legaled/ (follow "Discussion of Key Issues" hyperlink).

The exercises in this book can be modified to fulfill the particular learning outcomes and assessment goals of any course and make ongoing assessment both possible and manageable for professors. Professors now have ready-made legal analysis exercises with annotated sample answers they can use to incorporate multiple assessment opportunities covering an array of legal topics. Professors may use any of the exercises to track students' performance and provide faculty feedback, and the even-numbered exercises to encourage collaborative group work and peer-assessment and develop students' self-assessment skills. Professors may rely on the annotated sample answers to provide students with guidance on the applicable legal rules, relevant precedent cases, possible arguments, and organization for their written analysis.

HOW INTENDED AUDIENCES CAN USE THIS BOOK

This book is suitable for a number of audiences—each can use the exercises for different purposes.

For the Pre-Law Student

Even before law school begins, pre-law students can use this book to gain familiarity and practice with the analytical building blocks that they will soon be expected to master. Soon-to-be law students can start to work on legal analysis as part of a law school preparatory course or at their leisure, before law school starts.

To begin work with the book, pre-law students can start with the basic concept that underlies legal reasoning. Pre-law students can do this by working through the Orientation to Critical Thinking chapter and checking their responses against the sample answers. This chapter is an appropriate beginning, because the exercises are drawn from everyday life, devoid of all overtly legal concepts. The sample answers are just that—samples of how the questions could be answered. Students' answers may differ from the samples, but students' answers should follow the structure that makes up legal reasoning.

Next, pre-law students can try their hand at rule-based reasoning exercises. These exercises provide a rule of law and a fact pattern. Students can apply the rule to the facts and again compare their answers to the sample answers. Pre-law students who feel confident with rule-based reasoning can proceed to the basic analogical reasoning cases and then to exercises with statutes.

Once they start law school, students who have already worked through a number of the 100 exercises will approach law school assignments with greater competence and confidence.

For the Law Student

Law students must use legal analysis skills immediately upon starting law school. Legal analysis remains at the core of law students' work throughout law school and beyond: in their legal writing classes, on law school exams, on the bar exam, on the multi-state performance test, and in practice. This book provides 100 opportunities to develop and hone those important skills without first learning new substantive law—all information students need to work the exercises will be at their fingertips.

New law students can examine and work through straightforward examples of analogical reasoning in the Introduction to Legal Reasoning chapter. Law students can then practice with the simplest form of legal reasoning—rule-based reasoning that takes a legal rule and applies it to a set of facts. Law students can progress through rule-based reasoning exercises, starting with simple rules and facts and progressing through multi-part rules and more extensive facts patterns. Once students see how rule-based reasoning works, they can expand their repertoire with analogical reasoning.

Statutes too are a key component of legal reasoning, so two chapters are devoted exclusively to this important source of law: Chapter V, Statutory Analysis for Success, and Chapter VI, Statutes with Legislative History. In these chapters, students can see how statutes and cases interact, and how legislative history plays a role in legal analysis.

Students need not wonder whether their performance is up to par—they can immediately check their work against the sample answers. Through the exercises, students can develop a keen understanding of rule-based and analogical reasoning with these 100 unique opportunities to practice.

For the Law Professor

Law professors often note that students need more legal analysis practice. But professors are already hard-pressed to complete bar exam and other topics in available class time, leaving little time for legal analysis practice. Law professors can, however, refer students to this book, to supplement students' analysis skills while keeping class time for bar exam and other topics. Through the exercises, professors can increase the depth of students' analysis through the paced exercises, adaptable to any analysis paradigm. Significantly, students can self-assess with the sample answers provided within the book for even-numbered exercises. If a graded assignment would better fit the class's needs, the professor can assign an odd-numbered exercise—answers to these exercises appear only in the teacher's manual.

Legal writing professors in particular can turn to this book as a source of exercises and supplemental work. The problems can be assigned at any point in the semester either as written or adapted to particular needs. Exercises can also be expanded to include a research component beyond the sources included here. The exercises are grouped by form of legal reasoning, with additional exercises covering statutes with cases and statutes with legislative history.

For the Academic Support Professional

As employers and the American Bar Association increasingly emphasize the need for practice-ready law school graduates, more law schools are expanding their academic support offerings and adding supplementary writing courses such as Remedial Legal Writing. Students seeking academic support may at first be perplexed by legal analysis. These students would benefit from practicing their legal analysis skills by working through selected exercises in the book.

Any one of the exercises can serve as an assessment tool to determine the student's strengths and weaknesses. After the diagnostic exercise, an academic support professional may select additional exercises for the student to try. The student can then self-assess with the even-numbered exercises.

GENERAL STRUCTURE OF THE BOOK

This book contains five separate categories of exercises: Orientation to Critical Thinking, Rule-Based Reasoning, Analogical Reasoning, Statutes with Cases, and Statutes with Legislative History. Each category represents a distinct area of legal reasoning and analysis that law students must master. Within each category, the exercises start at a Beginning level, with basic concepts and fact patterns. The exercises increase in difficulty and sophistication, progressing through exercises at an Intermediate level, and ending with exercises at a Skilled level. The Intermediate and Skilled exercises use more complicated fact patterns, increased numbers of cases and statutes, and more extensive answers.

Chapter I: Orientation to Critical Thinking

This section eases students into legal analysis with exercises based on everyday examples drawn from non-legal scenarios. The exercises are lively and user-friendly, to draw students into legal analysis without intimidation. Through these exercises, students can see that they already instinctively use rule-based and analogical reasoning, and that legal reasoning is an extension of their existing skills. (Contains Exercises 1 through 9).

Chapter II: Introduction to Legal Analysis

Here, students learn that no matter which legal analysis paradigm their school uses, for example, IRAC, CRAC, CRRPAC, or others, the paradigms contain the same foundation and can be used to practice their analysis with this book. This chapter contains an equivalency chart that shows how the different paradigms are in fact close cousins to one another, with common elements. Students can be confident that their school's particular form of analysis is compatible with the exercises.

Chapter III: Rule-Based Reasoning for Mastery

In this chapter, students start practicing legal analysis. Paced exercises give students a legal rule to apply to a factual scenario. Students need not have any background on the particular legal issue—each exercise is free-standing, ready for students to try. Additionally, students need not worry about citation to authority for these exercises. These exercises are designed to simulate the legal reasoning process most widely used on law school essay examinations, where students apply the relevant rule(s) to the facts to construct arguments and predict the likely outcome and focus less on citation to authority.

The Beginning-level exercises contain fewer facts and less complicated law. Once students have gained confidence with exercises in the Beginning and

Intermediate levels, they are ready to take on the more challenging scenarios and law contained in the Skilled exercises. After completing all the exercises, students will be able to work confidently with the application of legal rules to fact patterns. (Contains Exercises 10 through 34).

Chapter IV: Analogical Reasoning with Depth

Once students are comfortable applying rules to facts, they are ready to practice with the basic building blocks of common law: cases. In this chapter, students start with simpler exercises using one or two cases as precedent to analyze a factual scenario. Exercises increase in complexity until students are using multiple cases to analyze a complex factual scenario. Students seeking additional confidence as they prepare for exams can work through all the exercises until they are fully at ease with the important skill of legal analysis. (Contains Exercises 35 through 64).

Chapter V: Statutory Analysis for Success

Legal analysis inevitably involves statutory analysis, but the interaction of statutes and cases is not always easy to understand. In this chapter, students can see how cases, and at times, regulations, influence the interpretation of statutes. Students can begin with the early exercises, which contain simpler statutory provisions and fewer cases. After gaining confidence with the Basic-level exercises, students can practice with exercises at the Intermediate and Skilled level. (Contains Exercises 65 through 89).

Chapter VI: Statutes with Legislative History

First-year legal writing courses and other first-year law school courses often touch on statutory analysis using legislative history. The generally cursory treatment of these topics often leaves students confused and needing practice. Only practice can put students at ease with these numerous and arcane principles. Students can see how various aspects of legislative history might be used by trying the exercises themselves and checking their answers against the samples. (Contains Exercise 90 through 100).

Chapter VII: Written Sample Answers

This chapter contains complete and thoughtful answers to all the book's even-numbered exercises. Each answer thoroughly and completely analyzes the exercise, demonstrating how students can answer that exercise. In addition, the answers are annotated so that students can see features that their answers should contain.

For students, the sample answers permit independent study and self-checking, until the student is producing answers that contain the same key points as the samples. For professors, the sample exercises free up valuable time that would otherwise be spent crafting a complete sample answer. (The accompanying *Teacher's Manual* contains the same complete sample answers but for all 100 exercises.)

The sample answers reflect a number of different writing style choices, any of which is widely accepted. The answers all, however, follow the organization most widely used in predictive memo documents: law and case illustrations are set out before the application of law to fact, and arguments are identified for all parties involved.

To Access a Case, Statute, or Regulation for an Exercise

To access a case, statute, or regulation for an exercise, you may use your LexisNexis Custom ID and Password on LexisNexis's website at www.lexis.com. In addition, our blog site at www.legalwritinginbrief.com contains links to access a case, statute, or regulation for an exercise, further information about LexisNexis student resources, and other helpful materials. You may also consult the following open access sites to retrieve a case, statute, or regulation:

- LexisNexis Communities at http://www.lexisnexis.com/community/portal/,
- Cornell's Legal Information Institute at http://www.law.cornell.edu/federal/opinions.html,
- FindLaw at http://www.findlaw.com/casecode/supreme.html and http://caselaw.findlaw.com/summary/,
- Google Scholar at http://scholar.google.com/,
- Justia at http://law.justia.com/,
- Open Jurist at http://openjurist.org/, and
- The Public Library of Law at http://www.plol.org/Pages/Search.aspx.

If you have any questions, you may contact LexisNexis's support team at lawschoolbooksupport@lexisnexis.com.

TABLE OF CONTENTS

About the Authors... vii

Acknowledgments ix

Preface xi

Goals of this Book xiii

How Intended Audiences Can Use This Book xvii

General Structure of the Book.. xix

Chapter I: Orientation to Critical Thinking (Exercises 1-9)..............   1

Chapter II: Introduction to Legal Analysis..   13

Chapter III: Rule-Based Reasoning for Mastery (Exercises 10-34)....   21

Part 1:   Beginning Rule-Based Exercises (Exercises 10-19) 23

Part 2:   Intermediate Rule-Based Exercises (Exercises 20-29)..................... 43

Part 3:   Skilled Rule-Based Exercises (Exercises 30-34)............................... 69

Chapter IV: Analogical Reasoning with Depth (Exercises 35-64).....   85

Part 1:   Beginning Analogical Exercises (Exercises 35-42) 87

Part 2:   Intermediate Analogical Exercises (Exercises 43-53) 107

Part 3:   Skilled Analogical Exercises (Exercises 54-64)................................. 143

Chapter V: Statutory Analysis for Success (Exercises 65-89)   177

Part 1:   Beginning Statutory Exercises (Exercises 65-72)............................. 179

Part 2:   Intermediate Statutory Exercises (Exercises 73-82)........................ 199

Part 3:   Skilled Statutory Exercises (Exercises 83-89) 233

Chapter VI: Statutes with Legislative History (Exercises 90-100)....   255

Part 1:   Beginning Statutes with Legislative History (Exercises 90-93)....... 257

Part 2:   Intermediate Statutes with Legislative History

(Exercises 94-97) 273

Part 3:   Skilled Statutes with Legislative History (Exercises 98-100) 285

Chapter VII: Written Sample Answers with Annotations   299

Index of Exercises by Legal Subject Matter 475

CHAPTER I

ORIENTATION TO CRITICAL THINKING

ORIENTATION TO CRITICAL THINKING
EXERCISE 1

A jogger runs along a beach, past a sign that says, "Fine $100 For Littering." A few steps past the sign, the jogger pauses to eat a banana. He throws the skin on the ground and continues to run. A police officer in training sees the skin fall. She recalls that her supervisor did not issue a littering ticket to a person who poured coffee on the ground. The supervisor did, however, issue a ticket to someone who threw a candy bar wrapper on the ground.

Should the police officer ticket the jogger? Why or why not?

ORIENTATION TO CRITICAL THINKING
EXERCISE 2

Using the rule provided below, determine whether April Jefferson violated the City Ordinance prohibiting cell phone usage or text messaging while driving.

Cell Phone Usage Rule:

The City Ordinance for Cell Phone Usage or Text Messaging provides that it is a moving violation and unlawful to use a wireless communication device to talk or listen to another person on the telephone or to view, send, or compose an electronic message or engage other application software while operating a motor vehicle.

Fact Pattern:

April Jefferson ("Jefferson") hopped in her new Ford Mustang convertible and headed downtown to meet her best friend for lunch. She placed her cell phone and purse on the passenger seat, let down the top on her car, and started to drive north on Kansas Street. The weather was great, clear and sunny. Jefferson could not wait to meet her friend; she had not seen her in months.

Jefferson slowed down at a crosswalk because some kids were standing at the corner. She then picked up her phone to take a quick look at the directions to the restaurant. She left them visible on the phone because she did not want to get lost and risk being late. Realizing that she was not too far away from the restaurant, she sent her friend a text, typing "almost there."

Jefferson noticed the voicemail message icon was lit on her phone. Once the kids crossed the street, she started driving and picked up the phone to check her voicemail message. She clicked on the "call voicemail" option and heard a couple of rings. The recording stated, "You have no new messages." "That darn icon," Jefferson thought. "It never seems to work right." She tossed her phone back on the passenger seat.

Jefferson drove about 50 feet to the next intersection and heard a siren. There was a police officer right behind Jefferson, signaling for her to pull over to the curb. Jefferson pulled over immediately. Officer Talbot had been watching Jefferson use her cell phone and told Jefferson she violated the City's new ordinance prohibiting cell phone use and texting while driving. Officer Talbot issued Jefferson three separate moving violations for: (1) viewing the driving directions, (2) texting, and (3) using the phone.

Jefferson admits she used her phone but does not believe she violated the new law. Please advise whether Jefferson violated the City Ordinance with her conduct. Address each of the separate alleged moving violations.

ORIENTATION TO CRITICAL THINKING

EXERCISE 3

Using the rule provided below, determine whether Jonathan violated his parents' dating rule.

Parents' Dating Rule:

If you are under 16 years old, you cannot go on a date without a chaperone. You may go on a date without a chaperone once you turn 16 years old.

Jonathan's Case:

A few weeks ago, Jonathan left his house and caught a bus to meet his girlfriend, Sarah, at the movies. Jonathan was 15 years old. He arrived at the movie theatre early and waited for about 20 minutes until Sarah arrived. While waiting, Jonathan purchased two tickets to see the Rocky Horror Picture Show. He had heard it was a classic, must-see movie. When Sarah arrived, they walked in and bought some popcorn and drinks. They selected two seats at the rear of the theatre, which was nearly full. After the movie ended, Jonathan and Sarah walked a few blocks to the Arabian Arcade, an Arabian Nights theme arcade with staff dressed as genies and magic carpets hanging throughout the building. In the sitting area, the booths were decorated with gold coins and candles and even had drapes that could be pulled closed for privacy.

The arcade was quite crowded, but Jonathan and Sarah found an empty booth and shared some snacks for about an hour. Afterwards, they played a few games. Around 9 p.m., Sarah spotted her next door neighbor at the arcade and asked for a ride home. Jonathan called his parents on his cell phone and told them he would be home soon.

When Jonathan arrived home, his parents asked where he had been all evening. He explained he met Sarah at the movies and then went to the arcade. He told them everything. Jonathan's parents then informed him he was grounded for violating their dating rule.

Please advise whether Jonathan violated his parents' dating rule. Clearly explain your answer. Lead with your conclusion and then apply the dating rule to Jonathan's case. Provide the arguments for Jonathan and his parents. Be sure to identify any assumptions that you are making in answering this question. End with your conclusion.

ORIENTATION TO CRITICAL THINKING

EXERCISE 4

Jordan was standing right outside a side entrance of the city mall. There was a sitting area with a few tables with benches. A small fountain also added a nice attraction to the scene's serenity. Several kids were playing on the slide and see-saw in the sandy children's area. Their parents sat and chatted at one of the tables nearby. Jordan noticed a "no smoking" sign posted on the exterior of the building. It read: "Be courteous to other patrons and please refrain from smoking." Below the text there was a diagram picturing a cigarette marked out with a big red cross.

Jordan had never seen the "no smoking" sign before this visit. In fact, he recalled seeing other people smoking while sitting at one of the tables. "Must be something new," he thought to himself. The city had not passed any ordinances prohibiting smoking in public places but the mall obviously decided to be a front-runner in the fight against public smoking. "No worries," Jordan thought. "Good thing I quit months ago. I just need my handy cigarette substitute to keep me calm."

Jordan then pulled out an electronic cigarette. An electronic cigarette, also called an e-cigarette or vaporize cigarette, is a battery-powered device that provides inhaled doses of nicotine or non-nicotine vaporized solution. The vapor provides a flavor and physical sensation comparable to inhaled tobacco smoke. However, no real tobacco smoke or combustion is actually involved in its operation. The electronic cigarette emits a vapor that resembles smoke but is largely water-based. The cigarette substitute allows Jordan to gradually reduce his nicotine intake and lessen his dependency over time. It provides a real smoking experience without the fire, flame, tobacco, tar, carbon monoxide, ash, stub, or smell found in real cigarettes.

One of the mall employees walked outside and spotted Jordan smoking. Jordan nodded and smiled, and the employee went back inside the mall. A few minutes later, a security guard exited the mall and ordered Jordan to put out his cigarette. Jordan tried to explain that it was not a cigarette but an electronic copycat. "We don't care," shouted one of the parents. "You are setting a bad example for our kids." The security guard then told Jordan that he had to either stop smoking or leave the premises.

Jordan felt humiliated, as a crowd began to gather near the exit. Did Jordan violate the mall's no-smoking policy? Provide the arguments for Jordan and the security guard.

6

ORIENTATION TO CRITICAL THINKING

EXERCISE 5

One Sunday, Cho-Hee Kim ("Kim") called her son to come by her house and give her a ride to the store. The store was several blocks from her home and, given her age and health, Kim knew she could not make the walk on her own. Her son did not answer the phone so Kim decided to ride her mobility scooter down the street to the store. "What could it hurt?" she thought. "And the warm afternoon sun could be good for me."

Kim gathered her purse, placed her sun hat in the scooter's basket, and took a seat. She then rode her mobility scooter out the front door of her home, down the driveway past the sidewalk, and into the street. Her scooter is one of the best selling four-wheel electric scooters on the market. It has a wider wheelbase for better stability and can even handle rough terrain. The scooter's design is like a motorized wheelchair and it works well for both indoor and outdoor use. It has a drive range up to 30 miles per charge and can reach a maximum speed of 9.5 MPH. Her model also has a safety package, which includes lights, horn, turn signals, and mirrors.

As Kim entered the street, she turned to the right to stay in the bicycle lane that was marked with a large white-lined boundary. The bicycle lane gave her plenty of room to maneuver her scooter. "The weather is fantastic! I'm glad I decided to get outside," she said. After a few blocks, a couple of bicyclists crossed the lane's boundary to move ahead of Kim and her scooter. "I guess there isn't enough room for all of us," she smiled to herself.

Suddenly, a police officer appeared and flagged Kim to stop. The officer approached Kim and told her that she could not drive in the bicycle lane. "This lane is meant for cyclists, not scooter operators like you. You should get on the sidewalk," the officer explained. Kim was very confused and insisted that it made more sense for her to ride to the store in the bicycle lane.

Should Kim be prohibited from using her mobility scooter in the bicycle lane? Provide the arguments for Kim and the officer.

ORIENTATION TO CRITICAL THINKING

EXERCISE 6

Keith Washington ("Washington") lives on campus in a residence hall at the University of Lakes ("Lakes"). Washington is an A student and a star player on the baseball team. Washington's fellow students like and respect him, but students in his academic classes sometimes wish he did not earn the top score on practically every test.

A week before a particularly difficult calculus exam, some fellow students were discussing Washington's annoying habit of securing the one A+ in most of his classes, especially math classes. "It sure would help if Washington would just be gone from the class," said one student. "Well, how is that going to happen?" said another. "Maybe he'll get into trouble for something," said a third. "He's not perfect." The first student remembered something that Washington had recently done. "You know, I think he broke the harassment policy. During orientation two years ago, he asked me out, and I said he shouldn't call me because I was dating Jeff at the time. Then he called me two months ago to ask me out because he had heard that Jeff and I had broken up. Check the harassment policy—I think we can easily cool his jets a little. By the time he gets this sorted out, one of us will have the top grade in calculus."

As all Lakes students learn at orientation, the residence hall has a strict "no stalking or harassment" policy. The policy in its entirety reads as follows: "You may not stalk or harass any fellow resident. Stalking is unwanted following or communication. Following or communication is unwanted if the recipient has stated that the contact should stop. Residents who stalk or harass another resident will be expelled from the residence halls." The policy was put into place four years ago by the resident council. When the policy was put into place, the council made the following announcement: "This is a safety rule. The new rule will make students safer, and students who cannot follow the rule will be dismissed from the residence halls. No student should have to live in fear."

Washington's fellow student refers him to the residents' council for calling her after she asked him not to. She alleges that he broke the stalking and harassment policy. You are a new member of the residents' council, and you are charged with deciding how to treat Washington's alleged violation of the policy. The council votes on which of the following actions to take—the council can take more than one action: (1) find a violation, (2) find no violation, or (3) find that the policy should be revised and suggest revisions. How do you vote and why?

ORIENTATION TO CRITICAL THINKING

EXERCISE 7

Hillary Jones ("Jones") was working in her back yard when she noticed her engagement ring missing from her hand. "Oh no!" she exclaimed. She thought back over where she had been during the past few days, and she remembered that she had made two trips to the Bigshop grocery store. She called the store to check on whether anyone had turned in a ring. In fact, someone had, two days before. Jones rushed to the store and checked with the customer service desk where the Lost and Found bin was located. "My ring! Can I have it back, please?" she said. The clerk looked at her sadly. "No, I'm sorry. Look at the policy."

The policy read as follows: "AS A COURTESY TO OUR VALUED CUSTOMERS, WE COLLECT ALL LOST AND FOUND ITEMS. DUE TO SPACE AND STORAGE LIMITATIONS, ALL ITEMS NOT CLAIMED AFTER 24 HOURS BECOME PROPERTY OF THE STORE. THANK YOU." The clerk pointed out that the ring had been turned in forty-eight hours before. "But this is a $2,000 ring," Jones exclaimed. "And it's tiny—how could this possibly have caused a storage problem?"

The clerk explained that two days ago, she had to keep a child's blanket because the owner did not return until three days after it had been turned in. "That was a tough one," said the clerk. "I didn't even check with the manager because the answer was so clear. Rules are rules, and this is the owner's policy." The clerk went on: "My strict instructions are to apply the rules equally. But you're welcome to talk to our manager on duty." You are the manager on duty, and the store owner is unreachable. What do you do with the ring, and why? The owner trusts you to use your judgment in any situation in which she is unreachable.

9

ORIENTATION TO CRITICAL THINKING

EXERCISE 8

Chris, Sophie, and Nick are young children who want to go swimming in their neighborhood pool. They are trying to figure out whether their parents will let them swim in the pool under the current weather conditions. Today, the weather is cloudy and rainy, with a light wind. There is no sign of thunder or lightning, although the children heard distant thunder a few hours ago. The children are desperate to swim, so they try to use past situations to predict their parents' answer.

Chris remembers a day three weeks ago when the family was swimming, when suddenly, there was a loud clap of thunder. "You must get out of the pool immediately!" his parents had said.

Sophie remembers another day when there were dark clouds and a strong wind. "You cannot swim until this clears up," the parents had said. "Safety first."

Nick recalls another day when the family was in the pool, and a light rain suddenly started to fall. The clouds were white and fluffy, and there was no wind, lightning, or thunder. "This seems fine," said the parents. "But listen for thunder and watch for lighting. If you see a dark cloud, tell me immediately. It's better to be safe than sorry."

Chris chimes in with another anecdote. One day several months ago, there was a strong wind blowing and the clouds were gray when the children wanted to swim. "I'm not sure what's going on," said their mother. "Let's just wait until this goes away."

Will the parents let them swim? What is the parents' synthesized rule for swimming in inclement weather?

ORIENTATION TO CRITICAL THINKING

EXERCISE 9

Will Rebecca Syed successfully become a partner at Dominguez & Thompson LLP?

Background Facts

Dominguez & Thompson LLP is a large full-service law firm. The firm has market-leading strengths in the employment, real estate, financial services, energy, technology, and life sciences sectors. The firm's practice areas can be broadly grouped into three categories: litigation, transactions, and counseling/regulatory work. Dominguez & Thompson has a core base of clients ranging from start-up companies to leading corporations. The firm is uniquely positioned to become a global powerhouse and expand its roster of clients given the firm's tradition of hiring top, cross-industry legal talent and its commitment to diversity, all of which brings valuable perspectives, experiences, and strengths to the firm.

Dominguez & Thompson is well known for its multi-faceted approach to handling client matters. The firm's attorneys work collaboratively across practice groups to share their strong knowledge of clients' industries, solve clients' problems efficiently, and keep clients continuously abreast of current trends and standards in the marketplace. Dominguez & Thompson takes a proactive approach to serving the needs of clients and has an unwavering dedication to their interests.

Rebecca Syed ("Syed") joined Dominguez & Thompson immediately upon her graduation from law school. She started her practice in the firm's real estate department and remained there for two and a half years. She then transferred to the firm's regulatory section and worked in that field for four years. Syed recently joined the employment section. The partners and attorneys in both the real estate and regulatory sections were sad to see Syed leave, but they supported her decision to move.

Syed is a former president of the local bar association and is active in the Junior League. In her early years at the firm, Syed consistently billed approximately 2,000 hours on client matters. Given her recent transition to the employment group, Syed bills fewer hours on client matters and instead attends workshops to develop an expertise in employment law.

Syed has worked for a number of the firm's longstanding clients. Because of her excellent representation, a few of these clients have hired the firm to handle new legal matters. For example, one of Syed's clients, a local school district, initially retained the firm to negotiate a real estate transaction for a new football stadium and later hired the firm to litigate an employment dispute involving a teacher.

This month, Dominguez & Thompson will decide whether it should offer Syed a promotion to partnership. Syed has been an associate at the firm for seven years. The firm has made the following recent decisions on partnership.

Christopher Preston

Christopher Preston ("Preston") has been recognized by *Law & Politics* as a "Super Lawyer" in the regulatory field. Preston is a member of various community service organizations and is an active member of the firm's Pro Bono Committee. Preston's social commitments and networking activities often cause him to bill fewer hours than the firm's target of 2,100 hours per year for senior associates. He roughly averages 1,850 billable hours per year on client matters. Last year, Preston brought three new clients to the firm. In addition, attorneys in other departments in the firm often ask him to consult on projects. Toward the end of his seventh year of practice at the firm, Preston received an offer to join the firm's partnership and accepted the promotion.

Denise Conway

Denise Conway ("Conway") is a tax attorney and has an LLM in employee benefits. Prior to joining the law firm, she worked for the federal tax court as a judicial law clerk. Conway works long hours on client matters and typically bills 2,100 hours per year. She often does not attend client events or other firm functions given her huge workload. Moreover, she has few opportunities to work with attorneys in other departments. Conway is a smart lawyer and strives to keep her clients happy. The firm, however, did not extend Conway an offer for partnership. Conway was in her seventh year of practice at the firm at the time of her partnership decision.

Carmen Pilaro

After graduating from law school, Carmen Pilaro ("Pilaro") worked as an education and employment attorney for seven years at a small law firm. Always involved in local politics, Pilaro ran for and won a seat on the state trial court. She remained a judge for thirteen years before losing her seat in a highly contested judicial election. Immediately after the election, the firm offered Pilaro a position as a senior partner and she accepted. Although she had not practiced in several years and did not bring any clients with her to the firm, the firm looked forward to having such a well-known name on its roster of attorneys.

Question

Will Syed successfully become a partner at Dominguez & Thompson? Base your prediction on the scenarios presented above. What will the firm consider in making its decision? Provide the arguments in support of your position.

CHAPTER II

INTRODUCTION TO LEGAL ANALYSIS

Legal problem-solving begins with the "law." The law originates from several sources such as constitutions, opinions issued by courts, statutes enacted by legislators, rules and regulations passed by administrative agencies, and executive orders issued by the president or a governor. When you are faced with a legal problem you need to solve, you first must identify the relevant legal issue(s) presented by the facts. Next, you must determine the law that applies to the legal issue(s) and facts. And then, you must apply the law to the facts to predict or determine the likely outcome of the case. The process of ascertaining the legal issue and relevant law and applying the law to the facts is called "legal analysis."

Legal analysis is the main skill you will use as a lawyer. It is an art—the lawyer's ultimate creative tool—and a technique that separates novice legal minds from expert practitioners. As you engage in legal analysis, you will form an opinion of the case and employ one of the many legal reasoning techniques to brainstorm and develop arguments for the parties involved in the case. There are many forms of legal reasoning that lawyers use in practice including, but not limited to, rule-based reasoning, analogical reasoning, policy-based reasoning, and narrative reasoning. This book focuses on rule-based reasoning (Chapter III), analogical reasoning (Chapters IV and V) and policy-based reasoning (as applicable throughout the exercises). In addition to these specific forms of legal reasoning, this book provides a series of exercises in Chapter VI to hone your ability to interpret statutory provisions using tools of construction such as the plain meaning doctrine, legislative history, policy, and canons of construction.

You likely learned about each of the forms of legal reasoning that are the subject of this book in your introductory legal analysis and writing course. This book supplements that knowledge and encourages you to complete an objective analysis of the facts for each exercise, as you would for a predictive memorandum. You should approach each exercise thinking about the relevant law and the viable arguments that you could make for all parties involved. That way, you will receive the most legal analysis practice, strengthen your analytic skills, and gain a better understanding and appreciation for the strategy involved in solving legal problems.

To begin, we start with a brief overview of the specific forms of legal reasoning and other analytical skills that you will practice in this book.

Rule-Based Reasoning

Rule-based reasoning is the simplest form of legal analysis and a skill that you will use largely in your doctrinal classes and on law school examinations. In practice, rule-based reasoning is generally employed in specific situations: when deciding an issue of first impression, which is one that the court has yet to address; when there are no analogous prior cases to apply to the client's facts; or when the application of law (the legal rules) to the facts is very simple, direct, and straight-forward and does not necessitate any case illustrations or examples to explain the resulting analysis.

When using rule-based reasoning, you apply the legal rules directly to the client's facts to predict the outcome. For example, consider the tort of battery. There are several requirements to prove battery: (1) intent, (2) contact, (3) hostile or offensive contact, (4) causation, and (5) damages. Now, focus on the second requirement: "contact." Prior cases help to refine your understanding of the term "contact." In particular, you will learn from these cases that direct contact between the defendant and the plaintiff's person is not required to show "contact." Sufficient contact is found when the defendant touches or strikes something that the plaintiff is holding or that is closely associated with the plaintiff (such as the horse a plaintiff is riding).

Assume that your client, Oliver, wants to sue Natasha for battery. Oliver and Natasha have been competing against each other since they were in elementary school. Now in eighth grade, the two prepared to compete in the school's spelling bee contest. They practiced for months. After several rounds, Oliver placed first in the competition and Natasha was the runner up. Natasha was furious and could not believe that Oliver won the last round and the $500 prize. The next day, Natasha saw Oliver walking down the hall holding a stack of books in his arms. She leaned against the lockers, waited until Oliver walked by, and knocked the books out of his hands to the floor. She did not touch Oliver's arms or his hands. Natasha immediately started to laugh but, as she watched Oliver try to collect the many books scattered on the floor, she started to feel bad. Natasha then stooped down to help Oliver pick up the books. Was there "contact" under the law?

A short answer to this question applying rule-based reasoning could read as follows:

Natasha's act of knocking the books out of Oliver's arms satisfies the contact requirement. Direct contact between the defendant and the plaintiff's person is not required to show "contact." Sufficient contact is found when the defendant touches or strikes something that the plaintiff is holding or is closely associated with (such as the horse a plaintiff is riding). Although Natasha did not hit Oliver's

Applies the legal rule directly to the facts.

arms or hands, she did hit something that he was holding. The stack of books essentially served as an extension of Oliver's physical person. Therefore, Natasha in fact made contact with Oliver's person (in particular, his arms and hands) as needed to satisfy battery.

Analogical Reasoning

Analogical reasoning is the form of legal analysis most widely used by lawyers. Unlike rule-based reasoning, analogical reasoning requires you to compare the client's situation to the facts in the prior case(s) and argue by analogy or distinction. With analogical reasoning, your position is either that the precedent case is analogous to the client's facts and thus warrants the same outcome or, that the precedent case is distinguishable from the client's situation and, as a result, the client's case should have a different outcome.

For example, using the same factual scenario provided above, assume there is a prior court case, *Martin v. Wynn*,* in which the court determined that the defendant's act of slapping a hat off the plaintiff's head constituted sufficient contact for battery. The court reasoned that the defendant's hitting the plaintiff's hat was akin to touching the plaintiff's body.

An answer to the question about Natasha and Oliver applying analogical reasoning could read as follows:

Natasha's knocking the stack of books out of Oliver's arms satisfies the contact requirement. Direct contact between the defendant and the plaintiff's person is not required to show "contact." Sufficient contact is found when the defendant touches or strikes something that the plaintiff is holding or is closely associated with (such as the horse a plaintiff is riding). For example, in *Martin v. Wynn*, the defendant slapped a hat off the plaintiff's head. The court held that the defendant's act constituted contact for a claim of battery since the defendant hit an object that was closely associated with the plaintiff's physical person. Similar to the defendant in *Martin v. Wynn*, Natasha made contact with an item closely associated with the plaintiff. Although Natasha did not hit Oliver's arms or hands, she did hit something that he was holding, the stack of books. The books were essentially an extension of Oliver's physical person. Therefore, just as the court concluded for the parties in *Martin v. Wynn*, Natasha in fact made contact with Oliver's person.

> Compares the prior case to the client's facts and identifies a factual similarity.

---

* This is a fictitious case.

15

Statutory Interpretation

For statutory interpretation problems, your objective is to determine the legislative intent. In other words, you should ask, what did the legislature actually intend or mean by the statutory language or provision at issue? You should begin your analysis with the statutory language and the plain meaning doctrine. Then, you should address any legislative history such as prior bills, floor debates, committee reports, and conference statements, and rely on any relevant purpose language, whether provided in the statute itself or gleaned from a legislator's remark.

Inference Statements

Whenever you engage in legal analysis and determine the arguments for the parties involved, you will identify specific factual support for each position or make a case comparison. Further, it is important that for each fact or case comparison, you provide a clear inference statement to create a fully developed and cogent argument. An inference statement is the legal significance or relevance of the facts or case comparison that you have identified. You should ask yourself, how do these facts or case comparison support my conclusion or position on this issue? What do these facts or case comparison show or prove? Why do these facts or case comparison matter? Your answers to these questions should be incorporated into your argument.

Readers can draw different interpretations from a fact or piece of evidence. Thus, you must clearly and succinctly explain the legal significance of the fact or case comparison included in an argument so that your reader will know which inference you intend. See the example below that illustrates the importance of stating clear inferences in an argument.

FACT	INFERENCE	CONCLUSION
The defendant's fingerprint was on the gun.	The defendant placed his fingerprint on the gun when he shot the victim.	The defendant shot the victim.
The defendant's fingerprint was on the gun.	The defendant placed his fingerprint on the gun while he was cleaning the gun several months before the shooting incident. He did not handle the gun at any other time—in particular, when the victim was shot.	The defendant did not shoot the victim.

Notice, in the example, each argument relies on the same supporting fact (which is not in dispute) but draws a different inference or interpretation from the fact. Without the inference statement, the argument is unclear and incomplete and the reader is left to fill in the gap. As a lawyer, your role is not only to identify the supporting fact or evidence but also to explain its relevance. You should not leave the inference or interpretation of the fact or case comparison to chance or misinterpretation.

Organization

Now let's turn your attention to how to organize your analysis. As mentioned above, this book emphasizes that no matter which legal analysis paradigm, acronym, or mnemonic your school uses, for example, IRAC, CRAC, CRRPAC, or others, the paradigms contain the same foundation and any one of them can be used to practice your analysis with this book. Below is an equivalency chart that shows how the different paradigms are in fact close cousins to one another, with common elements throughout. You can thus be confident that your school's particular brand of analysis is workable for practice with the exercises in this book. The equivalency chart defines the common elements and includes a description of language that we generally use in our annotated sample answers to guide you through each step of the legal analysis and decision-making process.

Paradigm Equivalency/Comparison Chart

IRAC	CRAC	CRRPAC	CREAC	TREAT	General Description Referenced in the Annotated Sample Answers
Issue	Conclusion	Conclusion	Conclusion	Thesis	**Conclusion:** Lead with a conclusion sentence that identifies the legal issue and predicts the likely outcome of the case.
Rule	Rule	Rule	Rule	Rule	**Law:** Follow with the law section that includes:
		Rule Proof	Explanation	Explanation	(1) the applicable legal standard or rule(s) for the legal issue (whether provided in the exercise or distilled or synthesized from the precedent case(s)) and

IRAC	CRAC	CRRPAC	CREAC	TREAT	General Description Referenced in the Annotated Sample Answers
					(2) for analogical reasoning problems, real-world illustration(s) or example(s) of the legal standard from relevant precedent case(s).
Application	Application	Application	Application	Application	**Application/ Argument:** Apply the law to the facts of the case, develop argument(s) for each party, and objectively evaluate each party's position. Lead with the strongest argument (affirmative argument) and then provide the argument for the opposing party (counter-argument). Follow with a rebuttal that challenges the counter-argument and reaffirms the leading affirmative argument.

IRAC	CRAC	CRRPAC	CREAC	TREAT	General Description Referenced in the Annotated Sample Answers
Conclusion	Conclusion	Conclusion	Conclusion	Thesis	**Conclusion:** End with a conclusion sentence that restates your position. May include a brief summary or recap of your analysis.

Now let's get started and turn your attention to the legal analysis exercises in the next chapter, Chapter III Rule-Based Reasoning for Mastery.

CHAPTER III

RULE-BASED REASONING FOR MASTERY

PART 1

BEGINNING RULE-BASED EXERCISES

RULE-BASED REASONING FOR MASTERY

EXERCISE 10

Using the law provided in the Rule Section, determine whether the proposed covenant not to compete is reasonable in terms of geography. Do not address the other factors.

Rule Section:

In general, a covenant not to compete is valid provided the employer and the employee make certain binding promises in the agreement and the covenant itself is reasonable in terms of time, geography, and scope of activity. With respect to geography, courts have found that non-compete clauses that cover areas where the employee did not actually work for the employer are overly broad and unenforceable. A covenant's terms are unreasonable if they are greater than what is required to protect the employer's goodwill or business interests, or if they impose an undue hardship on the employee.

Fact Pattern:

Reginald Brooks ("Brooks") just received the employment contract for the Regional VP position with his new employer, Johnson Publishing Company, Inc. ("JPC") and seeks your advice. Brooks has asked about the enforceability of certain provisions in the contract that prohibit him from working for competing publishing companies. Currently, Brooks is the Vice President of Sales and Marketing for Ice House Publications in Dallas, Texas. Brooks will be the new South Central Regional Vice President of Sales, Marketing, and Operations for JPC. JPC is the world's largest African-American-owned publishing company. JPC has established businesses not only in publishing but also in cosmetics, television production, and fashion. The company's brands, which include *Fashion Forward* and *Jet-Setters' Lifestyle* magazines and Brilliant Beauty Cosmetics, are household names and trusted sources around the globe. Brooks has over 10 years of experience managing sales, marketing and personnel at the district, regional, and corporate level for both start-up and established retail and publishing companies.

Brooks's new position with JPC will be located in Houston, Texas, and his employment contract will provide that Texas law governs the terms of his employment with JPC. Brooks will be responsible for sales, marketing, and operations for the entire South Central region, which includes Texas, Arkansas, Louisiana, and New Mexico. As of right now, Brooks's duties at JPC generally will include increasing publication sales and company market share, developing and implementing innovative marketing strategies, reducing management and sales associate turnover, and overseeing any new office openings in the South Central region. He also will manage a staff of approximately 75 people, including district managers and administrative personnel. Brooks will also be responsible for the design and marketing of new company brands or products that will be launched in the South Central region.

There is a covenant not to compete in the contract. JPC is concerned about the growing number of competing business in the publishing industry, all vying for a larger percentage of the urban market. JPC does not want its competitors to receive an unfair advantage by hiring Brooks and learning all of JPC's "tricks of the trade." For example, Brooks explained that, if he or JPC terminates his employment, JPC does not want Brooks to work for any other publishing company for at least two years. The length of time could be longer. JPC has not set a definite period yet.

Also, JPC does not want Brooks to work for any major company that advertised in a JPC publication or any company that solicits business from JPC's advertising clients, as to prevent JPC's advertising clients from discovering any confidential pricing or demographic information. A large portion of JPC's gross revenues comes from advertising sales.

As part of his employment, Brooks will be privy to confidential customer lists and various company marketing strategies. Brooks will also receive initial and on-going specialized training at JPC conferences. According to JPC, the marketing strategies that will be taught at the initial training enabled JPC to become a leading publishing company. As he has done for other positions in the past, Brooks will agree to return all company manuals, customer lists and other proprietary information upon his termination. He will also agree not to disclose any of such information after his termination.

The Regional VP position is a new one and JPC does not want to commit to a term contract right now but may consider it in the near future. So, either Brooks or JPC may terminate Brooks's employment at any time with or without advance notice.

Please advise whether the proposed covenant not to compete is reasonable in terms of geography. Do not address the other elements.

RULE-BASED REASONING FOR MASTERY
EXERCISE 11

Using the rule set out in the rule section, please state whether Giles Snider has a viable argument that the homeless shelter should allow him to keep his greyhound at the shelter. Please explain your answer.

Rule Section:

The Americans with Disabilities Act ("ADA") requires that public entities make reasonable modifications to policies, practices, or procedures, when such modifications must be made in order to avoid disability-based discrimination. The modification need not be made if the public entity can demonstrate that the modification would fundamentally alter the nature of the services, program, or activity.

A service animal may be permitted in an animal-free area as an accommodation. The ADA defines a "service animal" as one individually trained to do work or perform similar tasks for the benefit of an individual with a disability. An animal may provide comfort or amelioration of symptoms to an individual with a disability, but this is not sufficient to be considered a "service animal" under the statute. To be a "service animal," an animal must have abilities that qualify it as a "service animal"—the animal must have abilities that are beyond those typical of the breed or of dogs in general.

Fact Pattern:

Giles Snider ("Snider") lives in a city-run homeless shelter. He suffers from anxiety and depression. Some of his happiest moments are spent with his greyhound, Arthur. Arthur is a senior dog and very placid. Arthur used to race in greyhound races, but he was adopted out as a pet when he could no longer race. Arthur is quiet and does not bark.

For the past few weeks, Snider has argued with the homeless shelter's manager about Arthur. Snider wants to keep Arthur with him at all times, including in the shelter. The manager, however, states that Arthur is not a service animal and cannot be admitted into the shelter. "Do you know what would happen if I let every guy with a dog bring the dog into the guest rooms? It would be nothing but barking in here." Snider argues that Arthur is different from a normal dog, because he has learned Snider's habits. When Snider is suffering a serious bout of depression, Arthur knows that something is afoot, and he stays especially close to Snider until the bad spell has passed.

Once, when Snider considered harming himself, Arthur pushed a bottle of pills away from Snider's hand. "This dog is not just a regular dog. He saved me from overdosing. Without him, I'm lost." The shelter manager insists, however, that Snider take Arthur with him to a shelter that will accept pets, even though that shelter is less desirable, smaller, and less comfortable.

As part of a pro bono outreach that your firm is conducting, you are counseling Snider. He asks you: "Can I keep my dog in the shelter? Can't we force the shelter to have Arthur? Is the law really that cruel?" How do you respond? Please assume that Snider is a person with a disability.

RULE-BASED REASONING FOR MASTERY
EXERCISE 12

Using the rule set out in the rule section, please state whether Rick Harridan has a viable claim against your client, the Hills Hotel, based on the rat bite Rick Harridan sustained during a wedding at the hotel. Assume that all other elements except those described in the rule below are met. Please explain your answer.

Rule Section:

The following rule applies to the hotel: "Every dwelling place, shelter, apartment complex, or hotel shall be kept in good repair and condition. No property owner shall be held liable for particular harms, however, unless the owner knew or had reason to know that a dangerous condition existed on the premises."

Fact Pattern:

The Hills Hotel is an elegant and popular hotel in Detroit's business district. The thirty-floor hotel is popular with business visitors. In addition, the large ballroom is perfect for weddings, which take place at the hotel almost every weekend.

One weekend, a prominent Detroit couple held their wedding reception at the hotel. They invited over 400 guests, and a live band played. The decorations and flowers were spectacular, with rose petals strewn on the floor and double-layered silk chair covers. The lighting alone cost $15,000. Two wedding planners circulated to ensure that the guests' needs were met at all times.

The couple, Joey and Marie Fisher ("Joey" and "Marie"), was thrilled with the hotel's fine service and attention to their guests. Joey, a bond trader in the financial district, had paid a considerable amount of money toward the reception, and he felt the reception was well worth the high cost. He was particularly dismayed, then, when an unthinkable incident happened, right after the first dance.

Joey's boss, Rick Harridan ("Harridan"), was reaching toward the carved beef table when a large rat stepped out from behind the beef. The rat walked calmly toward Harridan and bit him on the wrist. Harridan shrieked as he raised his arm and tried to shake off the rat; unfortunately, the rat clung to his wrist. Harridan shook his wrist sharply once more, and the rat dropped off and scurried away. Harridan's wrist bled, and he winced in pain. Joey immediately called for medical help, and the hotel provided a doctor.

Joey apologized profusely to Harridan, who was rather shaken. Harridan's wrist did not heal well, and the bite became infected. Harridan had to take two weeks off work to receive high-grade intravenous antibiotics. Even after the wrist healed, Harridan's range of motion was somewhat restricted. Six months after the incident, Harridan sued your client, the Hills Hotel, based on the injuries he received.

The Hills Hotel's general counsel wants to know whether Harridan's claim is viable. The general counsel believes that the hotel should not be responsible for a rat attack that he sees as random. In speaking with hotel employees, you learn that two weeks before the Harridan bite incident, a hotel porter fell over a rat while taking luggage from a guest at the hotel entrance. The porter said that he had never seen a rat at the hotel before that night. That particular rat was sitting in the doorway until the porter fell over it. In addition, adjacent to the hotel is an alley that contains trash bins from several area businesses. The hotel's trash is kept in a large, locked and fenced trash bin, placed away from the hotel. Hotel employees park near the alley, but they never walk down the alley. Instead, they take a longer way around. "Too many rats!" said a desk clerk. "We all know better than to walk down there."

In addition, two months after the lawsuit was filed, a hotel housekeeper quit employment with the hotel, stating that she found a rat under a bed and developed a fear of going into the hotel's rooms.

The hotel maintenance man told you that he had been instructed to put down rat bait two years before the Harridan incident took place. He did so, and the rats ate all the bait. Nothing more has been said about rat control since that time. The maintenance man refused to state whether he had seen any rats since the bait was laid, repeatedly stating only that he liked his job.

RULE-BASED REASONING FOR MASTERY
EXERCISE 13

Using the rule set out in the Rule Section, determine whether the prosecution should charge Rob Smith with burglary.

Rule Section:

In the state of Mirabella, where Mirabella City is located, a person commits burglary if the person: (1) breaks and (2) enters (3) a habitation of another (4) with intent to commit a felony therein (5) at night.

Fact Pattern:

Rob Smith ("Smith") was down on his luck. He was working as a handyman in Mirabella City, but the jobs were few and far between. He owed money to a tough guy who had started threatening him. He was working on a small job hanging pictures in the hallway of a large house when the homeowner started doing some yard work outside. "Just make yourself comfortable on those chairs when you're finished," said the homeowner, motioning toward some chairs in the hallway.

Smith finished his work just as the streetlights became brightly lit. He decided to look around the house and see if he could help himself to some property to sell quickly. He walked down the hallway and saw a half-open door. "Mind if I go into the study for a while?" he yelled. Hearing nothing in response, he walked toward the door and squeezed past it. As he moved past it, he nudged the door and it opened a few more inches. Upon entering the room, he saw two laptop computers on a desk. He decided to steal the laptops and sell them.

He grabbed the laptops quickly and shoved them into a bag. Just as he was about to leave, the homeowner ran toward him. "What on earth!" she screamed at him. "Oh no you don't, buddy." She grabbed a decorative lasso off the wall, whirled it three times over her head, and threw it expertly toward Smith. The rope tightened around him, and he was instantly captured. He dropped the bag containing the laptops. "OK, lady, my mistake, let me go and I won't hurt you." The woman laughed: "Oh really? You won't hurt me? What if I hurt you?" She pulled the rope and dragged Smith toward her backyard.

"Stand there until the police come!" she commanded, guiding Smith toward an island in the middle of an ornamental pond. "What if I don't?" asked Smith. "Well, fine with me, but it may not be OK with the alligators." She pointed towards one of several shadowy, bumpy shapes just below the pond's surface. Smith was mortally afraid of alligators, so he crouched down and stayed still. The police arrived within minutes. "There's your man," the woman said to the police. "He thinks there are alligators in the pond, but there are only alligator statues. Worked like a charm." The police arrested Smith.

Should the prosecution charge Smith with burglary? Assume that the theft of two laptops amounts to a felony.

RULE-BASED REASONING FOR MASTERY
EXERCISE 14

Using the rule set out in the Rule Section, determine whether the Good Samaritan law applies to Dr. Smith's care of Sandra Simmons.

Rule Section:

This is the text of Indiana's Good Samaritan law:

Any person, who in good faith gratuitously renders emergency care at the scene of an accident or emergency care to the victim thereof, shall not be liable for any civil damages for any personal injury as a result of any act or omission by such person in rendering the emergency care or as a result of any act or failure to act to provide or arrange for further medical treatment or care for the injured person, except acts or omissions amounting to gross negligence or willful or wanton misconduct.

Fact Pattern:

Sandra Simmons ("Simmons") went to sleep one evening feeling a little tired. She had spent a busy day at work, and she did not feel very well. She hoped that an early night and a good night's sleep would cure her.

She woke up at 2:00 a.m. with a severe pain in her chest. Her chest hurt when she breathed, and she felt weak and extremely tired. Simmons had a good friend who was a family practice physician, so Simmons called her friend immediately. "I'm in pain, Mary," said Simmons. Dr. Mary Smith lived nearby, and she said that she would come to Simmons's house and examine her.

When Dr. Smith arrived, Simmons was lying on the bed, moaning. "Mary, I'm in pain," she said. "Please help me." Dr. Smith examined Simmons and took her vital signs. "You seem OK overall," Dr. Smith said. "Let me listen to your heart again." Dr. Smith listened carefully. She told Simmons that she most likely had pleurisy, a painful disease of the pleural (lung) cavity's lining. "The best thing to do is rest." Dr. Smith told Simmons that she should be checked out in the morning by her regular doctor, just to make sure.

In the morning, however, Simmons felt even worse. She got up and staggered slightly as she tried to cross the room. She felt excruciating pain, and she reached out for the phone to call 911. As she began to talk to the 911 operator, she slumped down and passed away. As it turns out, Simmons had suffered a massive heart attack, and she did not have pleurisy at all. Her earlier symptoms had been early signs of a massive heart attack.

Simmons's estate sued Dr. Smith for negligence. Dr. Smith responded by asserting that under Indiana's Good Samaritan law, she has no liability to Simmons's estate. Simmons's estate has hired you to represent it. The first question is whether the Good Samaritan law applies. There is no case law or legislative history on point.

Do you think that the Good Samaritan law applies to Dr. Smith's care of Simmons?

RULE-BASED REASONING FOR MASTERY
EXERCISE 15

Using the rule set out in the Rule Section, determine whether Sue Sanders was properly served in the lawsuit.

Rule Section:

Under Washington law, service must be effected as follows:

[B]y delivering a copy thereof, as follows:

(9) If the suit be against a company or corporation other than those designated in the preceding subdivisions of this section, to the president or other head of the company or corporation, secretary, cashier or managing agent thereof or to the secretary, stenographer or office assistant of the president or other head of the company or corporation, secretary, cashier or managing agent.

. . . .

(14) In all other cases, to the defendant personally or by leaving a copy of the summons at the house of his usual abode with some person of suitable age and discretion then resident therein.

Service made in the modes provided above shall be taken and held to be personal service.

Further, Washington case law indicates that instead of handing papers to a defendant, the process server can leave papers in a place where they can be easily retrieved. This manner of service also constitutes valid service of process.

Fact Pattern:

Roy Riddle ("Riddle") owns a rental car company in Seattle, Washington. After Sue Sanders ("Sanders") rented a car for two weeks without paying, Riddle decided to sue her for the rental money. He hired an attorney, who drew up a petition and retained a process server to serve Sanders with process.

On a rainy Monday morning, the process server approached Sanders's apartment to serve her with process. Sanders saw the process server at the door and opened it. She was expecting a package and had no idea she was about to be served with a lawsuit. "I have some legal documents for you," said the process server and handed the documents to Sanders. Sanders reached out her hand but then quickly retracted it. She did not touch the documents at all. "Oh no you don't," she said.

Sanders and the process server stood staring at one another for a second, and then Sanders jumped backwards and quickly slammed the door. At the same time, the process server reached out his hand with the documents, and the door hit the documents. The documents fell out of the process server's hand and hit the floor. "You have been served!" yelled the process server over a clap of thunder. Rain started to fall on the documents as they lay on the ground.

For three days, Sanders did not pick up the documents. Eventually, a wild animal came and took them for bedding. Sanders heard no more about the lawsuit until six months later, when she heard that a default judgment had been entered against her. She calls you to ask whether she was properly served in the lawsuit.

To advise her, you review the Washington law regarding service of process, which is set out in the Rule Section.

Was Sanders properly served?

RULE-BASED REASONING FOR MASTERY
EXERCISE 16

Using the law provided in the Rule Section, determine whether there is adequate consideration to create and support a legally enforceable agreement between Taylor Michel and the leasing agent, Felipe Arribe.

Rule Section:

A legally enforceable agreement or contract must have valid consideration—mutuality of obligation. Consideration is a bargained-for exchange of promises. A promise for a promise is sufficient consideration to support a contract but if a promise is *illusory*, there is no valid consideration offered and, therefore, no enforceable contract between the parties. A promise is illusory if it fails to bind the promisor, such as when the promisor retains the option of discontinuing performance. An illusory promise is no promise at all. If there is no binding promise or obligation between the parties, there is no legally enforceable agreement or contract.

Fact Pattern:

Taylor Michel ("Michel") is the owner of Beautiful Bouquets. Her business provides a variety of individual fresh flowers and unique floral arrangements for all occasions. Michel rents office space for her business in a mid-sized building in downtown Riverdale. She uses the space to meet with customers, store inventory, and create her arrangements.

Felipe Arribe ("Arribe") owns the building in which Michel leases space. Arribe also serves as the leasing agent for the building. The building has ten floors. The offices on the perimeter have a window that faces the outside and a window that faces the atrium. The offices in the center of the building have a window facing the atrium. Businesses located on the perimeter of the building are in the best position to market to potential customers. Business owners can place signs in both office windows so that passersby can view any announcements.

Arribe's leasing office is on the first floor near the elevators. In addition to the leasing office, there are several businesses on the first floor, including a deli shop, a health clinic, a beauty shop, two barbershops, an alterations business, a dental office, a travel agency, a mortgage and lending company, a small conference room, and a space with the mailboxes for each office. Given the number of businesses there, people are constantly walking around the first floor. In addition, some people enter the building simply because they are drawn to a sign in the window.

Michel's office is on the tenth floor in the center of the building. Very little foot traffic comes to the tenth floor. Michel believes that her business sales would increase dramatically if she were located on the first floor, even in the center of the building. Last month, while buying her lunch in the deli, Michel learned from the beauty shop owner how a recent style promotion doubled his monthly sales. The owner explained that he placed a sign in the window offering a "wash and perm" for a discount of $30 and had no fewer than fifteen new customers that month. Michel wants to have the same opportunity to attract new customers but knows that she needs to secure an office on the first floor to have the most success. She spoke with Arribe on a number of occasions about her desire to move to an office on the first floor.

On February 14, Arribe walked around the building to check for any needed repairs and stopped by Michel's Beautiful Bouquets. Michel was busy inside working on last minute Valentine's Day gifts. "Hi, Felipe," Michel said. "How's it going? Are there any openings downstairs yet?" Arribe replied, "You know, we usually have at least one vacancy during the holiday season. Hey, can you put together one of your fanciest arrangements for me for my wife's Valentine's Day gift? I somehow managed to forget that today was the day. Can you believe that? In exchange, when the holiday season comes around and if I am in an especially giving spirit, I will make sure you get first dibs on any vacant offices on the first floor. They come at a premium rate though." Michel responded, "That sounds good. I'll make a basket and bring it down to your office before I leave for the day."

Michel made a basket containing a floral arrangement and chocolates. She left the basket on Arribe's desk with a note that read "No charge. Enjoy your evening!" Michel then walked out the building to her car.

Shortly after the Thanksgiving holiday in November, Michel noticed that the office space for one of the barbershops was empty. She thought to herself, "It shouldn't be long now. I can't wait to move into my new space." Michel had been saving extra money each month to accommodate any increase in rent for a prime location. The following week, maintenance workers placed a nameplate on the empty office. It read "Lauren Oliver, PsyD, Clinical Psychologist." Michel went to Arribe's office immediately to ask about the vacancy.

"Felipe, you were supposed to give that vacant office to me, remember? We made a deal. You promised," Michel explained. "What promise?" Arribe asked. "On Valentine's Day, I made a basket for your wife, free of charge, and you said that I could get the next vacant office on the first floor," Michel said. "Oh that, I was just talking," Arribe replied, "You can't hold me to that. This is a business, not a barter system." Michel exclaimed, "It was a valid contract. That first floor office is mine!" "Nonsense," Arribe stated, "I made no such agreement and, even if I had, it wouldn't be binding. Plus, the new tenant paid rent for six months in advance!"

Does a valid and legally enforceable agreement or contract exist between Michel and Arribe, the leasing agent? In particular, is there sufficient consideration to support the agreement?

RULE-BASED REASONING FOR MASTERY
EXERCISE 17

Using the law provided in the Rule Section, determine whether the proposed covenant not to compete is reasonable in terms of scope of activity. Do not address the other factors.

Rule Section:

In general, a covenant not to compete is valid provided the employer and the employee make certain binding promises in the agreement and the covenant itself is reasonable in terms of time, geography, and scope of activity. With respect to scope of activity, courts have decided that an industry-wide exclusion is unreasonable. In addition, restraints on activity will be unenforceable if they extend to clients with whom the employee had no dealings while he worked for the employer. A covenant's terms are unreasonable if they are greater than what is required to protect the employer's goodwill or business interests, or if they impose an undue hardship on the employee.

Fact Pattern:

For this exercise, refer to the fact pattern provided in Exercise 10.

Please advise whether the proposed covenant not to compete is reasonable in terms of scope of activity. Do not address the other elements.

Using the rule set out in the Rule Section, please state whether Tanisha Smith and Mary Green have a viable assault claim against Bob Elliott. Please explain your answer.

Rule Section:

The tort of assault requires that the plaintiff reasonably believe, based on the defendant's conduct, that the defendant had the present ability to inflict serious bodily harm upon the plaintiff. The present ability need not be actual, but apparent. Words alone may result in liability for assault if, together with other circumstances and the defendant's acts, they create a reasonable belief by the plaintiff that the plaintiff is in reasonable apprehension of an imminent offensive or harmful contact. In determining whether an "apprehension of anticipated physical force" is a reasonable reaction by the plaintiff, courts look to the defendant's actions and words together with the circumstances.

Fact Pattern:

The Buff People Gym is in Los Angeles, California. It is open twenty-four hours a day and has a juice bar and sauna. It has reasonable prices and attracts a broad clientele of urban professionals, college students, and others who seek a good workout in an understated environment.

After their workout one Sunday evening, Tanisha Smith ("Smith") and Mary Green ("Green") left the gym at about 9 p.m. They bought a smoothie and strolled toward the exit. The two women had parked far from the gym, as Sunday night was one of the busiest nights in the gym. As they opened the door to leave, they saw a sign warning patrons to take extra care in the parking lot and avoid leaving valuables and other items that might create criminal opportunities.

They zigzagged through the parking lot on foot, laughing and discussing the tough spinning class they had attended. "He said to feel the burn, and man, I felt it!" said Green. "I know what you mean," said Smith. "We must have burned five hundred calories, no joke." They reached the end of the parking lot and could not see Smith's car. "Well," said Green. "What now? Do you remember where we put it?" Smith said she thought they had parked on the other side of the parking lot. The parking lot was emptying out, and a cloud shifted and covered the moon completely.

"Let's really think now," said Smith. The two walked to the other side of the parking lot. They walked through a very dark area, where the one streetlight serving that corner of the parking lot was not working. "I'm getting scared," said Smith. "Where on earth is the stupid car? Where?" Green grabbed her hand.

Suddenly, a man stepped out from behind one of the hedges that marked the parking lot's perimeter. He was tall and muscular, wearing workout clothes and gym shoes. He carried a gym bag and appeared to be about twenty years old. His face was unshaven. The two women stopped short, realizing that they were all alone with the tall stranger. He looked down, said nothing and started to walk away. Then he turned around and walked back, standing close to the two women.

He looked at them with a level gaze and said in a conversational tone: "Know what? I'm a thug. What do you think of that?" For three seconds, nobody moved a muscle. Then Smith quickly handed her wallet to the man and started to run away. "Come on, Mary, let's go." Green took her wallet out and handed it to the man. "We're out of here, it's all yours. Just let us go." The man did not leave, move, or say anything further. As Green and Smith ran away, they turned around and saw the man still standing there.

"That was so odd," said Green. "I'm shaking," said Smith. They called the police, and reported the incident. The man, who was still in the parking lot, was quickly apprehended. The district attorney did not prosecute the man, whose name was Bob Elliott ("Elliot"). In an interview with the district attorney, Elliott said that he was not intending to rob anyone, just to try out a new tough-guy persona that he was developing with heavy workouts at the gym. "I was stunned and afraid when they gave me their wallets. Were they crazy?" he said to the assistant district attorney who handled his case. "Why would someone just hand over a wallet? I was just trying to be impressive and sort of cool. They must be real wimps. In fact, I have a severe back injury from a motorcycle accident last month. I could not have hurt them even if I had wanted to. Good Lord."

Green and Smith believe that a crime was committed against them, and they are upset that the district attorney did not pursue charges. They have come to you seeking grounds to sue Elliott civilly. You have been asked to determine whether Green and Smith have a claim of assault, based on the rule set out above.

RULE-BASED REASONING FOR MASTERY
EXERCISE 19

Using the law provided in the Rule Section, determine whether Brewer & Hoffman LLP's advertisement of its legal services violated the attorney disciplinary rules prohibiting misleading communications of an attorney's services.

Rule Section:

The Model Rules of Professional Conduct generally provide that an attorney cannot make a misleading communication about his services. An advertisement reciting an attorney's achievements may be misleading if the attorney includes a statement that could lead a reasonable person to form an unjustified expectation that the attorney could obtain the same results for other clients in similar matters, without reference to the specific factual and legal circumstances of each client's case. Further, an unsubstantiated comparison of the attorney's services with the services of other attorneys may be misleading if the advertisement presents the comparison with such specificity as would lead a reasonable person to conclude that the attorney could substantiate the comparison. If a communication includes an appropriate disclaimer or other qualifying language then the statement may not create unjustified expectations or mislead a prospective client.

Fact Pattern:

Brewer & Hoffman LLP hired a marketing firm to design a new advertisement of its legal services for several publications in the local area. The firm placed the following advertisement in over thirteen different publications.

---

*Accidents can happen at any time
and they can quickly change your life.*

Brewer & Hoffman LLP
The Premier Personal Injury Law Firm

---

*With more than 20 years of trial experience and a comprehensive
support network,
we offer the track record and resources
you need to win a settlement.*

**CALL NOW
(319) 555-HURT
WE CAN HELP!**

The State Bar adopted the Model Rules of Professional Conduct to regulate the activities and services of the attorneys who are licensed and practice in its jurisdiction. A few days later, the State Bar received a copy of the firm's advertisement that was included in the Yellow Pages. The State Bar contacted the firm and advised it to cease further publications, as the advertisement violates the rules of professional conduct. The State Bar does not have a rating system for licensed attorneys.

Does the firm's advertisement violate the rules of professional conduct? In particular, do any of the statements constitute misleading communications under the rules of professional conduct? Please explain your position.

PART 2

INTERMEDIATE RULE-BASED EXERCISES

RULE-BASED REASONING FOR MASTERY

EXERCISE 20

Using the law provided in the Rule Section, determine whether the statements made by Rhoades about Weatherly were published or communicated to a third party as required for a slander claim. Do not address any other issues.

Rule Section:

The law provides that an aggrieved party may bring a slander suit against a speaker for false and defamatory statements about him that are published or communicated to a third party without any legal excuse or permission to do so under the law. The speaker's statements must be about the aggrieved party. The speaker need not specifically name the aggrieved party if those who heard the statements know him, are acquainted with him, and understood that the defamatory publication referred to him. Further, the statement must be communicated to and heard by someone (other than the aggrieved party) who is capable of understanding, and did so understand, the comment's allegedly harmful meaning. Also, the speaker may be held responsible for remarks that she actually did not intend to make to other people where she created such an unreasonable risk that the comments would be overheard by others.

Fact Pattern:

Gina Rhoades ("Rhoades") works at ReproNation, International ("ReproNation") in the main office. ReproNation is one of the leading reprographic and digital imaging companies in the United States. The company has an international presence, as there are hundreds of locations throughout the United States, Canada, Mexico, Europe, the Middle East, the Far East, and Russia. Houston is the largest location and the main office. There are a number of departments at ReproNation including Digital Services, Color Printing, On-Site Services, Document Logistics, Customer Service, Human Resources, Legal, and Recycling. Rhoades has an entry-level position in the Document Logistics Department recording the company's courier services and pick-up and delivery appointments. She has worked at ReproNation for approximately two years.

Mike Weatherly ("Weatherly"), Rhoades's supervisor, joined ReproNation about six years ago. He has worked in the Document Logistics Department the entire time. Rhoades and Weatherly are on the same logistics team, Team B. There are five teams in the Document Logistics Department, Teams A, B, C, D and E. Last month, the leader for Team B was transferred to the Dallas office. Donna Richards ("Richards"), Director of Document Logistics, then appointed Weatherly as the new team leader for Team B. Team leader is a coveted management position at the company. Team leaders receive company stock, year-end bonuses, increased vacation time, and a company car. Prior to becoming the Director, Richards was the leader for Team D for many years.

The week that Weatherly was appointed new team leader, Rhoades had a conversation with Pamela Chavis ("Chavis"), a member of Team E, in the ladies' restroom on the third floor, which is located directly across the hall from the company break room. Rhoades and Chavis both work on the fourth floor. That particular third-floor restroom is used by employees from all departments. The restroom has a separate lounge area with a bench, a chair, and a table. The lounge is the first area you reach as you enter the restroom. Employees sometimes use the lounge area to take a quick nap or to just get away. A door separates the lounge area from the main part of the restroom, which contains mirrors, sinks, and toilet stalls. This door is usually closed. That day, however, the door was slightly propped open by the custodian's cart. The custodian was cleaning one of the stalls during their conversation.

The following conversation took place between Rhoades and Chavis, as they stood in front of the sink area:

> Rhoades: Can you believe he's team leader now?

> Chavis: All I can say is good for him.

> Rhoades: I mean really, Pam. He's straight loopy! Most of the time, he doesn't know whether he's comin' or goin'. How can he lead us?

> Chavis: Big Mike's been here longer than us. He knows the ropes.

> Rhoades: Well, I hear he knows the ropes alright. There's been some extracurricular activities going on with him and the head lady, Richards.

> Chavis: Girl, I heard somethin' like that too.

> Rhoades: She's the one who gave him the promotion. That's one way to move up the ladder.

> Chavis: You're so crazy! I've got to get back to my desk. See you later.

> Rhoades: See ya.

Rhoades acknowledged that a few words may be out of place but guaranteed that this exchange accurately represents the substance of the conversation. She maintains that it was harmless banter between two coworkers. After they finished talking, Chavis left the restroom. Rhoades remained in the restroom for a few minutes longer to freshen up her makeup. Later that afternoon, Chavis sent Rhoades an email stating that, when she left the restroom, she saw Freda Higgins ("Higgins") from the Accounting Department. Higgins was lying on the bench and appeared to be taking a nap. Rhoades did not see Higgins when she left the restroom.

The next day, Weatherly called Rhoades into his office. Weatherly told Rhoades that he knew about her conversation with Chavis in the ladies' room. Rhoades does not know how he heard about the conversation. He also told Rhoades he spoke with someone in the Legal Department who said Weatherly could sue her for defamation for implying that he was incompetent and had an affair with his boss. Weatherly threatened he could win a large sum of money. He insisted she stop talking about him and focus on her work performance.

Rhoades cannot believe Weatherly was so upset about what she said to Chavis. They were pretty good friends before he became team leader. Rhoades is very concerned about her future at ReproNation and says that she cannot afford any problems or an expensive lawsuit. She really needs her job.

Please advise whether Rhoades's statements about Weatherly were published or communicated to a third party. Do not address any other issues (such as whether the statements were in fact defamatory or offensive).

RULE-BASED REASONING FOR MASTERY
EXERCISE 21

Using the law provided in the Rule Section, determine whether Taylor Simon committed extreme and outrageous conduct toward his teacher, Olivia Ruiz. Do not address any other issues.

Rule Section:

In order to establish a claim for intentional infliction of emotional distress, the plaintiff must show, among other things, that the defendant's conduct toward the plaintiff was extreme and outrageous. To be extreme and outrageous, the defendant's conduct must be so outrageous in character and so extreme in degree as to go beyond all possible bounds of decency, and to be regarded as atrocious and utterly intolerable in a civilized community. Generally, liability for intentional infliction of emotional distress has been found only in cases in which a recitation of the facts to an average member of the community would lead him to exclaim, "Outrageous."

Insensitive or rude behavior does not amount to outrageous behavior. Further, the fact that an act is intentional or malicious does not mean the defendant's conduct was extreme and outrageous. In addition, a defendant who conducts himself toward others with mere insults, indignities, threats, annoyances or other trivialities has not displayed extreme and outrageous behavior. Moreover, plaintiffs are expected to be hardened to occasional inconsiderate and unkind acts. The test for determining what conduct is extreme and outrageous is basically a subjective one and the court will consider the context and relationship between the parties.

Fact Pattern:

Taylor Simon ("Taylor") is an 18 year-old senior in high school who has a reputation for being a class clown. He won the title for "Most Funny Senior" and received his own page in the school's yearbook to display his favorite pictures and quotations. In addition to being funny, Taylor can be a bully at times. He does not pick fights with students but will tease them continuously. He shows no mercy. He makes jokes about his classmates' clothes, hair, shoes, taste in music, dance moves—practically anything about which a high school student is self-conscious. He finds satisfaction in making the whole room laugh at the object of his sharp tongue. Despite his bullying conduct, however, Taylor has plenty of friends at school.

Olivia Ruiz is Taylor's chemistry teacher. Ms. Ruiz is one of the best teachers in the school but she is the toughest one too. Several of Ms. Ruiz's students went on to college, majored in chemistry, and became successful pharmacists. Ms. Ruiz expects her students to be ready for each class, to complete all assigned readings and homework, and to do their best at all times. She tests her students at the end of each month and gives them pop quizzes about once a week. By the end of the year, the students are ready to take her final exam. She has very high, but achievable, expectations of her students.

Ms. Ruiz really cares about her students and always puts their needs first. Although she is a good teacher, she still has to deal with very difficult personalities at times and hostile students who receive failing grades from her in chemistry. Ms. Ruiz often mentions to other teachers that she is stressed and overworked. One day, Taylor overheard Ms. Ruiz tell several teachers that she could not wait to leave for vacation, and she had even considered taking an early retirement. Taylor wished that Ms. Ruiz would leave the school. He struggled in her chemistry class and dreaded facing another pop quiz or being called to the board to answer a question. He rarely prepared for chemistry class and found the subject quite boring.

One evening while watching television, Taylor decided that he wanted a new look—a hairstyle like his favorite pop star, Justin Bieber. He picked up a pair of scissors to give himself a quick trim and made an awful mistake. The scissors slipped and he cut too much of his hair. He tried to remedy the problem by cutting in other places to even out the style but, rather than looking like his idol, he resembled a cockatoo. Taylor put on a baseball cap and said, "I'm never taking this hat off my head."

That Friday in chemistry class, Taylor sat quiet in the back of the room, as to not draw any attention to himself. He had on his baseball cap and used his chemistry book to shield his face from his classmates. "Man, Taylor is quiet today," one student remarked. Ms. Ruiz walked in the room and sat at her desk. "Good morning class," she said with a big smile. "Let's begin by diagramming a few compounds from last night's homework. When I call your name, please come to the board. Erika, answer question #1. James, question #2." The students went to the board and started writing. "Taylor, why don't you answer question #3? And please take that hat off your head. You know the rules." "I didn't finish the homework, Ms. Ruiz. I don't know the answer," Taylor explained to avoid getting out of his seat. Ms. Ruiz responded, "That's okay, Taylor. Your classmates will help you. Go to the board and take off that hat."

Taylor stood up slowly and removed the baseball cap from his head. As he walked down the aisle, the other students started pointing at him and laughing. "What did you do to your hair?" they shouted. As payback for all of his harassing comments, the students' laughter roared, and some of them even fell to the floor holding their stomachs. Ms. Ruiz looked up at Taylor and chuckled slightly. She tried hard to hide her expression. "I'm sorry, Taylor. You may return to your seat and put your hat back on."

Taylor was furious. He had never been on the receiving end of a crowd's laughter and it was more than he could handle. He decided to take his anger out on Ms. Ruiz and get even for his embarrassment. Taylor wanted to make teaching unbearable for her. He planned to pull some harmless pranks to make Ms. Ruiz feel as bad as he did last week. "And just maybe," he thought to himself, "she will take an early vacation or leave teaching altogether." He did not plan to hurt Ms. Ruiz in any way. "Maybe I'll get some pictures in the yearbook for this one," Taylor said as he smiled.

The following Monday morning, Taylor placed a Whoopee cushion in Ms. Ruiz's chair. When she walked into class, Ms. Ruiz sat down and made a loud and embarrassing noise. All of the students started laughing loudly. "That's enough. Everyone be quiet!" Ms. Ruiz shouted. "Wow, don't lose your head, Ms. Ruiz," Taylor responded. "Thank you for your concern, Taylor. Why don't you start us off today by reciting the periodic table," Ms. Ruiz stated. "What's a periodic table?" Taylor asked. The class started to laugh again. Every time Ms. Ruiz attempted to speak to regain control over the class, Taylor would place his hand over his mouth and say, "loser." A few students came to Ms. Ruiz's defense and told Taylor to stop. The other students continued to laugh. Ms. Ruiz told Taylor to go and stand in the hall. Once Taylor left the room, the class became quiet. Ms. Ruiz was very disturbed by Taylor's behavior and made a note to contact his mother. As she wrote, her hand began to tremble. She put down the pen and told the class to open their books and read chapter fifteen.

While the students read, Ms. Ruiz opened her desk drawer to get her migraine medicine. She felt tension in her neck and knew a major headache was developing. She opened the drawer and, as she reached inside, a frog leaped out the desk. Ms. Ruiz was so startled that she screamed loudly and jumped in the air. The students asked, "What happened?" Once they saw and heard the frog, they resumed their laughter. Ms. Ruiz decided to go home early and start fresh on Tuesday. She spoke to the principal's assistant, and he called for a substitute teacher.

The next day, Ms. Ruiz entered the school with the principal. They exchanged pleasantries, and Ms. Ruiz turned the corner toward her classroom. When she walked in the room, she saw a large picture posted on the chalkboard. The face was hers, but the body was someone else's. The person was dressed in a skimpy two-piece bathing suit. The picture left very little to one's imagination. Ms. Ruiz was in shock. "Oh, no!" she shouted. "I hope no one has seen this yet. I would be absolutely devastated." She immediately ran to the board and tore down the picture. She ripped it to shreds and threw it in the trash. Ms. Ruiz then went to the teacher's lounge to get some coffee. Ms. Ruiz was shaking so much while she poured her coffee that she spilled most of it on the counter. She picked up a few napkins and cleaned up the mess. When she leaned down to throw away the napkin, she noticed the same horrible picture in the trash. Another teacher said, "Don't worry, Olivia. I saw the picture this morning and put it in the trash. I don't think anyone else saw it." Ms. Ruiz left the lounge without saying a word.

Little did Taylor know Ms. Ruiz had suffered a devastating loss three months ago. Her father passed away after a long battle with cancer. Ms. Ruiz did not share the news with her class and decided not to take a break from work. She felt that keeping her routine helped her to focus. When she was alone, the grief would overwhelm her and she would cry nonstop. Her doctor prescribed her a mild anti-depressant and some anti-anxiety and sleeping pills. He advised her to take some time off from work, but Ms. Ruiz continued to teach. Ms. Ruiz stopped taking the medications after two months and began to feel like her old self. She had even started watching Sci-Fi movie marathons again.

As Ms. Ruiz walked back to her classroom from the teacher's lounge, she noticed students pointing at her and laughing. "What's so funny?" she shouted. "You," one student responded, "You're all over the web thanks to Taylor. Look. You have over a thousand hits already." The student gave Ms. Ruiz her phone and showed her the picture on YouTube. It seemed that every student had seen it. Ms. Ruiz ran to her classroom, grabbed her purse, and ran out of the school.

When Ms. Ruiz got home, she immediately ran to her medicine cabinet and took two pills for anxiety. She then threw herself on the couch and let out a big sigh. She eventually fell asleep. After a short nap, she woke to several messages on her phone. The principal's assistant had called several times to check on her. She decided to turn off her phone and just rest. She felt very unnerved and on edge. She looked down at her arm and noticed red welt marks on her forearm. She was experiencing hives again, just as she did after her father's death. Ms. Ruiz took a long bath and went to bed. She did not have an appetite for any food.

The next morning, Ms. Ruiz still had no appetite, and she had a pounding headache. She barely got any rest the night before because, when she closed her eyes, she kept envisioning the poster-sized picture of her and the students jeering at her. She called the school and explained that she needed to take a few sick days off from work. She then took her migraine medicine and another anxiety pill and went back to bed.

A few days became a few weeks. Whenever Ms. Ruiz left home to go to work, she became ill. She grew more and more anxious as she approached the school doors. "I just need some more time off," she thought to herself, "It's long overdue anyway." She decided to take an indefinite leave of absence but knew that it would be hard on her financially. She had very little money in her savings account and still owed a large amount for her father's funeral and her own doctor's bills. Ms. Ruiz called one of her good friends to get some advice, and she told Ms. Ruiz that she should sue Taylor for intentional infliction of emotional distress. "It's his fault that you are so sick and can't work. He and his family should pay," her friend explained. Ms. Ruiz agreed and felt as if she had no other viable options.

Please advise whether Taylor's conduct toward Ms. Ruiz was extreme and outrageous. Do not address any other issues (such as whether Taylor's actions caused Ms. Ruiz's emotional distress or whether her distress was severe).

RULE-BASED REASONING FOR MASTERY

EXERCISE 22

Using the rule of law set out in the Rule Section, determine whether the parties created a contract to convey the nail salon.

Rule Section:

With regard to a contract, a person's behavior is judged by its outward expression rather than the person's internal and secret intentions. A person is understood to have the intentions that her words and acts would reasonably mean. Mental assent is not required to establish a contract; rather, if the person's words and acts have a single reasonable meaning, then the person's undisclosed intentions have no effect. A contract is not invalidated based on intoxication unless the intoxicated person cannot understand the consequences of the document being signed.*

Fact Pattern:

Tiffany LeGrand ("LeGrand") owns a popular nail salon in New Orleans, Louisiana. She started out as a manicurist, gradually gaining a loyal clientele. After five years as a manicurist, she became a partner in the business. Last year, her partner retired, and LeGrand took over the business in its entirety. She hired an extra employee, because the salon was so popular and busy. With her managerial responsibilities and bookkeeping tasks, LeGrand was constantly busy.

As the business continued to grow, LeGrand saw her family less and less frequently. After six months, LeGrand's family became increasingly tired of being put on the back burner. When LeGrand was two hours late to the family Thanksgiving celebration, LeGrand's mom had to speak up. "This salon!" she said. "It's becoming a nightmare and dividing our family! We hardly know you anymore." LeGrand was upset, and her eyes filled with tears. "Mom, this is all for our family. If I can make this work, it's great for all of us. You know there's nothing more important to me than you!" The two hugged, and LeGrand promised to see her family more often.

LeGrand's intense pace continued, however, and the salon required almost all of LeGrand's time. "How are you ever going to meet someone if you don't slow down?" asked her best friend, Cheryl Townsend ("Townsend"). "I don't think that will ever happen for me," said LeGrand. "I'm busier than I've ever been. But it's so much fun to see my dreams come true!" At night, as she locked the salon's door,

---

* *Lucy v. Zehmer*, 84 S.E.2d 516 (Va. 1954).

LeGrand sometimes thought about whether the salon was the right business for her at this time. She continued to work hard, however, and remained totally committed to the business.

One Friday night, she went out with three of her best friends, including Townsend. The three friends were all successful businesswomen, and they met at a martini bar downtown. LeGrand ordered and quickly drank an apple martini. The three chatted, and after an hour or so, they moved to another bar. They ordered lime mineral water and appetizers this time, and the conversation turned to work. About an hour later, LeGrand turned to Townsend and put her hand on her friend's shoulder. "Girl," LeGrand said, "You know what I just decided? I am so tired of all the salon work! I would sell it in a heartbeat. I am DONE!" LeGrand raised her water glass in a mock toast.

"You would not," said Townsend. "That place is your baby." "Maybe it was," said LeGrand. "But not anymore. I'm tired of it, and it's coming between me and my family. Put a fork in it, I'm done!" Townsend was puzzled. "I've never heard you talk like this before. But if you put it on the market, let me have a first bid. My grandmother left me some money, and I've always liked nails. I would take it over with no problem. I bet I could grow it even more."

"Why not?" said LeGrand. "I'm in a mood to do anything. Let's sign it up now! But not before I have a turn on the dance floor." LeGrand danced for a while, and she returned with a beverage napkin. "Look, here's my price. Bet you can't pay it." She laid down a napkin with a number on it: $900,000. The napkin had a note on it that said, "I, Tiffany LeGrand, will sell Deluxe Nails to Cheryl Townsend for $900,000. Close in 30 days." LeGrand had signed her name on the napkin. Townsend looked at the napkin for a second. She signed her name, looked up, and smiled. LeGrand responded, "Done! I sold it, and I feel so good." "Wow," said Mary Granger, one of the other friends. "You are going to be so happy without that salon," she said. LeGrand abruptly stood up and said that she was feeling strange. She headed to the bathroom. "I've got to call a cab," she said. "My asthma is acting up again."

The next day, LeGrand woke up late to the sound of the phone ringing. It was Townsend. "Hi there! I'm sending over an inspector to check out the salon building," she said. LeGrand suddenly remembered the events of the previous evening. "OK, I know we were all excited last night, and I was sick and tired of the salon, but I'm not really ready to sell yet. I was just making a little joke. Maybe we could talk in a few years. It really is my baby, and I'm not ready to throw in the towel." Townsend was taken aback. "What do you mean? I moved money into an account so I could buy it. A deal's a deal. You can't go back on it." The discussion continued, with both women upset. Finally, LeGrand said, "It's my nail salon, and I'm not selling! You're my friend, but if we're going to stay friends, you've got to drop this."

Townsend refused to drop it, and instead called you, her attorney, for advice. Did Townsend and LeGrand make an enforceable contract regarding the nail salon? In answering the question, please use only the statement of the rule set out above.

RULE-BASED REASONING FOR MASTERY

EXERCISE 23

Using the rule of law set out in the Rule Section, please determine whether the commercial described in the fact pattern below was a valid offer.

Rule Section:

New York law provides the following:

It is quite possible to make a definite and operative offer to buy or sell goods by advertisement, in a newspaper, by a handbill, a catalog or circular or on a placard in a store window. It is not customary to do this, however, and the presumption is the other way . . . Such advertisements are understood to be mere requests to consider and examine and negotiate; and no one can reasonably regard them as otherwise unless the circumstances are exceptional and the words used are very plain and clear.

The exception to the rule that advertisements do not create any power of acceptance in potential offerees is where the advertisement is clear, definite, and explicit, and leaves nothing open for negotiation. In that circumstance, it constitutes an offer, acceptance of which will complete the contract.

Further, a statement that is clearly a joke does not give rise to a contract; if the statement is not clearly a joke, the question is whether a reasonable person would consider the statement to be a joke rather than a serious offer.

Fact Pattern:

Cheryl Townsend ("Townsend") was the new owner of Deluxe Nails, a thriving nail salon in New York City. Under its previous owner, the salon had grown to be a local institution. Women gathered there not just for nail care, but for conversation over coffee and the welcoming environment. When Townsend took over, she wanted to put her own mark on the salon. She immediately renamed it Celebrity Nails and painted the store bright pink, instead of the previous light beige. She was delighted to own such a popular business, and for about three months, she happily took in the considerable profit that the salon produced.

Townsend made other changes in addition to the salon's name. She lowered the manicurists' hourly wage, and she removed the flex-time options that had previously been available. The manicurists were unhappy with the changes, and several of the most popular manicurists left. Townsend ended the practice of offering complimentary coffee or bottled water. "Too expensive!" she remarked to a customer who complained.

After a few more months of Townsend's ownership, business started to slump. Townsend reinstated the free coffee and bottled water, but still the customers stayed away. Townsend decided to take steps to increase business. She thought for several days about a promotion that would really create a splash. "I've got it!" she finally decided. She put together the advertising campaign and launched it on January 1st. The campaign consisted of a television commercial, billboard, and flyer posted on the salon's door.

In the TV commercial, an announcer dressed as Lady Gaga spoke straight into the camera: "If you want nails like a celebrity, come to Celebrity Nails. Come to the salon once, and you'll have nails like me. Come three times, and you'll be more glamorous than ever before. Come ten times, and you'll have a record contract! It worked for me!" The commercial then showed the faux Lady Gaga excitedly signing a contract, throwing the pen over her shoulder, winking, and then showing nails with glitter all over them. "It's all in the nails, baby," she said to the camera with a pout, as the shot faded and the address of Celebrity Nails appeared on the screen. At the bottom, large words appeared in pink letters: "Free celebrity glitter with every manicure!"

The commercial was a hit, and soon business increased. Customers loved the new faux Lady Gaga commercial, and many customers joked about the celebrity lifestyle that their new nails would supposedly bring. "It's all in the nails, baby," they said to one another, holding their nails up with a laugh.

Townsend was thrilled with the results of the advertising campaign, and she planned a sequel to the TV commercial. She was taken aback, then, when she was served with a lawsuit one morning. It stated that the customer had been to the nail salon ten times but did not have the promised record contract. The lawsuit alleged that the commercial had effectively set out a promise, and it had not delivered. "Please provide a record contract immediately," the lawsuit read, "or pay $1,000,000 in damages." Townsend gasped. "There's no way I can afford this," she explained to you in your office. "Do I have to deal with this? Can we win?"

Townsend asks you to find out whether her commercial really did amount to an enforceable offer to enter into a contract. What do you think? Please use the rule of law above to answer the question.

RULE-BASED REASONING FOR MASTERY
EXERCISE 24

Using the rules set out in the Rule Section, determine whether Jonas and Susan Gomez have a viable negligence claim against the manager of the bar for starting John Remy's car when he was intoxicated.

Rule Section:

A person is generally under no duty to help a stranger. But once a person voluntarily undertakes to assist another and the other relies upon the assistance, the person must assist with reasonable care. This is the case even though the person was not under any force or pressure to perform the act in the first place:

> [O]ne who undertakes to do an act or perform a service for another has the duty to exercise care, and is liable for injury resulting from his failure to do so, even though his undertaking is purely voluntary or even though it was completely gratuitous, and he was not under any obligation to do such an act or perform such service, or there was no consideration for the promise or undertaking sufficient to support an action ex contractu based thereon.

In addition, anyone who does an affirmative act is under a duty to others to exercise the care of a reasonable man to protect them against an unreasonable risk of harm arising out of the act.

Fact Pattern:

John Remy ("Remy") and Bob Gidet ("Gidet") went out one Friday night to celebrate Gidet's thirtieth birthday. They started out with two cocktails each at a bar in downtown Atlanta, and then they went to another bar, which had a live band. The two sipped drinks for a couple of hours, and then Gidet said that he had to go home. "I'm tired and a bit tipsy," he said. "Thanks for the awesome birthday celebration—you're the best. I think I'm leaving my car here, and I'm cabbing this one, man." He called a cab and climbed into it. "Do you want to join me?" he asked Remy. "No thanks," said Remy. "I love this band, and I really want to see it through. You go ahead." Gidet was a bit worried that Remy might try to drive home. "You'll cab it too, right?" he asked. "Don't worry," said Remy. "I'm not an idiot."

Remy sat through a few more songs and decided to order another drink. "One shot of tequila, please, with two lime slices," he said. The bartender looked at Remy and replied, "Dude, I can't serve you. You've had a couple too many. Next time, bud." Remy was pretty upset that he could not have another drink. "I've been here all night! I'm not that badly off, man," he said loudly. Remy tried to bang his hand on the table in anger, but his hand missed the table and caused

Remy to lurch sideways on his chair. "I'm going to another bar. Forget you guys. Who needs this kind of harassment?"

Remy walked out to the parking lot. He climbed into his car, almost slamming his hand in the car door. He turned the key in the ignition, and the engine turned over but did not start. Remy tried it again, with the same result. He looked at his headlight control switch and saw that his headlights had been turned on for the entire time that he had been at the bar. "Oh no," he said. "Now I've got to find a jump."

He went back into the bar and walked up to the same bartender who had just refused to serve him. "I'm heading out as fast as I can, man, but now my stupid car won't start." The bartender called the hostess stand and asked the manager to jump start Remy's car. "This guy is a good patron, and now he's stuck. Can you help him out with a jump?" Rob Fuller ("Fuller"), the manager on duty, pulled out some jumper cables and drove his car over to Remy's. Remy sat on the curb and stared into space. "How many drinks have you had?" asked the manager. "Let's see," said Remy. "One tequila, two tequila, three tequila, four! Four, dude! Plus the beers, of course. Woo-hoo!" Fuller hooked up the cables, and the car eventually started. "Thanks," said Remy. "Your bartender cut me off just now, but I appreciate your help. Now let me get going!"

Remy jumped into the car and drove away. On the way home, he drove through a red light and broadsided a car driven by Jonas Gomez, whose wife, Susan, was in labor. Fortunately, no one was seriously injured, although the husband's arm was broken in the impact and the wife suffered some bruises. The couple is now suing Remy and the bar. The theory of liability against the bar is that the bar's manager undertook a duty toward Remy, and that the manager was negligent in starting Remy's car when the manager knew Remy was drunk. Based on the rule of law above, does the couple have a viable claim?

RULE-BASED REASONING FOR MASTERY

EXERCISE 25

Using the rules set out in the Rule Section below, determine whether Sam Sarvino's statement to the police regarding the shooter should be admissible as an exception to the hearsay rule.

Rule Section:

Hearsay is an out-of-court statement offered to establish the truth of the matter asserted. Hearsay is generally excluded at trial because the declarant is not available to be cross examined. In addition, hearsay statements are generally not made under oath, and the fact-finder cannot judge the declarant's demeanor.

There are exceptions to the hearsay rule for statements made under circumstances that indicate the statement's trustworthiness. One such exception is for statements made while the declarant believes that death is imminent and does not believe that he or she will recover. Federal Rule of Evidence 804(b)(2) states that a dying declaration is an exception to the hearsay rule:

> (2) *Statement under belief of impending death.* In a prosecution for homicide or in a civil action or proceeding, a statement made by a declarant while believing that the declarant's death was imminent, concerning the cause or circumstances of what the declarant believed to be impending death.

To be admissible, a dying declaration need not be made immediately before the declarant's death. Indeed, the declarant need not actually die. To be admissible, the declarant of a dying declaration must first be unavailable to testify. In addition, the declarant must have had the impression that death was near. A declarant need not state that he or she believes death is imminent. Rather, the belief can be inferred from the circumstances surrounding the declaration and from the declarant's condition.

Fact Pattern:

You are a summer intern in the district attorney's office. You have been asked to help research some issues concerning a shooting incident involving two friends. The victim, Sam Sarvino ("Sarvino"), suffered three gunshot wounds but recovered after several weeks in the hospital. The night of the shooting, Sarvino and the defendant, Tim Roberts ("Roberts"), had gone out bar-hopping. They were having a good time when Roberts asked Sarvino whether Sarvino was still dating June Watson ("Watson"). Sarvino responded, "Whose business is that? Mine, that's all. Be quiet." In fact, Watson had broken up with Sarvino two weeks before, but Sarvino still hoped to win Watson back.

Roberts had been drinking heavily, and he persisted in his questioning. "Well, are you or aren't you? If not, well, then back off. Maybe I can ask her out." Sarvino was furious. "Watch it friend, or you'll get more than a date. You'll get a knuckle sandwich." Roberts laughed. "Are you serious, man? Really? Who talks like that, anyway? Daffy Duck?" Sarvino spun around and punched Roberts hard in the mouth. "There's your knuckle sandwich. Still think it's so funny?" Roberts, still reeling backwards, pulled a gun from the messenger bag he always carried. "You're right," he said. "It's no longer funny." He shot Sarvino three times in the arm and chest. Sarvino fell immediately, and Roberts panicked. "What have I done? This is my best friend!" He ran away, hopped on a bus, and was soon miles away from the crime scene. When the police arrived, Sarvino was lying on the ground, gasping for air.

Sarvino was losing blood rapidly, and ten minutes after the shooting the ambulance had not arrived. Some police officers who had arrived quickly on the scene did their best to provide first aid, but the injuries were profound. After a few more minutes, the ambulance arrived. The EMTs gave Sarvino some oxygen and an IV drip and loaded him into the ambulance. The police officers jumped into the ambulance next to the stretcher and tried to talk to Sarvino about a suspect. "Who did this to you?" they asked. Sarvino tried to speak but could not. He laid his head down and moaned.

"OK, let's get to the hospital," said one of the police officers to the other. They jumped into their squad car and followed the ambulance. At the hospital, Sarvino continued to lose blood rapidly.

One police officer said grimly, "This guy's not long for this world. Let's get what we can about the shooter." The other officer turned to Sarvino and said, "Who did this to you?" Sarvino lifted his head. "Roberts. Roberts did it. He did me in." Sarvino laid his head back down and took shallow breaths. "And as soon as I get out of here, I'm going to get him back, real bad," Sarvino added. "Whoa, don't think that way," said one of the police officers. "That way is the wrong way. Let's think about getting him the right way—prosecuting him. What happened between you and Roberts?" Sarvino started to think back to all the good times he and Roberts had shared. "It was dumb, just a dumb thing," Sarvino said. "I'm not saying anything else." Sarvino closed his eyes. "I want to be friends with him again. I do. Or I don't, I don't know. I feel sick."

Fortunately, Sarvino recovered from his injuries. He and Roberts met up some months later, and they decided to be friends once again. Sarvino laughed. "I'm not sure what I was thinking. 'Knuckle sandwich,' seriously. Who talks like that?" Roberts rubbed his jaw. "Well, you got me pretty good, buddy. Jaw broken in two places and four teeth out. What did I do to you?" Sarvino pointed to his chest. "Well, the two bullets in my chest and one in my arm weren't exactly a walk in the park. But what good does it do to stay angry? Who do I have if I don't have you, man? We never should have started all this." The two hugged, and they decided right there and then not to press charges against each other. Sarvino flew to Mexico and planned to stay at his vacation home until the whole incident blew over.

Undaunted, however, the assistant district attorney assigned to the case prosecuted Roberts, even though Sarvino did not want to press charges and was not available to testify. The assistant district attorney wants to introduce at trial Sarvino's statements to the police officers under the "dying declaration" exception to the hearsay rule. The assistant district attorney has asked you to determine how the judge will rule. You locate the legal rule set out above. Will the judge admit Sarvino's statement under the dying declaration exception to the hearsay rule?

RULE-BASED REASONING FOR MASTERY

EXERCISE 26

Using the rule set out in the Rule Section, please state whether the Sweeneys are likely to be held strictly liable for Hilda Storey's injuries. Please explain your answer.

Rule Section:

A dog's owner is strictly liable for damage caused by a dangerous dog. Liability only arises, however, if an owner keeps a dog after the owner discovers that the dog is dangerous. In order to hold an owner liable, the plaintiff must show that the owner knew, or should have known, of the animal's propensity to do the same mischief as the mischief at the basis of the plaintiff's claim. The knowledge should be of the type that would put a reasonable person on notice of the dog's tendencies, such that the owner knew or should have known of the dog's tendencies. The knowledge can come from other people, from experiences, or from observation of the dog. The mere fact that a dog belongs to a breed that tends to be more aggressive is insufficient; the evidence must pertain to the particular dog at issue.

Fact Pattern:

Hilda Storey ("Hilda") and her husband Skip Storey ("Skip") were taking their usual walk in the evening. They lived in a quiet neighborhood where people enjoyed taking evening walks or bike rides. The Storeys took a slightly different route from their usual one due to some construction on their usual route. The two were discussing the day's events when Hilda saw a gate swing open and a big shape rush toward her out of the darkness. Her initial impression was of a large mouth and sharp teeth. She then heard a snap of teeth close to her, and she felt a rush of air as the jaws snapped shut. She heard a loud howl, followed by three loud, sharp barks. The dog—a large German Shepherd—stood on the path before her, eyes narrowed, teeth bared, and ears back. It stared at her and gave a long, low growl.

Hilda startled and jumped backwards. She tripped over a hole in the lawn, falling backwards. She put a hand behind her back to steady herself, but she fell heavily on the side of the concrete pathway. She fractured her tailbone and broke her wrist. She was in the hospital for two days and spent three months in twice-weekly physical therapy appointments.

Hilda sued the dog's owners for the injuries she received. The dog's owners are Pat Sweeney ("Pat") and his wife, Mary Sweeney ("Mary"), who came to your office when they received the lawsuit. "We don't understand this," Pat said to you. "Duke has always been a terrific dog. He catches rats in the back yard—you should see him! He shreds them. He's great with the grandkids. I don't know how he got out of the yard. Sometimes he's able to get out, but he's never rushed at anyone that way. He's only ever barked at the mailman. One time last year there was a new mailman, and boy, did Duke ever get upset! Barking and rushing! And I guess Duke must have somehow got out of the gate when he rushed that mailman. But Duke is protective of us all, that's all. He's never hurt a fly, except for those old rats."

Mary chimed in to sing Duke's praises. "With my disability, I'm at home most of the day. I feel so much better knowing that Duke is around. He's so friendly to family, but so tough with outsiders. And that's the way it should be, right? He doesn't attack at all. He just lets people know he's around. You know, growling a bit and so on. But he's a sweetie when it counts. You should see him with babies—adorable."

As part of your investigation, you speak with the Sweeneys' neighbor, Jack Swan ("Swan"). Swan tells you that he is afraid of Duke. "That dog looks vicious to me. I don't go near it. With a German Shepherd, you never know." When further pressed, Swan can't tell you about any particular incident in which Duke bit or rushed a person. "I know a vicious dog when I see one, and that's one," Swan said.

You talk to the Sweeneys' neighbors on the opposite side of the street. They like Duke, because they believe he helps keep the neighborhood crime rate low. "He's a good dog," reports Suellen Smithey ("Smithey"). "He barks at strangers, really loudly. When he sees someone he doesn't like, he'll open up the gate and jump on them. I don't know if the owners have ever seen that, but I have. Fedex won't deliver there, I know that. The Sweeneys have to pick up their packages at the main office because of Duke. Mary is always complaining when she has to go to the main office, because it's inconvenient. Duke ran over a Fedex delivery person, and that was enough. I figured the Sweeneys must know, because they live at the house. People usually run away after they've been jumped on by Duke. I sure would, anyway. But he knows me, so it's all fine between me and Duke." You may assume that Smithey's testimony is truthful.

In view of the rule above, are the Sweeneys likely to be held strictly liable for Hilda's injuries? It is undisputed that the dog's actions caused the injuries.

Using the rule set out in the Rule Section, please determine whether the doctrine of res judicata will apply to the issues raised in the fact pattern.

Rule Section:

Res judicata, also known as "claim preclusion," is a doctrine designed to ensure that claims, once litigated, are not subject to re-litigation. The doctrine does not apply, however, unless the following four elements are met: (1) the same parties (or those in privity with the same parties) must be involved in the second lawsuit that were involved in the first lawsuit; (2) the initial judgment must have been rendered by a court of competent jurisdiction; (3) there must have been a final judgment on the claim's merits; and (4) both the first and second lawsuit must concern the same claim.

For purposes of the first element, privity can be based on a variety of grounds. Privity may be based on the parties' similar interests, such as an interest in the same result, or it may be based on participation in the first lawsuit. To claim privity, however, the party must be one who would have been bound by an opposite judgment, if the judgment had been different. The party claiming privity cannot, therefore, be a stranger to the judgment.

Once these elements are met, res judicata bars parties to the second lawsuit from bringing up claims and defenses that were actually raised or that could have been raised in the first lawsuit. If the party did not raise a claim or defense in the first lawsuit but could have done so, then that party is considered to have waived that claim or defense.

Offensive res judicata is the use of a prior judgment by a plaintiff who is a stranger to the previous judgment, against a defendant in the prior lawsuit. Offensive res judicata aims to prevent the defendant in the previous lawsuit from asserting a defense that was or could have been asserted in the previous lawsuit. Offensive res judicata is not generally permitted or encouraged.

Fact Pattern:

The Ants-Away Corporation had thirty employees and was doing well, until an economic recession hit the company hard. Clients dropped their pest control service, and Ants-Away had trouble meeting payroll. Before the recession, the company had a generous benefits package that permitted employees to accrue vacation and roll over unused vacation days from year to year or cash them out for extra pay. When the recession hit, the company laid off five employees and no longer permitted employees to accrue, roll over, or cash in any vacation days at all. Employees had to take any time off as unpaid time.

When the company announced that any accrued vacation would be taken away without compensation, Rick James ("James"), a ten-year Ants-Away employee, decided to sue. His claim proceeded to trial, and he was awarded the value of the ten days of vacation that he had accrued that year. He had already used all his vacation days that had accrued in previous years, so the maximum he was entitled to was ten days of vacation.

A fellow employee, Sally Sorren ("Sorren"), saw the success of James's lawsuit and decided to file her own. She sued for the value of all her accrued and unused vacation days, which totaled seventy-six days. Her vacation days had been accrued over seven years, and she had not used any of them. When Sorren was hired, she was given an employee handbook that explained the policy in full. Two years ago, the employee manual was discontinued in favor of a book of "Employee Rules" that simply explained the rules for the lunchroom and mentioned nothing about vacation at all.

She sued Ants-Away for breach of contract and violation of employment statutes, just as James had done. Ants-Away asserted the same defenses that it had asserted in the James lawsuit, but it also asserted the defense of waiver. It is undisputed that the court was a court of competent jurisdiction and that Ants-Away could have raised the defense of waiver in the first lawsuit, but chose not to.

Sorren wishes to assert the claim of unjust enrichment as well. It is undisputed that James could have raised this claim but chose not to.

You represent Sorren. Can you successfully assert res judicata so that Ants-Away's waiver defense is barred? Can Ants-Away assert res judicata so that Sorren's unjust enrichment claim is barred? Why or why not?

RULE-BASED REASONING FOR MASTERY

EXERCISE 28

Using the rule set out in the Rule Section below, determine whether Lois Lory's statement to Charlene Campbell regarding the stolen car—and Campbell's lack of a response—is admissible under the "adoptive admission" exception to the hearsay rule.

Rule Section:

Hearsay is an out-of-court statement offered to establish the truth of the matter asserted. Hearsay is generally excluded at trial because the declarant is not available to be cross-examined. In addition, hearsay statements are generally not made under oath, and the fact-finder cannot judge the declarant's demeanor.

There are exceptions to the hearsay rule for statements made under circumstances that indicate the statement's trustworthiness. One such exception is for statements that are offered against a party and adopted by that party.

A statement is not hearsay if it is offered against a party and is a statement of which the party has manifested an adoption or belief in its truth. A statement is considered to be adopted by the party if it is made in the party's presence, the party understood the statement, and the party could have denied the statement but did not.

Fact Pattern:

Lois Lory ("Lory") went out one evening with her friend, Charlene Campbell ("Campbell"), for a celebration of Lory's fortieth birthday. The two met at a restaurant on Fourth Street in Austin, Texas, and drank a martini each. The two women were talking about their college days and the fun they had had. "Of course, I never did anything seriously bad," said Campbell. "Just pranks and that sort of thing." Lory said, "Me too, I never did anything really bad either. The worst I did was swim in a campus fountain. That's it." The two women kept drinking and reminiscing about their college days.

After a few hours passed, the two started walking down Fourth Street together. Suddenly, Lory saw a beautiful yellow Ferrari. She turned to Campbell and said: "Look! The keys are in it. We've never, ever done anything bad. This is our one chance to do something bad but not so bad. Let's just take it for a turn around the block. The owner will never notice." Campbell grabbed Lory's arm and pulled her along the sidewalk. "Don't be ridiculous. This is nuts. Let's just grab another drink and cab it home. You don't need to start a criminal career at this point!" Lory agreed and walked into the martini bar.

A couple of hours later, the two women emerged from the bar. The Ferrari was still parked near the bar, and the keys were still in the ignition. "Oh baby, that car's calling to me! Just a little ride, Charlene." Campbell was very tired, and she knew Lory would not give up unless she was able to at least sit in the car. "OK, then, get in the car. But don't go anywhere." The two women climbed into the car, and Lory turned the key in the ignition. The engine roared, while Lory squealed with delight. "Stop, stop, stop, stop, STOP THE CAR!" screamed Campbell. Lory put her foot on the accelerator and tossed her head. "Here we go!" she screamed. The car took off with a sudden jerk and then stopped. Campbell was unused to the car's sensitive controls, so when she hit the accelerator again, the car shot forward. For about ten seconds, Lory and Campbell flew down Fourth Street in the Ferrari, their hair blowing in the wind. "Isn't this glorious?" yelled Lory. "Sure," said Campbell, "but you need to STOP now." With a bone-jarring crash, the car hit a hot dog stand on the sidewalk. Hot dogs flew everywhere, and the vendor screamed in fear. "What on earth?" he cried, as he jumped out of the speeding car's path.

The car skidded down the sidewalk, hitting a newspaper stand and crushing two parked bicycles. The car finally came to a halt in front of a crowded restaurant. A few seconds later, two Austin police officers descended on the car. "Get out of the car immediately," one of the officers yelled. "Put your hands on the hood. Don't try any funny business."

Lory and Campbell jumped out. The police officers arrested both of them and took them to the police station for booking. At the crowded police station, Lory and Campbell sat side by side, handcuffed on a bench alongside seven or eight noisy college students who had been arrested for disorderly conduct. Lory turned to Campbell and said, "Well, I guess that's our first car theft. We did it, didn't we?" Campbell looked away, audibly sighed, and brushed away a tear. She said nothing. "I wish those college students would be quiet," Campbell said, a few moments later. Suddenly, a booking officer asked the two to walk toward the camera and have their photographs taken. They spent the night in jail.

Two weeks later, Campbell is out on bail and meeting with you in your office. She wants to discuss the charges against her—automobile theft and conspiracy to commit automobile theft. "I was totally against anyone stealing that car," Campbell said sadly in your office. "It wasn't my idea, I was against it, and I told her not to do it. So how can I be charged with this? I don't get it." You tell her that the assistant district attorney plans to introduce Lory's statement before booking: "Well, I guess that's our first car theft. We did it, didn't we?"

You research the law and find the rule set out above. Can the prosecutor use Campbell's silence against her as an adoptive admission? Please use only the rule set out above and address only this issue.

RULE-BASED REASONING FOR MASTERY

EXERCISE 29

Using the rule set out in the Rule Section, please state whether Linda Smith can successfully assert the spousal testimonial exclusionary privilege and avoid testifying against her husband. Please explain your answer.

Rule Section:

Federal Rule of Evidence 501 provides:

> The privilege of a witness, person, government, State, or political subdivision thereof shall be governed by the principles of the common law as they may be interpreted by the courts of the United States in the light of reason and experience. However, in civil actions and proceedings, with respect to an element of a claim or defense as to which State law supplies the rule of decision, the privilege of a witness, person, government, State, or political subdivision thereof shall be determined in accordance with State law.

The rule set out above is supplemented by common law as set out below:

> In a criminal case, a spouse need not testify against his or her spouse. The marital testimonial privilege is meant to preserve marriages and avoid the stress on marriages and families that would occur if a spouse were to testify against his or her spouse. The privilege belongs to the witness-spouse rather than the defendant. In other words, one spouse may testify against another if he or she chooses to do so. The privilege extends to all matters that a spouse might testify to against a spouse, such as statements regarding acts and statements regarding statements made in the presence of third parties. The statements need not be confidential. In addition, the privilege includes statements made before the parties were married.

> The privilege must be narrowly construed, and it is not absolute. The privilege runs counter to the general rule that the public should have the benefit of every person's testimony. So, the privilege does not apply once a marriage ends, and it does not apply when spouses are joint participants in a crime.

Fact Pattern:

Linda Smith ("Linda") and her husband Bobby Smith, ("Bobby"), married three years ago in a simple ceremony on the beach in Florida. They started a life in the suburbs, with Linda working as a teacher and Bobby selling insurance.

Bobby provided excellent service to his clients, and before long, he had developed an extensive clientele of executives and other business leaders. While speaking with his clients, Bobby learned all about their stresses and concerns, and he realized that the executives sought relaxation and peace in their fast-paced lives. The state in which Smith lives does not permit the sale of marijuana. Despite marijuana's illegal status, Bobby started to market marijuana to his executive clients. His marijuana sales were brisk, and his insurance sales rose in tandem with his marijuana sales.

"This is fantastic!" Bobby said to Linda one evening. Linda was less than thrilled. "So, you did it, you started selling drugs?" Linda asked. Bobby explained that he wasn't selling any "hard stuff," just marijuana, in the form of leaves as well as chocolate-based baked goods. Linda was aghast. She could not believe that her hard-working husband had stepped into illegal sales. That night, they had a serious argument about the direction their lives were taking. Bobby defended his new lifestyle, and he pointed out the tremendous amounts of money that the tandem businesses could bring in. He argued that this was the way to a successful life.

Linda was disappointed that Bobby could not see the ethical problems with leading a lifestyle based on illegal business dealings. She was also worried about the connections with suppliers that Bobby would need to have. "What if they come to our house?" Linda asked. She had no intention of being in the house when a drug deal might go bad. "Drugs mean guns, guns mean danger, and the whole thing can go south. How can we ever start a family like this? I've got to leave here and think about all this." Linda left the house that night and stayed away for three weeks.

In the meantime, Bobby embraced his new business dealings. He saw himself as a sort of executive counselor, bringing security and relaxation in the form of insurance and marijuana, respectively. He found the people in marijuana sales to be friendly and relaxed. His supplier, Shelley Stowers ("Stowers"), became a particularly close friend. Bobby often confided in Stowers as his marriage became increasingly strained. "She just doesn't understand me any more," Bobby complained to Stowers one evening. "Not like you. You understand the need for an extra business—insurance just won't give me the kind of lifestyle I deserve. Marijuana is a win-win. You understand that, and she doesn't. Seriously, the further I feel from her, the closer I feel to you."

Bobby grew his business and expanded his marijuana sales to include real estate professionals. Linda could hardly believe that Bobby refused to leave the criminal lifestyle, and she told him that she might never return to him. In the following six months, Linda and Bobby's marriage continued to disintegrate as Bobby grew closer to Stowers. Linda and Bobby tried to work out their differences, but Bobby was committed to his marijuana clients. He refused to give up this line of work, and Linda continued to express her distaste for—and fear of—Bobby's new business. "This isn't us," Linda said. "This is not the direction I want to go, anyway. I just can't do it. I'm sorry, this may be the end."

When Bobby heard this, he started to think twice about his new line of work. "Maybe I don't need all this," he said. The two briefly reconciled, and Bobby quit selling for three months. After a while, though, he started to become bored with selling insurance. His insurance clients kept asking him for marijuana, and he could not resist selling for long. Once Linda realized that Bobby had returned to the criminal lifestyle, she left him for good. Bobby then returned to a romance with his supplier, Stowers. Two months after his return to marijuana sales, Bobby moved in with Stowers. They started to make a life together, and a few months later, Stowers realized she was pregnant with Bobby's child. Bobby had not yet filed for divorce from Linda, mainly because the businesses had kept him so busy.

Bobby's businesses—legal and illegal—were thriving. He almost forgot that marijuana was illegal, until he heard a knock at the door late one night. The police had come to raid his house, based on a tip. Bobby was arrested, along with Stowers. Both were charged with marijuana sales and possession. As they sat in the back of the police cruiser, Stowers told Bobby that perhaps Linda would not have to testify against him. "The last guy I supplied for walked free, because the only witness was his wife—she couldn't testify against him. Find out about it. And if it doesn't work, maybe you and I could get married. Then they wouldn't be able to make me testify against you!"

Is Stowers's legal analysis correct? Can Linda assert the marital testimonial privilege and avoid testifying against Bobby? If Linda and Bobby divorced and Bobby married Stowers before trial, could Stowers successfully assert the marital privilege?

PART 3

SKILLED RULE-BASED EXERCISES

RULE-BASED REASONING FOR MASTERY

EXERCISE 30

Using only the statements of law provided in the Rule Section, determine whether the alleged contract between Mary Flores and Sharisse Walker is supported by consideration. In addition, is it subject to the statute of frauds? Do not address any other issues.

Rule Section:

A contract must be supported by consideration. If a promise is to be enforceable, there must be consideration for the promise. Mutual obligations can furnish sufficient consideration to support an enforceable contract.[*]

The statute of frauds requires that certain contracts be in writing. That is, a promise or agreement governed by the statute is not enforceable unless it is reduced to writing and signed by the person or party who is to be charged with the promise or agreement. However, this requirement applies only if the agreement is not to be performed within one year from the date of its making.[**] An agreement need not be reduced to writing if it is to be completed within a year of its making.

In determining the contract's length of time for performance, if no term is given, a term of reasonable duration may be implied. In addition, if the contract calls for an act to be performed that could conceivably be performed within a year, then the contract does not fall within the statute of frauds. When the time for performance is not expressly stated in the contract, courts are to determine a reasonable time for performance as viewed by the parties at the time the agreement was made, rather than under any circumstances or facts that might have arisen afterwards.

Fact Pattern:

Sharisse Walker ("Walker") and Mary Flores ("Flores") worked together as toll booth attendants. They had known each other for over twenty years and were best friends. They were both divorced and each had adult children. They spent time together almost every weekend, and the two liked to vacation together as well.

---

[*] *See Hall v. Hall*, 308 S.W.2d 12 (Tex. 1957).

[**] Tex. Bus. & Com. Code Ann. § 26.01 (West 2011).

One evening, Walker asked Flores if she wanted to come to Las Vegas with her. "I had a dream that I won on a slot machine," said Walker. "I mean big winnings." Flores laughed. "Sure, haven't we all had that dream?" Walker said she hoped Flores would come too. "It would be a blast! And who knows, we might win! With all my medical expenses lately, that would be a blessing." Flores declined. "I'm just not that much into gambling. Besides, I can't afford it. And you're on crutches with your illness—are you sure this is a good idea?" Walker refused to give up. "Come on, you'll either be here, bored, or happy in VEGAS! Let's just go. You'll have fun. I have some frequent flyer miles that we can use, and I'll even pay the hotel and expenses. And I'll be fine on the crutches. I'm pretty good about getting around, aren't I?"

Flores eventually agreed. "You know, you're right. We might as well go. I want to see the Grand Canyon anyway, and this might be my only chance. If you're sure you don't mind paying. I've had so many expensive house repairs lately." Walker said she didn't mind paying, and the two booked their tickets and hotel. They planned to stay just two nights, then return to keep their work commitments. In advance of the trip, the two day-dreamed about what they would do with the winnings. "I'd buy a house, cash, just like that," said Walker. Flores said she would travel and eat in exotic restaurants. "I'd try a new cuisine every night: Moroccan, Ethiopian, Japanese, every single one of them. But I wouldn't spend it all at once. I'd be that one person in a million who actually waits to get and spend the money—or maybe not!"

Finally, the two left for Vegas. On the airplane, they talked excitedly about the shows they would see and the people-watching they would enjoy. "But let's not forget about my magic slot machine from my dream," said Walker. "If we just do that, all our dreams can come true. You know, my dreams of a wild spending spree and your dreams of a long-lasting, careful, wise lottery win. Maybe you'll be the first careful lottery winner in history."

In Las Vegas, Walker and Flores had a great time looking at the casinos and people-watching on the Vegas Strip, just as they had planned. "You know, you were so right about this trip," said Flores. "If it weren't for you, I'd be sitting at home doing nothing. You are such a good friend." Walker hugged her. "And you are my lucky charm!" said Walker. "With you here, I'm going to win big, just like in my dream. Anything we win, we split, right?" Flores laughed. "Whatever you say; sounds good to me." Walker suggested that they head over to the slot machines. "In my dream, the magic slot machine was in the Paris Casino, so let's go there." Flores pointed out that there is no such thing as a magic slot machine. "What, you think all these casinos were built on magic slot machines? I don't think so." Walker told Flores not to be such a downer. "Look, someone's going to win, and it might as well be us. You and me—winning together." Flores shrugged her shoulders. "OK, we'll do this together. One for all and all for one, I'm there for you. If I win, we win. If you win, we win."

The two walked over to the Paris Casino and started playing. They spent $57 on slots and won $11. At 2:00 a.m., they returned to their hotel. "I'm not giving up," said Walker. "Let's go back tomorrow." Flores laughingly agreed. "You are nothing if not stubborn," Flores said. The following day, they played the Paris Casino slots again. "I'm getting tired of the slots," said Flores. "Can't we just go see the Blue Men again? I love those guys. They're so mysterious with their crazy blue heads." Walker reluctantly agreed. "Well, OK. Let me just play one more dollar coin. Can you put it in for me? I really need to sit down. My legs are acting up, even with the crutches." Flores said, "Of course," as she walked over to the machine and dropped in the coin. "This one's for you, my best friend ever!" The machine lit up. It started to flash. And then a siren went off. A sign above the machine started flashing, "BIG WINNER BIG WINNER."

"We won!" said Walker. "Let me go get my winnings," said Flores. "OK, sounds good," responded Walker. "But you mean *our* winnings, right?" she called out as Flores walked away. Flores did not respond. For the next two days, the two shopped and partied in Vegas. They had a terrific time, dining at the best restaurants and watching shows. On the third day, Flores turned to Walker and said, "So, what you would you like as a present—a car, maybe, or a mink coat?" Walker responded, "Why would you give me a present? I just want what we agreed on— half of the winnings." Flores said, "Well, I can't really do that. I have a lot of commitments at home. Plus, the payout is just $95,000 per year for twenty years. That's quite a lot of money, but it's nothing really when you consider the expenses I will have with my new home, new car, and new vacation home. Besides, people press the slot machines different ways. It's the special way I pressed it that won. I'd love to give you a nice present, though." Walker was amazed. She said quietly, "But we said we'd split it all, anything we won. What happened?" Flores said, "That was never a real agreement, just chit chat. I didn't count that as a real promise."

The two continued to disagree, all the way home to San Antonio, Texas. "Why did you pick such a long payout?" asked Walker. "I would have preferred a lump sum, so I could pay off debts and buy a house with cash." Flores bristled, "Well, no one asked you, did they. The casino asked me. Me, because I'm the winner. They gave me the choice—all at once, payment over five years, or payment over twenty years. I always imagined it would be best to take the money over a long period of time. They said that people who get it all at once usually end up doing something crazy. And that's not me. I'm not crazy. Plus, I know what's mine and what belongs to other people!" Walker started to cry. "I never wanted to fight with you, ever, Mary. You are one of my greatest friends, and now I see it all slipping away. Gone. Does it have to end this way?" Flores just sighed and looked away.

After the two returned home, Walker continued to call Flores and ask about her share of the winnings. Flores had her telephone number changed, and she refused to speak to Walker. A few days later, a man identifying himself as Flores's lawyer called Walker. "Please stay away from my client. She has no interest in talking to you about her winnings. It's best if you forget all about this." Walker asked about the friendship. "I don't know about that," said the lawyer. "She asked me to contact you and give you this message, so I guess the friendship is over. Sorry about that." Walker has decided to look into suing Flores for her share of the winnings. She contacted you and asked your firm to represent her and review her situation. You and two other associates are looking into the law that will apply to this case.

In researching the law, you find the rules stated above, concerning consideration and the statute of frauds. Is the alleged contract between Flores and Walker supported by consideration? Is it subject to the statute of frauds?

RULE-BASED REASONING FOR MASTERY
EXERCISE 31

Using the rules set out in the rule section below, determine which party—Jones or the Marino family—has the right to keep the dog.

Rule Section:

A contract can be subject to rescission in case of mutual mistake. The mistake must, however, be material, affecting a fact or facts that are at the very basis of the contract. There must be clear proof of the mutual mistake. The mistake cannot be slight, and it cannot be inconsequential. Only if the mistake is fundamental to the parties' contract is rescission for mutual mistake appropriate or reasonable. A court can look beyond the four corners of the agreement in evaluating a mutual mistake.

An animal, even if lost, is privately-owned personal property. The captor of a lost animal does not acquire ownership of it unless the animal is abandoned. Property is abandoned if the owner intentionally gives up ownership of it.

A bailment contract, express or implied, is created when one person delivers personal property to another's possession in trust for a specific purpose, pursuant to an agreement that the owner will have the property returned to him, or that the property will be accounted for or kept for the owner to reclaim it. In the case of a bailment, possession of the property is given to the bailee, but the original owner retains ownership of the property. Ownership is not transferred with possession of the property. A party who wrongfully sells or otherwise disposes of bailed property outside the bailment agreement has converted the property.

A contract requires offer and acceptance. A contract must be definite enough that each party can determine what it is to do. If the parties agree on the terms and show an intent to be bound, they create an enforceable contract.

Every contract carries with it an implied covenant of good faith and fair dealing. Bad faith implies fraud, whether actual or constructive, or the intent to mislead or deceive.

Fact Pattern:

A year before she came to your law office, Hannah Jones ("Jones") was living in Miami, Florida with her two children and her beloved greyhound, Hugo. Hugo was a retired racing greyhound and was then fourteen years old. He was a gentle dog and a great family pet. Even when the children bothered him, he remained quiet and unaggressive. As a Florida resident, Jones kept a constant eye on the weather, especially in late summer. One morning in early September, Jones saw on television that a hurricane was approaching. She started to plan the family's evacuation. Unfortunately, Hugo could not fit into the car when the car was loaded with the children and their belongings.

As the hurricane gathered strength and continued on track toward Miami, Jones struggled with her options. She called her mother in Tampa, to see if she could take Hugo for a few days. Her mother could not—she was feeling unwell and did not want the extra responsibility. Jones remembered a local shelter, and she took Hugo to the intake office. "I just need help until the hurricane passes," Jones said. "OK," said the person behind the reception counter. The receptionist was out for an appointment, and the shelter manager was taking her duties when Jones came in. "We can take him. Just sign this form, and wait until at least two days after the hurricane to come and get him. Just make sure you're back in fifteen days from now, or things could become difficult with keeping the animals. Oh, and there's a $120 hurricane shelter fee for this."

MIAMI RESCUE AND SHELTER (MRS)

I hereby acknowledge that MRS is a shelter for displaced animals in crisis or emergency. As an owner of an animal placed with MRS, you must pick up your animal within 15 days of placement. If you do not pick up your animal within 15 days, MRS may dispose of the animal as MRS sees fit. This may include adoption or euthanasia.

Thank you for taking care of Huge in this emergency. I am giving him to you for care with the understanding that if I can't come back in 15 days due to a hurricane emergency, you will call me at 832-228-7474 if you can't take care of him and he will be picked up. Thank you, HJ

Jones signed the agreement, but she added some additional language at the bottom of the notice. "I added some notes, OK?" Jones said as she handed it back. "Please take care of him. Hugo, baby, I love you. Be safe." The shelter manager looked at the form. "Looks good," she said. Jones handed over the $120 fee, kissed Hugo on the nose, and watched as he was led away to the kennels. Jones quickly returned to her apartment and continued to gather her belongings for the evacuation. She traveled two hundred miles north to a small hotel and waited with her children.

The following day, the storm hit. Jones's apartment was severely damaged by wind and rain, as well as rising water. Jones drove back to Miami to survey the damage, but the three blocks around her apartment had been blocked off by police. She returned to the evacuation hotel and looked online for an undamaged apartment in Miami. Unfortunately, many other people were looking for the same thing, and Jones had few choices. She had particular difficulties finding a complex that would allow her to keep Hugo, as he exceeded the pet weight limit at most complexes by about fifty pounds.

In the meantime, MRS was overwhelmed with pets after the storm. Many residents had simply left pets at home when the owners evacuated—the families were unable to fit the pets, family members, and possessions into their vehicles as they fled the city in advance of the storm. Communication with owners was difficult, as many people were unable to return home to their damaged properties. Many animals had to be shipped to other shelters, as MRS was inundated with animals every day. In addition, many shelter employees were dealing with their own storm-related problems and could not work regular hours. The files became disorganized, and the regular file clerk quit due to her family's problems with the storm. Hugo stayed at the MRS shelter for three weeks after the storm, but then he became separated from his file, and the shelter manager decided he should be adopted out.

"Hey, big guy," said the shelter manager to Hugo on Hugo's twenty-first day at the shelter. "You're a handsome fellow!" Hugo sniffed the manager's hand politely and looked around. "You survived that storm? I don't know your real name, so I'll call you Lucky. Lucky, it may be time for you to have a forever family!" The manager talked to the animal supervisor. "We'll have an adoption day on Saturday," announced the manager to her staff. "Let's publicize it and get the public out here."

The Marino family had been watching the storm-related news for two weeks and was moved by the plight of the families affected by the storm. The Marinos' house had been spared, and they wanted to help. They saw the announcements about the shelter's adoption day. "If we couldn't keep our hamster, Charlie," said the oldest boy, Christopher, "I would want someone to adopt him. We should adopt a storm animal. We've got room, and it's the right thing to do." The parents smiled at him. "You know, even though it's a big responsibility to have another pet, we should all do our part. Let's go find a new family member!" They went to the shelter adoption day that weekend. Twenty-three days after Jones had placed him at MRS, Hugo was adopted by the Marinos. "He's so cute," said the middle child. "He's sort of a chocolate color. Let's name him Hershey!"

Before the Marinos could take Hershey home, they had to sign a contract. According to the contract, the family adopted Hershey in return for $100. The Marinos promised to care for Hershey, to keep him vaccinated, and to keep identification on him at all times. They left happily with the dog and welcomed him to his new home.

At the same time Hugo was adopted, a little over three weeks after the storm, Jones finally found an apartment willing to take the family and Hugo too. "Thank goodness!" she exclaimed as she talked to the apartment manager. "I'll go get my dog and move in tomorrow." Jones went to the shelter and talked to the receptionist. "I'm ready to get Hugo. Thank you so, so much for taking him. Here, I have a donation to the shelter to express my thanks." The receptionist looked through her file of active animals. "I don't see a Hugo. Was he a hurricane dog?" Jones gasped. "A 'hurricane dog'? What do you mean, a 'hurricane dog'?"

The receptionist explained that a number of dogs were admitted to the shelter during the hurricane. "We had so many dogs that we had to send some to other shelters. Maybe your Huck went there. Check Tampa or St. Petersburg maybe. Good luck." Jones was incensed. "He is *Hugo*, and I need you to find him now! I am living with no furniture, out of my apartment, and trying to put my life back together, and you are so heartless!" The receptionist brought the manager, and eventually the group pieced together the events that took Hugo to the Marino family.

"He's been adopted out under a contract," said the shelter manager. "There's nothing we can do. The family sent me a photo of Hershey—I mean Hugo—dressed up in baby clothes, surrounded by kids and dog treats. They are so into that dog."

Jones has come to your office to find out how she can get her dog back. Given the legal rules set out above, how do you advise her?

RULE-BASED REASONING FOR MASTERY
EXERCISE 32

Using the rule set out in the rule section, please state whether the dog-scent lineup evidence should be admitted. Please explain your answer.

Rule Section:

The relevant rule of evidence provides as follows:

If scientific, technical, or other specialized knowledge will assist the trier of fact to understand the evidence or to determine a fact in issue, a witness qualified as an expert by knowledge, skill, experience, training, or education, may testify thereto in the form of an opinion or otherwise.

Scientific evidence should only be admitted at trial if it is reliable. Where scent lineup evidence is concerned, the scientific evidence is based on training rather than scientific methods. In such situations, there are three questions that determine whether the field produces reliable scientific evidence. These questions are: (1) whether the particular area of expertise is a legitimate one; (2) whether the expert will testify on matters within that field of expertise; (3) whether the expert correctly uses the principles of that field.

The issue of scent lineup evidence's admissibility has not been addressed in this jurisdiction. Scent-tracking evidence, on the other hand, has been admitted when the owner or trainer can show that the dog and the trainer are both properly qualified and respected in and outside the courtroom. A dog is qualified if (1) it is a member of a breed of dog known for its acute sense of smell, (2) the dog has been trained in discerning one human scent from another, (3) the dog has a history of being reliable in identifying and discerning scents, (4) the dog was given the suspect's scent, (5) the scent was given to the dog while the scent was still effective.

The dog's trainer is qualified if the trainer has significant qualifications in the field of dog scent tracking and scent lineups.

In addition, the particular application of the scent evidence must be fair and objective. A scent line-up is fair and objective if it follows accepted principles in the field and addresses the additional concerns set out below:

At a minimum, a scent lineup should use four or five samples. The samples should be placed at least six feet apart, and any alert should be repeated at least twice. Careful records should be kept, and the alert should be described in detail.

The technique should address the following concerns*:

(1) Trainer influence—dogs, particularly those on a leash, pick up on subtle cues that tell the dog the result the trainer would like to see. Dogs like to please trainers and will give that result.

(2) Sample contamination—lineups typically include scent from the suspect and four or five other people. All the scents should be fresh and the same age, as scent disappears as it ages. The samples should be handled so that they are not contaminated. Scents are best stored in individual glass jars at room temperature, out of direct light.

(3) Accuracy and reliability—because the dog itself cannot express what it saw, records should be carefully kept. Successes and failures should be recorded in detail.

Fact Pattern:

Six months ago, a burglary took place on a quiet residential street north of the city. No suspects were found until a second burglary took place four houses down on the same street. Immediately after the second burglary, police arrested a suspect who was found on the driveway with electronics from the burglarized home.

The suspect provided a scent sample, and detectives worked with Deputy Downs and his bloodhounds on a scent line-up. Deputy Downs is well known in the area for his work with bloodhounds. The bloodhounds have tracked and found escaped convicts on at least four occasions. In one famous incident, the bloodhounds tracked and found a convict whose trail was over a week old. Downs himself has a bachelor's degree in marketing. He has no formal training in scent lineups, but he has worked in the police department with the K-9 unit for over twenty-five years. He has written four articles about police work with dogs for the "Police Today" magazine, which is a health and wellness publication of the police union.

Downs's dogs are both bloodhounds. As puppies, they were selected for their excellent temperaments and ability to differentiate one human scent from another. They trained for two years with the FBI in the field of scent identification. They are each now ten years old, and they work full time with the police department, and they have lived with Downs since they were puppies. They have worked with the Federal Bureau of Investigations as well as the Bureau of Alcohol, Tobacco, and Firearms to locate and apprehend criminals. Their experience to date has been in tracking rather than scent line-ups. The FBI has, on the other hand, used scent lineups to rule out suspects in important cases concerning national security.

To prepare the scent line-up, Downs took his samples from the duffle bag, which also serves as his workout bag. He separated the samples' plastic baggies from one another, then took the sample from the suspect and placed it on a piece

---

* Scott Henson, *Scent Lineups by Dogs Don't Pass the Smell Test*, GRITS FOR BREAKFAST (July 13, 2009), http://gritsforbreakfast.blogspot.com/2009/07/scent-lineups-by-dogs-dont-pass-smell.html.

of gauze. The suspect's sample was ten days old, while the samples from other people—known as "foil" samples—were four weeks old. He placed scent from four other people on other pieces of gauze, and he literally lined them up, ten feet apart. He let the dogs sniff each scent. Next, Downs took the "foil" samples and placed them with scent from the crime scene. The leashed dogs were permitted to sniff each one, and they were told to look for one that was connected to a sample from the first set. Downs explained later that both dogs alerted to the scent at position two, which was the position of the suspect's scent.

No one but Downs was able to see any reaction from the dogs—they simply appeared to look around and at the door during the entire process. Downs testified that only he understood the dogs' reactions; Downs himself was aware of which scent was the suspect's. Upon questioning, Downs testified that because he was the only person who could understand the dogs' reactions, no one could review the dogs' performance. Because there were no outwards signs of an alert, Downs did not take any notes of the dogs' performance.

Two experts also testified at the hearing on this issue. The first expert, Dr. Sonya Simons, a professor of biochemistry and veterinary medicine, testified on behalf of the State. She is a co-author of the book *Scent Tracking Today*. She said that the scientific literature supports the theory that each person has a unique scent, and that dogs can differentiate between humans because of dogs' strong sense of smell. She testified that scent evidence should always be used in conjunction with other evidence, and that it is better used to exclude people from suspicion rather than to identify suspects. She said that scent lineups are not like DNA evidence, and that there are limits to their reliability. She testified that in her opinion, Downs followed the best practices developed by the K-9 law enforcement community. Downs said that in other countries, it is common to use multiple dogs in the line-up, as Downs did.

The second expert, Dr. Dan Flores, testified on behalf of the defendant. He is a biochemist and research scientist in ecology. He has published several articles on dog scent line-ups. He testified that a properly trained dog should be able to identify a person's scent. He testified that if a person uses multiple dogs in a line-up identification process, the dogs may copy one another and reinforce a mistake. In addition, he criticized the fact that Downs used a leash on the dogs, as he may have accidentally suggested the correct scent. Furthermore, Downs did not use "negative lineups" in which the defendant's scent is excluded altogether. Negative lineups test the accuracy of the initial line-up, so that the handler can see whether the dog is simply alerting out of habit or guesswork.

Scent lineup evidence has not yet been addressed by this court, or by any court in this state. It is undisputed, however, that courts in this state have admitted various types of dog-related evidence, such as dog-tracking evidence to establish probable cause to search a building and evidence of a dog's reaction to drugs to establish probable cause to detain a suspect.

You are a briefing attorney for a judge who must decide whether to admit the scent-lineup evidence. It is undisputed that Drs. Simons and Flores are qualified. You find out that thirty-seven states admit scent lineup evidence; four do not.

RULE-BASED REASONING FOR MASTERY

EXERCISE 33

You are a clerk for a federal judge. Using the rule set out in the rule section, please advise the court if it should grant the prosecution's request for authority to prospectively acquire exact information on the location of a cell phone by using Global Positioning System and cellular network enhancing technology. Please fully explain your answer.

Rule Section:

The Fourth Amendment to the United States Constitution states that "[t]he right of the people to be secure in their persons, houses, papers, and effects against unreasonable searches and seizures, shall not be violated, and no Warrants shall issue but upon probable cause, supported by Oath or affirmation, and particularly describing the place to be searched, and the persons or things to be seized."

To obtain information such as location information, law enforcement must either show that the information can be obtained incident to an arrest pursuant to a valid arrest warrant or obtain a separate search warrant.

An arrest warrant based on probable cause contains the "limited authority" to go into a house or other home, such as an apartment, in which the suspect resides and where the arresting authority believes the suspect is located. If the state presents enough evidence to convince a court probable cause exists, then the suspect ideally would permit law enforcement to enter his home. However, a suspect has a reasonable expectation of privacy in his own home, and the arrest warrant provides an exception only for those situations in which law enforcement knows where a suspect lives and has a reasonable belief the suspect is within that location. The "limited authority" of an arrest warrant is restricted even further: law enforcement may not, in the absence of exigent circumstances, enter the house of a person not named in an arrest warrant, even if law enforcement has a reasonable expectation the subject of the arrest warrant is within.

A search warrant also must be based on probable cause. With regard to search warrants, "probable cause" means probable cause to believe that the information sought will in and of itself be evidence of a crime. When applying for a search warrant, law enforcement must generally show that the evidence it wants to obtain will be evidence of a crime. The evidence to be found must have some nexus to the alleged illegal activity. The government may use a search warrant to locate and detain a defendant when the government can show probable cause that the defendant is in a certain place.

Fact Pattern:

The judge for whom you clerk receives a request from law enforcement for a warrant to obtain detailed location data for the subject of an arrest warrant, John Jones ("Jones"). Law enforcement plans to present the search warrant to the Flippy Telephone Company so that Flippy will provide law enforcement with the relevant records. Law enforcement knows Jones uses a Flippy phone, and law enforcement wants to obtain location data from the cell phone company.

More specifically, law enforcement seeks a search warrant that will permit thirty days of continuous on-demand monitoring of the suspect's location through cellular phone and Global Positioning System ("GPS") data. A good quality GPS receiver can pinpoint the user's location to within a few meters; with enhancing technology, it can provide real-time location data to within a few inches. The GPS function on a phone can be disabled by the phone's user. Law enforcement has requested that if GPS data is not available, the company provide cell-site positioning information. This information is obtained from the cellular phone service, which does not normally maintain location data on its customers. The company can, however, obtain location data by sending a signal to a particular telephone, which in turn will return location data to the company based on cell phone towers. This process, called "pinging," cannot be detected by the user.

Law enforcement's application explains that the suspect, Jones, is a drug kingpin who has been difficult to locate and arrest. Law enforcement has no indication Jones is evading arrest; however, the only information law enforcement has about Jones is that he owns and uses a particular cellular telephone.

Law enforcement has not made any claim that the location data it seeks will be evidence of a crime. Essentially, law enforcement simply needs help finding Jones so as to execute the arrest warrant and states that the information sought will assist in locating the suspect. In this case, law enforcement argues a search warrant should issue simply because the information sought will help find the suspect. First, law enforcement claims the arrest warrant for Jones contains sufficient authority to obtain the location data under the Fourth Amendment. Second, in the alternative, law enforcement asserts that obtaining a search warrant for this type of location data is permissible to assist law enforcement in finding and apprehending a suspect.

Your judge informs you that this case presents an issue that is at the nexus of arrest law and search warrant law. That is, is the search a "reasonable" one that can be made in the execution of an arrest warrant, or is the proposed search one that calls for an exception to the usual warrant requirements? Your judge also informs you that it is undisputed that the subject of an arrest warrant has a reasonable expectation of privacy in his movements and location. Law enforcement has made no attempt to show exigent circumstances in this case.

RULE-BASED REASONING FOR MASTERY

EXERCISE 34

Using the rules set out in the Rule Section below, determine whether the class of people who purchased Hot Mamba lipstick was properly certified for purposes of a class action lawsuit.

Rule Section:

To be certified, a purported class must meet four requirements: numerosity, commonality, typicality, and adequacy of representation. Alabama Rules of Civil Procedure provides as follows:

> (a) Prerequisites to a Class Action. One or more members of a class may sue or be sued as representative parties on behalf of all only if (1) the class is so numerous that joinder of all members is impracticable, (2) there are questions of law or fact common to the class, (3) the claims or defenses of the representative parties are typical of the claims or defenses of the class, and (4) the representative parties will fairly and adequately protect the interests of the class.

(1)   The class must be so numerous that joinder of all members is not feasible. Joinder of all class members need not be impossible, but must be too difficult or inconvenient to be feasible. Numerosity does not mean a particular number, but rather is considered on a case by case basis. Approximation of the number is to be expected in the class action context.

(2)   A class must also have common questions of law and fact. All of the questions of law or fact need not be common. Rather, there should be a core of common facts.

(3)   The typicality requirement means that the named plaintiffs' claims are essentially the same as those of all the class members. A claim is typical of the class's claims if the claim is based on the same underlying facts and events as the other class members' claims. The individual facts may differ slightly, but where the class members and the representatives complain about the same conduct, the typicality requirement is probably satisfied.

(4)   Adequacy of representation means both the adequacy of the named plaintiffs and the class counsel. In other words, will the named plaintiffs have interests antagonistic to the other class members? With regard to class counsel, the issue is whether the class counsel has the qualifications, experience, and ability to carry on the litigation as it should be.

Class certification is reviewed on appeal for abuse of discretion.

Fact Pattern:

Reptile Cosmetics is a high-end cosmetics company. It sells makeup in only the finest department stores, and it is able to maintain a high profit margin due to its cutting-edge formulations and fashionable colors. Two years ago, Reptile Cosmetics introduced another new concept: makeup containing actual reptile extract. In certain proprietary studies, women stated that reptile extract seemed to make their skin smother and more elastic. Reptile Cosmetics acted on this information and quickly introduced its Smooth as Snake line of cosmetics, which consisted of skin care, lipsticks, foundations, eye shadows, concealers, and liquid eye liners.

The lipstick line contained actual snake extract, and one red lipstick was named Hot Mamba, due to the Black Mamba extract that it contained. The box was a distinctive grey color, like a Black Mamba snake, and the box was textured like snake skin. Unfortunately, the African supplier to Reptile Cosmetics had misunderstood the exact ingredient that Reptile Cosmetics had requested. Instead of compiling the shed skins of Black Mambas and creating a paste from them, as the company had requested, the supplier harvested the Mamba venom and made a paste from that. Rushing to bring the product to market, Reptile Cosmetics truncated its usual testing process and spot-checked only a few lipsticks for quality issues. The lipstick was in thousands of stores within weeks.

About a week after the product was launched, Reptile Cosmetics received its first few complaints. Women called, wrote, and emailed, complaining of sore, stinging lips. Several said that they felt ill. Reptile Cosmetics could not understand the issue. The company had used animal extracts before, always with success. They worked backward through their supply chain, trying to discover the problem. As the three-week investigation progressed, more complaints poured in. Reptile Cosmetics considered recalling the product, but it was selling so well. "Let's keep it on the shelves through Christmas," said the CEO of Reptile Cosmetics. There must be a lot of satisfied folks out there—we're just hearing from a few that don't like the product."

Two days into the new year, Reptile Cosmetics received a call from a hospital emergency room. "My lips are on fire!" screamed a woman. "Your crazy lipstick is doing all this!" When he heard of this incident, the CEO decided to pull the product off the shelves. "We're done," he said. "Nothing is worth all this drama."

Within weeks of the company's decision to pull the lipstick off store shelves, women injured by the Hot Mamba lipstick had organized themselves on a Facebook page and retained counsel. They knew that Reptile Cosmetics's head office was in Alabama, and they prepared to sue in Alabama. Their counsel prepared a petition that asserted causes of action under the Uniform Commercial Code ("UCC"). All states except Louisiana have adopted some version of the UCC. The plaintiffs' legal theory was that the description of Hot Mamba was an "express warranty" under the UCC. In addition, they alleged that the product was not fit for its intended purpose and that it therefore breached its implied warranty of fitness for its intended purpose, which is a deceptive trade practices claim.

Julie Jordan ("Jordan"), Sue Molina ("Molina"), and Jolina Montgomery ("Montgomery") were the named class plaintiffs. Jordan and Molina had both bought the lipstick for themselves and applied it at home within a day or two of purchase. Montgomery had been given the lipstick as a birthday present; she applied it two weeks after purchase. Jordan and Molina suffered stinging lips and shortness of breath, while Montgomery suffered dizzy spells and asthma from the lipstick. Other potential class members suffered stinging lips, shortness of breath, and shock when they learned that the lipstick contained actual Mamba venom.

To represent them, the plaintiffs selected a firm headed by Montgomery's brother. Montgomery was always very close to her brother, and she wanted him to be involved because she trusted him. The firm, called the Montgomery Firm, usually handled criminal defense cases in a small Alabama town, but Bob Montgomery was delighted to receive the class action case. This was the firm's opportunity to start a new line of business: nationwide consumer class actions. Their criminal defense cases had been drying up a little, and they were ready to move onto something else.

Even though criminal law had been their sole area of expertise, the Montgomery Firm's lawyers were ready to learn something new. Their criminal clients had always been appreciative, and clients had elected them "Super Lawyers of Pine Bluff" five years in a row. They planned to read some treatises on class actions and contact some lawyers who had represented large classes before. "This will really start out our class action practice with a splash!" exclaimed Bob Montgomery. "This case will be in the headlines from the start. Don't worry, this will be like law school for us all over again—but we can do it. We've got the right stuff!" The firm expected more than five thousand members to be in the class.

Montgomery was particularly eager to turn over a new leaf in his practice, as he had been disciplined by the Alabama bar for failure to communicate with clients and for misappropriating client funds. The disciplinary action took place two years ago, and the firm has not committed any missteps since that time.

The plaintiffs were delighted when their class was certified. Reptile Cosmetics appealed immediately, claiming that class certification was improper. Reptile Cosmetics argued that the class did not meet any of the requirements for class certification. The Montgomery Firm prepared a response to the appeal. Their conduct and filings to date in this case have been exemplary, and they have worked without any compensation to date for over a year.

You are the briefing attorney in the court of appeals that is hearing this appeal. You've been asked to state whether you believe the class was properly certified. Please explain your answer.

CHAPTER IV

ANALOGICAL REASONING WITH DEPTH

PART 1

BEGINNING ANALOGICAL EXERCISES

ANALOGICAL REASONING WITH DEPTH

EXERCISE 35

Using the case listed below, determine whether Ms. Olivia Ruiz suffered from severe emotional distress, as required for a claim of intentional infliction of emotional distress.

Background Facts

This exercise stems from the fact scenario for Exercise 21. Taylor, an 18-year-old high school student, committed a series of acts to embarrass his teacher, Ms. Ruiz. Please review the background facts in Exercise 21 and advise whether Ms. Ruiz experienced severe emotional distress. Do not address any other issues (such as whether Taylor's actions were extreme and outrageous or whether Taylor caused Ms. Ruiz's emotional distress).

The case for this exercise is:

- *Clayton v. Wisener*, 190 S.W.3d 685 (Tex. App. 2005)

ANALOGICAL REASONING WITH DEPTH

EXERCISE 36

Using the cases for this exercise, determine whether Antonio Garza had apparent authority to consent to Officer Ada Lee's request to search Sylvia Trenton's business premises.

Background Facts

At 6:00 a.m., Officer Ada Lee ("Officer Lee"), a veteran on the Chicago police department, responded to a call reporting suspicious activity in the warehouse district in Chicago, Illinois. The dispatch officer gave her the physical address located next door to Paint Your World, a paint business owned by Sylvia Trenton ("Trenton"). Paint Your World sells and mixes both interior and exterior paint for homes and businesses. As Officer Lee approached the address, she did not notice any people or movement. She decided to check the entire block to be sure. She parked her vehicle along the front curb and walked along the row of businesses, peering into the windows to see if anyone was there. There were six stores on the block, some of which had a loft layout. Officer Lee was not familiar with any of the businesses or their owners. Most of the businesses had opened recently under the city's urban renewal development grant.

Officer Lee knocked on each front door and turned the doorknob to make sure the door was locked. Paint Your World was the last business on the block. As with the other stores, Officer Lee knocked on the door and turned the doorknob. No one answered. She then walked around the corner to the back alley to investigate the area further. She noticed a middle-aged man leaning against the wall. He was smoking a cigarette. He wore a white smock over his clothes. The smock was dingy and had some stains on it. He stood near the back door to the paint business. The back door was propped open with a long piece of wood. The man did not appear startled by the officer's presence.

"Hey, I got a call about some suspicious activity here. Did you hear me knocking?" Officer Lee asked.

"I thought I heard someone at the front door," Antonio Garza ("Garza") revealed.

"Do you have any identification?" Officer Lee inquired.

"Yeah," Garza said as he threw his cigarette to the ground and tapped the butt with his foot. "It's inside next to the computer. I was about to pay some bills online."

"Can I follow you inside to take a look around?" Officer Lee stated.

"Sure," Garza responded. Garza turned around, kicked the makeshift doorstop, and pushed the back door open fully. It was completely dark and quiet inside the building. Officer Lee did not hear any activity, not even the ticking of a clock. Garza went to the far side of the room to turn on the lights.

"Here's my wallet, right next to the computer," Garza said. He picked up his wallet and handed his driver's license to the officer. Officer Lee studied the license.

"Can I go use the john?" Garza interrupted. "It's an emergency. I'll even leave the door open a bit."

"Let me check it out first," Officer Lee stated. Garza led the officer to the men's restroom and she looked around to make sure everything was fine. "Go ahead," she directed to Garza.

Officer Lee walked a few steps back to the showroom floor. About a minute later, she noticed a box on the computer table. Inside the box in plain view, there was a large plastic bag containing a bunch of dark green leaves. Officer Lee's many years of training allowed her to identify the substance in the bag instantly as marijuana. At that moment, Trenton appeared at the top of the stairs.

"What are you doing in here? This is my store and we are closed," Trenton said as she walked to the bottom of the stairs.

"Antonio Garza let me in," Officer Lee replied.

"He can't let anyone in here. He doesn't work here. He owns the deli a few stores down. I just let him use my computer and the restroom for a few minutes since the one restroom in his store is being repaired and his internet line is down," explained Trenton.

"And where were you?" Officer Lee asked.

"I was upstairs sleeping. Like I said, we are closed and we don't open until 10 a.m.," Trenton responded rudely. Then, out the corner of her eye, Trenton spotted the bag of marijuana. She tried to walk in front of the table to block the officer's view of the box.

"Well, Garza gave me permission to enter and, since this is your store, I am placing you under arrest for drug possession. I already saw the drugs in the box," Officer Lee stated authoritatively.

Officer Lee charged Trenton with possession of a controlled substance. She read Trenton her Miranda rights and placed handcuffs on her. Garza returned from the restroom and watched in shock as Officer Lee arrested Trenton. At her trial, Trenton moved to suppress the evidence seized at her store, arguing that Garza, the neighboring storeowner, lacked sufficient apparent authority to consent to the officer's entry into and search of her business premises.

Did Garza have apparent authority to grant Officer Lee's request to enter Trenton's business? Do not address whether Garza voluntarily consented to the search.

The cases for this exercise are:

- *United States v. King*, 627 F.3d 641 (7th Cir. 2010)
- *United States v. Sandoval-Vasquez*, 435 F.3d 739 (7th Cir. 2006)

ANALOGICAL REASONING WITH DEPTH
EXERCISE 37

Using the case for this exercise, determine whether Joel Ralph had apparent authority to contract on behalf of Sunshine Hamburger Grill with Lonnie Garrett, the director of Adventure Express Summer Camp.

Background Facts

Shannon Crowe ("Crowe") owns Sunshine Hamburger Grill ("Sunshine Grill"). The restaurant is a mainstay in the Hartford, Connecticut community. Sunshine Grill uses gluten-free ingredients, fresh vegetables, and farm-raised natural meats to prepare its meals. The restaurant's specialty is gourmet hamburgers, but it also serves sandwiches, chicken, pasta dishes, and baked goods. Sunshine Grill has one location and it is always busy. The restaurant also provides catering services for special local events.

Lonnie Garrett ("Garrett") is the director of Adventure Express Summer Camp ("Adventure Express") in Hartford. Adventure Express is a camp for children with learning disabilities and physical challenges. The camp strives to provide a safe and supportive environment for children who often struggle in their daily lives. The camp has tons of activities, such as swimming, hiking, baseball, arts and crafts, and music lessons. Adventure Camp works hard to subsidize the majority of the costs for the campers. Garrett spends a lot of time planning fundraising events and writing grants to foundations and government agency projects.

One fundraising event that Garrett instituted is First Fridays Lunch and Greet ("First Fridays"). Through First Fridays, Garrett planned to promote the camp's mission and services and encourage contributors and potential donors to visit the grounds and spend time with the campers. For the first gathering, Garrett invited the campers, their parents, and current donors to First Fridays. She asked each donor to bring at least one friend. She planned to encourage guests to add Adventure Express to their list of charities. At the same time, she would have an opportunity to increase the camp's mailing list.

For the inaugural First Fridays, Garrett also decided to use Sunshine Grill's catering services. She searched online for the restaurant's website and clicked on the contact page. The restaurant did not list a specific number for catering so she picked up the phone and called the general number listed on the website. Crowe answered the phone.

"Good afternoon, this is Shannon with Sunshine Grill. How may I help you?" Crowe asked.

"Yes, I want to order lunch for a big event that I am having at my campgrounds next Friday. I hope it is not too late. I plan to have at least 100 people here. About half of the attendees will be children and youth," Garrett explained. "What do you suggest?"

"Well, it all depends on your budget and dietary needs. How much are you working with? Do you require vegetarian meals too?" Crowe inquired.

"Well, our budget is a bit small and I would like to have some vegetarian meals on hand, just in case. I gave you a call because your food is always so good and fresh. I have never had a bad meal at the restaurant and decided to try your catering services," Garrett said.

"Thank you for the compliment. We strive to do our best and make our customers happy," Crowe replied. "Let's see what we can go for you." For the next twenty minutes, Crowe discussed meal and pricing options with Garrett. Garrett finally decided on the best arrangement and cost for her budget. Crowe then confirmed the order and prepared the contract.

"Okay, it looks like we are almost done. I will fax the contract to you. Please review it carefully, sign it, and fax it back to me before we close at 9 p.m. today. Then, you can mail the original to me in a day or so," Crowe instructed. "I just need a signed copy today so I can finalize your order. How does that sound?"

"Great! You have been so helpful. Thank you, Shannon," Garrett stated.

"It's my pleasure. Let's see, we have a delivery of Friday at 10 a.m. Joel will arrive at your camp probably around 9:45. He'll take care of all of your needs."

"Joel, got it. That sounds good. Anything else?" Garrett asked.

"No, just be sure to send me the signed contract today," Crowe reminded Garrett.

"Will do. Thank you," Garrett said.

"Thank you," Crowe replied and hung up the phone.

The next Friday, Joel Ralph ("Ralph") arrived at the camp at 9:45 a.m. to deliver lunch. Ralph drove to the campgrounds in Sunshine Grill's van. The restaurant's logo, a yellow smiling face with a hamburger, was on both sides of the van along with the restaurant's phone number. The van was white with the logo and text in yellow, red, and black, the same colors as the restaurant. A few campers gathered near the van. Ralph exited the van and slid open the side door. He grabbed two trays of brownies and two jugs of lemonade and turned toward the children.

"Yay! Brownies and lemonade!" the children cheered in unison.

"Howdy!" Ralph interrupted. "Where can I find Ms. Garrett?" he asked. A camper showed Ralph to Garrett's office. Her door was open.

"Excuse me, Ms. Garrett. Hi, I'm Joel Ralph from Sunshine Grill," he said. "Where should I set up?"

Garrett looked away from her computer and saw Ralph standing in her doorway with his arms full of food and drinks. He had on dark colored shorts and wore a t-shirt with the restaurant's logo on it and a New York Yankees baseball cap. "Nice to meet you, Mr. Ralph," Garrett responded. "You are here right on time. Let me show you to the cafeteria. We will be in there. Do you need any help?"

"No, I've got it taken care of. I have my dolly outside in the van. It will just take me a few trips. No problem at all," Ralph explained.

"Great," Garrett said as they walked to the cafeteria. "Here is the cafeteria. I would like the food to be placed on those tables along the wall. There a few smaller tables for drinks and the desserts."

"Got it," Ralph said.

"Now, let me show you how to get back to your van," Garrett told Ralph as she directed him outside. Once outside, Garrett saw the restaurant's van with the logo on the side. "What a pleasant design," she thought to herself.

Garrett stood outside while Ralph unloaded the van. A few children asked to help him and Ralph yielded. He let them carry a few of the lighter items like plates, cups, and utensils. After about thirty minutes, Ralph was finished. He closed the van's doors and reached through the front window to get his clipboard. He then jogged over to where Garrett stood.

"Well, I'm finished, Ms. Garrett. I just need you to sign this delivery acknowl-edgment form right here on the dotted line. Feel free to review the form," Ralph explained.

"Okay." Garrett read the document and flipped up the top page to sign. She then noticed the restaurant's price list, contracts, and order forms. The contracts and order forms were blank with the restaurant's name printed at the top and in the spaces designated for the restaurant. "Do you have a price list and order form that I can keep?" she asked Ralph.

"Sure. I have a whole stack of them in the van. Let me get you some," Ralph said and walked back to the van.

When Ralph returned, Garrett said, "You know what, I will go ahead and place my next order now. You are right here and have the forms. I just want to get the same deal unless you know of any other specials."

"No, I don't," Ralph replied.

"Do you think it would be cheaper if I ordered ice tea instead of lemonade? What about cookies instead of brownies?" she asked.

"I'm not sure but I can check the price list and then add it up," Ralph responded. "But, for what it's worth, the kids sure started cheering when they saw the brown-ies and lemonade," he remarked.

"Well, let me get what I ordered for today's event," she decided.

"Okay," Ralph said. He reviewed Garrett's current order and marked the same items and prices on the new order form and contract. "When do you want this delivered? Write the day and time here."

Garrett wrote the delivery date and time in the space provided. She signed the contract and handed both documents back to Ralph. "I think I'm supposed to give you a copy of this contract. Here it is," Ralph stated and gave Garrett a copy of the contract.

"Thank you," she said.

"No, thank you for your business," he responded. Ralph then got in the van and drove back to the restaurant.

When he returned to the restaurant, Ralph gave Garrett's order form and contract to Crowe. "What's this?" Crowe asked. "Joel, these prices are all wrong. We had to raise our prices for all catered events, starting with those scheduled for next month. Gosh! I have to fix this." Crowe immediately picked up the phone to call Garrett.

"Hi, Ms. Garrett, this is Shannon at Sunshine Grill."

"Yes. Hi Shannon," Garrett replied. "Thank you again for the wonderful service. Our First Fridays lunch event was a huge success and everyone raved about the food. I look forward to the next one."

"About that, I hate to bother you, but there is a problem with your sales contract. It has the wrong prices for the meals that you ordered," Crowe stated.

"What do you mean?" Garrett asked.

"We recently had to raise our prices to deal with skyrocketing costs," Crowe explained. "Joel should not have taken your order or completed this document with you. He's our delivery guy, not a salesperson."

"I'm sorry, Shannon, but we have an agreement. I cannot afford a higher price right now and must insist that you honor our contract," Garrett maintained.

Crowe believes the agreement that Ralph, her delivery person, made with Garrett is unenforceable, as Ralph had no authority to contract on the restaurant's behalf. In the absence of actual authority, did Ralph have apparent authority to contract with Garrett on Sunshine Grill's behalf? Further, did Garrett justifiably rely on his authority to contract? Do not address whether there is an offer, acceptance, or consideration for the contract. Focus on the existence of apparent authority and justifiable reliance.

The case for this exercise is:

- *Nowak v. Capitol Motors, Inc.*, 255 A.2d 845 (Conn. 1969)

ANALOGICAL REASONING WITH DEPTH

EXERCISE 38

Using the case set out after the problem, determine whether Samuel Waters can successfully claim that All About Kids negligently hired its employee, Javier Thomas.

Background Facts

This scenario stems from the negligent repair of the crib Samuel Waters ("Waters") purchased from All About Kids for his three-year-old son, Damon, which is discussed in Exercise 49.

A few weeks after he purchased the crib, Waters called All About Kids to request some repair work on the crib. The All About Kids employee, Javier Thomas ("Thomas"), arrived and disassembled and fixed the crib. He then reassembled the crib and even polished the wood. Waters was quite pleased with his attention to detail and quick work. Thomas, however, did not properly repair the crib or reassemble it. Notably, Thomas failed to secure key hinges on the crib adequately. Waters was not aware of this problem. Then, one evening, Damon's crib collapsed and he suffered serious injuries from the fall.

Waters later learned that Damon's crib had been negligently repaired and assembled by Thomas. Waters contacted All About Kids and informed the company that he intended to file suit against it for negligently hiring Thomas.

Thomas's supervisor at All About Kids, Andrew Scavo ("Scavo"), was shocked by the news about Thomas's poor workmanship. Although it was about eight months ago, Scavo remembered the day he hired Thomas to work for the company. It was a Saturday morning, quite early, when Thomas walked into the store. He asked to speak with a manager about employment. Scavo happened to be on the floor giving instructions to the crew stocking the shelves. The cashier pointed in Scavo's direction, and Thomas walked over to him. He introduced himself with a very firm handshake and a nice big smile. Thomas said, "Good morning, sir. My name is Javier Thomas, and I am looking for a job as a salesperson or an installation guy. I am really good with my hands and have been in this business for some time now." Scavo shook his hand and led him to a corner of the store where they could talk in private.

Thomas then told Scavo about his recent work experience with The Home Store and his side business installing home products such as flooring and furniture. "I've pretty much done it all. No job is too big or small for me," Scavo stated. When Scavo asked Thomas about his business, Thomas told him that he unfortunately had to close its doors due to the bad economy. "I understand," Scavo replied. "It has been rough on everyone. And for some reason, we are still experiencing a high turnover rate here. I can't hire folks quick enough. You definitely came in at the right time."

Scavo and Thomas chatted for about 25 minutes when Oscar Martinez ("Martinez"), a veteran employee at All About Kids, walked in and spotted Thomas talking to Scavo. Martinez walked over to the two men and politely interrupted their conversation. Martinez told Scavo, "Sorry to interrupt, Andrew. Remember, this is the guy I've been telling you about. He's great, a hard worker. I have known him for years. I'm just glad he finally got a chance to come in and apply to work here." Martinez shook Thomas's hand and headed to the employee lounge.

Scavo then asked Thomas if he had some time to complete an application form. Thomas said "of course" and Scavo walked him to the information desk. He handed Thomas a short application form that asked for his full name, address, telephone number, social security number, and work history. The form also instructed applicants to list three references, two of which had to be work-related. Thomas wrote down Martinez's name and phone number as a reference.

While Thomas continued to complete the application, Sarah Mitchell ("Mitchell") walked through the front door. Mitchell is a long-time customer of All About Kids. She runs a local childcare center and purchases several items from the store each month. She is on a first-name basis with most of the staff. Mitchell recognized Thomas and said, "Hey Javier! I see you're filling out an application. So long to The Home Store. I hope you get the job!" Scavo overheard Mitchell's well wishes to Thomas. About 15 minutes later, Thomas handed his application form to Scavo. Scavo told him, "I'm glad that we had a chance to talk today. I will be in touch. By the way, how soon could you get started?" Thomas responded that he could start work as early as that afternoon.

Later that day, Scavo reviewed Thomas's application. He noted Thomas's experience with The Home Store and his personal business, and Martinez as his reference. He then ran a quick search on the Internet for Thomas's business but did not find any information. Scavo typically required two work-related references but had a good feeling about Thomas. He decided to call and offer Thomas an installation/repair position.

Thomas started work the following Monday morning. He jumped right in and started handling customer calls and requests. He performed on-site installations about four times a week. He took care of repair calls about once a month. Scavo noticed that Thomas was not only a quick learner but also a good team player. When other employees fell behind, Thomas would pick up the slack or ask how he could help.

About three months after Thomas started, he showed up intoxicated for work. Scavo noticed it immediately, reprimanded him, and sent him home without pay. "We cannot and will not tolerate this behavior, Javier," Scavo exclaimed. "Our insurance costs are through the roof and things like this don't help. You are a good employee, but I will fire you if this happens again." Thomas said, "I'm really sorry. It won't happen again. I just had a really bad night. My wife told me she wanted a divorce. Can you believe that? 20 years of marriage down the drain. We were high school sweethearts. I know this is more than you want to know. I promise. It won't happen again." Scavo put a note about his reprimand in Thomas's file.

Since Waters's notice that he plans to file suit against All About Kids, the company's legal team discovered that Thomas had a less than stellar employment record at The Home Store. Over the course of his three-year term at The Home Store, Thomas received about eight customer complaints, ranging from no-shows or tardiness for installation appointments and unsatisfactory work to inappropriate conduct. The average employee in the installation department averaged about two complaints or incidents per year. The legal team ran a search on Thomas's business but did not locate any information on the Internet. They contacted the local Better Business Bureau (BBB) and learned that his company had a rating of D on a scale of A+ to F. The factors that lowered his business's rating included 25 complaints filed against the business and Thomas's failure to respond to half of those complaints. Several of the complaints were not resolved. Although the team did not receive detailed information about the nature of those complaints, the BBB representative stated that the complaints ranged from billing issues and contract disputes to warranty and product issues.

All About Kids has already indicated that it will vigorously defend against Waters's claim of negligent hiring. Can Waters raise a successful claim under California law against All About Kids for negligently hiring Thomas?

The case for this exercise is:

- *SeaRiver Maritime, Inc. v. Indus. Med. Servs., Inc.*, 983 F. Supp. 1287 (N.D. Cal. 1997)

ANALOGICAL REASONING WITH DEPTH

EXERCISE 39

Using the cases below, determine whether Reynaldo Perez was constructively discharged.

Background Facts

Reynaldo Perez ("Perez") interviewed at the popular Malloy's Department Store ("Malloy's") in Los Angeles, California. He sought a position as a department manager, specializing in shoes and accessories. During a break in his interviews, he filled out an application form. The application form included the following language: "Thank you for applying to the Malloy's family of companies. We appreciate your time and interest. Malloy's hires and retains hard-working people. If you are hired with us, please keep in mind that our employment relationship will end whenever we determine that it should. Good luck in the application process!"

Perez had several years of experience in shoes and accessories with another company, as well as a degree in marketing and sales. Malloy's hired him, and he started work at an annual salary of $47,000, plus benefits and vacation days. During his new employee orientation, he received an employee manual that, among other things, outlined the company's history and explained the company holiday schedule. The manual also contained the following language:

> Welcome to the Malloy's family! We hope for a long and productive employment relationship with you. We reward hard work and productivity. On the other hand, if you do not perform your job as you should, you will be fired. You can be fired any time, for any reason. We hope you remain a loyal and productive member of the Malloy's family for many years.

Perez enjoyed his work at Malloy's, and he connected well with the customers. After two years with the company, he received his first bonus of $5,000. "You reached an important sales milestone," said his supervisor. "Your department has sold more shoes this year than in any past year, and it's only November! Well done, Perez."

Perez was quickly promoted to store manager, and in five years' time, he was regional manager. His salary increased to $170,000, plus bonuses tied to store sales within his region. His supervisors continued to praise his work and sales results. Each year, Perez received a performance evaluation. From the day he started at Malloy's to the day he left, his evaluations were uniformly good. After five years, company president Edwina Malloy ("Malloy") told him that she had never seen evaluations as good as Perez's, and that if Perez continued to perform at this level, his job would always be safe. "We don't just fire people around here, Perez. We don't do that. Stick with us, and you'll be fine."

Perez stayed at Malloy's for a total of twenty years, rising to the level of national vice president of the company. At the celebration of his twenty-year anniversary with the company, the president approached him to shake his hand. "What a success story, Perez!" she said. "You have brought our company back to a strongly competitive position. By the way, my nephew, Billy Malloy Meagle, will be starting as your assistant next week. Please show him everything you know, as I want him to be a key player. He just finished his Master of Business Administration degree, and he can hardly wait to get to work. He's twenty-eight years old, and you will love his energy." Perez agreed to help Meagle learn the ropes at Malloy's. Over the next few months, Meagle and Perez worked together, and Meagle shadowed Perez through his day. Before long, Meagle was alongside Perez making presentations to the Board of Directors, and Perez was proud of Meagle's progress.

Perez was surprised when Malloy called him into her office one day to discuss a new assignment. "Look, Perez, you've been great and all, but it's time for new blood. You're going to be Meagle's assistant now, and he will be the vice president." "But what have I done wrong?" asked Perez. Malloy said that he had done nothing wrong at all, but that business is business, and that's what the company needed right now.

Perez returned to his office and called his wife. He explained that he did not feel wanted at the company, and she urged him to resign. "You don't have to stay there," she said. "Tell them you're leaving immediately." Perez decided to wait. He returned to Malloy's office and told her that he was fine with the change in his assignment. After a year, however, he started to feel depressed that he was still working for his former subordinate. Meagle continued to ask Perez questions every day, and even the chairman of the board said that Perez undoubtedly knew more than anyone at the company about the shoe and accessory aspect of the business. Meagle came into work late, and Perez kept working long hours. Finally, he had had enough. He went to Malloy's office and said that unless he could get his own job back, he was leaving effective immediately. "Well, we hate to see you go," said Malloy. "But OK. We're going to be reducing the size of our executive staff at some point anyway, so you're probably on the right track. Good luck." Perez went home, distraught. Two weeks later, he called your law firm.

The partner in charge is considering bringing a number of different claims, but first, she would like you to answer the following question: Did Perez resign, or did Malloy's actions essentially force him to resign? In other words, was Perez constructively discharged?

The partner gives you just one case that she thinks will be sufficient to answer the question: *Turner v. Anheuser-Busch, Inc.*, 876 P.2d 1022 (Cal. 1994). For the partner's next project on this case, see Exercise 67.

ANALOGICAL REASONING WITH DEPTH

EXERCISE 40

Using the cases below, determine whether the default judgment entered against Home Stuff Stores, Inc. can be set aside.

Background Facts

You are a new law clerk at a small Houston firm. One day, a senior partner comes into your office, looking flustered and exclaiming, "Look at this! By one day!" You quickly learn that a judge has entered a default judgment against Home Stuff Stores, Inc. ("Home Stuff"). Home Stuff has retained your firm in its efforts to have the default judgment set aside.

Apparently, customer Lillian Diller ("Diller") sued Home Stuff for damages suffered when she allegedly slipped and fell in the houseplants section of the store. (Home Stuff's in-store video shows Diller walking to a wet area in the store, looking around, and then lying gently on the floor. After a few seconds, she starts screaming.) Diller's counsel served the lawsuit upon Home Stuff's corporate office in Fort Worth. It is undisputed that service was properly perfected and that manner and mode of service were proper according to the rules. There is no jurisdictional or other defect on the face of the petition. An answer was due in the 295th Civil District Court in Harris County at 10 a.m. on the Monday following the expiration of 20 days following service.

Home Stuff has a large in-house legal department, and legal assistant Deb Howe ("Howe") initially reviewed the lawsuit and determined that it should be handled by Smith & Smith LLP, the firm that handles all of Home Stuff's routine Texas litigation. Howe emailed her supervising attorney for approval to retain counsel—unfortunately, the supervising attorney was on vacation in Africa, and he had lost his Blackberry at the airport. He did not otherwise receive the message.

Five days later, Howe called June Smith ("Smith"), a partner at Smith & Smith, to advise her that the lawsuit would be faxed over as soon as Howe received approval. Then Howe left town for a legal assistants' conference in Florida. Smith was in the middle of a trial in Arizona, but she left a message for a junior associate asking him to watch out for the lawsuit, which she referred to as "yet another Home Stuff slip-and-fall." The junior associate was busy with other matters too, but he made a mental note to watch for the lawsuit. Two days later, the junior associate left the firm suddenly and joined another firm. In the meantime, Smith had won her trial, and she returned to the office. She had completely forgotten about the Home Stuff lawsuit.

On the Friday before the answer was due, the supervising attorney at Home Stuff returned from his safari and emailed his approval to Howe. Still jetlagged, he reviewed the lawsuit and placed the documents in Howe's chair without looking at the answer date. Howe was home sick from work on Monday and Tuesday.

On Tuesday morning, Robert Holder ("Holder"), a solo practitioner representing Diller, telephoned Home Stuff's general counsel and left two messages stating that Home Stuff should file an answer or risk default. The general counsel was attending a board meeting, but when she received the messages, she immediately telephoned outside counsel to find out the answer's status. Later that day, Holder appeared in court and moved for a default judgment. Just before the close of business on Tuesday, a messenger arrived at the courthouse with Home Stuff's general denial.

Unfortunately for Home Stuff, the judge had already reviewed the motion for default and granted a default judgment at noon that day. The hearing on damages is set for two weeks from now. (Another lawyer in your firm is handling research related to the damages hearing, so you need not address that issue.)

Today, five days after the default judgment was entered, Home Stuff's general counsel wants your firm to advise her as to whether a motion for new trial is likely to be successful. To be successful, your motion must show that (1) the failure to file an answer was due to accident or mistake rather than conscious indifference, (2) the defendant can set up meritorious defense in the lawsuit, and (3) the plaintiff will not suffer delay or other injury if the motion is granted. Please analyze just the second element, explaining whether you think Home Stuff can succeed in setting up a meritorious defense in the lawsuit.

Please use the following case to answer the question:

- *State Farm Life Ins. Co. v. Mosharaf*, 794 S.W.2d 578 (Tex. App. 1990).

ANALOGICAL REASONING WITH DEPTH

EXERCISE 41

Using the case for this exercise, determine whether the officer's search of Frank Bahls's desk drawer was a constitutionally permissible warrantless search incident to his arrest.

Background Facts

Frank Bahls ("Bahls") owns and operates a tax preparation business on the southwest side of Houston, Texas. Bahls shares a two-story office building with three other businesses. Bahls's office and an insurance company are located on the first floor, with Bahls's office on the left and the insurance company on the right. On the second floor, there are two more businesses, a real estate agency and a mortgage company. Each business has a private office with a door that locks. The business owner is the only person with a key to each respective office. Each office space measures approximately 10 feet by 10 feet.

The four businesses share a reception area located on the first floor in the center, just past the front door. Bahls's office is located six feet past the reception area. The reception area has a desk and five chairs for clients. The four business owners recently hired a new receptionist. The receptionist arrives at 7:45 a.m. Monday through Saturday and typically opens the front door of the building. The receptionist only has a key to the front door. As a client enters the building on the first floor, the receptionist greets him, calls the business owner, and either asks the client to wait in the reception area or directs the client to the appropriate office. On average, there are three clients sitting in the reception area at any one time during the week.

The businesses also share a restroom and small kitchen area, both of which are on the first floor behind the receptionist's desk. The restroom is on the left side of the building and the kitchen area is on the right side. On the first floor, there also is a back door between the restroom and kitchen. The back door leads directly outside to four covered parking spaces that the business owners use daily.

On Tuesday at 10:30 a.m., two Houston Police Department (HPD) officers, wearing their official uniforms, stood a short distance from Bahls's office building. The officers waited for their informant to return. Officer Julio Hernandez, who stood six feet and two inches tall, weighed about two hundred and ten pounds. His partner, Officer Loretta Benson, stood five feet and six inches tall and weighed approximately one hundred and forty pounds. About ten minutes later, the officers' informant walked out of Bahls's office building and down the street to meet them.

The informant told the officers that she just purchased five hundred dollars' worth of counterfeit bills from Bahls for two hundred and fifty dollars. The informant showed the officers the counterfeit money. The informant also told the officers that she did not see any weapons in Bahls's office, and she was almost certain

Bahls had more counterfeit money in his possession. She described the layout of the first floor and mentioned there were at least three people in the reception area. Lastly, the informant revealed that Bahls had received a telephone call as she was leaving his office, and she heard him discussing an important meeting at noon. After verifying that the currency purchased by the informant was indeed counterfeit, the officers rushed to the office building to arrest Bahls. Fearing that he would destroy any potential evidence or leave the building for his meeting, the officers did not wait for an arrest or search warrant.

The officers quietly entered the front door of the building and motioned to the receptionist and clients waiting in the reception area to exit the building.

"What's going on?" the receptionist asked as he picked up his belongings.

"Sir, please do not ask any questions and just do as we have asked. Leave the building. We want to make sure everyone is safe," Officer Benson stated firmly. The receptionist and the clients who were in the reception area walked out the front door. The receptionist forgot to mention the business owners were upstairs.

The officers walked past the reception desk and down the hall to Bahls's office. The front door was wide open. Bahls sat at his desk, which faced the front door. The two officers appeared in the doorway.

"Frank Bahls, you are under arrest for counterfeiting," Officer Hernandez said.

Shocked, Bahls pushed his chair back and started to stand. "Freeze," both officers shouted in unison as they raised their guns. The other business owners in the building heard the commotion and remained in their offices with the doors locked.

"Don't make any sudden moves," Officer Hernandez shouted. "Show me your hands. Now, carefully and slowly stand and move away from the desk." Bahls stood up, raised his hands above his head, and moved two feet to the right of his desk. Bahls was five feet and nine inches tall. He weighed one hundred and eighty pounds.

There was a clear path between the front door of the office and the place where Bahls stood next to his desk. As Officer Benson held her gun pointed at Bahls, Officer Hernandez walked to Bahls, patted him down, and grabbed his arm. He escorted Bahls toward the office door. Officer Benson then searched Bahls's office for counterfeit money and any related evidence. Meanwhile, Officer Hernandez guarded Bahls as they both stood in the doorway to Bahls's office. Officer Hernandez did not handcuff Bahls. Officer Hernandez read Bahls his *Miranda* rights and tried to ask Bahls questions about his counterfeiting operation, tax business, and recent sale to the informant. Bahls and Officer Hernandez stood about four feet from Bahls's desk. (See the diagram of Bahls's office at the end of this exercise.)

Officer Benson continued to search Bahls's office and sat in his desk chair. She moved a cup of coffee to the far left and flipped through some documents on his desk. She opened the center desk drawer and rummaged through the items inside. She then looked down slightly to her right and saw two drawers stacked one on top of the other. Officer Benson pulled on the drawers, but they would not open.

"These drawers are locked. Bahls, where is the key?" Officer Benson asked. Bahls ignored the officer, and Officer Benson repeated her question. "Don't make me break the lock."

"The key is right in front of you. It's on the key ring on the desk," Bahls responded reluctantly. Officer Benson picked up the key ring and tried to open the drawers using one key at a time. The last key opened the drawers successfully. She searched the top drawer and did not find any useful information. She then opened the bottom drawer and found an unregistered gun on top of a stack of counterfeit one hundred dollar bills.

"We've got him!" Officer Benson claimed. "With the informant's testimony, we should have more than enough evidence to send him away for a long time."

"I want a lawyer," Bahls said. Officer Hernandez stopped questioning Bahls, grabbed his arm, and escorted him outside the building to the patrol car parked a few feet away. The officer placed Bahls in the back seat.

The United States Government charged Bahls with illegal counterfeiting of United States currency and unlawful possession of an unregistered firearm in violation of federal laws. At his trial, Bahls's defense counsel moved to suppress the evidence seized during the search of Bahls's desk drawer, arguing the officer conducted an unconstitutional search incident to arrest.

Was the officer's search of Bahls's drawer a valid warrantless search incident to his arrest? Do not address whether Bahls's arrest was valid or whether the officers had probable cause to arrest him. Focus on the reasonableness of the officer's search of Bahls's desk drawer as a search incident to his valid arrest.

The case for this exercise is:

- *United States v. Yanez*, 490 F. Supp. 2d 765 (S.D. Tex. 2007)

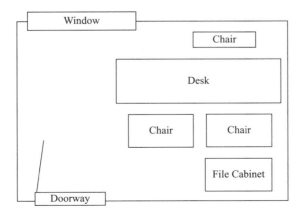

ANALOGICAL REASONING WITH DEPTH

EXERCISE 42

Using the cases below, determine whether there is any merit to Julius Johnson's battery claim against Pierre Washington.

Background Facts

Pierre Washington ("Washington") and Julius Johnson ("Johnson") are college friends who like to play golf together at the local municipal golf course. The two have been friends since high school, and they like to discuss their academic successes and challenges, their social lives, and other life issues as they play a relaxing round of golf. One Saturday, the two were teeing off on the ninth hole. Washington had had a difficult week at college, and he was quiet and a bit grumpy. Johnson had had a great week, and he was talking excitedly about his good exam grade and promising date that night. "Buddy, I am on a roll!" he said. Washington tried to be enthusiastic for his friend. "That's great," he said flatly. "Good for you." Johnson heard the lack of enthusiasm in Washington's voice. "What's up?" said Johnson. "Nothing, man," said Washington. "I'm happy for you. I'm just not having a great week myself. Go ahead and swing."

Johnson grabbed a driver and stepped up to take his shot. The club made firm contact with the ball, and the two watched the ball as it flew over grass and far above the sand traps. It continued to fly closer to the green, where it bounced and started rolling toward the pin. "Whoa," said Johnson. "It's getting awfully close to the hole!" The ball rolled more slowly and then approached the hole. It skipped over a small rough patch, slowed slightly, and then dropped into the hole. "I can't believe it!" cried Johnson. "Wow, you score again, my friend. High five!" said Washington. Johnson was still stunned at his hole in one and did not hear Washington's comment at all. Washington approached Johnson for the high five and thought Johnson was holding up his hand. Washington raised his hand to meet Johnson's, but the two hands did not meet—instead, Washington hit the side of Johnson's head by accident.

"What the heck?" said Johnson. "My ear hurts!" Washington apologized, but Johnson was injured. "Why'd you do that, man?" said Johnson. "I know you had a bad week, but come on." Washington was surprised at his reaction. "Of course I didn't do it on purpose. You're being ridiculous." Johnson's ear continued to hurt, and he went to the doctor later that day. As it turns out, Johnson had a ruptured ear drum and required treatment. A few months later, Washington heard from Johnson's lawyer. The lawyer said that if Washington did not pay immediately for the treatment, Johnson would sue Washington for civil battery. Washington has contacted you to find out if there is any merit to Johnson's battery claim—what is your opinion?

Please use the following cases to answer Washington's question:

- *Paul v. Holbrook*, 696 So. 2d 1311 (Fla. Dist. Ct. App. 1997)
- *Gatto v. Publix Supermarket, Inc.*, 387 So. 2d 377 (Fla. Dist. Ct. App. 1980)

PART 2

INTERMEDIATE ANALOGICAL EXERCISES

ANALOGICAL REASONING WITH DEPTH
EXERCISE 43

Using the cases set out after the problem, determine whether Sasha Champion is liable to Veronica McPhee for conversion of McPhee's luggage and its contents.

Background Facts

Sasha Champion ("Champion"), the sole heir to the Champion Suites and Hotels chain, arrived in Miami, Florida on a direct flight from Los Angeles, California. Since she sat in first class, Champion was one of the first few passengers to exit the plane. The flight attendant quickly grabbed Champion's Louis Vuitton overnight bag from the overhead compartment and handed it to her.

"Have a great time on your cruise," the attendant told Champion.

"I plan to," Champion responded abruptly. "Since we arrived in Miami several minutes late, my driver will have to speed to the dock to make sure we get there well before the sailing time. I don't want to get caught in any long lines or large crowds."

"Sorry for the late arrival. I do hope you enjoyed the flight and my service today," the attendant said nicely.

Champion put on her Chanel shades and gave the attendant a smirk. Champion headed down the jet bridge toward the airport, picked up her telephone, and called her driver to make sure he was waiting down in baggage claim for her.

"We don't have any time to waste," she told the driver. "Be on the lookout for my matching Louis Vuitton luggage. I'm sure no one else has anything like it."

About fifteen minutes later, Champion reached the baggage claim area and found the baggage carousel for her flight. She spotted her driver who stood patiently at the carousel near the opening in the wall. A few seconds later, the red light flashed, the siren sounded, and the conveyor belt started to move.

"There's my bag. Quick, grab it. And there's the other one. Get it too," she directed her driver. The driver pulled both Louis Vuitton suitcases from the belt. Both suitcases had the classic Louis Vuitton style with monogram canvas and measured 18.5" × 26.3" × 9.8". "Great. We didn't have to wait too long at all. Let's get out of here and on our way to the dock," Champion instructed.

Champion motioned to the driver, and they both walked to the car parked outside. As they approached the car, Champion took off her jacket and placed it inside one of the large monogrammed Louis Vuitton suitcases. She quickly unzipped the top of the suitcase, near the luggage tag, and squeezed her jacket inside. She also placed a few items from her smaller overnight bag in the suitcase, including a plastic pouch carrying perfume, lotion, and nail polish and two magazines. She slid them through the small opening as to not waste time opening the entire suitcase. She then got in the back seat of the car while the driver placed the luggage in the trunk.

Meanwhile at the carousel, Veronica McPhee ("McPhee"), who also was a passenger on the flight to Miami, waited for her luggage to arrive. McPhee sat in the back of the plane and reached the carousel about ten minutes after Champion had left. As McPhee approached the belt, she noticed a Louis Vuitton bag and moved toward it. She pulled the bag off the belt and read the luggage tag. It read "S. Champion. 310-228-3685."

"Oh, this isn't my bag," she thought to herself. She placed it back on the belt, hoping no one saw her grab it. McPhee waited for almost twenty minutes for her suitcase to appear. She noticed that no one had claimed the Louis Vuitton bag that was still circling the belt. When the conveyer belt stopped moving, McPhee removed the suitcase and headed to the airline's service desk.

"Hi, how may I help you?" the representative asked.

"I think someone took my suitcase. I checked a brand new Louis Vuitton suitcase that I just received as a graduation gift. It has the LV design all over it and is the large model, just like this one here. Actually, they are identical. This suitcase belongs to S. Champion. It was left on the belt. My suitcase is missing," McPhee explained.

"I am so sorry. Write down your phone number here and let me see your baggage claim ticket so that I can make a report in our system. I will hold on to this bag and try to contact the owner. In the meantime, I suggest that you call the number too. One of us is bound to reach someone soon. Here is my card," the representative stated.

"I really hope so. I am a bridesmaid in my cousin's wedding tomorrow. My dress is in that suitcase and I cannot replace it at this late date. It's a designer dress," McPhee explained. "My cousin is going to kill me," McPhee said as she let out a big sigh.

McPhee left the center and immediately called the number on the luggage tag. Her call went to voicemail. She left a detailed message on Champion's phone, explaining the situation and that she desperately needed her luggage to be in her cousin's wedding. She called back four times in a row and kept getting voicemail.

A week later, McPhee received a call from Champion about her suitcase. Champion explained that she was on a cruise and had not realized her mistake until after the ship set sail. She saw McPhee's name and contact information on the luggage tag and opened the suitcase to find McPhee's belongings in the bag. She knew there was no way to return the suitcase until the ship docked again or returned to Miami. She apologized for the mistake and offered to deliver the suitcase to her.

"Thanks, but no thanks!" McPhee exclaimed. "My cousin's wedding was ruined! I couldn't walk down the aisle as a bridesmaid and felt horrible about it. Yeah, I definitely want my suitcase back, but I deserve even more for what you put me through this past week. My lawyer will be contacting you soon." She then hung up the phone.

Champion disregarded McPhee's tirade and told her driver to deliver the suitcase to the address on the luggage tag. When McPhee received the suitcase, she opened it up and discovered her dress was damaged and had huge stains on it. "Unbelievable. The dress is ruined," she murmured to herself. "I cannot wait to tell my lawyer about this."

Is Champion liable to McPhee for conversion of McPhee's Louis Vuitton suitcase and its contents? Do not address whether there is sufficient damage to McPhee to support a conversion claim. Rather focus on the main elements for conversion presented in the cases. Champion has already indicated that she will vigorously defend against McPhee's claim for conversion.

The cases for this exercise are:

- *Seymour v. Adams*, 638 So. 2d 1044 (Fla. Dist. Ct. App. 1994)

- *Warshall v. Price*, 629 So. 2d 903 (Fla. Dist. Ct. App. 1993)

- *Ciamar Marcy, Inc. v. Montiero Da Costa*, 508 So. 2d 1282 (Fla. Dist. Ct. App. 1987)

Using the cases below, determine whether Culinary Delights had a reasonable business expectancy in securing the food services contract with Samuel Bennett University.

Background Facts

Samuel Bennett University ("SB University") is currently accepting bids for its food services contract. SB University is a private four-year university located in Riverdale, Virginia. SB University has two undergraduate divisions and a graduate school of law. The enrollment for the undergraduate divisions is about 7,500 students and for the School of Law is 700 students. The total faculty count is approximately 650 members. All freshmen and sophomores live in campus housing and have easy access to the Cooper Dining Hall, which is located near most of the dormitories. There are four sorority houses near campus with dining rooms. Each house provides regular meals to its residents. There also is a snack bar and another large dining hall located in the Marion L. Tyson University Student Center. The student center also contains a lounge space, meeting rooms, and a movie theatre. There are four other full-service dining halls on campus, one of which is Kosher. All students in the undergraduate and graduate divisions may use the dining halls located on campus. The law school building has a snack and coffee bar and a small cafeteria. During examination periods, the law school provides 24-hour snack and coffee service to students.

The successful bid for the food services contract with SB University will need to provide nutritious meals to all of the dining locations on campus, including the full service dining halls, the sorority dining rooms, and the snack and coffee bars. In addition, the company will need to service special catered events and provide a variety of food service options, such as meals on the run or to go and vegetarian selections. SB University has a tradition of maintaining an excellent dining pro-gram. In past years, SB University's Dining Services has received a number of awards for its flexible and nutritious menu options, innovative themed dining events, and gourmet catering services. SB University expects its next food service vendor to maintain the same high quality standards. Although SB University has no complaints with its current provider, university rules require the school to seek competitive bids for its food services program once every five years.

Amaka Ukwu ("Ukwu"), the new Vice President for University Dining Services, will make the final decision regarding the successful bid, after consulting with a committee comprised of faculty, students, and university administrators. Since she is brand new to the University, Ukwu plans to review each bid with fresh eyes and to consider all of the factors involved, including, but not limited to, the cost to SB University and its students, the company's resources, meal plan options, and food variety. The University employs a blind bidding process at the initial level that requires applicants to redact all identifying information as much as possible.

Culinary Delights is a relatively new food service provider with its headquarters in Richmond, Virginia. Culinary Delights has two food services contracts with colleges. These contracts are with Bates College and Harper Community College ("HCC"), both located in Virginia. Each contract has a four-year term. Bates College has about 1,350 undergraduate students and 400 graduate students. The faculty includes 143 full and part-time members. Bates College has three full-service dining halls and two smaller cafes with snack bars and coffee counters. HCC has a student body of approximately 4,500 students and 420 full and part-time faculty members. HCC does not provide housing for its students. Given that most of its students commute to campus, HCC has only one large dining hall for students located in the center of campus. There is a separate dining center for HCC faculty.

Culinary Delights provides a variety of meal plan and food options to both colleges and caters special events. Last year, for its work at Bates College, the company received the Bronze Award for a catered special event and an Honorable Mention for its Mardi-Gras themed dinner. Culinary Delights received favorable recommendations from Bates College and HCC to support its application for the food services contract with SB University. Culinary Delights is an active participant in the National Association of College & University Food Services ("NACUFS") organization. The company's head chef competed in the organization's annual culinary challenge and won third place. The company received the organization's "Rising Star" award after its first year in business. Culinary Delights also works diligently with Virginia's Campaign to Promote Environmentally-Friendly Practices.

Recently, Tanya Bowen ("Bowen"), an Executive Assistant to the Chief Operations Officer at Culinary Delights, resigned from the company and accepted the position of Assistant Director of Customer Relations at Tasty Cuisine. Tasty Cuisine is a competing food service company also located in Virginia. Since Bowen did not have an administrative position at Culinary Delights, she did not have a non-compete clause in her employment agreement with the company. While at Culinary Delights, Bowen had access to company materials such as proposals, menu items, and bid documents. In particular, Bowen attended various planning meetings and strategy sessions for Culinary Delight's bid to SB University. Bowen took detailed notes for the company's minutes. In her new position at Tasty Cuisine, Bowen assisted the team in preparing a bid to submit to SB University.

Tasty Cuisine specializes in nutritious meals and has several food services contracts with colleges and universities in the Virginia and Maryland area. Notably, Tasty Cuisine provides food service to three medium-sized colleges, each with an enrollment of about 4,500 students and 350 faculty members. Each campus has three full-service dining halls and a few snack bars. These colleges are the company's largest clients. Tasty Cuisine is a member of NACUFS and participates in all of the organization's annual competitions. Although the company has never placed in the chef competition, the company's President and employees have received a number of special recognition awards for their service to the food services industry. To support its application to SB University, Tasty Cuisine submitted favorable recommendations from its largest clients and two of the small colleges that it services.

After reviewing the five proposals submitted for the food services contract, Ukwu selected Tasty Cuisine as its new service provider. A week later, representatives with Culinary Delights met with Ukwu to discuss its bid and receive feedback on its performance. Ukwu informed Culinary Delights that it ranked the company's bid for the new contract second among the five proposals submitted. She also told the representatives that the company's bid was very close to Tasty Cuisine's winning bid in terms of projected costs and meal plan and food options. Culinary Delights later learned that Bowen participated in preparing Tasty Cuisine's bid. Bowen admits that she took a number of documents about Culinary Delight's proposed bid when she resigned from the company. Culinary Delights's counsel sent Bowen a letter stating the company's intent to file suit against her for tortious interference with a business expectancy. Bowen contends that Culinary Delights did not have a valid business expectancy with SB University, only a hope in securing the contract.

Did Culinary Delights have a reasonable business expectation in acquiring the food services contract with SB University? Do not address any other issues (such as whether Bowen knew about the business expectancy or whether she intentionally interfered with the relationship).

The cases for this exercise are:

- *Am. Tel. & Tel. Co. v. E. Pay Phones, Inc.*, 767 F. Supp. 1335 (E.D. Va. 1991)

- *Levine v. McLeskey*, 881 F. Supp. 1030 (E.D. Va. 1995)

- *Muir v. Navy Fed. Credit Union*, 744 F. Supp. 2d 145 (D.D.C. 2010)

ANALOGICAL REASONING WITH DEPTH

EXERCISE 45

Using the cases below, determine whether Danielle Conway disaffirmed or repudiated her contract with *Celeb Look*[24] *Magazine* within a reasonable time after she reached eighteen years of age, the age of majority.

Background Facts

Danielle Conway ("Conway"), a seventeen-year-old high school student, walked through the neighborhood mall and paused in front of a boutique. She gazed at the mannequins in the window and wondered whether the store had the purple jumpsuit in her size. "I could never afford that outfit," she thought to herself as she walked away. She then felt a light tap on her shoulder.

"Hi. Can I speak to you for a minute?" a salesperson asked, holding a clipboard.

"Sure, why not?" Conway responded.

"Let me tell you about a new magazine called *Celeb Look*[24]," the salesperson stated. "It's innovative and better than anything you have seen on the market. Look at this first issue. We have real celebrity stylists who contribute articles and offer beauty advice and fashion tips. We even have writers who follow reality stars and provide readers with the real deal on their daily routines and events."

"This is really great," Conway remarked. "I hope to attend fashion design school one day in the near future. It's on my to-do list. And I simply love all of the reality shows out there today. I never miss an episode of the *Kardashians*."

"Well then, this is the magazine for you," the salesperson said. "If you sign up today, you can receive our special offer of twenty-four issues at a discounted price of $2.50 an issue. That is fifty percent less than the newsstand price. Also for your subscription, you will receive twenty-four hour access to our interactive site and blog where you can learn more about celebrity fashion and sightings. On our site, you can watch live interviews of Hollywood stars and post questions that you would like to ask the celeb. Of course, we also encourage viewers to post general comments about each interview to continue the dialogue. The site never sleeps and you can tune in at any hour. In addition to all of this, we sponsor monthly competitions for our subscribers to submit their articles, editorials, or fashion designs. You could become a star one day."

"I'm game. What do I need to do?" Conway asked.

"Just complete this subscription agreement and sign your name below," the salesperson explained.

Conway took the clipboard and checked the box next to "Yes, I want a new subscription to *Celeb Look*[24] *Magazine*." She then wrote her name, address, and telephone number in the designated spaces. She checked the box to receive twenty-four issues at $2.50 each and marked the option for billing at a later date in four equal installments. She signed her name, wrote "June 11" in the date line, and handed the contract to the salesperson. The salesperson quickly reviewed the document to verify that it was complete. He then removed the carbon copy and gave it to Conway.

"Look out for your first issue in the mail," the salesperson instructed. "It should arrive in a couple of weeks. Here is your access code for the companion website. You can log on immediately with this code. If you misplace it, simply call the 800 number on your copy of the agreement and give them your last name and address. You can call that 800 number if you have any questions or problems. Thank you for your business and enjoy your shopping this afternoon."

A few weeks later, Conway received her first issue of *Celeb Look*[24]. She flipped through the pages of the magazine. She was amazed at the photography and detailed helpful information provided in each column. Conway became more excited as each new issue arrived in the mail. She had fun filling out the questionnaires and completing the style, personality, and relationship quizzes and games.

Conway received her first bill for the magazine six months after she signed the contract. Conway's mother gave her a check for $15.00. Conway immediately sent the requested payment to the magazine's publisher. Two months later, on February 20, Conway celebrated her 18th birthday. Conway received a new two-year gift subscription to *Celeb Look*[24] *Magazine* from her best friend, Monica Calhoun. "Thank you, Monica!" Conway exclaimed. "Now, I can toss out my subscription and enjoy more issues for free."

Conway continued to receive issues of the magazine under her original subscription agreement. She used her access code to log on to the website and watch celebrity interviews. She even posted a few comments in the chat room and submitted a couple of articles for the site's editors to consider. Conway eventually started to receive two copies of each new issue once her gift subscription began.

Four months after her birthday, in mid-June, Conway received the next payment notice in the mail. She picked up the phone and called the 800 number to cancel her subscription. A representative answered the phone on the second ring.

"*Celeb Look*[24] *Magazine*, how may I help you?" the representative asked.

"I need to cancel my subscription," Conway stated.

"Can you please provide me with your last name and address so that I can pull up your account?" the representative responded.

"Yes, Conway. C-O-N-W-A-Y. I live at 7103 Westbrook Lane, Cincinnati, OH 45213," Conway provided.

"Here you are," the representative said. "Oh, you still have a year left on the special offer. You got a great deal. The monthly rate is much higher now given the magazine's popularity. Well, Ms. Conway, we are very sad to lose your business, but we still need to receive payment for your second installment of $15.00 under the agreement. We, of course, will not request full payment for all twenty-four issues. With your cancellation, you will not receive any future issues, but you need to pay for those you have already received."

"I think you are mistaken. I shouldn't have to pay anything since I was too young to sign that contract. I was only seventeen years old at the time," Conway revealed.

Celeb Look[24] Magazine disagreed with Conway's position and requested immediate payment on her account. The publisher has a zero tolerance policy for failed payments and past due accounts and vigorously pursues all available collection methods.

Did Conway disaffirm or repudiate the contract that she signed as a minor with *Celeb Look[24] Magazine*? Do not address any other issues (such as whether there was an offer and acceptance or sufficient consideration for the contract). Focus on whether Conway successfully repudiated the magazine subscription agreement.

The cases for this exercise are:

- *Muller v. CES Credit Union*, 832 N.E.2d 80 (Ohio Ct. App. 2005)

- *Weiand v. City of Akron*, 233 N.E.2d 880 (Ohio Ct. App. 1968)

- *Herschede Motor Car Co. v. Bangham*, 1926 Ohio Misc. LEXIS 1079, 26 Ohio N.P. (n.s.) 232 (Ct. Com. Pl. 1926)

ANALOGICAL REASONING WITH DEPTH

EXERCISE 46

Using the cases set out after the problem, determine whether Tara Smith's detention by Wow Electronics Stores was for a reasonable length of time for purposes of the shopkeeper's privilege defense to false imprisonment. Do not address the other elements of the shopkeeper's privilege.

Background Facts

Wow Electronics Stores, Inc. ("Wow") has reported a possible claim by an elderly woman named Tara Smith ("Smith"). Smith was detained at a Wow store on suspicion of shoplifting; she is ninety years old. Smith is threatening to sue for false imprisonment. Wow plans to assert the shopkeeper's privilege, which is a defense to false imprisonment. The shopkeeper's privilege permits shopkeepers to detain suspected shoplifters under certain circumstances.

To succeed in this defense, the shopkeeper must establish that the detention was: (1) based on reasonable suspicion; (2) reasonable in length of time; and (3) reasonable in manner. You need not assess the reasonableness of the suspicion or reasonableness in manner, just the reasonableness in length of time.

Retiree Smith was shopping alone in a Wow store. Smith was looking for a gift for her granddaughter. Smith's granddaughter liked the band Five Boys, so Smith was looking for a CD of Five Boys' music. When Smith found the Five Boys in the CD section of the store, she looked through the various CDs. Smith's granddaughter had told her the name of the most recent CD, but Smith could not remember the name. She dug through her purse, and as she did so, a CD slipped off the shelf and fell into her purse. Smith did not notice that the CD had fallen into her purse, so she continued to look for the CD her granddaughter wanted. Elated, Smith finally found the "Five Boys 4Ever" CD. She walked happily past aisles of televisions toward the checkout stand and paid for the CD.

As she reached the exit, two security guards grabbed her by the arms. Instinctively, she brushed off their hands. One guard announced loudly, "Don't try to attack me, lady. I'm Captain Johnson of the Wow Asset Protection Team. What are you doing with that CD?" Smith tried to explain that she had just paid for the CD.

The guard pulled Smith roughly by the arm, saying "Not that one, lady. The one in your purse!" By this time, a small group of shoppers had gathered. One shopper said, "Look at that old lady! A thief!" The guard took Smith's belongings and locked her in the Assets Protection Guest Lounge. The "guest lounge" was actually a small, windowless room that locked from the outside. It contained no furniture but a dusty chair. The room had no telephone, and Smith was denied the use of a telephone when she requested one to call her son. Smith was scared. She sat in the room without any contact from other people for one hour. After an hour, a manager yelled through the door, "We're working on reviewing the tapes, but the television just broke. Looks like you may be in the clear—or just lucky this time. Do you mind waiting a bit longer?" Smith jumped up and said, "NO! I don't want to wait! I need to go home and take my medication!" After another twenty minutes, the manager came back. "Looks like you're in the clear. We can see that the CD just fell into your purse by accident. Off you go! Come back and see us."

Smith feels humiliated, and she intends to sue for false imprisonment. In such cases, Wow asserts the shopkeeper's privilege. Was the detention reasonable for a reasonable amount of time, for purposes of the shopkeeper's privilege?

The facts set forth above are undisputed. Our client, Wow, confirmed these facts from store videotapes and witness interviews.

The applicable cases are set out on the following pages.* The cases for this exercise are:

- *Guijosa v. Qwik-Mart Stores, Inc.*

- *Willard Dep't. Stores, Inc. v. Silva*

---

* These cases are fictitious and/or adopted, in part, from actual cases. You need not worry about Bluebook citation form for this exercise, as there is no reporter information provided.

ANALOGICAL REASONING WITH DEPTH
CASES FOR EXERCISE 46

Salvador GUIJOSA and Rogelio HERNANDEZ

v.

QWIK-MART STORES, INC.

June 30, 2000

Plaintiffs appeal from a verdict in favor of Qwik-Mart in a civil action alleging false imprisonment. We affirm.

Salvador Guijosa and Rogelio Hernandez (together "plaintiffs") filed this suit against Qwik-Mart, claiming false imprisonment.

The claim arises from an alleged shoplifting incident at the Qwik-Mart store. Trial testimony conflicted about whether Guijosa was wearing a baseball cap when he entered the Qwik-Mart. All parties agreed Hernandez wore a baseball cap when he entered the store. While shopping, Guijosa tried on hats from a sale bin and decided to purchase two. Rhonda Liburdi, a loss prevention associate, testified she saw Guijosa tear off the price tag and place the hat on his head. Guijosa paid for some hats at the checkstand. Liburdi asked the cashier if they paid for the hats on their heads; the cashier replied no. Liburdi stopped the two in the front vestibule of Qwik-Mart, telling them she was detaining them for taking the hats without paying.

Liburdi requested they proceed to a security office at the back of the store. She asked a coworker, David Opfer, to assist her. Guijosa was the only one of the two who spoke English. He told Liburdi the hats belonged to them. Hernandez and Guijosa both testified that Guijosa's cap had been purchased the previous day. Guijosa also told Liburdi that the two would make a statement to the police. Liburdi called the Shelton police, who arrived approximately 20–30 minutes later.

In the meantime, Guijosa and Hernandez were placed in an unused employee break room, which contained chairs and a vending machine. Guijosa and Hernandez were locked in the room, but they were offered beverages and the use of a telephone. They were treated respectfully by staff at all times.

The shopkeeper's privilege creates a defense for retailers in an action for unlawful detention, arising from a shoplifting investigation for shoplifting taking place at their retail establishment. Under the common law, in any civil action brought by reason of any person having been detained on or in the immediate vicinity of the premises of a mercantile establishment for the purpose of investigation or questioning as to the ownership of any merchandise, it is a defense to the action that the person was detained in a reasonable manner and for not more than a reasonable time to permit such investigation if the owner, employee or agent had reasonable grounds to believe that the person so detained was committing or attempting to commit larceny or shoplifting on such premises of such merchandise. A "reasonable time" shall mean the time necessary to examine employees and records of the mercantile establishment relative to the ownership of the merchandise.

Plaintiffs maintain on appeal that the privilege did not apply in this case as a matter of law because the detention went beyond a "reasonable time" and was not performed in a reasonable manner.

Generally, the reasonableness of a shopkeeper's detention as a whole depends upon the facts and circumstances of the case. Other jurisdictions examining the time-specific issue under a shopkeeper's privilege statute have looked to all the circumstances of the detention to determine whether the time was "reasonable." "Reasonable time" is the time necessary to examine employees and records of the mercantile establishment relative to the ownership of the merchandise. This necessarily requires an examination of the entire circumstances of the detention.

The question of whether a shopkeeper detained a shoplifter for a "reasonable time" may be dependent upon the circumstances of the specific case. A suspect requiring special help, such as a handicapped person, an elderly person, or a minor, should be treated with special concern. But still, as a matter of public policy, storeowners should be able to hold suspected shoplifters for a reasonable amount of time to determine whether they have sufficient evidence of theft to contact police. It would be unfair to merchants to set a particular period of time, only to have it run out when a proper and careful investigation is underway.

The approximately 20–30 minutes in this case that plaintiffs waited for the police to arrive was not an unreasonable amount of time for Liburdi to attempt to get their statements, and investigate ownership of the merchandise. Furthermore, it is persuasive that Qwik-Mart's procedures were efficient and well organized.

With regard to the manner of detention, that element too depends on the facts of the case. Indicia of unreasonable manner may be humiliation, uncomfortable conditions, denial of basic necessities during detention, and the like. Locking a suspect in a room is inherent in detention, so that alone cannot constitute unreasonableness in manner. The detention here was performed with respect and consideration, so no complaint can be made on that basis. Affirmed.

WILLARD DEPARTMENT STORES, INC., Appellant,

v.

Lyndon SILVA, Appellee.

May 13, 2003.

Willard Department Stores, Inc. accused Lyndon Silva of shoplifting. Silva was tried in criminal court for theft charges stemming from this incident and was found not guilty. After his acquittal, Silva brought a civil action against Willard, alleging false imprisonment. A jury found Willard liable and awarded Silva past and future damages of $10,124.01 and $3,000.00, respectively, and punitive damages of $50,000.00. Willard contends there was no evidence or factually insufficient evidence to support the jury's findings of false imprisonment.

Silva was a hairstylist and testified that, while working at his place of employment, he received three shirts as a gift from a customer who has since returned to her native country. He explained that, because he and his roommate liked to dress alike, two of the three shirts were the same. Silva further testified he had his picture taken with the shirts at the salon where he worked. This picture was shown to the jury.

On June 12, 1997, Silva went to the Hancock Mall, where one of his friends was opening a new hair salon. Silva also took the three shirts, because he and his roommate had decided to exchange them. After touring the new salon, Silva went to his car, retrieved the three shirts, and went to Willard. Silva testified the customer who had given him the shirts had also given him the receipt with the gift, in case he wanted to exchange them.

Silva first attempted to return the shirts at the cosmetics/accessories counter, but was told he needed to exchange them at another department. While at the cosmetics/accessories counter, Silva purchased a back brush; the receipt indicated this purchase was made at 1:06 p.m. At 1:27 p.m., Silva purchased a Tommy Hilfiger shirt, making him eligible to purchase a Tommy Hilfiger travel bag being used as a promotional item. Another receipt indicated he purchased this travel bag at 1:31 p.m.

Silva testified he began to experience a headache and asked directions to the water fountain so he could take some medicine. According to Silva, a Willard security guard, Kevin Rivera, stopped him while Silva was on his way to the water fountain. Rivera was an off-duty police officer who was in uniform, with his "gun on [his] hip." Silva testified Rivera accused him of theft and placed him on the floor and handcuffed him. Silva said the officer emptied Silva's shopping bag onto the floor. Silva told the officer he had receipts for the items, including the three shirts. When the receipt for the shirts was not found in the bag, Silva said he begged the officer to go outside and check his car for the receipt. The officer instead took Silva, while handcuffed, up the escalator to an empty office. Silva said there were a lot of people watching. He also testified that no one asked him for an explanation and that, while in the office, the officer and a woman made fun of him. He stated that, when the city police arrived to take him into custody, Rivera again placed him on the floor with his knee in his back, and exchanged handcuffs with the city police. Silva said there were onlookers lined up to watch when he was escorted back downstairs and taken to the waiting police car.

Silva later produced a receipt for three shirts purchased at Willard June 2, 1997. All three shirts were the same style and price as the three Silva was accused of stealing. However, two of the SKU numbers did not match exactly those written on Willard's internal report about the incident. Silva's explanations of these discrepancies between the SKU numbers included a difference in sizes (delineated by the end numbers of the SKU numbers), a sales clerk scanning one item multiple times instead of scanning the individual tags on similar items, and a misidentification of the merchandise.

As its first point of error, Willard contends there was no evidence, or only factually insufficient evidence, to support the jury's finding of false imprisonment.

To prevail under a false imprisonment claim, a plaintiff must prove (1) willful detention, (2) without consent, and (3) without authority of law. Willard contends the third element is missing in this case. Willard bases this contention on the shopkeeper's privilege, which grants an employee the authority of law to detain a customer to investigate the ownership of property, so long as (1) the employee has a reasonable belief the customer has stolen or is attempting to steal store merchandise, (2) the detention was for a reasonable amount of time, and (3) the detention was in a reasonable manner.

Here, the first component is met. The second component of the shopkeeper's privilege is whether the detention was for a reasonable amount of time. Silva testified he did not know the length of time he was detained by Willard. The last receipt obtained from Willard by Silva was marked 1:31 p.m. Wallace testified she first noticed Silva around 1:30 or 1:45 p.m. She observed him for about fifteen minutes until he went into a dressing room for five or six minutes. Shortly after this, Silva was approached by Rivera and taken upstairs. The police report denotes the patrol officers arrived on the scene at 3:23 p.m. to transport Silva to jail.

Willard contends the evidence shows Silva was detained for approximately one hour, perhaps a little longer. Silva agrees the detention lasted an hour or so. Willard contends that, even if the detention was longer than an hour, there was no evidence this was an unreasonable amount of time for Rivera to question Silva and the store employees, and to talk with officers at the police department and prosecutors at the district attorney's office. In *Resendez*, the court held the ten to fifteen minutes in that case was not unreasonable as a matter of law. *Id*. The court, however, made its decision "[w]ithout deciding the outer parameters of a permissible period of time." *Id*. Here, both sides agree the detention was for at least an hour. Considering the totality of the circumstances, we cannot say Silva was detained for an unreasonable length of time.

The third component of the shopkeeper's privilege is whether the detention was in a reasonable manner. Again, Willard contends there was no evidence the detention was not reasonable. Silva testified, however, that Rivera accused him of theft and placed him on the floor and handcuffed him. Silva said the officer emptied Silva's shopping bag onto the floor. Silva testified people were around him when he was taken upstairs in handcuffs and when he was later escorted to the police car. He further stated the officer and a woman made fun of him while he was being detained upstairs. Silva stated that, when the city police came to take him into custody, Rivera again placed him on the floor with his knee in his back and exchanged handcuffs with the city police. He further testified that he asked Rivera many times to check his car for the receipt, but these requests were ignored and that, during the entire time he was detained, no one asked him for any explanation.

Silva's testimony provided the jury with evidence the detention was not conducted in a reasonable manner. Although the descriptions of the detention by Silva and Rivera were different, when parties introduce conflicting testimony in a jury trial, it is the duty of the jury to determine which witness is more credible. The verdict indicates the jury found Silva's story more credible than Rivera's.

Generally, the reasonableness of a detention is a question of fact for the jury to decide. Silva's testimony was more than a scintilla of evidence to support the jury's finding. Affirmed.

ANALOGICAL REASONING WITH DEPTH

EXERCISE 47

Using the cases set out after Exercise 46, determine whether Tara Smith's detention by Wow Stores was reasonable in manner for purposes of the shopkeeper's privilege defense to false imprisonment. Do not address the other elements of the shopkeeper's privilege.

Background:

Wow Electronics Stores, Inc. ("Wow") has reported a possible claim by an elderly woman named Tara Smith ("Smith"). Smith was detained at a Wow store on suspicion of shoplifting; she is ninety years old. Smith is threatening to sue for false imprisonment. Wow plans to assert the shopkeeper's privilege, which is a defense to false imprisonment. The shopkeeper's privilege permits shopkeepers to detain suspected shoplifters under certain circumstances.

To succeed in this defense, the shopkeeper must establish that the detention was: (1) based on reasonable suspicion; (2) reasonable in length; and (3) reasonable in manner. You need not assess the reasonableness of the suspicion or reasonableness in length of time, just the reasonableness in manner.

Further Facts and Cases:

For this exercise, please refer to the facts and cases in Exercise 46.

ANALOGICAL REASONING WITH DEPTH

EXERCISE 48

Using the cases set out after the problem, determine whether the building in question is an "inhabited dwelling house" for purposes of a first-degree burglary conviction.

Background Facts

Mike Jossery ("Jossery") is a successful criminal defense lawyer. He is known for his strong work ethic and diligence in defending every case. He works long hours at his office in the city and commutes home to the suburbs late in the evening. Jossery can be seen at all hours of the night working at his desk. His office is within a suite of offices on the 56th floor of a high-rise office building in the downtown business district. Jossery shares the suite with other criminal defense lawyers. Those lawyers also work day and night, and the lawyers, clients, and witnesses are in and out of the offices at all hours. The suite of offices is open during business hours and locked at night. Jossery likewise keeps the door to his own office unlocked during the day and locked at night, including when he works at night. Cleaning crews work throughout the offices between about 8 p.m. and 10 p.m.

Before and during trials, Jossery works his hardest. He has even been known to sleep at the office. He does not like to do this, though, because the office does not have a bed or shower. In addition, Jossery has to go home and feed his three dogs. When he does sleep at the office, he sleeps on the couch inside his own office. He keeps a pillow, quilt, and slippers at the office for this purpose.

One evening over the Memorial Day weekend, Jossery was preparing for trial. He had planned to go out of town for the holiday, but an important case was about to go to trial. He cancelled his plans and started a marathon trial prep session. After a full day and evening of work, he became so tired that he could hardly look at his computer. He decided to take a break before reading some more cases. He lay down on his couch and closed his eyes. He had been sleeping for about an hour when he awoke to the sound of the office door closing. Apparently, one of his former criminal clients, Shelley Moran ("Moran"), had noticed during an office interview that Jossery kept a magnificent antique clock in his office. She had heard that Jossery was out of town for the holiday, so she returned to the law office, picked the lock of both the suite and Jossery's office, and stole the clock without disturbing Jossery.

When Jossery awoke, he looked around his office and was horrified to see that the clock was missing. He ran to his video surveillance cameras and reviewed the tapes. He recognized Moran immediately, and the tape clearly showed her carrying the clock out of the office.

Moran is being prosecuted for first-degree burglary. Is Jossery's office an "inhabited dwelling house" for purposes of first-degree burglary?

The cases for this exercise are:*

- *Villalobos v. State*

- *Fond v. State*

---

* These cases are fictitious and/or adopted, in part, from actual cases. You need not worry about Bluebook citation form for this exercise, as there is no reporter information provided.

ANALOGICAL REASONING WITH DEPTH

CASES FOR EXERCISE 48

Jason VILLALOBOS

v.

STATE

January 10, 2002

Defendant appeals his conviction for first degree robbery and burglary. He contends that an occupied motel room, such as that where this crime took place, is not an "inhabited dwelling house" as required for conviction of this crime.

On the evening of November 7, 2000, Roy Anthony Miller rented a room at the Peppertree Motel in Ontario. Miller was alone in the motel room for an hour or two, waiting for a friend. Miller heard a knock on the motel room's door. Miller looked out the peephole, but did not see anyone. He then looked out the window and saw defendant Villalobos and another man standing to the side of the window. He had seen Villalobos before but did not know who he was.

Villalobos and the other man told Miller that they were going to rob him. The two men pointed knives at Miller and ordered him to the floor, but allowed him to lie on the bed instead. Villalobos searched Miller and removed $500-$700, a wallet and change from his pockets, and took his watch and a necklace.

Under this jurisdiction's law of burglary, any burglary of an "inhabited dwelling house" is burglary of the first degree. "Inhabited" means currently being used for dwelling purposes, whether occupied or not.

The issue before us is whether a motel room, which is rented on a transient or temporary basis, is "inhabited" within the meaning of those statutes. In order to determine whether, or when, an overnight lodging place qualifies as an inhabited dwelling, we must examine the principles underlying the first degree burglary law.

This jurisdiction's burglary law stems from the common law policy of providing heightened protection to the residence. The peace of mind and security of the residents is sought to be protected, rather than the property. Burglary laws are based primarily upon a recognition of the dangers to personal safety created by the danger that the intruder will harm the occupants in attempting to perpetrate the intended crime or to escape and the danger that the occupants will in anger or panic react violently to the invasion, thereby inviting more violence.

A person is more likely to react violently to burglary of his living quarters than to burglary of other places because in the former case persons close to him are more likely to be present, because the property threatened is more likely to belong to him, and because the home is usually regarded as a particularly private sanctuary, even as an extension of the person. In keeping with the purpose of the statute, the term "inhabited dwelling house" has been given a broad, inclusive definition. Thus, although an inhabited dwelling house is a place where people ordinarily live and which is currently being used for dwelling purposes, it need not be the victim's regular or primary living quarters in order to be deemed an inhabited dwelling house. Rather, the inhabited-uninhabited dichotomy turns on the character of the use of the building.

The proper question is whether the nature of a structure's composition is such that a reasonable person would expect some protection from unauthorized intrusion. Thus, a temporary place of abode, such as a weekend fishing retreat or even a jail cell may qualify.

People have an expectation of freedom from unwarranted intrusions into a room in which they intend to store their personal belongings, sleep, dress, bathe and engage in other intimate, personal activities. Obviously, whether one burglarizes a private home or a hotel room, there is a much greater possibility of confronting the resident and a substantial risk that force will be used and that someone will be injured, than if one burglarized a building that was not intended for use as habitation such as a warehouse.

We are at our most vulnerable when we are asleep because we cannot monitor our own safety or the security of our belongings. It is for this reason that, although we may spend all day in public places, when we cannot sleep in our own home we seek out another private place to sleep, whether it be a hotel room, or the home of a friend. Society expects at least as much privacy in these places as in a telephone booth—a temporarily private place whose momentary occupants' expectations of freedom from intrusion are recognized as reasonable.

Of course, a motel room may be "occupied" for purposes other than use as a temporary dwelling, and thus not be "inhabited" for purposes of the burglary and robbery statutes. A motel can be rented as a place to transact business, licit or illicit. It is also not uncommon for people to rent motel rooms to conduct legitimate business meetings or transactions. The rooms are "occupied" while these transactions or meetings take place, but they are not "inhabited" unless they are also being used as a place of repose. Here, it was undisputed that Miller intended to stay overnight in the motel room and to sleep there. In light of that evidence, Miller was using the motel as a temporary habitation. Affirmed.

Philip FOND

v.

STATE

April 5, 2000

On appeal of his conviction for first-degree burglary, Fond contends that a locked psychiatric hospital is not an inhabited dwelling house for the purpose of first-degree burglary.

On May 2, 1997, Birgit C. entered Oakwoods Hospital for treatment of depression and substance abuse. Fond was also a patient residing at the hospital.

The next day when Birgit awoke from a nap in her room, she encountered Fond. Fond grabbed her purse and jewelry and ran out of the door. Fond contends that a psychiatric hospital is not an inhabited dwelling house for the purpose of first-degree burglary.

Under our law, every burglary of an inhabited dwelling house is burglary of the first degree. An inhabited dwelling house is a structure where people ordinarily live and which is currently being used for dwelling purposes. It need not be the victim's regular or primary living quarters. The term "inhabited dwelling house" has been given a broad, inclusive construction.

Here, Birgit was assigned a hospital room in which she stayed overnight and in which she was staying at the time of the robbery. That is sufficient to make the room her dwelling house for purposes of first degree burglary. That her stay in the room was less than 24 hours, or that she had a roommate or that her room did not have locks on the inside does not detract from its status as a dwelling house.

Fond contends that the test for first degree burglary is whether a reasonable person would expect some protection from unauthorized intrusions. Fond argues that Birgit had no reasonable expectation of privacy. He points to evidence that the staff and other patients had access to her room.

No doubt Birgit expected the staff to enter her room for purposes related to her treatment. But there is no evidence she expected that the staff could use her room for their own purposes no matter how unrelated to the operation of the hospital. Thus she could reasonably expect to be free from unauthorized intrusions by the staff.

There was also evidence that Birgit had a reasonable expectation to be free from unauthorized intrusions by other patients. Sherri Lewitz, the hospital's director of quality and risk management, testified that patients have an expectation of privacy and it is impermissible for other patients to enter their rooms. If a nurse saw another patient enter a room, the nurse would intervene and direct the patient out of the room. That the nursing staff failed to direct Fond out of Birgit's room does not mean Birgit had no reasonable expectation of privacy.

The burglary of an inhabited dwelling is more serious than other types of burglaries because it violates the victim's need to feel secure from personal attack. People simply need some place where they can let down their guard and where they can sleep without fear for their safety. It is difficult to imagine anyone with a greater need for a feeling of security than a patient in a psychiatric hospital. For such a patient a hospital room may represent a special place for repose.

Affirmed.

ANALOGICAL REASONING WITH DEPTH

EXERCISE 49

Using the cases set out after the problem, determine whether Samuel Waters can successfully claim that he was closely related to the victim, present at the scene of the accident, and aware that the event caused injury to the victim, his son Damon. Do not address whether Waters suffered emotional damages, as that element requires additional expert testimony.

Background Facts

Samuel Waters ("Waters") is a single father raising his three-year-old son, Damon, in Long Beach, California. Waters works as a bookkeeper in a hardware store. As the bookkeeper, Waters manages the store's cash flow and provides the owner and accountant with necessary reports to make the right business decisions. One night a week, Waters has to work late after business hours to reconcile invoices, to raise purchase orders, and to match those purchase orders against invoices that are received from suppliers.

When Waters has to work late, he hires a babysitter from Sitters-R-Us, a well-known and reputable child-care business. Sitters-R-Us prescreens candidates and verifies all references. Waters usually asks for Tatiana to watch Damon. Tatiana has worked for Waters in the past, and he is quite comfortable with her. Plus, Tatiana gets along well with Damon and knows the toddler's evening bedtime routine. She even knows Damon's favorite toys. Damon's favorite stuffed animal is his *Yo Gabba Gabba Brobee* cuddle pillow. He cannot fall asleep without it. Tatiana also does not mind the video monitor that Waters uses to keep an eye on Damon while he is sleeping.

Last month, Waters had a particularly stressful week and had to work three nights in a row to reconcile the store's accounts. Luckily, Tatiana was available to sit for Waters each night. On the last night, Tatiana arrived at Waters's home around 6 p.m. and gave Damon his dinner at 7 p.m. By 8 p.m., she ran Damon a bath. After Damon's bath, Tatiana put Damon's pajamas on him and placed him in his crib. Tatiana then turned on the video monitor so that Waters could view Damon's evening routine and know that he is okay. The Live Web Watch Baby Monitor transmits secure video via the internet directly to Waters's PC. The Live Web Watch Baby Monitor is known for its superior image and audio quality. Waters was able to see his son's first steps with the baby monitor. Damon now runs circles around the house.

After Tatiana read Damon two stories, she turned off the light, turned on the musical mobile, and left the room. She closed the door behind her. Tatiana forgot to place Damon's Brobee pillow in the crib with him. She left it in his toy chest. Although Waters could not see Damon on his PC screen, he could hear him breathing and turning around in the crib over the soft music coming from the mobile above his bed. About an hour after Tatiana turned off the light, Waters heard a series of creaking sounds and several snapping noises like sticks breaking in half. He then heard a loud crash followed by loud cries. Waters stared at this monitor and screamed, "Damon!" He grabbed his car keys and ran out the door.

Tatiana heard the crash too and immediately ran upstairs to Damon's room. She found the baby crying beneath the rubble of the broken crib. The mattress did very little to break his fall or protect him from injury. Tatiana called 911 and waited for the paramedics to arrive. She also called Waters's office but did not reach him. She then called his cell phone and told him what happened. Waters had been trying to reach her at his home since he ran out of the office, but the phone line was busy. Waters arrived home just in time to ride with Damon in the ambulance to the hospital. Damon suffered serious injuries from the fall, but he fully recovered over time.

Waters later learned that Damon's crib, the Cradle of Love model, had been negligently repaired and assembled by an employee at All About Kids, the store from which Waters purchased the crib. At the time of Waters's purchase, the Cradle of Love model was a top seller. The Cradle of Love crib is a wooden crib that can be used when a baby is young and then, in the later years, converted to a twin-size bed by using an optional conversion twin rail kit. The Cradle of Love model does not have a fixed side for added stability like most other cribs on the market. Its design allows for easy movement and placement. Other manufacturers use a static crib side that purportedly makes the crib extra baby-safe.

A few weeks after the purchase, Waters called All About Kids to request some repair work on the crib. The All About Kids employee arrived and disassembled and fixed the crib. He then reassembled the crib and even polished the wood. Waters was quite pleased with his attention to detail and quick work. The All About Kids employee, however, did not properly repair the crib or reassemble it. Notably, he failed to secure key hinges on the crib adequately.

Waters wants to sue All About Kids for negligent infliction of emotional distress, and the company has already indicated that it will vigorously defend against his claim.

In order to establish negligent infliction of emotional distress under California law, the claimant must show that the he was (1) closely related to the victim, (2) present at the scene of the injury-producing event, (3) aware that the event was causing injury to the victim, and (4) as a result, suffered emotional distress. Can Waters satisfy the elements of closely related, presence, and awareness in California? Do not address whether Waters suffered emotional damages, as that element requires additional expert testimony. You may use any part of the following cases.

The cases for this exercise are:

- *Thing v. La Chusa*, 771 P.2d 814 (Cal. 1989)

- *Wilks v. Hom*, 3 Cal. Rptr. 2d 803 (Ct. App. 1992)

- *Scherr v. Hilton Hotels Corp.*, 214 Cal. Rptr. 393 (Ct. App. 1985)

ANALOGICAL REASONING WITH DEPTH
EXERCISE 50

Using the cases for this problem, determine whether Beth Cohen is barred from asserting her defamation claim against Adrian Lucas under either the doctrine of either equitable estoppel or the doctrine of equitable tolling. Do not address promissory estoppel or any other equity doctrines used to prevent a limitations defense.

Background Facts

Beth Cohen ("Cohen") and Adrian Lucas ("Lucas") are co-workers at Automated Systems, Inc. ("ASI") in Albany, NY. Cohen and Lucas often eat lunch together on Fridays and even have attended a few weekend events outside of the office. Cohen enjoys Lucas's company and considers Lucas a good friend and mentor. Cohen started working at ASI only two years ago whereas Lucas has been there for seven years. Cohen learned the ropes about the company from Lucas. She put that information and direction to good use and quickly became a Department Supervisor. She is one of five supervisors at the company and the only female supervisor. Cohen now hires, promotes, and trains all of the staff in the company call center. She supervises no fewer than twenty employees at one time. She hopes to one day become a Regional Manager. Lucas, on the other hand, has no aspirations for management. He worked in the mailroom for a number of years and now works as a clerk in the front office. He enjoys the flexibility his position provides and does not want a job that would require him to work nights or weekends.

According to Cohen, Lucas knows everything about everybody at ASI. Lucas is known as the company "rumor mill" and the go-to person for the "scoop." Lucas knows that some of what he says is pure gossip and unfounded drivel, but he insists that his comments have been confirmed on several occasions. Further, Lucas is right. For example, Lucas predicted the early departure of the company's CEO last fall due to bad health. Further, Lucas knew before anyone else that the company planned to replace its longtime Network Systems Director with one of his high school classmates, Raymond Drummond. In addition, when the company's treasurer divorced his wife and married his secretary six months later, no one in the office was shocked since Lucas had already sent around emails to several employees discussing the treasurer's affair with his secretary. Cohen has received many of Lucas's email messages that comment freely on an employee's inappropriate work attire, or a co-worker's love life, or predict a likely turnover in company structure. She even looked forward to their Friday lunch to hear some of the information firsthand.

Cohen continued to work hard at ASI and received several recognitions for her stellar service to the company. The company awarded her "Supervisor of the Month" on more than one occasion. Then, in February, Cohen overhead some employees in the lounge talking about a supervisor who was having an affair with a call center employee in the supervisor's department. Although Cohen could not

131

understand every word, she did hear the employees mention an email that went around the office and the first name of the call center employee, Reginald. "I have a Reginald in my department. But surely, they can't be talking about me," she chuckled to herself. "And Reggie is half my age. He's just a baby. We went to lunch a few times, but that's it." The employees looked up, saw Cohen, and immediately ended their conversation. They continued eating in silence. Cohen said hello, walked over to the microwave to heat her lunch and then left the lounge.

After months of out-of-town meetings and conferences, Cohen and Lucas finally went to lunch in June. They met at one of their favorite Chinese restaurants. During lunch, Cohen told Lucas about the incident in the lounge area where the employees mentioned an affair between Reginald and his supervisor. She then asked Lucas whether he had heard anything about her. Lucas said no and told her not to worry so much. She explained how much she wanted the company to promote her to Regional Manager by the end of the year and that such a rumor suggesting she had such poor discretion could derail all of her efforts and ruin her professional reputation. The current regional manager told her that he planned to retire in November and that she would be a natural choice for the position. He confided in her that he intended to speak with the Director of Service on her behalf later that month. Lucas smiled and told Cohen she would be an excellent Regional Manager.

Lucas knew he had gone too far this time. He had sent the email about the affair back in February. He had seen Cohen and Reginald go to lunch many times while she continued to cancel their lunch appointments. In a panic, he called his friend, Raymond, who headed the Information Systems Department. Lucas wanted to see if he could remove his sent email from the company's network. Lucas explained the situation with Cohen and said that he did not want Cohen to find out about the emails or the comments he wrote about her. Raymond told Lucas that the company could fire him for tampering with company emails and he refused to help at first. However, after much pleading, Raymond agreed and explained to Lucas that it would take some time. Lucas indicated that he sent only one email to several employees and had not spoken about the affair in any other setting. Raymond assured Lucas that he would work to delete the email from the company's server by the end of the week.

To be safe, Lucas sent an email to his distribution list asking them to delete any messages pertaining to Cohen. He did not reference the affair and only used the first initial of Cohen's first name. While Cohen stood over her secretary helping him correct a letter, his email notification box appeared on his computer screen. Cohen caught a glimpse of the message from Lucas: "Please delete all emails about B sent back in February. Check your inbox and file folders please." Cohen knew that Lucas had gotten himself in trouble again. She shook her head and continued to work.

In late October, Cohen was in a car accident and suffered severe back injuries. The ambulance rushed Cohen to the hospital and the doctors immediately began surgery. She remained in the hospital for two months and then started intensive physical therapy as an outpatient. She stayed at home and friends and neighbors drove her to appointments. Cohen's treating physician did not release her to return to work until several months later. During her recovery, Cohen learned that that the company promoted Howard Nguyen ("Nguyen") to Regional Manager. Despite her hard work, Cohen did not receive the position.

When Cohen returned to the office in February of the following year, she went to Nguyen's office to congratulate him on his new position. She also called to schedule a meeting with the Director of Service. Since she had been gone for a while, Cohen wanted to make sure she had the latest information on the company's system procedures. Cohen met with the Director in early March. The meeting started well. The Director welcomed her back and commended her on meeting all of her goals for the prior year despite being out for several months. She then told Cohen that she had a very promising future with the company and advised her to work harder to stay out of office gossip. Puzzled, Cohen asked, "What office gossip?" The Director mentioned Lucas's email that went around the office last year. She explained, "I usually don't put much stock into what he says, but the appearance of any impropriety by a supervisor can be troublesome. Of course, I didn't receive the email, but I saw a print out on my secretary's desk."

Cohen is furious and plans to sue Lucas for defamation, namely, for the libelous statements he made about her in his email to company employees. Lucas claims that Cohen waited too long and that New York's one-year statute of limitations bars her from filing a defamation claim. According to Lucas, Cohen had until the end of February of this year to file any suit. Cohen concedes that the applicable limitations period is one year, but maintains that either the doctrine of equitable estoppel or the doctrine of tolling suspends the limitations period and prevents Lucas from pleading statute of limitations as a defense.

Please determine whether the facts of her case warrant the tolling or estoppel of the limitation period. Do not address promissory estoppel or any other equity doctrines used to prevent a limitations defense. In addition, do not address whether the facts support a viable defamation claim. Focus on the limitations defense. You may use any part of the cases for this problem.

The cases for this exercise are:

- *Zumpano v. Quinn*, 849 N.E.2d 926 (N.Y. 2006)

- *Gen. Stencils, Inc. v. Chiappa*, 219 N.E.2d 169 (N.Y. 1966)

- *Kotlyarsky v. New York Post*, 757 N.Y.S.2d 703 (App. Div. 2003)

ANALOGICAL REASONING WITH DEPTH

EXERCISE 51

This exercise builds on the facts and concepts in Exercise 40.

You are a new law clerk at a small Houston firm. One day, a senior partner comes into your office, looking flustered and exclaiming, "Look at this! By one day!" You quickly learn that a judge has entered a default judgment against Home Stuff Stores, Inc. ("Home Stuff"). Home Stuff wants to retain your firm in its efforts to have the default judgment set aside.

Apparently, customer Lillian Diller ("Diller") sued Home Stuff for damages suffered when she allegedly slipped and fell in the houseplants section of the store. (Home Stuff's in-store video shows Diller walking to a wet area in the store, looking around, and then lying gently on the floor. After a few seconds, she starts screaming.) Diller's counsel served the lawsuit upon Home Stuff's corporate office in Fort Worth. It is undisputed that service was properly perfected and that manner and mode of service were proper according to the rules. There is no jurisdictional or other defect on the face of the petition. An answer was due in the 295th Civil District Court in Harris County at 10 a.m. on the Monday following the expiration of twenty days following service.

Home Stuff has a large in-house legal department, and legal assistant Deb Howe ("Howe") initially reviewed the lawsuit and determined that it should be handled by Smith & Smith LLP, the firm that handles all of Home Stuff's routine Texas litigation. Howe emailed her supervising attorney for approval to retain counsel—unfortunately, the supervising attorney was on vacation in Africa, and he had lost his Blackberry at the airport. He did not otherwise receive the message.

Five days later, Howe called June Smith ("Smith"), a partner at Smith & Smith, to advise her that the lawsuit would be faxed over as soon as Howe received approval. Then Howe left town for a legal assistants' conference in Florida. Smith was in the middle of a trial in Arizona, but she left a message for a junior associate asking him to watch out for the lawsuit, which she referred to as "yet another Home Stuff slip-and-fall." The junior associate was busy with other matters too, but he made a mental note to watch for the lawsuit. Two days later, the junior associate left the firm suddenly and joined another firm. In the meantime, Smith had won her trial, and she returned to the office. She had completely forgotten about the Home Stuff lawsuit.

On the Friday before the answer was due, the supervising attorney at Home Stuff returned from his safari and emailed his approval to Howe. Still jetlagged, he reviewed the lawsuit and placed the documents in Howe's chair without looking at the answer date. Howe was home sick from work on Monday and Tuesday. On Tuesday morning, Robert Holder ("Holder"), a solo practitioner representing Diller, telephoned Home Stuff's general counsel and left two messages stating that Home Stuff should file an answer or risk default. The general counsel was attending a board meeting, but when she received the messages, she immediately telephoned outside counsel to find out the answer's status. Later that day, Holder appeared in court and moved for a default judgment. Just before the close of business on Tuesday, a messenger arrived at the courthouse with Home Stuff's general denial.

Unfortunately for Home Stuff, the judge had already reviewed the motion for default and granted a default judgment at noon that day. The hearing on damages is set for two weeks from now. (Another lawyer in your firm is handling research related to the damages hearing, so you need not address that issue.)

Today, five days after the default judgment was entered, Home Stuff's general counsel wants your firm to advise her as to whether a motion for new trial is likely to be successful. To be successful, your motion must show that (1) the failure to file an answer was due to accident or mistake rather than conscious indifference, (2) the defendant can set up meritorious defense in the lawsuit, and (3) the plaintiff will not suffer delay or other injury if the motion is granted. Please analyze just the first element, explaining whether you think Home Stuff can succeed in showing that its failure to answer was due to mistake or accident, rather than conscious indifference.

Please use the following cases to answer the question:

- *Young v. Kirsch*, 814 S.W.2d 77 (Tex. App. (Tex. App. 1991)

- *State Farm Life Ins. Co. v. Mosharaf*, 794 S.W.2d 578 (Tex. App. 1990)

- *Southland Paint Co. v. Thousand Oaks Racket Club*, 724 S.W.2d 809 (Tex. App. 1986)

ANALOGICAL REASONING WITH DEPTH
EXERCISE 52

Using the cases for this exercise, determine whether the "force majeure" provision included in the contract between Natural One Corporation, the buyer, and GasPro, Inc., a processing plant and the seller, excused the plant's performance under the contract.

Background Facts

Natural One Corporation ("Natural One"), a Fortune 500 company based in Kansas, is one of the largest natural-gas distributors in the United States. Natural One connects natural-gas-liquids supply with key market centers and customers in Kansas, Oklahoma, Texas, New Mexico, and Arizona. The company's customers include local distribution companies, industrial customers like petroleum companies, and power generators.

Natural One purchases natural-gas byproducts such as natural-gas liquids ("NGLs") from local processing plants. GasPro, Inc. ("GasPro"), a processing plant headquartered in Topeka, Kansas, owns the nation's most sophisticated NGLs systems, employing innovative "green" technology. GasPro purchases raw natural gas produced from underground gas fields or surface oil wells, purifies the raw natural gas, and removes byproducts such as NGLs, natural-gas condensate, sulfur, and ethane. These byproducts are sold to companies like Natural One for distribution.

Although GasPro is not a publicly traded company, the business is well known for its focus on community and small businesses. Recently, GasPro received the "Monumental Stars Award" from the Kansas Department of Commerce for its support of family-owned businesses. The award included a cash prize of $10,000 donated by Natural One. Natural One placed an announcement about GasPro's award in the Topeka Business Journal. The announcement detailed GasPro's commitment to Topeka's small business community and attached a picture of GasPro's executives receiving the award from executives at Natural One. The Yearling family, who owns the main gas well that supplies GasPro with raw natural gas, also stood in the picture.

Natural One and GasPro have worked together on several ventures using natural gas and byproducts. Each arrangement and the companies' related obligations are included in detailed performance and purchase contracts. Last year, in January, GasPro (the seller) contracted with Natural One (the buyer) to supply Natural One with NGLs at a discounted market rate. Natural One agreed to take, purchase, and pay for the NGLs delivered to the company each month, and in turn, GasPro had a guaranteed buyer for its natural-gas byproduct. Specifically, the contract required Natural One to take a minimum volume of natural gas each month or pay for the gas as if taken. In turn, the contract stated that GasPro would deliver a certain targeted amount of NGLs to Natural One each month. If GasPro did not supply at least ninety percent of that monthly-targeted amount, then GasPro would have to pay Natural One the difference to reach ninety percent of the target.

The contract also included a "force majeure" provision that excused performance for events beyond the seller's control. In particular, the force majeure clause stated the following:

> Except for Buyer's obligation to make payment due for gas or NGLs delivered hereunder, neither party shall be liable for failure to perform this agreement when such failure is due to "force majeure." "Force majeure" shall mean acts of God, fires, floods, acts of the public enemy, wars, riots, epidemics, strikes, lockouts, industrial disputes, civil disturbances, interruptions by government or court orders, present and future valid order of any regulatory body having proper jurisdiction, inability to obtain easements, right-of-way or other interests in realty, or any other cause beyond Seller's control.

Greg Lombardi ("Lombardi"), Natural One's chief executive officer, met Ramon Flores ("Flores"), GasPro's senior processing engineer, at GasPro to sign the contract. The lawyers for both companies attended the meeting. While signing the contract, Flores mentioned to Lombardi that he needed to get Martha Yearling ("Yearling"), whose family owned the gas well, on the phone to tell her to start production. Lombardi met the Yearling family at the awards program but had already known of them given that few family-owned wells still existed in Kansas. Flores commented that he wanted to get started as soon as possible on working toward the monthly target. Lombardi and Flores then shook hands, solidifying another profitable venture between the companies.

After Lombardi left, Flores called Yearling and notified her of the new contract with Natural One. The Yearlings had worked with GasPro on most of their contracts with Natural One, and the family was familiar with the expectations. Flores explained the specific minimum delivery requirements, and the parties discussed the amount of raw natural gas that the Yearlings would need to supply to GasPro for GasPro to meet its contractual obligation to Natural One. GasPro agreed to pay the Yearlings a competitive rate for their gas supply and sent a team to the Yearlings' property to inspect the well and ensure its readiness and capabilities.

In the beginning, the Yearlings' well produced a steady supply of approximately 10,000 barrels of raw natural gas per day, and the family provided GasPro with sufficient gas to process for byproducts. For the first two months under the new contract, GasPro delivered enough NGLs to Natural One to exceed the monthly-targeted amount. Natural One paid GasPro for each delivery in a timely manner.

Then, in March, production from the Yearlings' well declined from 10,000 barrels to 5,000 barrels per day. The Yearlings continued to extract gas from their well but could not meet GasPro's supply needs. Martha Yearling called Flores and explained, "This was bound to happen one day. Our well has run dry. We have exploration projects underway but may not locate a viable site this year." That month, GasPro supplied Natural One with only thirty percent of the targeted amount, well below the agreed upon ninety percent.

As provided in the contract, Natural One requested that GasPro pay the difference to reach ninety percent. GasPro refused, maintaining that its performance under the contract was excused by the "force majeure" clause. Further, GasPro emphasized that it would have to contact other companies and purchase raw natural gas at a higher rate to supply Natural One with the required amount, thereby reducing the company's profit margin on its arrangement with Natural One. Natural One insists that GasPro's failure to perform constitutes breach of their agreement.

Please determine whether the "force majeure" provision excuses GasPro's non-performance under the contract. Provide the arguments for GasPro, the supplier, and those for Natural One, the buyer. You may use any of the listed cases for this exercise.

Use the following cases for this exercise:

- *Hutton Contracting Co. v. City of Coffeyville*, 487 F.3d 772 (10th Cir. 2007)

- *City of Topeka v. Indus. Gas Co.*, 11 P.2d 1034 (Kan. 1932)

- *Benson Mineral Grp. Inc. v. N. Natural Gas Co.*, No. 86-1903, 1988 U.S. Dist. LEXIS 17581 (D. Kan. Apr. 28, 1988)

ANALOGICAL REASONING WITH DEPTH

EXERCISE 53

Using the cases set out after the problem, determine whether Ready Realty, LLC deprived Marisol Martinez, the owner of Vegan Yoga Sanctuary, of the covenant of quiet enjoyment and constructively evicted her from the premises she leased from the company.

Background Facts

Marisol Martinez ("Martinez") is the owner of the Vegan Yoga Sanctuary in Palestine, Illinois. As is explained below, she moved out of her original yoga studio in October and recently found a new studio. Martinez offers special yoga instruction that incorporates nutritional classes and training focusing on a vegan or meatless diet. She advocates for a holistic approach in wellness and works to help her clients improve their physical, emotional, and spiritual health. She holds group yoga classes throughout the week and schedules individual training sessions. She even provides shopping excursions to grocery stores and arranges group-dining trips to local vegan restaurants. When Martinez first leased space for her business from Ready Realty, LLC ("Ready"), she renovated her studio space at her own expense. She worked hard to create a peaceful and tranquil environment in her studio. She wanted her clients to think of her sanctuary as a retreat from everyday life.

The busiest day for yoga classes was Saturday morning. About eight people attended the 8 a.m. and 10 a.m. classes on Saturday. The other classes during the week averaged about three to five students. Some classes did not have any participants, especially during the harsh winter months. During those times, Martinez worked on administrative matters, strategized about new marketing efforts, and designed new yoga routines. She also started to build out a room in the back of her shop for massage therapy and aromatherapy. The room had a massage bed, candles, and several holes in the walls for sound-system installation. Martinez remained hopeful that her unique concept of combining vegan nutrition with yoga fitness would grow in popularity soon.

The Vegan Yoga Sanctuary was located in a small strip center with four other businesses. Martinez signed a three-year lease with Ready one year ago. Section 16 of Martinez's lease with Ready provided the following:

> Section 16. *Quiet Enjoyment.* Tenant, upon paying rent and performing all the other covenants and conditions aforesaid on Tenant's part to be observed and performed under this Lease, shall and may peaceably and quietly have, hold, and enjoy the Demised Premises . . . free from disturbance by Landlord or anyone claiming by, through or under Landlord. . . .

Martinez's business was located at one end of the center. When she moved in, there was a small empty storage area next to her business and a large business space next to this storage space. The larger business space, the largest in the center, which holds a maximum of 150 people at one time, also was empty. Next to the vacant suite, there was a tax preparation business, and a Goodwill Donation Center was at the opposite end of the center from Martinez's business. Parking for the center is limited, with only a dozen parking spaces.

New Business

In February this year, Thomas Duong ("Duong"), a leasing agent for Ready, informed Martinez he planned to locate another dance studio in the business space next to Martinez's. He explained that the small empty storage space would sit between the Vegan Yoga Sanctuary and the new business. Duong described the new business as a country line-dancing studio and mentioned the studio owner would be required to do soundproofing. He handed Martinez one of the business's brochures that highlighted both group and individual classes and promised food, fun, and exercise all in time for the local rodeo events. The business name, JJ's Country Time ("Country Time"), appeared in bold on the front of the brochure.

Country Time opened on March 1. Martinez immediately began objecting to Duong that the music coming from the line-dancing business was too loud and could be heard in her studio. She also complained in person to JJ Woodrow ("Woodrow"), the owner of Country Time. In response, Duong directed Woodrow to install insulation as required by the terms of his lease. Country Time promptly installed the insulation, but Martinez continued to complain that the noise from the studio was disrupting her business. She left several messages with Duong. In one message, she exclaimed, "How can we focus on these complicated yoga moves and maintain serenity when all we hear are stomping hooves coming from next door? And it's not just the loud music. It's the dancing. I swear it's as if the walls are coming down around us!"

Duong then agreed to pump insulation into the wall space between Country Time and the vacant storage space between the two businesses. Ready completed this insulation at the end of March. After this was done, Duong told Martinez he and Ready considered the matter closed. Thereafter, Martinez lodged a few additional complaints about the noise with other leasing agents at Ready. Her last official complaint about the noise was in April. No other businesses in the center filed any noise complaints—not even the tax preparation business located directly adjacent to Country Time.

As word spread about the new line-dancing studio, the classes began to fill up with eager first timers. The best-attended class was on Thursdays at 7 p.m. To capitalize on the crowd, in mid April, Country Time started *Thursday's Thriller Bar-B-Que Dinner*. The studio not only provided nonstop line-dancing instruction but also served hearty barbeque dinners with sausage links, potato salad, and all the fixings. Approximately forty people attended the Thursday evening class each week. The other classes averaged fifteen to twenty participants. Many retired people attended more than one class weekly. Country Time offered a special monthly rate with unlimited class visits for seniors.

As the business grew, so did the crowds coming to the center. Typically, Country Time's customers used all of the parking spaces in the front of the center. As a result, many of Martinez's clients had to park in a nearby neighborhood. Also, her clients sometimes arrived late for classes or consultations because they could not find nearby parking.

In May, Martinez called Duong to complain about the lack of parking for her clients. The other businesses had filed similar complaints. That week, Duong decided to allocate three spaces for each business. He installed "Reserved" signs and a warning with a number to call in case a vehicle was towed. He sent a letter about the new parking policy to each business in the center and included a number for a local towing company. Martinez received three reserved spaces directly in front of her studio for her business. Despite the signs, Country Time's customers continued to park in the wrong spaces.

In late May, Duong visited Martinez's studio. She was finishing a yoga class for beginners. Two students were in the class. Once the class ended, Martinez asked Duong to walk with her to the back room. She turned to Duong and said, "I had hoped to use this room for massages and aromatherapy, but it's ruined now." "What do you mean? Why?" Duong asked. "Don't you smell that? A horrible meat smell is infiltrating this back room and my studio. It's really bad on Thursday nights. My clients refuse to come back here. Most of them are vegan. Or they are starting the transition to a meatless diet. The smell of meat makes them ill," Martinez explained. Duong told Martinez he understood her concerns but he really did not smell anything offensive.

Duong knew about Country Time's barbeque dinner and class, and he had even attended a couple of events. Country Time's lease did not prohibit such dinners or installing a commercial size oven. Country Time had a full-size oven in the back of the studio and the owner cooked most of the meals there. After his discussion with Martinez, Duong spoke with Woodrow and asked him to help prevent smells in Martinez's massage room by opening the back window when he cooked meals. Woodrow agreed. When Martinez followed up with Duong about the smell, Duong told her he had spoken with Woodrow and even put in a request to have Ready personnel check the distribution ductwork and piping through which the smell might be traveling.

Several months passed. Country Time's business continued to thrive. The local newspaper featured the new sensation of country line-dancing in a front-page article with a colored photo of a class in session. Martinez's business did not fare as well. She experienced a steady decline in clientele.

Martinez did not pay rent in September, and in October she abandoned her studio in the strip center without notifying Ready. A few weeks later, she called Duong and told him she found a new space that better suited her needs and gave her peace of mind. Duong informed Martinez that she owed rent for September and the remaining rent due under her three-year lease. Martinez refused to pay.

According to Martinez, when she closed her studio and vacated the premises in October, Ready already had constructively evicted her from the premises by allowing Country Time to operate in the center. Martinez then notified Duong that she planned to sue Ready for the disturbing noise, bad odor, and lack of parking for her clients and intended to recover her lost profits, moving costs, and the difference in rent.

Ready has already indicated that it will vigorously defend against Martinez's suit and will counterclaim for past due rent and future rent owned under her lease. Can Martinez successfully sue Ready for breach of contract based on the theories of constructive eviction and breach of the covenant of quiet enjoyment?

The following cases are for this exercise:

- *St. Louis N. Joint Venture v. P & L Enters., Inc.*, 116 F.3d 262 (7th Cir. 1997)

- *Metro. Life Ins. Co. v. Nauss*, 590 N.E.2d 524 (Ill. App. Ct. 1992)

- *Applegate v. Inland Real Estate Corp.*, 441 N.E.2d 379 (Ill. App. Ct. 1982)

PART 3

SKILLED ANALOGICAL EXERCISES

ANALOGICAL REASONING WITH DEPTH

EXERCISE 54

Using the cases set out after the problem, determine whether Marisol Martinez vacated the leased premises in a reasonable amount of time as required for her claim of constructive eviction.

Background Facts

This scenario stems from Marisol Martinez's ("Martinez") claim of constructive eviction from the business space that she leased from Ready Realty LLC ("Ready"), which is discussed in Exercise 53.

Martinez is the owner of the Vegan Yoga Sanctuary in Palestine, Illinois. The Vegan Yoga Sanctuary was located in a small strip center with four other business spaces. Through her business, Martinez offers special yoga instruction that incorporates nutritional classes and training focusing on a vegan or meatless diet. She advocates for a holistic approach in wellness and works to improve her client's physical, emotional, and spiritual health. She holds group yoga classes throughout the week and schedules individual training sessions. She even provides shopping excursions to grocery stores and arranges group-dining trips to local vegan restaurants. Martinez renovated the studio space at her own expense. She also started to build out a room in the back of her shop for massage therapy and aromatherapy. The room had a massage bed, candles, and several holes in the walls for sound system installation. Martinez worked hard to create a peaceful and tranquil environment in her studio. She wanted her clients to think of her sanctuary as a retreat from everyday life. Martinez remained hopeful that her unique concept of combining vegan nutrition with yoga fitness soon would grow in popularity.

Martinez raised concerns about loud noise coming from another tenant, Country Time, in April. Then in May, she complained to Thomas Duong ("Duong"), Ready's leasing agent, about the lack of parking for her clients in front of the center and the awful smell of meat permeating her back room and studio space. After these complaints in May, several months passed without Martinez again communicating with Ready. Country Time's business continued to thrive. The local community newspaper featured the new sensation of country line-dancing in a front-page article with a colored photo of a class in session. Martinez's business did not fare as well. She experienced a steady decline in clientele.

Martinez started to look for a new location during the summer. She hoped to find some specials on leasing agreements such as one month free or a waiver of security deposit. Oftentimes, leasing agents offer special summer deals for new clients. She needed to find a business space that she could afford. The decline in her business left her with very little savings to start over.

Martinez read countless advertisements in the local business journal and newspaper and found many available suites, but most of them were located inside a large office building. These locations would not help in her marketing efforts. She wanted a storefront office space that could be seen easily by passersby. She knew her business provided unique services, uncommon to most local residents, and she wanted the opportunity to draw unfamiliar community members to her new business. She also needed adequate space for her yoga sessions and a separate room for massage and aromatherapy services. The yoga space under her current lease was rather large with wood floors and mirrors on the walls. She spent her own money to add more mirrors and incorporate a Zen theme throughout the space. She also planned to finish the sound system. In addition, one day soon she hoped to install a full bathroom with two standing showers and a changing room and paid special attention to those listings that provided additional square footage for room to build.

Martinez had learned from the experience with Ready and did not want to sign a new lease in a center that had a nearby restaurant or dance studio. Ideally, she wanted to be located near other businesses that provided services that worked well with her business plan. For example, Martinez believed that she could get more business from residents using a nail spa or eating at a vegan or vegetarian restaurant in the same center. Martinez called about a few listings and visited approximately two locations each month. One of those locations included a Bikram Hot Yoga Studio that would directly compete with her business model. She saw the studio and immediately decided to cancel her tour of the property.

Martinez did not pay rent in September and, in October, she abandoned her studio in the strip center without notifying Ready. A few weeks later, she called Duong and told him she found a new space that better suited her needs and gave her peace of mind. Duong informed Martinez that she owned rent for the month of September and the remaining rent due under her four-year lease. Martinez refused to pay.

According to Martinez, when she closed her studio and vacated the premises in October, Ready already had constructively evicted her from the premises by allowing Country Time to operate in the center. Martinez then notified Duong that she planned to sue Ready to recover her lost profits, moving costs, and the difference in rent due to the disturbing noise, bad odor, and lack of parking for her clients.

Ready has already indicated that it will vigorously defend against Martinez's suit and will counterclaim for past due rent and future rent owned under her lease. Ready also maintains that Martinez waived any claim for constructive eviction given that she waited several months to vacate the leased premises. Did Martinez abandon the leased premises within a reasonable amount of time?

The cases for this exercise are:

- *Auto. Supply Co. v. Scene-in-Action Corp.*, 172 N.E. 35 (Ill. 1930)

- *Shaker & Assocs., Inc. v. Med. Techs. Grp. Ltd.*, 733 N.E.2d 865 (Ill. App. Ct. 2000)

- *Dell'Armi Builders, Inc. v. Johnston*, 526 N.E.2d 409 (Ill. App. Ct. 1988)

ANALOGICAL REASONING WITH DEPTH

EXERCISE 55

Using the cases for this exercise, determine whether the evidence is sufficient to convict Lynette Wilson ("Wilson") of robbery. In particular, address whether Wilson completed a taking of the store's property by violence or intimidation and, therefore, committed robbery.

Background Facts

Freda's Fine Things is a boutique store in Fredericksburg, Virginia. One Saturday afternoon, Wilson walked into the store and headed straight to the back toward the clearance section. She took her time perusing the racks of clothes. She pulled a couple of items from the racks and went to the dressing room to try them on. While she was in the dressing room, an attendant asked Wilson if she needed any other sizes. Wilson said no and explained to the attendant that the colors simply did not work for her. The attendant then asked Wilson to leave any items that she did not want to purchase in the dressing room. Wilson replied, "Okay." A few minutes later, Wilson left the dressing room and went back to the store floor. She left the clothes in the dressing room.

Wilson spent about ten minutes in the section for women's shoes and then spotted the cosmetic area. "They may have what I need," she thought to herself. Wilson walked over to the counter. She was surprised to see such an extensive selection of perfumes. The salesperson was busy helping another customer on the opposite side of the counter. The salesperson had her back to Wilson and could not see her. Wilson stood in front of the tester bottles and started looking for bottles that were at least half full. "Man, some of these perfumes cost about seventy dollars. I can sell most of these and keep the really nice ones for myself," Wilson mumbled. Wilson quickly looked around and did not see any salespeople or guards in the area. She then selected the best bottles and discreetly placed them in her bag. "This is a great find," Wilson whispered. "I cannot believe they have a tester of Chanel No. 5 out in the open. It's at least two hundred dollars." Wilson tried to make sure she looked up periodically to avoid drawing too much attention. Wilson realized that she could not hold too many bottles in her bag and planned to stop when she had ten bottles.

While Wilson was focusing on her bag, a customer, Sunny Charles ("Charles") approached the cosmetic counter, saw Wilson, and instantly got a puzzled look on her face. "Hey, what are you doing? Aren't those the tester bottles?" Charles asked Wilson. Wilson ignored her. Charles then asked, "Can I at least try on the *Play* by *Givenchy*? It's the one in the purple bottle, right there in front. I really don't want any trouble. I just need to buy a gift for my sister, and I'm running late." Again, Wilson ignored Charles and continued to select perfumes and load them in her bag. Seconds later, Wilson quickly placed the tenth bottle in her bag. Charles then called to the salesperson who asked her to be patient while she finished with a customer. Frustrated, Charles stormed off to find a security guard.

While Wilson stood at the counter, the store's undercover security guard, Amare Sitota ("Sitota") watched Wilson as she placed the perfume bottles in her bag. Sitota was dressed in plain clothes. He stood behind a column in the women's shoes department so that Wilson could not see him. Sitota saw the customer speak to Wilson and watched Wilson place the final bottle of perfume in her bag. Wilson immediately turned to leave the store. She took a few steps, and Sitota ran to stop her. He leaped in Wilson's path and shouted, "Where do you think you are going? Hand over the bag and the perfume." Wilson took a running start and slammed Sitota to the ground. She jumped over him and ran out the door. Because she had been discovered, Wilson threw her bag into the garbage can as she ran out the door.

The authorities apprehended Wilson and charged her with robbery of the store's perfume. The Commonwealth of Virginia plans to take the robbery case to trial, but Wilson's attorney, Jonathan Cho ("Cho"), insists there is insufficient evidence to support a robbery conviction. Cho offered to discuss a plea for the lesser-included offense of larceny. The Commonwealth wants to know whether it can successfully try Wilson for robbery. Please examine the robbery elements (namely, taking the property of another by violence or intimidation) in light of the cases below and provide the arguments for the Commonwealth and Wilson.

The cases for this exercise are:

- *Green v. Commonwealth*, 112 S.E. 562 (Va. 1922)

- *Mason v. Commonwealth*, 105 S.E.2d 149 (Va. 1958)

- *Beard v. Commonwealth*, 451 S.E.2d 698 (Va. Ct. App. 1994)

ANALOGICAL REASONING WITH DEPTH

EXERCISE 56

Using the cases set out after the problem, determine whether Brian and Anita Cooper can successfully claim that they adversely possessed a strip of land within the property of their neighbor, Ladelle Standish.

Background Facts

Brian and Anita Cooper live in a small home located on two acres of land in Islesboro, Maine, population 603. Islesboro is an island located three miles to the west of Lincolnville Beach, Maine. Islesboro was originally a fishing colony, where families settled to fish for lobster, crab, and various species of fish. Over the years, however, it has become known less for fishing and more for the celebrities and investment bankers who own vacation homes on the island. Islesboro counts John Travolta and Kirstie Allie among its more famous part-time residents.

Brian and Anita Cooper are lifelong Islesboro residents of modest means. Brian is a lobster fisherman and Anita helps with fishing tasks and works in a small café on the island. The Coopers' property on Islesboro has been in the family since 1880. The Coopers' home is located on two acres of beautiful beachfront property. The couple has fished for lobsters in the waters off the property for their entire lives, as their grandparents did before them. Around 1984, however, the lobster catch became inconsistent, and the Coopers' income declined.

The Coopers' property is adjacent to a three-acre property owned by film actress and singer Ladelle Standish ("Standish"). She purchased the property in 1983 after commanding her first $5 million fee for a film role. Standish spends most of the year in Los Angeles, California, but she stays at her Islesboro property for a total of about eight weeks per year—four weeks in the summer and four weeks over the Thanksgiving holiday. The Standish property consists of water-front land, with a white, four-bedroom wooden house. The land around the house is mowed, with flowerbeds and decorative statues, but the acre closer to the beach is kept wild. Standish enjoys walking down to the beach to watch the sunset reflected in the water and observe the many species of birds that are drawn to the wild, grassy terrain.

Despite the differences in wealth and lifestyle between the island's longtime and new residents, relations between the two groups are generally good. Some year-round residents complain about the loud parties that some celebrities throw, but most of the celebrities go out of their way to ease any tensions between themselves and the year-round residents. When a new celebrity arrives on the island, others quickly explain that most celebrity residents permit the longtime residents to use the celebrities' land for recreational or other occasional purposes when the celebrities are not in residence. Under this arrangement, year-round residents have benefitted from additional space in which to picnic, play, and even graze their livestock.

148

In 1985, after a particularly lean lobster season, the Coopers' main fishing boat developed serious engine problems. The Coopers had to borrow $5,000 to replace the boat, more than they earned for the entire season of lobster fishing. The couple was at serious risk of foreclosure on their property. "Can't we somehow make more money off this land?" Anita wondered aloud, looking around at the mansions that were so close to the Coopers' land. Just at that moment, Anita's eyes landed on the back cover of a Maine tourist brochure. The brochure showed a photograph of a beautiful bride, posing next to a wicker altar. "Ready to tie the knot? Share your love at our beautiful Maine chapel. Make your wedding dream come true!"

"Yes! This is it!" Anita exclaimed, and she set about researching the wedding industry. In 1986, the Coopers finalized their plan to earn extra money from their property's desirable location by hosting destination weddings. They incorporated "Barefoot Beach Weddings" and created a portable shell-covered arch for the ceremonies themselves. The only problem was that near the beach, the Coopers' property was rather rocky. When the first wedding took place in June of 1987, the bride requested that all wedding party members wear white clothes and shell crowns. She also requested that they walk barefoot down the rocky aisle. The wedding ceremony did not go well, with the bride cutting her foot twice on rocks and the ring bearer tripping and bursting into tears. "Nasty, nasty rocks!" he wailed, as members of the wedding party searched for smooth rocks to stand upon through the lengthy ceremony's painful conclusion. "This was supposed to be a *barefoot* wedding," hissed the bride at Anita afterwards. "I need a 20 percent refund." Anita and Brian complied.

After that debacle, the Coopers tried to work out a solution that would keep the weddings barefoot and natural, but also safe and pleasant. They looked around their property for a better place to hold the weddings. Seeing no rock-free area on their own property that was large enough, they looked at Standish's adjacent land. That land was kept unmowed and wild near the beach, but was grassy rather than rocky. It had beautiful spruce trees and a decorative rock birdbath. If mowed, it would be perfect for beachside weddings. "Look, she's never even here," said Anita to Brian. "We're the real residents of this island." With that, the two decided to hold the ceremonies on an area inside Standish's land.

The Coopers mowed a one hundred by thirty-foot area, which was entirely inside the Standish property. The Coopers stopped mowing at a picturesque, bubbling stream that ran across the Standish property, down to the beach. Also, next to the stream—still on the Standish property—was a slight rise in the terrain, which became the new altar area. They moved the shell-encrusted shelter over to the Standish property and started a new marketing campaign in national bridal magazines, with photographs of the grassy property and bubbling stream.

The weddings on the new, rock-free ground started in earnest in September of 1987, and the Maine destination wedding concept was a great success. For the first two years, a wedding would take place about once every three to four weeks during the summer, with music, dancing, and sometimes hundreds of guests. The venue's most popular feature was the bubbling stream. It became known as the "Stream of Good Fortune," and couples from all over the country came to hold their weddings at this location and drink from the lucky stream. After business took off in the third year, there were weddings almost every week in May, June, and July, and the property was constantly abuzz with vendors and visiting couples. In the winter months, from November to February, very few weddings took place due to the harsh Maine weather.

The Coopers took care of all the Standish property they used. They trimmed the trees of dangerous branches and picked up any debris after storms. During the summer months, they mowed the strip of property, and they placed bright white ant-killing powder on the grass. When neighborhood children would try to play on the area surrounding the shell-encrusted shelter, the Coopers would ask them to leave.

One special feature of the Coopers' weddings was the availability of tame deer for wedding photographs. The Coopers kept four tame, collared Maine deer on their property, and they allowed the deer to graze freely through the Standish property as well. The deer in fact preferred the Standish property, because it was grassy rather than rocky.

In 1993, however, the wedding business slowed down as other destination wedding locations opened up. "All my friends prefer the Riviera Maya," said one bride-to-be. "Maine just isn't cool any more." From 1993 to 1998, the weddings slowed to one every eight weeks or so. In 1999, there was just one wedding all year. The ant killing powder faded and grass grew up over the altar area. Anita and Brian became frustrated with the situation and started bickering with one another. "If you spent more time on marketing our business than on buying Army surplus equipment on Ebay, maybe we wouldn't be in this mess," said Anita to Brian. "Wait a minute, maybe we can put that equipment to use," Brian responded.

Inspired by Brian's hobby, the two decided to open "Army Time" paintball game company. Clients were invited to join a team of three to five combatants, who then stalked each other in the woods on the Cooper property and on the Standish land, including the strip that used to be the wedding aisle and altar area. In keeping with the Army theme, the teams wore actual camouflage military surplus clothing and used converted M-16 rifles to shoot paint at one another. The Coopers erected an Army surplus tent on the Standish property, for use as part of the game. Each session of paintball cost $50, which limited the clientele to the affluent celebrity families on the island.

When the paintball business first opened in the spring of 2000, youths and adults from all over the island came to play. The summer of 2000 was busy, with paintball teams forming once a week. In the summer of 2001, business dropped off, with teams meeting about once a month. All of 2002 passed with just one paintball weekend camp. Brian and Anita found that once people had played once or twice, they rarely returned. Despite incentive plans and an aggressive marketing campaign in the island newsletter, they were unable to retain customers. In addition, the town council complained about the environmental impact—the red paint that occasionally splattered on the trees in the gaming area was unsightly and difficult to remove. And when one of the Coopers' tame deer was struck by paint while walking on the Standish property, Anita knew the business could not continue. "This deer is pink! This isn't right!" she cried while trying to scrub the paint off the deer's coat and collar. When a paint shot narrowly missed a Bald Eagle a few days later, the Coopers decided to return to the wedding business.

In 2003, the Coopers restarted the wedding business with a new marketing angle. They remodeled their house so that guests could stay there for a special group rate, and once again, business picked up. Business remained strong from the summer of 2003 to 2010, with eight to ten weddings each year, mostly in the spring and summer months.

One day in June of 2010, Standish was taking a rare weekend away from her busy film schedule to relax at her Maine property. She and her cousin, Linda Graves ("Graves"), walked around the property to look for birds, while they breathed the fresh, seaside air and talked about the character Standish was playing in her latest film. Standish saw a white shape at the end of her property. She took out her birding binoculars. "What on earth?" Standish said to Graves. "There is a bride over there, and she's drinking from my stream!" Graves exclaimed, "Wow, that is strange. I hope she doesn't get sick." Standish and Graves returned to the house and called the Coopers to find out what was going on. Standish quickly learned about the wedding business. "You can't have a wedding business on my land, using my stream!" said Standish. "Well, you never wanted that land," said Anita. "You're never even here. Besides, my nephew is a law student, and he says it's ours now, anyway. See you in court."

Standish wants to sue for trespass, and the Coopers have already said that they will defend by asserting a claim of adverse possession.

To establish adverse possession under the common law of Maine, the claimant must show that the possession was (1) actual, (2) open, (3) visible, (4) notorious, (5) hostile, (6) under a claim of right, (7) continuous, and (8) exclusive, all for a period of twenty years. Standish concedes that the Coopers' use was exclusive. Can the Coopers satisfy the remaining elements of common law adverse possession in Maine? You many use any part of the cases that follow.

- *Solomon's Rock Trust v. Davis*, 675 A.2d 506 (Me. 1996).

- *Striefel v. Charles-Keyt-Leaman P'ship*, 733 A.2d 984 (Me. 1999).

- *Webber v. Barker Lumber Co.*, 116 A. 586 (Me. 1922).

- *Clewley v. McTigue Farms, Inc.*, 389 A.2d 849 (Me. 1978).

- *Falvo v. Pejepscot Indus. Park, Inc.*, 691 A.2d 1240 (Me. 1997).

- *McMullen v. Dowley*, 418 A.2d 1147 (Me. 1980).

- *Weeks v. Krysa*, 955 A.2d 234 (Me. 2008).

ANALOGICAL REASONING WITH DEPTH

EXERCISE 57

Using the cases for this problem, determine whether Oscar Rogers and Margaret Frost satisfy the requirements for a common-law marriage under Kansas law. Address each of the elements for common-law marriage. However, with respect to the first element, you should address only age capacity (i.e. whether the parties were of the legal age to marry). Do not address mental capacity. The parties agree that no disputed facts challenge their mental capacity to marry under common law.

Background Facts

Year 1: They Meet

On January 1, Oscar Rogers and Margaret Frost met at a New Year's Eve party. Oscar, born on October 15, was 18 years old, and Margaret, born on February 26, was 19 years old. Oscar and Margaret had a great time at the party and talked the entire evening. They started dating immediately. Margaret really loved that Oscar was so romantic and a bit old-fashioned. Everyone told them they were too young to be in love, but they felt their relationship was very real—a modern day Romeo and Juliet. Oscar and Margaret spent most of their time together. Although Oscar had his own apartment in Northwest Topeka, he frequently stayed with Margaret at her apartment on Bassoon Street.

Year 2: Child and New Lease

More than one and a half years after they started dating, on December 6, the couple became proud parents of a baby boy, Oscar Gideon Rogers. Both Oscar and Margaret call him "Gideon." With a new child, Oscar and Margaret really needed more living space, so Margaret started to search nearby neighborhoods for the perfect home. Luckily, Margaret's favorite part of town, Highland Park, had a rental home available. Highland Park is one of Topeka's most famous historical neighborhoods. The neighborhood and its residents value family, community, and small businesses. Margaret worried whether they could find a rental home in their price range, but she eventually located a small guesthouse for rent.

Margaret parked her car and knocked on the door of the main house to inquire about the rental. The property owner, Mrs. Jordan Taylor, invited her in for tea. During the conversation, Mrs. Taylor openly expressed her reservations about an unmarried man and woman living together. She also explained the historical significance of the guesthouse and its many features. After she told Margaret the rental price, Margaret indicated the price was within their budget. Mrs. Taylor asked Margaret to bring her family over the next day.

The following day, Margaret, Oscar, and Gideon visited with Mrs. Taylor. Mrs. Taylor made sure to ask Margaret and Oscar whether they were married, and they both nodded in agreement. Both Oscar and Margaret signed the lease, Margaret signing as Margaret Frost Rogers.

Year 3: Move into New Home

Although they signed the lease in December, Margaret and Oscar did not move into their new home until January the following year. Oscar kept referring to the move as their "anniversary move" because they had met two years before in January. One evening, soon after they moved into their new home, Oscar and Margaret decided they wanted to sit outside and test their new outdoor heater. They stayed outside on their new patio for hours wrapped in a thermal blanket and seated right by the heater. While staring up at the sky, Oscar whispered to Margaret that he "would be hers forever." Margaret turned, faced Oscar, and repeated the same words to him.

Then on February 23rd, a few days before Margaret's birthday, Oscar gave Margaret a ring and necklace with a handwritten note that read: "To my loving wife, Love you forever, Oscar." The ring was a family heirloom. The ring had a ruby stone in the center surrounded by small diamonds. It was set in a gold band. The necklace was gold. Oscar always wanted his wife to have his family ring. He saved for months to purchase the necklace. Margaret knew that the ring belonged to Oscar's grandmother. Oscar bought himself a ring with a silver band from a pawnshop. Oscar wore his ring on the fourth finger of his left hand. Although she more often wore the ring on her left hand, Margaret wore the ring on the fourth finger of either hand, depending on what she was doing on that day or at that time.

Then in August, while planning a family vacation, Margaret used cheaphotels.com to book a room at the Sheraton in Kansas City. She used Oscar's credit card and booked the room under the name Margaret Frost Rogers. Later that same year, during a brief conversation with one of her wealthy neighbors, Margaret casually mentioned that she and Oscar had just returned from Las Vegas. Her neighbor bragged about her family's trip to Spain and Margaret claimed that she and Oscar stayed in the honeymoon suite at the Bellagio in Las Vegas. Margaret has never been to Las Vegas.

Although Margaret and Oscar both paid the household bills, Oscar paid most of them. Margaret had a part-time job, and Oscar made more money. Oscar was a night-shift manager at AppleTree's, a local family-owned restaurant. Sometimes, Margaret would visit Oscar at his job. One day, as she walked through the door, Oscar turned to a waiter and said, "Here comes my wifey now." Margaret smiled.

Oscar covered Gideon on his insurance plan, and Margaret typically received some medical coverage through her part-time jobs. It was cheaper for Margaret to have her own coverage rather than adding her to Oscar's medical plan. Oscar and Margaret paid the household bills from their separate checking accounts. Neither one was a signer on the other's individual checking account. They also had a joint saving account to which Oscar tried to deposit at least twenty-five dollars each month. Oscar completed the tax forms for both Margaret and himself. Margaret simply signed the documents. For the first year in their new home, Oscar and Margaret filed a joint tax return. In particular, Margaret's tax return indicated that she was married with one dependant, Oscar Gideon Rogers. The form listed her name as Margaret Frost.

After the household expenses were paid, Margaret and Oscar hardly had any money left for entertainment. They lived paycheck to paycheck and used the funds in their savings account for unexpected bills, namely, for baby Gideon. When Oscar mentioned having a wedding ceremony, Margaret kept saying that she wanted to wait until her grandmother, Elle Gutierrez, got better. There never seemed to be the right time, and they had so many bills to pay. Toward the end of the first year in their new home, Margaret and Oscar started to fight a lot about bills and money.

Oscar began communicating with his ex-girlfriend, Haley, on the telephone and through MySpace, a social networking site. Margaret also used a social networking site, Facebook. On her Facebook page, Margaret lists 86 friends. Her name appears as Margaret Frost and, under the relationship line, it states single. One weekend night in December, Oscar went with Haley to the movies in one of the busiest areas of town. Oscar's best friend, Aaron, saw him there with Haley. Oscar told Margaret about Haley, and she forgave him. They started going to a counselor that month.

Year 4: Loan from Grandmother and New Business

The following year, on February 14th, Margaret's grandmother, Elle Gutierrez, sent Margaret fifteen thousand dollars to start a cupcake business. Her grandmother also sent a note that read: "I am so happy to hear about your plans for your future. I think that opening a cupcake shop is a wonderful idea. You know I pray for you and that grandson of mine every day. I am happy that you are thinking about his future financial well-being, but what about his overall well-being? Child, what are you and that man of yours doing anyway? When is he going to make an honest woman out of you? You know that I've always been fond of Oscar. I just worry about you and that beautiful baby of yours. Well, enough of my preaching for now, I guess. You know that I just love you so much and want the very best for you. Love, Grandma El."

In addition to the money from her grandmother, Margaret secured a business loan to start the store. She found a great location, just one mile from their house, and hired a pastry chef, one of Oscar's former classmates. Oscar reviewed all of the loan documents that Margaret signed. Oscar did not sign any of the loan documents or the business formation documents. Margaret used the loan money and her grandmother's gift to open the cupcake store a few months later in June. She named the shop "Gideon's Cupcakes" after her son. Oscar was a signer on the business checking account. He reviewed and kept the books, opened business mail, and paid the vendors.

During the first few months of business, the store struggled financially. Oscar helped with the business and kept his full-time job at AppleTree's. Both Margaret and Oscar knew the business was a potential gold mine. It was the only cupcake place in Topeka. They decided to focus more on marketing efforts. At the end of the year that included the first few months of the business, Margaret filed her tax return as single and included a schedule for business deductions. Again, Oscar completed the paperwork, and Margaret signed the document.

Year 5: Newspaper Article about New Business and Increase in Sales

In January the following year, an article about the new cupcake store appeared in *The Topeka Gazette*. The article, titled *Happy Couple Opens Gideon's Cupcakes*, included a picture of Margaret and Oscar embracing each other in front of the cupcake shop. A couple of months after the newspaper published the article, sales at Gideon's Cupcakes increased. In addition, the business received a lucrative contract with a local restaurant to supply cupcakes for its dessert menu. The store received so many calls for orders that Margaret hired three more employees. Although it seemed that the financial difficulties would soon become a distant memory, it was too late to save the relationship.

Shortly after the spike in sales, Margaret and her son moved out of the guest home in Highland Park to Margaret's old apartment on Bassoon Street. They lived there with Margaret's cousin who had been subletting the apartment from Margaret for about three years. Although Oscar attempted several times to restore the relationship by visiting Margaret at her apartment, he eventually gave up on the relationship.

Oscar continues to provide for his son but fears he will eventually have to leave the guesthouse because he cannot afford to pay the rent any longer. Margaret has not offered any money for the lease since she moved out of the house. Oscar believes he is entitled to a share of the business's profits. Oscar has filed a divorce action against Margaret, but to receive a divorce decree, the parties first must have a valid marriage. In certain jurisdictions, marriage does not require a formal wedding ceremony that is legitimized by an authorized official such as a religious leader or judge. In these jurisdictions, parties may be married if they fulfill the requirements for a common-law marriage. Kansas is one of the states that recognize common-law marriage.

Oscar claims he and Margaret have had a common-law marriage since they moved in together into the guesthouse in Highland Park, over two years ago. The elements to prove a common-law marriage are: (1) capacity of the parties to marry (age and mental capacity); (2) a current marriage agreement between the parties; and (3) a holding out of each other as husband and wife to the public. Please analyze the merits of Oscar's claim that he and Margaret have a common-law marriage. Address each of the elements for common-law marriage. However, with respect to the first element, you should address only age capacity (i.e. whether the parties were of the legal age to marry), not mental capacity. No facts are disputed regarding their mental capacity to marry under common law.

The cases for this exercise are:

- *In re Estate of Antonopoulos*, 993 P.2d 637 (Kan. 1999)

- *Dixon v. Certainteed Corp.*, 915 F. Supp. 1158 (D. Kan. 1996)

- *Eaton v. Johnston*, 681 P.2d 606 (Kan. 1984)

- *Gillaspie v. E. W. Blair Constr. Co.*, 388 P.2d 647 (Kan. 1964)

- *Flora v. State*, Nos. 98,283, 98,284, 2008 Kan. App. Unpub. LEXIS 1006 (Kan. Ct. App. Dec. 19, 2008).

- *In re Pace*, 989 P.2d 297 (Kan. Ct. App. 1999)

- *In re Adoption of X.J.A.*, 166 P.3d 396 (Kan. 2007)

- *Pitney v. Pitney*, 101 P.2d 933 (Kan. 1940)

- *Schrader v. Schrader*, 484 P.2d 1007 (Kan. 1971)

- *State v. Johnson*, 532 P.2d 1325 (Kan. 1975)

- *Whetstone v. Whetstone*, 290 P.2d 1022 (Kan. 1955)

ANALOGICAL REASONING WITH DEPTH

EXERCISE 58

John Napoli retired after a twenty-year career with an organic grocery store, Carefree Foods Company ("Carefree"). Napoli was a Carefree founder, and he had spent his lifetime building the company. His employment contract called for him to receive, starting upon retirement, an annual pension equal to eighty percent of the average of his five highest years' compensation. Napoli was initially pleased with the amount, which was $140,000 per year.

After a few months, though, Napoli heard about other members of the executive team who had retired, and the pensions they were receiving. Apparently, those retirees were receiving payments on the same basis as Napoli. The one difference, however, was that those retirees' pension amount was calculated differently. Each executive, including Napoli, had received a bonus in his or her final year of service—Napoli's bonus was not included within the pension calculation (as part of the final year's compensation for purposes of the five-year average). For the other retirees, however, the company had added the bonus to the final year's compensation amount, so that the average of the five years' compensation was considerably higher.

Napoli asked the company about adding in his bonus, but the company declined to do so, offering no explanation. Napoli contacted you to represent him against the company, and you filed a declaratory judgment action in state court in Harris County, Texas.

Carefree immediately removed to federal court, properly citing diversity jurisdiction. For strategic reasons, Napoli prefers to stay in state court, and he has asked you to find a basis for remand to state court. You review the relevant law and do not find a basis. You then review Napoli's employment contract and find the following provision:

> Carefree irrevocably (i) agrees that any such suit, action, or legal proceeding may be brought in the courts of such state or the courts of the United States for such state, (ii) consents to the jurisdiction of each such court in any such suit, action or legal proceeding and (iii) waives any objection it may have to the laying of venue in any such suit, action or legal proceeding in any of such courts.

You believe that this clause provides a basis for remand. Please draft a persuasive argument explaining why, using the following cases:

- *City of Rose City v. Nutmeg Ins. Co.*, 931 F.2d 13 (5th Cir. 1991)
- *Perini Corp. v. Orion Ins. Co.*, 331 F. Supp. 453 (E.D. Cal. 1971)
- *McDermott Int'l, Inc. v. Lloyds Underwriters*, 944 F.2d 1199 (5th Cir. 1991)

ANALOGICAL REASONING WITH DEPTH

EXERCISE 59

Using the cases listed at the end of this exercise, determine whether Alan Harris can provide sufficient evidence that Kathleen Bergeron knew of his business expectancy and, therefore, can survive Bergeron's motion for summary judgment.

Background Facts

Assume the following facts are from the parties' depositions.

Alan Harris ("Harris"), a resident of New York, and Kathleen Bergeron ("Bergeron"), a resident of Florida, are both second-year students in the Forest Whitaker Television and Film Academy (the "Academy"). The requirements to gain entrance to the television program at the Academy are stringent. Each year thousands of budding writers, directors, and producers vie for the few slots available in the entering class. The school admits only forty students each year.

The Academy provides a hands-on approach to teaching its students about the television and film industry. Students take courses in the history of American motion picture and television, screenwriting, cinematography, film editing, directing, and television and video production. Students in the television division participate in a mock exercise in small groups in which they prepare a treatment (generally two to five pages) for a television show idea and practice pitching the idea to production company executives. The students have an opportunity not only to write a creative piece but also to role-play the parts of writer and producer, as group members take turns assuming each role.

The Academy has a library stocked with all the industry resources, sample treatments and scripts, and DVDs of movies and television shows. For example, at the front desk, students may request the latest issue of the *Hollywood Creative Directory*, a publication that contains updated contact information for production companies, television shows, and studio executives. Students have access to the same resources that executives, directors, writers, producers, and actors use in Hollywood and New York. Also, the library has five viewing rooms students may reserve for single-person use and three screening rooms students may use for large gatherings.

With the school's location in Washington, D.C., students have many opportunities to visit networks, studios, and production companies in New York City and key surrounding areas. Many of the Academy's students secure summer internships at top production companies and studios. Another draw to the Academy is its annual Production Company Fair (the "Fair"). The Academy hosts the Fair each February and many production companies and students attend. Production companies usually send only one or two junior associates to the Fair, as it takes place during "Pilot Season," the period from January to April during which writers submit and pitch ideas for new television shows. The companies need several people on hand at the office to field telephone calls and submissions during this season.

The Fair is a place for the Academy's students to network with production company staff, learn more about the business, exchange business cards, submit resumes, and discuss upcoming programming. Although the Academy's students are constantly working on new projects, they rarely submit a treatment to a production company at the Fair. Students mainly focus on connecting with the representatives and securing summer or permanent employment. The Academy feels this low-pressure dynamic has allowed the school to foster strong, long-term relationships with production companies. The companies' staff look forward to attending the Fair each year and appreciate that the students do not subject them to non-stop "sales pitches." The Academy, however, does not have an official policy that prohibits students from submitting a treatment or idea to a production company at the Fair or even requesting a follow-up meeting from a representative at the Fair.

The students at the Academy are very talented and competitive. The school encourages students to work on projects in small groups to foster a supportive and collaborative teaching environment, help students develop strong communication skills, and train students how to work well with others. Films and television shows are team endeavors, and the Academy prepares its students to succeed in the real-world entertainment industry.

Harris is one of the Academy's rising stars. He is never short of new ideas for a television show or movie script. He also is a gifted writer. In high school, Harris submitted a short story for a competition sponsored by the *Reader's Digest*. Harris won the contest and was the youngest winner to receive the grand prize of $5,000. Harris used his winnings to purchase *Final Draft*, a computer program designed for writing movie scripts, televisions shows, and plays. Since then, Harris has been writing and developing "spec scripts" (also known as speculative screenplays) for television shows and films.

Bergeron is in the same class as Harris. Bergeron has the potential to become a great lead writer one day. During their first year at the Academy, Harris and Bergeron were in the same small group. Bergeron and Harris spent a lot of time working together on class projects and vetting each other's television and movie ideas. Although the two were quite competitive, they somehow managed to work together on side projects. During their first year of school, they submitted a joint "spec script" for an original film idea. They based the script on their childhood experiences and their journeys to becoming students at the Academy and professional Hollywood industry insiders. Although they never sold their script, each continues to use it as a writing sample. Harris and Bergeron also worked on a spec script for the television show *Criminal Minds*, using all the established character and storylines. However, they never completed this script.

Bergeron often told Harris how much she admired his work ethic. She was familiar with Harris's routine. Each year since high school, Harris has submitted an idea (whether as a treatment or spec) to a production company. He continues to work on new ideas even though he has yet to secure a meeting with a production company about his work. Following Harris's lead, Bergeron started to write new treatments she hoped to send out by the next year. She believed their competitive nature would inspire her to work harder on several projects.

In February, both Harris and Bergeron attended the Academy's Fair. After about two hours visiting with production companies and fellow students, Bergeron spotted Harris at the booth for Cracking Up TV Productions LLC ("Cracking Up LLC"). Cracking Up LLC is a television production company with its headquarters in Washington, DC. The company, founded by a graduate of the Academy, has garnered much success with its innovative programming and access to a roster of talented writers. Bergeron noticed that Harris stood at the company's booth talking with the representative for about thirty minutes. Harris also handed the representative what appeared to be some papers in a folder, which the representative flipped through and then handed back to Harris. They continued to talk and even laughed a few times.

"What is he up to?" Bergeron thought to herself. Bergeron continued to watch as Harris shook the representative's hand and walked to the next booth. There, Harris picked up some materials and continued to the next table where a group of students were gathered watching a preview of a new television show.

"This is fascinating," Harris said. "When will it air?"

"This September," the company associate responded. Bergeron watched Harris as he visited the next few booths and approached the end of the aisle where she stood.

"Hey Alan, how's it going? Do you have any exciting projects going on these days?" Bergeron asked him.

Harris smiled and said, "Inquiring minds always what to know." He then walked away.

"You can tell me!" Bergeron shouted after him, but Harris quickly turned the corner.

The next day, Bergeron went to the library to view a video for her *History of the American Motion Picture* course. Harris also was at the library working at one of the tables in the lobby. Bergeron walked past the front desk and behind Harris. She decided not to disturb him as he was staring attentively at his computer screen. As she walked by, she noticed Harris was looking at the website for Cracking Up LLC and the company's contact page. Bergeron continued to the viewing room.

A week later, Bergeron overheard a small group of students in the lounge discussing Harris's idea for a new reality television show. She vaguely heard them mention the words "innovative," "zoologists," "San Diego," and "wildlife." She approached the group and asked what they were talking about.

"Harris is amazing!" one student said. "He has a treatment for this brilliant idea for a new reality show called *Wild Life*. It will document the crazy adventures of zookeepers, other staff, visitors, and animals at city zoos and wildlife parks. People will send in videos they tape on their cameras or phones, and Harris will air them. He also may reenact some incidents, like the tiger attack at the San Francisco zoo. It's going to be *Funny Videos* on steroids! Don't you just love the name, *Wild Life*? It's so creative."

"Love it? I wrote it! He stole my idea!" Bergeron yelled and then stormed out of the lounge. The students looked in Bergeron's direction, shrugged, and resumed their conversation.

When Bergeron returned to her apartment, she immediately called Harris, but he never returned her call. Bergeron eventually decided to get Harris's attention by filing a lawsuit against him. She filed it pro se. She even started a blog about the show and her lawsuit against Harris. She titled the site, *My Wild Life*. On her blog, she explained to readers how she created the reality show and her inspiration for the idea. She also provided daily updates about her pending lawsuit. She did not portray Harris in a positive light.

Harris had a meeting scheduled with the Production Manager for Cracking Up LLC. At the recent Fair, Harris had shared his treatment and pilot spec for his *Wild Life* reality show with the company's representative, Gregory Tibbs ("Tibbs"). Tibbs loved the idea and told Harris to give him a call to schedule a meeting with the Production Manager. Harris followed up with Tibbs, secured a meeting date and time, and immediately began to prepare his pitch. He practiced every day on what he would say and how he would say it. He thought of questions the Production Manager may ask him and reviewed all of his writing samples. He was so busy preparing for the meeting that he did not answer or return any calls unless they were from the production company.

Meanwhile, at Cracking Up LLC, the Production Manager asked Tibbs to pull together any information he could find on Harris to prepare for the meeting. Tibbs typed "Alan Harris" and "Academy" into the search bar and instantly came upon Harris's Facebook page. Tibbs reviewed the biographical information, printed the screen, and scrolled through Harris's list of Facebook friends. Tibbs continued to search, and after twenty minutes of clicking on links, he discovered Bergeron's *My Wild Life* blog.

"Oh no," Tibbs thought. "This is not good." Tibbs showed the blog to the Production Manager, and she instructed him to cancel the meeting until the dispute was fully resolved.

Harris filed suit against Bergeron in federal court for tortious interference with an economic advantage.* According to Harris, Cracking Up LLC learned of Bergeron's lawsuit against him and the blog she created about the show idea and, in turn, the company decided to cancel his pitch meeting with the Production

---

* Federal court jurisdiction in this case is based on diversity of citizenship (i.e. the parties are citizens of different states and the amount in controversy exceeds $ 75,000, *see* 28 U.S.C. § 1332).

Manager. As the matter escalated, Bergeron hired counsel to respond to Harris's complaint. She then filed a motion to dismiss, which the court denied, and later filed a motion for summary judgment, claiming she had no knowledge of Harris's business expectancy. The parties stipulate that District of Columbia law governs the tortious interference claim.

Under District of Columbia law, can Harris provide sufficient evidence that Bergeron knew of his business expectancy and, therefore, survive Bergeron's motion for summary judgment? Do not address the other requirements for a tortious interference claim (such as the existence of a valid business expectancy), as Bergeron bases her motion for summary judgment on the knowledge requirement only. For this exercise, incorporate the relevant standard of review for a summary judgment motion (which is explained in the cases) into your response.

The following cases are for use in this exercise:

- *Bennett Enters., Inc. v. Domino's Pizza, Inc.*, 45 F.3d 493 (D.C. Cir. 1995)

- *Nat'l R.R. Passenger Corp. v. Veolia Transp. Servs., Inc.*, 592 F. Supp. 2d 86 (D.D.C. 2009)

- *Nat'l R.R. Passenger Corp. v. Veolia Transp. Servs., Inc.*, 791 F. Supp. 2d 33 (D.D.C. 2011)

- *Muir v. Navy Fed. Credit Union*, 744 F. Supp. 2d 145 (D.D.C. 2010)

- *Register v. Pierce*, 530 So. 2d 990 (Fla. Dist. Ct. App. 1988)

- *Lake Gateway Motor Inn, Inc. v. Matt's Sunshine Gift Shops, Inc.*, 361 So. 2d 769 (Fla. Dist. Ct. App. 1978)

ANALOGICAL REASONING WITH DEPTH

EXERCISE 60

Congratulations! You succeeded in having the Napoli lawsuit explained in Exercise 58 remanded to state court. Your client is pleased that the lawsuit will go forward in state court. In the meantime, Carefree is not pleased, and has opted to appeal the remand order to the Fifth Circuit Court of Appeals.* In addition, you expect Carefree will file a motion to stay the state court lawsuit while the federal appeal proceeds.

Carefree plans to argue it will be irreparably injured if the stay is not granted, because Carefree is required by the employment contract to pay Napoli's legal fees. Carefree fears that any legal fees and work effort spent on the state court lawsuit will be wasted if the lawsuit eventually proceeds in federal court.

Your client of course wishes to oppose the motion to stay. Based on the cases set out below, do you think your client will succeed? What arguments can your client make? Please address all requirements except "success on the merits," because that requirement is analyzed in Exercise 58.

The cases for this exercise are:

- *Ruiz v. Estelle*, 666 F.2d 854 (5th Cir. 1982)

- *Wildmon v. Berwick Universal Pictures*, 983 F.2d 21 (5th Cir. 1992)

- *Belcher v. Birmingham Trust Nat'l Bank*, 395 F.2d 685 (5th Cir. 1968)

- *Lightbourn Equip. Co. v. Perkins Engines, Inc.*, 39 F. Supp. 2d 785, (N.D. Tex. 1999)

- *Gulf Cent. Pipeline Co. v. Motor Vessel Lake Placid*, 315 F. Supp. 974 (E.D. La. 1970)

- *Renegotiation Bd. v. Bannercraft Clothing Co.*, 415 U.S. 1 (1974)

- *McDermott Int'l, Inc. v. Lloyds Underwriters*, Nos. 91-0841, 91-0871, 1991 U.S. Dist. LEXIS 8776 (E.D. La. June 21, 1991)

---

* While a remand order based on grounds authorized by 28 U.S.C. §1447(c) is not appealable, a remand on grounds not authorized by that section is appealable. *See, e.g., Lightbourn Equip. Co. v. Perkins Engines, Inc.*, 39 F. Supp. 2d 785, 786 (N.D. Tex. 1999).

ANALOGICAL REASONING WITH DEPTH
EXERCISE 61

Using the cases and regulation listed below for this exercise, determine whether Greg Browning can bring a successful false imprisonment claim against Skyway Airline for his being detained and delayed on the tarmac for approximately three hours.

Background Facts

Greg Browning ("Browning") made plans for his trip to Augusta, Maine to attend his family reunion. He reserved a space for his dog at the kennel, asked his neighbors to pick up his mail, and wrote a list of items he needed to pack. Browning was excited about seeing his family but very nervous about flying. And this upcoming flight made him particularly anxious. Browning purchased his ticket from Dallas, Texas to Augusta on Skyway Airline ("Skyway") several months ago at a discounted price. Skyway's headquarters is in Dallas and the airline offers the most direct, non-stop flights to the East Coast from Dallas. His flight was scheduled to depart the following morning at 9:20 a.m. CST and arrive in Augusta at 2:00 p.m. EST.

On the outbound flight, Browning (and the other passengers) would fly on a Skyway jet (Embraer ERJ-175). Browning checked the dimensions for the jet and seating chart online at seatguru.com. According to the site, the Embraer jet has a small cabin space with twelve seats in first class and sixty-five seats in the economy section. On the left and right sides of the plane, there are only two seats in each row. The aircraft has two lavatories, one at the front of the plane and one in the rear of the plane. Passengers are limited to one carry-on bag given the limited overhead space in the bins. The idea of spending several hours in such a tight space made Browning's chest tighten. Browning even spoke with his doctor about his fear of flying, and his doctor prescribed him a mild drug to combat his anxiety. The doctor told him to take the pill as needed and gave him some breathing exercises to reduce stress.

Browning arrived at the airport early for his flight. He checked his two large bags and kept the small duffle bag holding his Kindle, magazines, prescriptions, and toiletries. He discarded his bottled water and made it through the security checkpoint in record time. By 7:00 a.m., Browning was waiting at the assigned gate to board the plane. "Maybe I'm too early," he thought to himself. "This waiting is giving me too much time to think about the flight. I really hate small spaces. I can't wait to get this over with." Browning decided to get up and walk around the airport. He spotted a deli and went inside to purchase a breakfast sandwich and coffee. He sat down at a counter, ate his food, drank his coffee, and read the *Wall Street Journal* that someone had left behind. He began to feel much better.

Around 8:45 a.m., the airline started to board the flight to Augusta. Browning's seat was 17B, an aisle seat toward the back of the plane. He was in the first group of passengers to board the plane. Browning handed his boarding pass to the Skyway representative, took a deep breath, and walked down the jetway to the plane. He found his seat and placed his duffle under the seat in front of him. He quickly sat down and fastened his seat belt. Browning looked out the window to give him a sense of more space. The airline loaded the entire plane in about twenty minutes. At 9:25 a.m., the flight crew closed the door and the pilot pushed the jet back from the gate. The plane rode on the tarmac for a while before coming to a complete stop. Browning assumed the plane was about to take off, but at 9:40 a.m. he heard the pilot's voice on the plane's intercom and PA system.

"Good morning, everyone," the pilot stated. "Our take-off will be delayed a bit. Although the weather appears to looks just fine outside your window, there is a severe weather storm heading our way that is temporarily grounding some flights, especially those headed eastward. The latest information is that we may leave in about forty-five minutes. Just sit back and relax. Please keep your seat belt fastened since we are on an active runway. If anything changes, I will turn off the seatbelt sign. Thank you." Browning instantly became nervous. He had mentally prepared himself for about four hours of flight time to Augusta but did not expect any delays. He reached down to open his bag and look for his anti-anxiety pills but could not find them. "I must have accidentally placed them in my suitcase," he thought to himself. Suddenly, storm clouds formed and the sky became dark. Browning saw lightning and heard roars of thunder.

About one hour later, Browning pushed the flight-attendant call button. The male attendant came to Browning's seat and asked what he needed. Browning asked him how much longer they would have to stay on the plane. The attendant explained the delay, reiterating the same information the pilot gave over the PA system, and told Browning to be patient. "We cannot control the weather. It can be a thorn in our sides." Browning took a deep breath and said, "I cannot breathe on this plane. I need to get off. It's just too small in here." Browning looked very flushed. "Let me get you some water," the attendant suggested and walked to the galley area.

When the attendant returned with the water, Browning explained, "I have a fear of flying. It has been over an hour, and we haven't gone anywhere. I cannot take much more of this." "Try to remain calm," said the attendant. "We shouldn't have to wait much longer." At the two-hour delay mark, several other passengers became agitated and hungry. The small jet carried a limited amount of supplies and food so the crew gave one snack to each passenger. There was more than enough water for everyone. As time passed, the lavatories became unpleasant and dirty.

The passenger seated next to Browning became worried about him. She noticed that he was sweating profusely and had trouble breathing steadily. He looked extremely nervous. She asked Browning whether he was okay. He said, "I just need to get off this plane!" "Are you in pain? Should I get an attendant?" she asked. "No, don't bother. They won't help. We're stuck here." The passenger looked out the window and told Browning, "The weather is clearing up. It won't be long now." A few minutes later, the pilot told passengers the storm had passed and all flight operations would resume. "Good news, we are cleared to leave. Not so good news, we are seventeenth in line to depart, which could take some time. Please remain seated with your seatbelts fastened to ensure your safety."

After three hours of delay on the tarmac, Browning stood up and walked toward the front of the plane. The female flight attendant saw him and said, "Sir, please return to your seat. The pilot has the seatbelt sign on." Browning tried to respond, "But, I. . . ." The attendant interjected, "Sir, please don't force me to take further action by notifying the airport authorities. We all are a bit anxious here. Please take your seat." Fearing any official reprimand, Browning returned to his seat. He felt very light-headed but managed to maintain consciousness. By this time, Browning's shirt was drenched from his sweating and aggravated nervous condition. About fifteen minutes after Browning returned to his seat, the pilot announced they were next in line for take-off. "Sorry for the extremely long delay and thank you for your patience. We will be taking off shortly," the pilot said.

A trip that should have taken about four hours became a seven-hour ordeal. Browning was traumatized by the experience. Even after he landed safely in Augusta, he had difficulty regaining his composure. He had nightmares about being trapped on the plane and had to take several doses of his anti-anxiety medication. Browning spent most of his vacation time in his hotel room rather than with his family at the reunion activities. He eventually decided to leave the reunion early and rented a car to drive back to Dallas. Browning refused to be held captive on a plane ever again. Once he returned to Dallas, he spoke to a lawyer about suing Skyway for false imprisonment for the poor treatment he received on his flight to Augusta and the crew's refusal to let him deplane. In particular, he sought damages for his emotional pain and suffering and the unexpected costs for his trip back home.

Please determine whether the facts of Browning's case support a claim for false imprisonment under Texas law (the incident took place on the tarmac in Dallas, Texas). Do not address any affirmative defenses that Skyway may have but rather analyze the specific elements for false imprisonment. You may use any part of the cases or regulation below for this exercise.

The cases and regulation for this exercise are:

- *Wal-Mart Stores, Inc. v. Rodriguez*, 92 S.W.3d 502 (Tex. 2002)

- *Wal-Mart Stores, Inc. v. Cockrell*, 61 S.W.3d 774 (Tex. App. 2001)

- *Fojtik v. Charter Med. Corp.*, 985 S.W.2d 625 (Tex. App. 1999)

- *Ray v. Am. Airlines, Inc.*, 609 F.3d 917 (8th Cir. 2010)

- *Abourezk v. N.Y. Airlines, Inc.*, 895 F.2d 1456 (D.C. Cir. 1990)

- Responsibility for Operational Control; Domestic Operations, 14 C.F.R. § 121.533 (2011)

ANALOGICAL REASONING WITH DEPTH

EXERCISE 62

Using the cases listed after the problem, determine whether Errol Isadore can successfully sue Mohamed Noor for battery.

Background Facts

Errol Isadore ("Isadore") arrived at T.F. Green International Airport in Warwick, Rhode Island with about one hour to spare before his flight's scheduled departure. Isadore prided himself that he had air travel down to a science. He knew exactly how early to arrive at the airport and had a fool-proof system for travel. He made sure he was ready for every contingency. In case of no food being for sale on a flight or a rather long delay on the tarmac, Isadore packed plenty of snacks, two sandwiches, and one large bottled water in his carry-on bag. Further, he always boarded the plane with a hot cup of coffee to steady his nerves and keep him alert. To insure it was sufficiently hot, he waited until the last minute before boarding to purchase the coffee from an airport vendor.

Per his usual routine, Isadore purchased a large cup of coffee from a stand in the airport about ten minutes before the attendant announced the start of boarding. He placed two creams and five packs of brown sugar in his pocket. He planned to add the cream and sugar once he sat on the plane.

Isadore was one of the first passengers to board. He had attained Elite Status in the airline's Frequent Flyer Program last year because of the many cross-country trips he had to take for business. As Isadore boarded the plane, he walked past First Class and let out a sigh. He usually sat in First Class but unfortunately had purchased his ticket at the last minute after all the seats in First Class had been reserved. He could not afford to take a later flight and risk being late for his lunch meeting. Isadore reluctantly walked through First Class to the Coach section. He found his seat on the aisle, 10C, pulled down the tray for the middle seat, and carefully placed his coffee on the tray. He then placed his carry-on bag under the seat. Lastly, he removed his jacket, placed it in the overhead bin, and took his seat.

Surprisingly, the rows near Isadore filled up rather quickly. Although there was no one seated next to him, three passengers sat in the row behind him and two passengers sat to his left. Isadore said hello to each of them as they passed his seat. They appeared to have boarded the plane together in the first group for frequent flyers. For the next several minutes, boarding passengers headed toward the seats in the back of the plane. Most passengers carried a medium-sized suitcase they had to place in the overhead bins. "Why must airlines charge for baggage?" Isadore thought to himself. "It does more harm than good and makes travel so burdensome these days." At that moment, he heard a passenger yell, "Ouch!" The offending passenger leaned forward and apologized profusely, "I'm so sorry, sir. I didn't mean to hurt you. This bag is so heavy and hard to lift."

Boarding continued for about ten minutes and then slowed down. Seeing a lull in boarding activity, Mohamed Noor ("Noor"), who sat directly behind Isadore, decided to go to the lavatory. Noor stands six feet tall and often has trouble getting up from a seat on a plane. He finds airline seats to be rather uncomfortable and restrictive. The tight space between the rows is even worse. The limited space for egress makes it difficult for someone of his size to maneuver easily. Noor wanted to use the lavatory before the attendant closed the plane doors and instructed everyone to remain seated. Noor positioned one hand on the top of Isadore's seat, which was in front of him, and his other hand on his own armrest to provide leverage. He pushed down with both hands, rose from his seat, and walked toward the back of the plane.

When Noor let go of Isadore's seat, the seat immediately thrust forward, jerking Isadore who had his cup of hot coffee in his hand. Noor did not know Isadore was preparing his coffee at that time. Isadore had just removed the lid and added the cream and sugar. He was in the process of taking a sip from the cup when his chair rebounded forward and bumped him, causing him to spill hot coffee in his lap. He instantly let out a shriek, "Darn it! It's so hot!" A flight attendant rushed right over to his aid. "The coffee burned me, and it's his fault!" Isadore exclaimed, as he pointed in Noor's direction. "He stupidly grabbed my chair!" Fearing he required medical attention, Isadore decided to deplane and possibly take a later flight. One flight attendant gathered Isadore's belongings while another spoke with Noor about the incident.

Isadore's attorney sent Noor a letter, stating his plans to file suit for battery unless Noor reimburses Isadore for his medical and flight expenses. Noor claims that Isadore cannot satisfy the elements for battery since he did not intend to injure or touch Isadore. He plans to defend himself vigorously against any battery claim and views this incident as a chance to shed light on the extremely uncomfortable seating arrangements on planes. Can Isadore successfully sue Noor for battery under Rhode Island law?

The cases for this exercise are:

- *Hennessey v. Pyne*, 694 A.2d 691 (R.I. 1997)

- *Picard v. Barry Pontiac-Buick, Inc.*, 654 A.2d 690 (R.I. 1995)

- *Proffitt v. Ricci*, 463 A.2d 514 (R.I. 1983)

- *Lee v. Gelineau*, Nos. Civ.A.93-3466, Civ.A.93-3468, 2001 Super. Ct. LEXIS 69 (Super. Ct. June 28, 2001)

- *Ghassemieh v. Schafer*, 447 A.2d 84 (Md. Ct. Spec. App. 1982)

ANALOGICAL REASONING WITH DEPTH
EXERCISE 63

Using the cases below, determine whether Gerard Grogan's contract with Quik Mobile Communications is voidable under Ohio contract law covering minors.

Background Facts

One day at school, Steve Jones ("Steve") told Gerard Grogan ("Grogan") about a sales promotion at Quik Mobile Communications ("Quik Mobile"). The deal would give new customers a free cell phone, three months of free service, and a discounted monthly rate, provided the customer signed a two-year contract with the company and agreed to an early termination penalty. Gerard had not heard of such a great deal for cell phone service and decided to stop by Quik Mobile to see if the company still had the promotion. Gerard did not have a cell phone and was very interested in owning one. Almost everyone in his tenth grade High School class had a cell phone, and he felt left out.

The next day, Gerard put on his Akron University t-shirt, khaki pants, and baseball cap, grabbed his wallet, and headed to Quik Mobile in Medina, Ohio. Gerard, who was rather tall for his age of sixteen, decided to drive his father's Chevy Suburban because it had extra legroom. He recently had passed the state's driving test and received his license. "I have to be sure to ask about a hands-free device for driving," Gerard thought to himself.

When Gerard walked through the door, a Quik Mobile sales associate, Hermann Weingarten ("Hermann") greeted him with a firm handshake.

"How are you today? Akron University—that's a good school," Hermann said.

"Yeah, and it has a great basketball team," Gerard replied.

"What can I help you with today—a new phone?" Hermann asked.

"Yeah, I heard that you guys have this promotion going that offers new customers a phone for free," Gerard stated.

"Yes, we do! But I have to warn you. The new phone with the promotion is a basic model. It doesn't have a lot of bells and whistles like some of the more recent models, but it gets the job done," Hermann explained. "Here it is. Take a look."

"This is better than I thought it would be. It's a flip phone with a keyboard. That'll make texting easy. Does it have any applications or games?" Gerard asked.

"Here is a list of all the services provided with the phone, including applications and games. And in that column on the right, there are the promotion features," Hermann directed. "Notice the discounted rate—only $30 per month with

169

unlimited texts and limited minutes. But who makes phone calls these days anyway, right?"

"I'm sold. What do I need to do now?" Gerard asked.

"All I need is a deposit, a credit card, and your signature on this service agreement with Quik Mobile, and I can get you all set up. The contract includes all of the terms you just read and we discussed. Take some time to look it over. Let me know if you have any questions," Hermann said. The agreement was a standard cell phone contract that complies with the procedures and disclosures required by the Federal Communications Commission (FCC) and state rules.

Gerard spent a few minutes reading the agreement and borrowed a pen from Hermann to sign the contract. He then handed Hermann a credit card with his photo printed on it.

"These new cards are great. They make it so there's no need to really check IDs anymore," Hermann commented.

Gerard picked out a black cell phone from the selection of available basic models, and Hermann went to the back office to program the phone. When Hermann returned to the sales floor, Gerard said he also needed to buy a car charger and hands-free device. Hermann placed the additional items in the bag.

"Okay, that will be $40 for the extras and $50 for the deposit, which will be applied toward your monthly service fee starting four months from now. I will place it all on your card. Remember, after the three-month promotion ends, your card will be charged the monthly service fee. And you will have to pay a penalty for any early terminations of the service agreement which includes the cost of the phone," Hermann reminded him.

"Okay, "Gerard stated. Before he left the store, Gerard picked up one of Hermann's business cards and placed it in his pocket. "Thanks for your help, man." Gerard could not wait to show his friend Steve his new phone.

About two and a half months later, while watching reruns of *The Simpsons*, Gerard saw a commercial for a new mobile phone company named Top Dog Cellular ("Top Dog"). Top Dog catered to young adults and had the newest 4G interactive cell phones in its inventory. For its grand opening in Medina, the company offered new customers their choice of a free phone and one month of free service. Customers were required to sign a one-year contract with an early termination penalty. The company also promised to pay one-half of any competitors' termination fees incurred by new customers.

Gerard immediately found Hermann's business card and gave him a call. A salesperson answered the phone on the first ring.

"Is Hermann there?" Gerard asked.

"This is Hermann. How can I help you?" Hermann responded.

"Hermann, this is Gerard. I don't know if you remember me. I signed up with you a couple of months ago. I need to cancel my contract with that promotion deal. I found a better one," Gerard explained.

"Oh, I really hate to hear that, Gerard. Of course, you are free to cancel your service contract at any time, but your credit card on file will be charged the early termination fee. Or you can come in and pay the fee in person. As you may remember, the penalty includes a processing fee and the cost of the free phone that you received as part of the promotion." Hermann replied.

"What? I don't have that kind of money, and that credit card is maxed out. Man, just cancel the contract. I was too young to sign it anyway. I'm just in high school. The contract probably isn't even legit," Gerard revealed to Hermann.

Can Gerard void his contract with Quik Mobile? Be sure to address whether the necessities (necessaries) exception applies. Also, even if you decide the exception does not apply, you should address whether Quik Mobile can enforce the parties' agreement under Ohio law if a court concludes Gerard purchased a necessity.

The cases for this exercise are:

- *Chambers v. Dunmyer Chevrolet Co.*, 58 N.E.2d 239 (Ohio Ct. App. 1943)

- *Davis v. Clelland*, 92 N.E.2d 827 (Ohio Ct. App. 1950)

- *Bramley's Water Conditioning v. Hagen*, 501 N.E.2d 38 (Ohio Ct. App. 1985)

- *Univ. of Cincinnati Hosp. v. Cohen*, 566 N.E.2d 187 (Ohio Ct. App. 1989)

- *Fifth Third Bank / Visa v. Gilbert*, 478 N.E.2d 1324 (Ohio Mun. Ct.1984)

- *Parkwood OB / GYN, Inc. v. Hess*, 650 N.E.2d 533 (Ohio Mun. Ct. 1995)

ANALOGICAL REASONING WITH DEPTH

EXERCISE 64

Using the cases listed below, determine whether Brian Clemens has standing to contest the state troopers' search of the car that he was driving.

Background Facts

While heading south on Interstate 64 just within the Newport News city limits, Virginia State Police Trooper Adam Anderson noticed a maroon colored Mazda 626 driving in the lane next to his. The driver of the Mazda was speeding and crossing over the lines. His erratic driving prompted the trooper to turn on the siren and signal to the driver to pull over. Brian Clemens ("Clemens"), the driver of the Mazda, saw the red lights in his rear view mirror and immediately pulled over to the side of the highway. Trooper Anderson got out of his patrol car and walked towards Clemens.

"Do you know why I stopped you?" Trooper Anderson asked.

"No, I don't, officer," Clemens responded nervously.

"You were speeding. The posted speed limit is sixty-five and you were going eighty miles per hour. And you kept crossing over the lines. Have you been drinking?" Trooper Anderson inquired.

"No, of course not, officer," Clemens replied. "I'm just trying to get to Virginia Beach to meet my buddies. I left Richmond late and was trying to make up some time."

"Let me see your license, registration, and insurance," Trooper Anderson directed.

"Okay. The registration and insurance are in the glove compartment, I think. This isn't my car. It belongs to my girlfriend's mother. I am just borrowing it. Is it okay for me to reach inside the glove compartment?" Clemens asked.

"If that's where the documents are located," Trooper Anderson replied. Clemens opened the glove compartment and sifted through the many items inside. He finally located the registration and insurance documents and handed them to the trooper.

"What is the car owner's name?" Trooper Anderson asked so that he could compare Clemens's answer to the name on the registration.

"Roberta Peterson," Clemens told the trooper. "And here is my license." Clemens handed his driver's license to the trooper.

"This license is expired by almost a year," Trooper Anderson stated. "Do you have a new one or some proof of renewal?"

"No, that's all I have on me," Clemens explained as he fidgeted in his seat.

"Okay. Turn off the car and wait right here. Keep both hands on the steering wheel," Trooper Anderson instructed. Clemens turned the engine off and placed his hands on the steering wheel. The trooper then walked to his patrol car to run the car's license and Clemens's license through the computer system. The system confirmed that Roberta Peterson owned the car and revealed that the state had suspended Clemens's license last year after he received two convictions for driving under the influence (DUI). As a precaution, Trooper Anderson called the police dispatcher for back up and walked back to the car.

"Explain to me again how you got this car," Trooper Anderson directed. Clemens started to perspire and his face became flushed.

"My girlfriend, Kelly, borrowed it from her mother about eight months ago when her car broke down. We haven't saved enough money to get Kelly's car fixed yet," Clemens began. "Kelly let me use the car to drive to Virginia Beach. I don't have a car. I used Kelly's car when it was working. I'd drive Kelly's car to work at least once a week or Kelly would drop me off at work. Kelly couldn't take me to Virginia Beach today because she had to work. So she let me drive it."

"So your girlfriend is at work? How will she get home if you have the car?" Trooper Anderson inquired.

"She said one of her coworkers would bring her home today. I plan to drive back to Richmond tomorrow morning," Clemens added.

"So does her mother, Roberta Peterson, know that you are driving her car to Virginia Beach?" Trooper Anderson asked.

"I don't know but Kelly knows I have the car. I haven't met Mrs. Peterson yet. She knows Kelly and I are dating. Kelly told her about me. I moved in with Kelly about two months ago," Clemens explained. "Mrs. Robertson isn't happy about our dating or living together, but she knows I live with Kelly. She thinks I'm too old for her daughter. I'm only ten years older than Kelly. And I'm not a leech. I help. I gave Kelly some money to give her mom for the car insurance and note. It wasn't a lot but it was something," Clemens responded.

"Okay. And you were coming from Richmond, right?" the trooper inquired.

"Yes, we live in Richmond but Kelly's mom lives in Petersburg. Her mom brought the car to Kelly in Richmond, and then Kelly drove her back home," Clemens explained.

"So, today, you set out to drive about one hundred and ten miles from Richmond to Virginia Beach. Did you make any stops along the way?" Trooper Anderson asked.

"When I left the apartment, I put some gas in the car and got it washed. I didn't want to show up in Virginia Beach in a dirty car. The gas station was just about two miles from the apartment," Clemens answered.

"Did you make any other stops?" Trooper Anderson asked.

"Twenty minutes ago, I went to the restroom at one of those rest areas on Interstate 64. It was maybe ten or fifteen miles back," Clemens added.

"So you have driven about eighty miles so far?" Trooper Anderson confirmed.

"I guess so. Well, yes, since I'm in Newport News now," Clemens responded.

Trooper Anderson then noticed that a state patrol car drove over to the side of the highway and parked behind his patrol car. "Just a minute," the trooper told Clemens. "Wait right here. Keep your hands on the wheel." Trooper Anderson walked towards the other police officer, Trooper Sunil Raghu ("Trooper Raghu"), and explained the situation to him. He told the trooper that Clemens was talking freely but acting quite suspicious. Both troopers walked back to the car in which Clemens sat. Clemens grew more nervous.

Trooper Anderson spoke first. "Your license has been suspended for nearly a year. You know you cannot drive with a suspended license," Trooper Anderson stated. "Step out of the car. We are placing you under arrest for driving illegally with a suspended license. The car will be towed and impounded."

Clemens got out of the car and Trooper Anderson pulled Clemens's arms behind his back and placed handcuffs on him. Meanwhile, Trooper Raghu started to search the car. He opened the glove compartment, removed the contents, and placed them on the passenger seat. He then slid his hands under the front seats.

Trooper Raghu discovered a bag of marijuana in the console between the seats, which prompted him to search further. Trooper Anderson escorted Clemens to his patrol car and placed him in the back seat. Trooper Anderson questioned Clemens about the marijuana, and Clemens admitted that he hid his recreational stash of marijuana in the console. When the trooper asked if there were any other drugs in the car, Clemens shrugged his shoulders.

When Trooper Anderson returned to the car, the troopers removed the panel from the front passenger door. There, they found more marijuana. The troopers estimated that the amount hidden in the door weighed about two pounds. The troopers continued to search the car. They found a few marijuana seeds but no other drug evidence. Trooper Raghu pulled a duffle bag from the back seat and rummaged inside. He took out the contents and placed them on the trunk of the car. Trooper Raghu did not find any weapons or drug evidence in the bag.

The Newport News Commonwealth Attorney's Office charged Clemens in state court for driving on a suspended license and drug possession with intent to distribute. The Commonwealth Attorney's Office, however, delayed prosecution of the state charges, and the United States Attorney's Office charged Clemens with drug possession with intent to distribute in violation of federal criminal law. In a pre-trial proceeding, Clemens moved to suppress the evidence seized by the state troopers during their search of the car. The Assistant United States Attorney objected to Clemens's motion, arguing that Clemens did not have standing to contest the automobile search. The trial court has not yet ruled on the motion.

Does Clemens have standing to contest the state troopers' search of the car? Do not address the validity of the search. Focus on whether Clemens has standing to challenge the search.

The following cases are for use in this exercise:

- *United States v. Carter*, 300 F.3d 415 (4th Cir. 2002)

- *United States v. Rusher*, 966 F.2d 868 (4th Cir. 1992)

- *United States v. Whitehead*, 428 F. Supp. 2d 447 (E.D. Va. 2006)

- *United States v. Sanchez*, 943 F.2d 110 (1st Cir. 1991)

- *United States v. Obregon*, 748 F.2d 1371 (10th Cir. 1984)

CHAPTER V

STATUTORY ANALYSIS FOR SUCCESS

PART 1

BEGINNING STATUTORY EXERCISES

STATUTORY ANALYSIS FOR SUCCESS
EXERCISE 65

Using the statute and case below, please draft the argument portion of your response to the judge.

Fact Pattern:

You are about to start your first trial—a negligence case in Indiana. You represent a global pharmaceutical company alleged to have falsified clinical trial results in order to minimize awareness of a potentially-lethal side effect. An experienced partner is working with you, but you are going to question witnesses and play a substantive role in the trial.

Neither plaintiff nor defendant requested a jury in this case, so you expect a bench trial. As you approach the bench for pre-trial motions, the plaintiff's lawyer speaks up. "We expected a jury. But today we realized that we forgot to request a jury. Our client has suffered serious injuries, and she wants her day before a jury of her peers. We want a jury, and we believe you would violate our client's rights if you deny her a jury. We base this on the Constitution of the United States of America, namely the Seventh Amendment. In addition, Article 1, Section 20 of the Constitution of Indiana guarantees our client a right to a jury trial. We hereby make an oral motion for a jury trial."

Your client, Big Pharmaceuticals, does not want a jury trial. Your defense relies on a number of technical arguments that you and your client believe will resonate more with a judge than a jury. In addition, the plaintiff has suffered serious injuries, and she is a sympathetic person and witness. So how do you respond to the plaintiff's motion?

Constitutional Provisions and Case:

You first locate the Seventh Amendment to the United States Constitution.

In Suits at common law, where the value in controversy shall exceed twenty dollars, the right of trial by jury shall be preserved, and no fact tried by a jury, shall be otherwise re-examined in any Court of the United States, than according to the rules of the common law.

U.S. Const. amend. IV.

You also find Article 1, Section 20 of the Constitution of Indiana.

Ind. Const. art. I, § 20.

In all civil cases, the right of trial by jury shall remain inviolate.

In addition, you find the case of *Hayworth v. Bromwell*, 158 N.E.2d 285 (Ind. 1959).

Please review these authorities and draft the argument that will be the basis of your response to the judge.

STATUTORY ANALYSIS FOR SUCCESS

EXERCISE 66

Using the statutory section and cases for this exercise, determine whether Brett Cullen is entitled to a mistake of fact charge at his trial for involuntary manslaughter and misuse of a firearm while hunting.

Background Facts

Hunting is a time-honored and popular recreational activity in Georgia. Georgia has more than ninety Wildlife Management Areas throughout the state, giving hunters access to almost one million acres of public hunting land. Georgia also has a number of privately owned hunting grounds. For example, Big Oak Plantation ("Big Oak") is a family owned and operated hunting area in Georgia, just about two hours south of Atlanta. Big Oak consists of approximately two thousand acres of fields and very heavy foliage with hardwood timber, planted pines, and ponds. For safety reasons, Big Oak allows only a maximum of ten hunters on the grounds, no more than four teams, at any one time. In addition, there are other rules that hunters must follow to ensure everyone's safety. For example, hunters cannot wear a red, white, or blue t-shirt or similarly colored socks beneath their camouflage because they may be mistaken for a turkey. In addition, hunters are instructed to handle their shotgun safely at all times.

Brett Cullen ("Cullen") and his wife, Vera Cullen ("Vera"), planned a weekend celebration at their home in Augusta, Georgia for their son's 21st birthday. The weekend event included a family barbeque on Friday and a turkey-hunting trip on Saturday and Sunday at Big Oak. The season for hunting in Georgia lasts for about two months (March 24 to May 15) and the season limit is three gobblers (male turkeys) per hunter. It is illegal in Georgia to hunt and kill a hen (female turkey). Cullen scheduled his hunting trip for the last weekend in the season.

On Friday, the Cullens hosted a spectacular barbeque in their backyard with a live band. They had plenty of food for all their family and friends who attended the bash. Cullen worked the grill while his wife served drinks, punch and beer. When Cullen took his breaks to drink beer with his son and cousins, Vera watched the meat on the grill. The band played until midnight and all of the guests left around 12:30 a.m. Cullen and his wife cleaned up all the trash from the party while their son went to bed. After washing the dishes, his wife told Cullen goodnight. Before he went to bed, Cullen spent a few minutes pulling together his gear for the hunting trip and set his alarm for 6:30 a.m.

Cullen shot up in his bed when the alarm sounded. He called out to his son and told him to get ready. Cullen's cousin, Bennie Miller ("Miller") and Miller's wife and sons, who had attended the Friday barbeque, arrived at Cullen's home around 7:00 a.m. They all piled into the van and drove about three and a half hours to Big Oak. Cullen drove the entire trip. They stopped two times, once for a quick breakfast at the Waffle House and a second time for a restroom break. They arrived at Big Oak around noon. As they walked through the front door of Big Oak's lobby, the clerk gave each of them a map of the grounds.

"Hi there, I hope you had a nice drive," she said. "Step right over here so that I can check you in." The clerk began to check them in and assigned their rooms. Meanwhile, Cullen and Miller discussed their hunting plans for the day.

Both Cullen and Miller had been to Big Oak many times before and had their favorite hunting locations on the grounds. They decided to hunt in two separate groups. Cullen indicated that he and his son would hunt in the "timber fields" area and Miller said that he and his wife and sons would hunt on the far side of the grounds in the "grove" area. Both locations were marked clearly on the map and located about a half mile from each other.

Big Oak's clerk listened to their discussion and wrote down their planned locations in the logbook. She then said, "Good choices. Here are your room keys. We have one other group here this weekend. I hope that you will get a chance to meet them. Also, we serve dinner in the main hall at 7 p.m. and snacks until 11:00 p.m. Be sure to stop by our store just in case you need any extra gear. We sell loads and ammunition, decoys like turkey fans, and turkey calls for gobblers and hens. We have everything that you could need."

After finishing with the check-in process, the Cullens and the Millers went to their guestrooms and changed into their hunting gear, which included camouflage body attire and face masks. The mask concealed the wearer's entire head, except for an opening over his eyes. Each hunter carried a 12-gauge shotgun with an autoloader. None of the shotguns had a scope. Each group had a cooler with drinks and snacks. About an hour later, Cullen, his son, Miller, and Miller's wife and sons met in the hallway outside their rooms. They set out for their respective hunting locations and planned to meet back at the lodge by 8:00 p.m.

At dusk, just as the sky was growing dark, it started to mist. "May start to rain soon," Cullen told his son. "I cannot believe we haven't seen a turkey yet. We've been at it for about four hours now and will have to pack up soon." As Cullen reached into the cooler for another beer, he heard a turkey gobble, a loud and aggressive sound. "Did you hear that?" he asked his son. "Look over there in those trees. I think I saw it fan out." Cullen then fired his shotgun in the direction of the heavy foliage, approximately fifty feet away.

Cullen's shot went through the trees and hit his cousin, Miller. Miller's wife screamed, "Oh no! Bennie's been shot!" Cullen ran in the direction of the shot and told his son to go for help. Miller died from a gunshot wound to his chest before any help could arrive. When the police reached the scene, Cullen admitted that he had fired the shot, killing his cousin. He was visibly shaken and dis- traught by what had occurred. "I thought he was a turkey. How could this have happened? I will never forgive myself," Cullen cried. While questioning Cullen's son, the officer smelled alcohol on his breath and asked him if they had been drinking. Cullen's son told the officer that he had drunk one beer and his father had maybe two beers.

A Georgia state grand jury indicted Cullen for involuntary manslaughter and misuse of a firearm while hunting. During plea negotiations, Cullen raised mistake of fact as a defense. He claimed that his cousin's death was a tragic incident but an accident, as he mistakenly believed that he was shooting at a male turkey. The prosecution rejected Cullen's explanation and refused to let him plead guilty to a lesser crime. The case was set for trial.

Is Cullen entitled to a charge for mistake of fact as a defense at his trial? Develop the arguments for the state and Cullen and determine which party has the stronger position.

The statute and cases for this exercise are:

- Ga. Code Ann. § 16-3-5 (2011)

- *Crawford v. State*, 480 S.E.2d 573 (Ga. 1997)

- *Clark v. State*, 386 S.E.2d 378 (Ga. Ct. App. 1989)

STATUTORY ANALYSIS FOR SUCCESS
EXERCISE 67

Using the statutory section and cases for this exercise, determine whether Reynaldo Perez had an implied contract of employment that could be terminated only for cause.

Background Facts

Reynaldo Perez ("Perez") interviewed at the popular Malloy's Department Store ("Malloy's") in Los Angeles, California. He sought a position as a department manager, specializing in shoes and accessories. During a break in his interview, he filled out an application form. The application form included the following language: "Thank you for applying to the Malloy's family of companies. We appreciate your time and interest. Malloy's hires and retains hard-working people. If you are hired with us, please keep in mind that our employment relationship will end whenever we determine that it should. Good luck in the application process!"

Perez had several years of experience in shoes and accessories with another company, as well as a degree in marketing and sales. Malloy's hired him, and he started work at an annual salary of $47,000 plus benefits and vacation days. During his new employee orientation, he received an employee manual that, among other things, outlined the company's history and explained the company holiday schedule. The manual also contained the following language:

> Welcome to the Malloy's family! We hope for a long and productive employment relationship with you. We reward hard work and productivity. On the other hand, if you do not perform your job as you should, you will be fired. You can be fired any time, for any reason. We hope you remain a loyal and productive member of the Malloy's family for many years.

Perez enjoyed his work at Malloy's, and he connected well with the customers. After two years with the company, he received his first bonus of $5,000. "You reached an important sales milestone," said his supervisor. "Your department has sold more shoes this year than in any past year, and it's only November! Well done, Perez."

Perez was quickly promoted to store manager, and in five years' time, he was regional manager. His salary increased to $170,000 plus bonuses tied to store sales within his region. His supervisors continued to praise his work and sales results. Each year, Perez received a performance evaluation. From the day he started at Malloy's to the day he left, his evaluations were uniformly good. After five years, Company President Edwina Malloy ("Malloy"), told him that she had never seen evaluations as good as Perez's, and that if Perez continued to perform at this level, his job would always be safe. "We don't just fire people around here, Perez. We don't do that. Stick with us, and you'll be fine."

Perez stayed at Malloy's for a total of twenty years, rising to the level of national vice president of the company. At the celebration of his twenty-year anniversary with the company, the president approached him to shake his hand. "What a success story, Perez!" she said. "You have brought our company back to a strongly competitive position. By the way, my nephew, Billy Malloy Meagle ("Meagle"), will be starting as your assistant next week. Please show him everything you know, as I want him to be a key player. He just finished his Master of Business Administration degree, and he can hardly wait to get to work. He's twenty-eight years old, and you will love his energy." Perez agreed to help Meagle learn the ropes at Malloy's. Over the next few months, Meagle and Perez worked together, and Meagle shadowed Perez through his day. Before long, Meagle was alongside Perez making presentations to the Board of Directors, and Perez was proud of Meagle's progress.

Perez was surprised when Malloy called him into her office one day to discuss a new assignment. "Look, Perez, you've been great and all, but it's time for new blood. You're going to be Meagle's assistant now, and he will be the vice president." "But what have I done wrong?" asked Perez. Malloy said that he had done nothing wrong at all, but that business is business, and that's what the company needed right now.

Perez returned to his office and called his wife. He explained that he didn't feel wanted at the company, and she urged him to resign. "You don't have to stay there," she said. "Tell them you're leaving immediately." Perez decided to wait. He returned to Malloy's office and told her that he was fine with the change in his assignment. After a year, however, he started to feel depressed that he was still working for his former subordinate. Meagle continued to ask Perez questions every day, and even the chairman of the board said that Perez undoubtedly knew more than anyone at the company about the shoe and accessory aspect of the business. Meagle came into work late, and Perez kept working long hours. Finally, he had had enough. He went to Malloy's office and said that unless he could get his own job back, he was leaving effective immediately. "Well, we hate to see you go," said Malloy. "But OK. We're going to be reducing the size of our executive staff at some point anyway, so you're probably on the right track. Good luck." Perez went home, distraught. Two weeks later, he called your law firm.

The partner in charge is considering bringing a number of different claims. One issue she would like you to resolve is whether Perez's employment was at will, meaning that either party could end the employment relationship for any reason, or for cause, meaning that the relationship could be terminated only for a specific reason. In other words, did Perez have an implied contract of employment that could be terminated only for cause?

Please use the following sources to answer the question:

- Cal. Lab. Code § 2922 (Deering 2011)

- *Guz v. Bechtel Nat'l, Inc.*, 8 P.3d 1089 (Cal. 2000)

- *Pugh v. See's Candies, Inc.*, 171 Cal. Rptr. 917 (Ct. App. 1981)

STATUTORY ANALYSIS FOR SUCCESS

EXERCISE 68

Using the statutory section and cases for this exercise, determine whether the librarian may have committed a battery.

Background Facts

Mary Seville ("Mary") was excited to explore her new neighborhood of Sarasota, Florida. She had moved to Sarasota for a new job and could hardly wait to make new friends. One Saturday morning soon after she moved into her new house, Mary visited the children's story hour at the local library. She brought her two small children with her, and she met several other parents. Over conversation and children's stories, she started to learn about the neighborhood. She was also happy to see that the library carried a copy of the new, bestselling romance novel by Parker Louise, *Tahiti Dreams: A Year of Island Love*. She quickly checked out the book and rushed home with her children to read it.

Three weeks later, she attended the children's story hour again. She sat with the parents, exchanged local news, and talked about school issues. Mary was relaxed and happy as she enjoyed her new friends. As story hour came to a close, Mary decided to head home. Mary had gathered a stack of books that she intended to check out, including several children's books and the next Parker Louise book, *Summer Boys of Bora Bora*. Mary walked over to the circulation desk, and the librarian checked out the books to Mary. The librarian stopped, however, when she reached the *Summer Boys of Bora Bora*. "Don't you know that this book is in high demand?" said the librarian. "Yes, of course," said Mary. "I'm happy to find it here. What a great library you have here in Sarasota!" "You know you still have it *Tahiti Dreams*. Why don't you give that one back first?" Mary replied, "Yes, I was going to bring it, but I forgot. I'm new to the city, and I had a lot on my mind this week. I'm sorry I still have the book, but I've finished reading it and will bring it back later this week." The librarian scowled but continued to check out the books.

Mary gathered her children and books before heading to the door. As she reached the exit, she saw one of her new friends whose children were at the same school as Mary's. "We have got to get the kids together," said Mary. Before she could finish her conversation, she saw the librarian running over to her. "Ms. Seville! The Tahiti book is OVERDUE," she said loudly. "You can't have another bestseller when you have an overdue bestseller!" Mary looked up, surprised and embarrassed in front of her new friend. Another mother from the story hour walked over to see what the problem was. "Is that the library policy?" asked Mary, rather shaken. The librarian responded, "I've been the librarian for twenty-nine years and three months, and it's MY policy!" she said.

Mary was upset, but would not be bullied by the librarian. "I am sorry, but I am not aware of that policy. That policy is not written down anywhere, and it is not the official policy of this library. I will bring the Tahiti book back as soon as possible, but I am going to keep the books I checked out. If I owe fines, I will pay the fines. Good day. Come on, children." Mary walked toward the door with her stack of books. The *Summer Boys of Bora Bora* book rested on the top of her stack of books.

The two other mothers stood awkwardly by the door. They did not know what to do or say. Mary walked briskly to the door, but the librarian stepped in front of her. "Oh, no you don't, Missy," said the librarian, and grabbed the book off the top of the stack. "Not in this town. Maybe that was OK in New York or wherever you came from, but it's not OK here. Don't you know you need to follow the rules? Now get out of here!" The other mothers looked sorrowfully at Mary as she left. "I'm sorry," said one. "That was awful."

Mary went home and tried to forget about the incident, but she felt humiliated. You are the district attorney assigned to Ms. Seville's case. She wants you to file charges against the librarian. You and another assistant district attorney plan to discuss possible charges in an afternoon meeting. You have been tasked with deciding whether the librarian may have committed a battery. What is your view, and why?

Please use the following sources:

- "Battery occurs when a person either actually and intentionally touches or strikes another person against the will of the other." Fla. Stat. § 784.03 (2001)

- *Malczewski v. State*, 444 So. 2d 1096 (Fla. Dist. Ct. App. 1984)

- *Clark v. State*, 746 So. 2d 1237 (Fla. Dist. Ct. App. 1999)

- *Williamson v. State*, 510 So. 2d 335 (Fla. Dist. Ct. App. 1987)

STATUTORY ANALYSIS FOR SUCCESS

EXERCISE 69

Using the statutory sections and case for this exercise, determine whether the City of Colby violated the provisions of the Kansas Open Meetings Act.

Background Facts

The City of Colby ("City") is located in Northwest Kansas and has a population of slightly fewer than five thousand residents. The City has a Mayor, a City Council, and a City Manager. The Mayor is elected at large and the City Council is comprised of eight members who are elected from each ward for a four-year term. The Mayor and City Council are responsible for setting City policy and approving the budget. The Mayor votes on City Council business only when there is a tie vote and has the power to sign or veto any ordinance passed by City Council. The City Manager handles routine administrative tasks that pertain to the City's operation and supervises City personnel. The Mayor presides at all City Council meetings, which are typically held in the Council's Room at City Hall.

City Hall is a historic building located in the center of town. The Council's Room is the second largest meeting room in City Hall and is often used for special events, presentations, group pictures, and media sessions. The Council Room is an ornate, richly finished space with a high-coffered ceiling and mahogany wood floors and doors. The room also features segmental arches over each large window. Most of the room's original hardware remains intact. Although the room has certain architectural significance, it does not have built in technology for audio and visual presentations.

There are three other rooms in City Hall that can accommodate group meetings: the Mayor's conference room, the Caucus Room, and the Community Room. The Mayor's conference room is connected to the Mayor's office. To reach the conference room, persons must check in with the Mayor's executive assistant and then walk through the Mayor's office to the conference room. The conference room is a long rectangular-shaped room, measuring about six hundred square feet. The room has a long conference table with seating for twenty people and additional chairs along the walls. It also has a projector mounted from the ceiling and a 161-inch diagonal motorized projection screen on one end of the room. The Caucus Room is the smallest space in City Hall. The room is approximately 144 square feet, and includes a small circle table with six chairs. The Community Room is the largest meeting room and is approximately 3,250 square feet with multiple uses. The Community Room can be divided into two smaller rooms, each approximately 1,500 square feet, and may be used for classroom space or a banquet or as a theatre room.

In January, a new nightclub opened in Colby near the city's high school and community center and a group of parents lobbied heavily to limit the business's operations and impact on the surrounding community. After the group obtained the signatures of about six hundred concerned citizens, a City Council member proposed a city ordinance that would roll back the closing hours of nightclubs and dance clubs from 3:00 a.m. to 1:00 a.m. six days of week and from 4:00 a.m. to 2:00 a.m. on Sundays. The City Council announced that it would meet at City Hall on the second Tuesday in March at 2:00 p.m. to address the proposed ordinance.

As people arrived for the City Council's meeting, personnel at the information desk directed them to the Mayor's conference room. The Council's Room was unavailable for the meeting, as it was under construction and being remodeled to add new technology including a projector, large screens, and an updated sound system. The Community Room was being used by several organizations preparing for the City's Annual Spring Festival ("Festival") and an elementary school practicing for the Festival's opening play.

Reporters for the local newspaper and television station, the parents' group, no fewer than twenty interested residents, and several students from the high school and community college attended the meeting. The room was very crowded, with standing room only. The room accommodated everyone who arrived. The Mayor, the members of City Council, and the parents' group sat at the conference table. Other attendees sat in chairs positioned along the wall or stood against the wall. Some students opted to sit on the floor near the door.

Sonia Weber ("Weber"), who owned a small dance club in Colby, arrived at the meeting just before it started. Weber was concerned that the ordinance could negatively affect her business. Over the years, Weber's club had developed a loyal following and managed to outlast many of the local businesses. As Weber approached the conference room, she noticed how many people had decided to attend the meeting. She managed to enter the room, carefully stepping over a few students who sat on the floor, but she did see any available seats. The room felt stuffy so Weber decided to stand near the entrance. She located a space between two occupied chairs and stood with her back against the wall, facing the far end of the conference table. The Mayor sat at the opposite end of the table from the room's entrance.

At the meeting, the City's Area Planning Commission presented a study on nightclub business operations and crime statistics involving such businesses. The parents' group noted their concerns over underage drinking and inappropriate activities by minors and their views on how late operation hours for nightclubs increase these dangers. The construction noise from the Council's Room interrupted the meeting a few times and caused speakers to pause. The Mayor's assistant went to the Council's Room to ask the contractors to take a break from hammering, but people standing near the room's entrance could still hear construction noise during the meeting. Several students spoke against the ordinance at the meeting. A few students were rather soft-spoken and Weber had trouble hearing their comments. As some speakers spoke in favor of the ordinance, some students made brief outbursts crying "Unfair!" A couple of attendees moved closer to the conference table to hear the discussion better.

Weber shifted her weight from one leg to the other leg, as she grew tired of leaning against the wall. Eventually, Weber decided to leave. Toward the end of the meeting, the Mayor's assistant circulated copies of documents that speakers presented at the meeting. The meeting lasted approximately two hours and twenty-five minutes. Weber left about forty-five minutes before the end of the meeting. After the City Council concluded the discussion, it voted to pass the ordinance, 6-to-2. Frustrated by her experience at the meeting, Weber challenged the validity of the City Council's vote, arguing that the City violated the Kansas Open Meetings Act ("KOMA").

Did the City Council violate the KOMA? Was the meeting to discuss and vote on the proposed ordinance "open" to the public as required under the KOMA? Develop the arguments for the City of Colby and Weber and determine which position is stronger. The parties agree that the City Council is a government body subject to the KOMA and that the City Council gave proper notice of the meeting.

The statutory sections and case for this exercise are:

- Kan. Stat. Ann. § 75-4317 (2010)

- Kan. Stat. Ann. § 75-4317a (2010)

- Kan. Stat. Ann. § 75-4318(a) (2010)

- *Stevens v. City of Hutchinson*, 726 P.2d 279 (Kan. Ct. App. 1986)

STATUTORY ANALYSIS FOR SUCCESS

EXERCISE 70

Using the statutory section and case for this exercise, determine whether Joshua Mantegna is a bona fide resident of Alabama for purposes of his divorce complaint filed in Alabama state court.

Background Facts

Joshua Mantegna ("Joshua") is married to Alexis Mantegna ("Alexis"). They own a home in Baltimore, Maryland and lived there together until Joshua began law school. After graduating from the University of Virginia, Joshua started working as a computer programmer at a small technology company in Baltimore. He worked at this company for three years before he applied to law school. Joshua applied to several top law schools throughout the country but received the best offer from the University of Alabama School of Law ("UA Law"). UA Law offered Joshua a merit scholarship for full tuition costs and a generous stipend for living expenses for three years. Joshua accepted UA Law's offer and immediately arranged for a trip to Tuscaloosa, Alabama to search for an apartment.

First Year of Law School

Joshua found an apartment close to UA Law's campus and signed a two-year lease, which gave him a significant discount on the monthly rent. He provided UA Law with his new apartment address, 1800 Links Blvd. Apt. # 1201, Tuscaloosa, Alabama 35405, and asked them to send all of his documents to this address. He also opened checking and money market accounts at the Alabama Credit Union to deposit his scholarship funds. In addition to these accounts, Joshua has a joint checking and savings account with his wife at Harbor Bank in Maryland.

Joshua's new apartment complex, The Links at Tuscaloosa, has several amenities including a business center, pool, exercise room, and recreation center. With Alexis's help, Joshua moved most of his personal belongings to Tuscaloosa and purchased furniture at a discount furniture store near campus. Joshua leased a two-bedroom apartment on the first floor near the exercise room. Joshua knew he would need to exercise daily to maintain a high energy level during his first year of school.

Joshua's assumption proved correct. He spent most of his time reading, studying, and meeting with his study group to discuss cases and assignments. He rarely saw his wife, Alexis. She visited him about once a month and often had to join him at study sessions with his classmates. She would bring a book to read or try to catch up on some work for her real estate clients. Joshua went home to Baltimore for the Thanksgiving holiday but decided to stay in Alabama during the winter holiday break. During the break, Joshua updated his resume and contacted local firms. The letterhead for his resume stated:

Joshua Mantegna

1800 Links Blvd. Apt. #1201, Tuscaloosa, AL 35405
(205) 247-3344 • jmantegna@gmail.com

Joshua finished strong in his first year, placing in the top ten percent of his class. He even landed a summer law clerk position with a local Tuscaloosa law firm that specialized in intellectual property and patent law. However, since the law clerk position was unpaid, Joshua worked evenings and weekends at Starbucks to supplement the stipend he received from UA Law.

During the summer, Alexis started to visit Joshua less frequently and often complained to him about the Alabama heat. It was clear to Joshua that Alexis did not like Tuscaloosa or Alabama. Joshua thoroughly enjoyed UA Law and the city. He learned more about the various art galleries and theatres in Tuscaloosa as he attended firm functions over the summer.

Second Year of Law School

At the start of his second year of law school, Joshua filed a change of address form with the United States Postal Service online. He selected the option for a permanent address change, provided the address for the home in Baltimore as the "old address," and listed 1800 Links Blvd. Apt. # 1201, Tuscaloosa, Alabama 35405 as his "new address." Joshua also mailed his resume to several firms, public interest organizations, and judges in Alabama. Joshua focused his job efforts mainly on legal positions in Alabama. However, when a classmate from the University of Virginia contacted Joshua about an internship with a federal judge in Washington, D.C., Joshua submitted his resume.

In September of his second year of law school, Joshua submitted an absentee ballot for the primary elections in Maryland. Later, in November, Joshua paid to have his Maryland driver's license, registration, and tags renewed. He completed the forms and mailed them to the Maryland Department of Transportation Motor Vehicle Administration along with his payment. Also, that same month, Joshua voted in the general elections in Maryland by absentee ballot. Joshua remained in Tuscaloosa during the holidays and had easy access to the law school's resources that were open during the break. The law library and computer lab had limited staffing hours but were open most days.

In January, Joshua filed his application to take the Alabama state bar examination. He paid the $750 fee for non-residents since he did not have an Alabama driver's license, which is required for the $450 application fee for residents. He also paid a down payment for a preparation course for the Alabama bar examination. Then, in April, Joshua filed his federal and Alabama state income taxes as "married filing separately." He provided the address for his apartment on both forms. At the end of his second year of law school, Joshua renewed his apartment lease for another year. He also learned that the judge in Washington, D.C. selected him to be his summer intern. That summer, Joshua worked in D.C. for seven weeks and lived at the Baltimore house with Alexis. Once the internship ended, Joshua returned to Tuscaloosa.

Third Year of Law School

Joshua continued to mail his resume to several firms, public interest organizations, and judges in Alabama. He received a few interviews and callbacks in August. Also, that same month, Joshua contacted a real estate agent to discuss purchasing a local property. The agent directed Joshua to her website and emailed him a number of listings. Joshua told the agent that he had saved some funds for a down payment and wanted to view some properties once he received an offer of employment.

After growing apart from his wife for some time, in October of his third year of law school, Joshua filed for divorce against Alexis in Alabama state court. Joshua also made plans to get an Alabama driver's license, vehicle registration, and tags in November. Alexis did not file an answer or otherwise respond to the complaint. Alexis maintains that the Alabama court does not have proper jurisdiction over the divorce action since Joshua is not a bona fide resident of Alabama. The parties do not dispute that Alexis is a resident of Maryland but disagree as to Joshua's place of residency.

Is Joshua a bona fide resident of Alabama for purposes of his divorce complaint filed in Alabama state court? Develop the arguments for Joshua and Alexis, relying on the relevant legal standard and precedent case. Determine which party has the stronger position.

The statute and case for this exercise are:

- Ala. Code § 30-2-5 (2011)
- *Fuller v. Fuller*, 991 So. 2d 285 (Ala. Civ. App. 2008)

STATUTORY ANALYSIS FOR SUCCESS

EXERCISE 71

Using the statutory sections and case for this exercise, determine whether the clawfoot tub that Melissa Ososki added to her master bedroom is a fixture or removable property under Oklahoma law.

Background Facts

In January, Melissa Ososki ("Ososki") signed a one-year lease for a third-floor apartment in a building owned by Jason Rutter ("Rutter"). The building was located in a historic neighborhood in Tulsa, Oklahoma. Ososki's apartment had two bedrooms and one bathroom in the hallway in between the two bedrooms. The bathroom had a large shower but did not have a bathtub. Ososki decided to use the larger bedroom as her master bedroom and the second bedroom as an office. The larger bedroom had enough space for a king-sized bed and a separate seating area. The seating area was near the window and had a stone tile floor whereas the rest of the room had carpet. Ososki decided to add a "clawfoot" or pedestal bathtub to her master bedroom in the tile floor area and create her own serenity space.

Ososki asked Rutter if she could install a clawfoot bathtub in her apartment. Rutter agreed, provided that she placed it on the tile floor and not on the hardwood.

"Sounds like it will be really nice, Melissa," Rutter responded. "Remember, you are responsible for any installation costs."

"Of course," Ososki said. "I will call a plumber next week." Ososki found a 60-inch clawfoot bathtub with a gooseneck faucet online for $1,200. The cost included the porcelain cast-iron roll rim tub, the gooseneck faucet, supply lines with shut off valves, and a drain with a chain and stopper. Ososki purchased the bathtub and requested rush delivery.

Once the bathtub arrived a few days later, Ososki contacted a local plumber about installation. Ososki described her new clawfoot tub to him over the phone and the plumber explained the installation process for rough-in plumbing. He also gave her an estimate. Ososki agreed with the cost and the plumber arrived the next day to complete the work.

"Nice tub," the plumber said. "It will fit perfectly in this corner on the tile floor. We can place it near this wall shared with the bathroom. That way, I can access the existing plumbing more easily."

"That makes sense," Ososki replied. "What will you need to do in here, exactly?"

"First, I will need to examine the existing plumbing and drill about three holes in the tile floor to run the pipes and secure them to the tub's faucet and drain. The holes will be about the size of a golf ball but, once done, you won't see them. They will be neatly covered by the piping hardware which is secured by nuts. I'll need to use a wrench to tighten the nuts. Then, after cutting off the water, I will cut back the existing plumbing to reach the new holes and reroute the supply lines. All of this plumbing is held in place by welding work and glue in certain parts. Next, I work on the tub. I will connect the claws or feet to the bottom of the tub using large screws. The tub will not be screwed directly to the floor. I also will install the tub's stopper assembly and secure the pipes, connecting them from the tub through the holes in the floor. Again, I'll use a wrench and nuts to keep it all in place. Lastly, I will install the tub's faucet assembly and make sure the water is running freely and it's all working properly. What's so great about this clawfoot tub is that it can sit practically in the middle of your seating area and not against the wall. The tub will not be cemented or attached to the wall. At any time, we can disconnect the tub from the pipes and replace it if you like."

"Yeah, that is the look I was going for but it sounds a bit difficult to achieve," Ososki said.

"It's not an easy project but definitely doable. I'll probably have to work through the weekend to complete it. You see, right now, the clawfoot tub is basically freestanding but, once I'm done, it will be connected to the pipes, which will be connected to the floor. Everything is basically held together by nuts, some screws on the tub, plumber's tape and putty, and my great work," the plumber stated with a smile.

"Well, I'll let you get to it then. I'm really excited to see the finished product. I will be in the living room if you need anything," Ososki stated as she left the room.

The plumber finished the job on time and the new clawfoot tub looked amazing in the bedroom. Ososki was pleased with the plumber's work. She added just a few finishing touches to the bedroom to complete her serenity theme. Ososki thoroughly enjoyed her new tub and used it several times a week, especially during the summer months.

Much later, in December, Ososki informed Rutter that she would be terminating her lease and vacating the premises at the end of her one-year term. She had purchased a new loft-style condo in the downtown Tulsa area. Rutter said that he was disappointed to see her go and wished all of his tenants could be as thoughtful as her.

Ososki started to pack her belongings and made arrangements to place her things in storage until her new home was ready. She also called the plumber to dismantle the clawfoot bathtub so that she could remove it and place it in storage. When the plumber arrived, Rutter saw him park his van in front of the apartment building. Ososki walked outside to meet the plumber and Rutter approached.

"Hi, Melissa," Rutter said. "Are you having some problems with your plumbing? You should have let me know. I could have taken care of it for no charge."

"Oh no, I'm not having any problems," Ososki responded. "I called the same plumber that originally installed my clawfoot tub to come out and disconnect and remove it for me."

"Remove it?" Rutter asked shockingly. "You cannot remove it. The tub and its components are fixtures, permanent parts of the property. They must stay here after you leave."

"How can that be? I paid a lot for that tub and I'm not leaving it here," Ososki stated firmly.

Is the clawfoot bathtub an immovable fixture or removable property? The parties agree that there was no agreement between them regarding removal of the disputed property and that the items do not constitute trade property. Develop the arguments for Ososki and Rutter, relying on the relevant legal standard and precedent case. Determine which party has the stronger position.

The statutes and case for this exercise are:

- Okla. Stat. tit. 60, § 5 (2011)
- Okla. Stat. tit. 60, § 7 (2011)
- Okla. Stat. tit. 60, § 334 (2011)
- *W. Nat'l Bank v. Gerson*, 117 P. 205 (Okla. 1910)

STATUTORY ANALYSIS FOR SUCCESS

EXERCISE 72

Using the statutory section and case for this exercise, determine whether Stellar Meats Company breached the implied duty of good faith and fair dealing in increasing the price for its turkey meat products under the open price term of its contract with Matsui's Meat Market.

Background Facts

Jiro Matsui ("Matsui") owns and operates Matsui's Meat Market ("MMM") in Englewood, Colorado, a city located forty-five miles outside of Longmont, Colorado. MMM has both a retail business and a restaurant. The company specializes in providing fresh, all natural, and locally grown products in its store and restaurant. MMM is well known for its ground turkey burgers and sausage patties. During the breakfast rush, there is always a long line for MMM's famous "T-breakfast bun" and "T-omelette," both of which include fresh ground turkey. In August, Matsui opened two more locations near Englewood, one in downtown Denver.

As Matsui's business grew, he began to examine additional cost-cutting measures more closely and approached Stellar Meats Company ("Stellar") about entering into a long-term contract for the purchase of turkey products. Stellar provides quality meat products to retailers and restaurants throughout the United States. The company's manufacturing plant is in Longmont, Colorado, and the company raises and processes the animals at this location. Stellar produces beef, chicken, and turkey products. In particular, Stellar sells a variety of fresh turkey products including ground turkey, turkey bacon, hams, jerky, hotdogs, and sausages. Stellar guarantees that its meat products do not have steroids, hormones, and antibiotics, and the animals are grain fed and humanely raised. In addition, the company promotes its competitive pricing and impressive customer loyalty and satisfaction rates.

Matsui spoke with a number of meat producers based in New Jersey, Ohio, Pennsylvania, and Delaware. Stellar was the only company located in Colorado. In October, Matsui decided on Stellar and entered into a contract to purchase all of its turkey meat products from the company. Since MMM was located just outside Longmont, the products did not have to be shipped to MMM and MMM saved substantial money on shipping costs. Further, during an unexpected product shortage or extremely busy time at the restaurant, Matsui or one of his employees could drive to Longmont to purchase additional turkey meat rather than wait for a scheduled delivery or pickup. Under the agreement, MMM promised to purchase all of its turkey meat supply from Stellar in exchange for competitive wholesale pricing. The contract provided the initial price $1.90 per pound of ground turkey. This price was 40 cents lower than the going market rate. Although the contract included the initial price term, Stellar retained the discretion to review and modify the price amount once each quarter (namely, January 1, April 1, July 1, and October 1). Given its preference for locally grown, natural products and the competitive pricing term, MMM signed the agreement with Stellar for a two-year term.

In January, officials at Stellar reviewed the agreement with MMM and decided that the price would remain at $1.90 per pound. Shortly thereafter, in February, the country experienced an outbreak of "mad cow" disease, a condition that affects the cow's nervous system. The Food and Drug Administration reported that people who consumed infected beef risked developing a similar brain disease and possibly death. After this announcement, throughout the country, beef sales declined and the demand for poultry increased dramatically.

In March, Stellar's Research and Marketing Team conducted a study that reviewed the market, consumer demand, and the national supply for meat products (including competing companies). The team concluded that, given recent events and the company's quality products, Stellar should increase the wholesale price per pound of its turkey products by at least two dollars. The company's CEO agreed that a price increase should take effect but decided to raise it to $3.00, rather than $3.90. Stellar's CEO informed Matsui that, pursuant to the contract terms, the price would increase from $1.90 to $3.00 per pound, effective April 1.

Matsui was outraged over Stellar's decision to increase the price under the contract by over fifty percent. Matsui immediately contacted a few other manufacturers and discovered that most of them increased their prices for turkey meat products by an average of thirty percent. The wholesale prices ranged on average from $2.30 to $2.60 per pound. Only one company in Delaware quoted a price of $2.95 per pound. None of these manufacturers were located in Colorado.

Matsui contends that Stellar cannot modify the price of the purchased items in this manner. The parties agree that certain provisions of the Uniform Commercial Code ("UCC"), which Colorado has adopted, apply to the terms of their sales contract. Colorado law and the UCC provide for an implied duty of good faith and fair dealing in contract terms. MMM claims that Stellar breached this covenant.

Did Stellar breach the covenant of good faith and fair dealing when it increased the price for turkey products under its agreement with MMM? Develop the arguments for Stellar and MMM, relying on the relevant legal standard and precedent case. Determine which party has the stronger position.

The statute and case for this exercise are:

- Colo. Rev. Stat. § 4-1-304 (2011)

- *Amoco Oil Co. v. Ervin*, 908 P.2d 493 (Colo. 1995)

PART 2

INTERMEDIATE STATUTORY EXERCISES

STATUTORY ANALYSIS FOR SUCCESS
EXERCISE 73

Using the statute set out below and the case that follows, explain whether a lawsuit filed by Sue Salopic and her parents against Roger Stallow and his parents will be subject to a motion to strike under the anti-SLAPP statute. Do not address any other issues.

Statute:

The Anti-SLAPP (strategic lawsuit against public participation) statute applies where "[a] cause of action against a person aris[es] from any act of that person in furtherance of the person's right of petition or free speech under the United States Constitution or the California Constitution in connection with a public issue." Cal. Civ. Proc. Code § 425.16(e) (Deering 2011).

An "act in furtherance of a person's right of petition or free speech under the United States or California Constitution in connection with a public issue includes (1) any written or oral statement or writing made before a legislature, executive, or judicial proceeding, or any other official proceeding authorized by law; (2) any written or oral statement or writing made in connection with an issue under consideration or review by a legislative, executive, or judicial body, or any other official proceeding authorized by law; (3) any written or oral statement or writing made in a place open to the public or in a public forum in connection with an issue of public interest; (4) or any other conduct in furtherance of the exercise of the constitutional right of petition or the constitutional right of free speech in connection with a public issue or an issue of public interest." *Id.* § 425.16(e).

Fact Pattern:

Sue Salopic was a junior at a Sacramento, California high school when she decided to start the school's first computer recycling program. She knew that many of her friends were given new computers every year, and they had difficulty finding a place to recycle their old computers without driving for miles. With this in mind, Salopic started the Campus Computer Collectors or "CCC."

Ten students joined immediately, and they started to discuss the location of their first collection post. "Just one point of business first. Well, obviously, I'm the president of CCC," said Salopic. The other students started to murmur, and one spoke out. "Why? I mean, we're all in the organization. Shouldn't we vote on a president?" "Well, you can vote next year, but this year it's me." At this competitive high school, officer positions in any organization were hotly contested, because all the students wanted their high school records to look as good as possible for college admissions. Salopic pressed ahead with the meeting and wrote down her own name as president in the official organization records of the school.

At the next meeting, the CCC members were still grumbling. "OK," said Salopic. "I heard that the drop area was not fully staffed last weekend. That is not going to work for this organization. You guys are going to have to step up if we're going to have any impact on the environment." "Are you sure you're talking about an impact on the environment and not your resume?" asked a student pointedly. Salopic stared down the student. "If it weren't for me, there would be no CCC, so forget it. Move on and create your own organization if you're jealous."

The meeting continued, and Salopic explained the plans for the new organization website. "This will be handy," she said, "because we can have constant updates about the next collection spot and even home pick-up of larger computer equipment. We'll have a forum for community discussion as well." The website was planned to go live in one week's time.

The CCC organization lurched through the semester, with some staffing of pick-up areas, a fall dinner, and a holiday gift exchange. Over the winter break, Salopic learned that she had been accepted to an ivy-league university—her first choice. She was elated, and she posted the great news on her Facebook page. At the same time, she started to notice some strange discussions in the CCC website community forum. A commenter called "AA" posted that the CCC "was just a sham organization designed to give Sue some resume fodder." Another called "JJ" posted the following message: "Sue's an egomanic! Sue made herself president of this nutty organization without an election! She needs to get a life and get a real resume. What a fool." Another said: "If you think Sue cares about the environment, then I've got a bridge to sell you." The most disturbing was posted by "LR": "Sue, you'd better head to your fancy ivy league school fast. Because watch your back if you stay here, you fake person."

As soon as Salopic saw the messages, she felt cold with fear. She ran to her parents. "Look! Just look at this!" The three of them pored over the messages, becoming more and more upset. Salopic and her parents talked about the messages all weekend, and they immediately shut down the website.

By Monday, Salopic and her parents had decided to take legal action. With your help, they found out the names of the students who had posted the messages, and they sued the students and their parents. One of the defendants' attorneys called you and said that you should non-suit the lawsuit, because the defense lawyers were going to file a joint motion to strike under the anti-SLAPP statute. You have heard of the anti-SLAPP statute, but you need to research further to determine whether the defendants' motion to strike is likely to succeed. Using the statute set above and the case set out below, do you believe the defendants' anti-SLAPP motion to strike will succeed?

- *D.C. v. R.R.*, 106 Cal. Rptr. 3d 399 (Ct. App. 2010)

STATUTORY ANALYSIS FOR SUCCESS

EXERCISE 74

Using the statutory section, regulations, and cases for this exercise, determine whether Randy Valladolid adequately substantiated his business travel expenditures as required under tax law.

Background Facts

Randy Valladolid ("Valladolid"), a professional sculpture artist, lives in Albuquerque, New Mexico. Valladolid has been creating sculptures since his teenage years. He received his Bachelor's degree in Art from New Mexico State University. He is a member of the National Sculpture Society, the oldest organization of professional sculptors in the United States, and an active participant in the Save Outdoor Sculpture Movement, an initiative created to document all monuments and outdoors sculptures in the United States and to help communities preserve the integrity and beauty of their artwork. Since graduating from college, several of Valladolid's pieces have been displayed in local galleries and museums. Valladolid also has sold two of his sculptures from his third sculpture series titled, "Roaming."

Despite these accomplishments, Valladolid has not been able to quit his nighttime job as a security guard at the New Mexico Museum of Art. He desperately wants to be able to focus all his energy on further developing his sculpture business. He registered his business name a few years ago and started to market a number of his sculptures online. However, business has never been Valladolid's strong suit. Therefore, when a friend told him about the Annual Artist Collective's Business Conference ("AACB Conference") in Dallas, Texas, he decided to attend. He also had a friend from college who lived in Dallas whom he had not seen in several years.

The theme for the AACB Conference was "Business Training for the Creative Mind." The conference included three full days of information, networking, and exchange with speakers and panel discussions on the "nuts and bolts" of launching a business, market research, financing, business plans, and branding. The conference also provided a two-hour session on negotiating contracts with cities, businesses, and private and public organizations. The conference organizer guaranteed that attendees would develop key entrepreneurial skills, strategies, and tools to turn their artistic gifts and passions into a lucrative career. The conference hotel was the Sheraton in downtown Dallas near the Convention Center and in the nationally renowned arts district. Valladolid, in particular, looked forward to visiting the sculpture gardens and the Plaza of the Americas.

Valladolid spent much of his limited savings to go to Dallas. He, therefore, claimed all of his travel expenses as business deductions on his tax return. He claimed the following amounts:

Annual Artist Collective's Business Conference

Conference Materials and Registration Fee	$ 450.00
Greyhound Bus Ticket	$ 122.00
Conference Meals (for 3 days)	$ 117.00
Conference Lodging (for 3 days)	$ 620.71
Taxicabs	$ 55.00

The Tax Commissioner disallowed all of Valladolid's deductions as business travel expenses and, in turn, found a deficiency in Valladolid's Federal income tax return. The Commissioner did not dispute the business nature of the conference but found that Valladolid failed to substantiate the requested amounts. The case proceeded to trial.

At trial, the parties admitted the following testimony and evidence regarding Valladolid's travel expenses:

Valladolid explained that he decided to attend the conference because of its focus on helping artists develop thriving businesses. To keep his costs down, Valladolid took a Greyhound bus from Las Cruces, New Mexico to Dallas, Texas, which cost $61.00 each way. A coworker gave him a ride to the bus terminal in Las Cruces, which was approximately 200 miles. He gave his coworker about $50.00 for gas. Valladolid paid his Greyhound bus fare in cash and did not have a copy of the receipt or the bus ticket. He did not realize he would need to submit the bus ticket but indicated that the current ticket price for travel from Las Cruces to Dallas on Greyhound's website was accurate. He paid a total of $122.00 for his round trip ticket.

Valladolid arrived at the conference on Wednesday, August 10, and checked into the hotel. He put down a credit card to cover any incidentals at the hotel but, at check out, paid his hotel bill in cash. He received a bill from the hotel. In support of his testimony, Valladolid submitted a copy of this bill from the Sheraton Hotel in Dallas from Wednesday to Friday (three days). The total for the hotel bill was $640.71, but he claimed only $620.71. The excluded amount was for movie rentals and purchases at the hotel snack bar. As for the conference registration and materials fee, Valladolid paid this charge with a money order at the conference registration desk and he did not keep the carbon copy of the money order. Nor did he contact the conference organizers for a copy of the money order or a receipt for payment.

To travel from the hotel to the conference and other venues, Valladolid took public transportation and cabs. The money he spent on cabs totaled $55.00. Valladolid submitted two receipts for cab rides. Each receipt provided the amount for the particular trip. The handwriting on each receipt was similar. In addition, the receipts provided the name of the taxicab company, Yellow Cab, but did not include the company's address or phone number.

Valladolid also produced a copy of the brochure and program schedule for the AACB Conference, which he printed from the organization's website. In addition, he submitted handouts from at least three conference sessions. He also produced pages from a notepad on which he took notes from the various conference sessions. He could not recall all of the sessions that he attended, but he identified many of the workshops, luncheons, and receptions that he participated in over the three days. In particular, he spoke highly of the information he learned from the two-hour session on contract drafting and negotiations.

Has Valladolid substantiated his travel expenses sufficiently by adequate records? Do not address whether the court would allow the deduction as a trade or business expense under relevant tax law. Focus on the substantiation requirements.

The statutory section, regulations, and cases for this exercise are:

- I.R.C. § 274(d) (2011)

- Treas. Reg. § 1.274-5T (2011)

- Treas. Reg. § 1.274-5(c) (2011)

- *Wilson v. Comm'r*, 82 T.C.M. (CCH) 899, 2001 Tax Ct. Memo LEXIS 339 (T.C. Nov. 14, 2001)

- *Gardner v. Comm'r*, 46 T.C.M. (CCH) 1283, 1983 Tax Ct. Memo LEXIS 245 (T.C. Sept. 1, 1983)

STATUTORY ANALYSIS FOR SUCCESS
EXERCISE 75

Using the statutory section and cases for this exercise, determine whether Lea Tomlin ("Tomlin") is a putative spouse under California law and, therefore, entitled to an equitable division of marital or quasi-marital property.

Background Facts

Lea Tomlin ("Tomlin"), a native of Midvale, Idaho, graduated from Boise State University ("Boise State") with a Bachelor's degree in Theatre Arts. After graduating from college, Tomlin married her longtime boyfriend, Trent McCoy, and settled down in Boise. Tomlin worked full-time as a project manager at Midvale Telephone Exchange, Inc. but still managed to star in several productions at the Boise Contemporary Theatre. She also worked as an adjunct instructor in the Theatre Arts Department at her alma mater, Boise State. As a teacher, she had the opportunity to share her experiences from college and the stage and even direct a few of the department's productions.

Tomlin has received rave reviews for her own performances, and after appearing in a number of plays, Tomlin competed in the Mrs. Idaho America competition. She won runner-up and landed a spot in a regional commercial for the Idaho Potato Commission. A national talent agent saw Tomlin's commercial and invited her to come to an audition in Los Angeles, California. The agent was so impressed with her performance that he paid for Tomlin's flight to Los Angeles.

Tomlin auditioned for a role on a new reality television show called *My Big City Life*. The reality show documented the trials and tribulations of three budding actors as they moved from the comfort of their small town homes to the big city of Los Angeles. Tomlin secured the role as the female actor and made plans to move with her husband, Trent, to Los Angeles. Tomlin had to start filming for the show immediately and left Boise the following month. Trent was to join her in Los Angeles in six months. Tomlin's agent found her temporary housing and an acting coach. Although this was a reality show, her agent expected this role to open the door to commercials and feature films.

After two months, Tomlin's husband called and told her he did not want to move to Los Angeles. The couple argued about the move over the next few weeks and decided to file for divorce. Although she was sad to end her marriage, she knew that it was for the best, as Trent would not have been happy in Los Angeles away from his family and friends. Tomlin decided to channel her sadness and focus on her craft.

My Big City Life aired in June and Tomlin garnered some fame. The public seemed to love her small town charm and naivety, candid descriptions of Hollywood actors, producers, and directors, and tales of long lines at auditions and nights of partying. However, as with many Hollywood productions, the show did not have high enough ratings to secure a second season. With the show's dismissal, Tomlin's five minutes of fame soon ended. She continued to audition for televisions and film roles but many of the casting agents and directors commented that they could not envision her in any role but as the actor in *My Big City Life*. Tomlin was effectively typecast.

A couple of months later, Tomlin took a position as a Production Assistant for the Fox Reality Awards Show. Her main job was to make sure the hosts, honorees, and awardees were ready to appear on stage and knew where to exit the stage. Back stage, Tomlin met Deepak Navar ("Navar"). A few years ago, Navar received the Favorite to Watch Award and his hit show, *Wild Life*, won the Choice Award at the Fox Reality Show Awards. *Wild Life*, another reality show, documents and reenacts the crazy antics and adventures of zookeepers and the animals at the nation's zoos. Navar was the show's host for five years. Since *Wild Life*, he has received offers to host game shows and talk shows and he has appeared in several films. Rumor also has it that *People Magazine* almost included Navar in its annual feature issue for the "Sexiest Man Alive."

Navar met his wife, Trinity Morgan ("Morgan"), on the set of *Blue Lagoon III: The Paradise Continues*. Morgan, a very talented singer, dancer, and actor, became famous on Broadway. On the big screen, she mainly appears in musicals and adaptations of stage plays. When they started dating, Navar and Morgan became an instant Hollywood power couple and a favorite of the public. The media described the couple as "Broadway meets Hollywood" and referred to them as "TriniDee" for Trinity and Deepak. They were inseparable and appeared to be in it for the long haul. Their relationship seemed to work even though Morgan lived in New York City and Navar spent much of his time in Los Angeles or on location.

When Tomlin met Navar at the awards show, he took an immediate interest in her. He remembered that she starred in *My Big City Life* and commented how much he liked the show. "It was a refreshing change of pace to watch someone with such values navigate the Los Angeles terrain," Navar told Tomlin. Tomlin and Navar had a few laughs and exchanged contact information.

A week later, Navar called Tomlin and asked her to meet him for drinks. She put him on hold for a minute, covered the phone, and screamed for joy. She was so happy that he called. She returned to the phone and agreed to meet him the next day at 5 p.m. for drinks. Navar selected the Blue Room Bar in Burbank. "It's pretty out of the way and private there," Navar explained.

When Tomlin arrived at the bar, she spotted Navar across the room wearing dark shades and a casual suit. Tomlin sat in the booth with Navar. "How are you?" he asked.

"Doing well," Tomlin replied. "And you?"

"Better now that you are here," Navar said. Tomlin smiled.

"I have a question. I know that you are married to Trinity Morgan. She's absolutely amazing. Why did you ask me to meet you?" Tomlin asked.

"Yes, Trinity and I are the 'it' Hollywood couple at the moment," Navar began. "But it is all smoke and mirrors, a story created by the press. The reality is we are not as happy as the media would have us. It's hard being married and famous actors."

"I see," Tomlin said. "I just don't know if I should be here with you. It doesn't seem right."

"Let's not worry about all of that right now. We are just two people having a drink," Navar said. "And I wanted to talk to you about some projects that I am working on. There could be a role for you."

Navar then waved to the waiter, who came over, and Navar ordered two dry martinis with blue cheese olives. Navar and Tomlin talked and laughed for hours. They made plans to meet the following weekend.

Tomlin and Navar had a whirlwind romance out of the public eye. They met at little known places around the Los Angeles area, mainly in the San Fernando Valley, and spent time at Navar's home in Encino, which was hidden behind a large brick wall and security gate. Morgan rarely visited this home, as she preferred life in New York City. Further, the paparazzi never caught Navar and Tomlin out together. Their affair remained private.

A month later, while getting ready for work, Tomlin saw an announcement about Navar and Tomlin: "TriniDee Calls It Splits: Trinity Morgan and Deepak Navar Separate after Six Years of Marriage, A Hollywood Record." *TMZ* broke the story. Tomlin sat on her bed and listened to the story. The reporter revealed very little but explained that reliable sources had confirmed the couple's plan to divorce. "He finally did it," she thought to herself.

The next week, Tomlin went to Navar's house for dinner. Tomlin asked Navar about his divorce from Morgan. "That's why I wanted to see you tonight," Navar said. "I wanted to tell you that I'm finally getting divorced." Navar then got down on one knee, gently grabbed Tomlin's hand, and said, "Lea, will you marry me?" He pulled a ring from his pocket and placed it on her finger. Without hesitation, Tomlin replied "Yes!"

"Let's not wait too long. What about eight or nine months from now?" Navar asked.

"That's plenty of time to arrange a dream wedding," Tomlin stated.

"You know, I think we should keep it very small and intimate, just you, me, the minister, and our two closest friends as witnesses. I've done the big wedding thing before and I want to go the opposite route this time," Navar explained.

"Okay. I've been married before too and don't mind a change of pace for us. I just want to be with you," Tomlin replied. "What do you think about the first Saturday in August?"

"Perfect," Navar said. "I'll make sure my agent carves out that date in my contract. I'm auditioning for an action movie next week and hope to get the lead role."

"I'm sure you will. You are the best," Tomlin encouraged him. "What about a wedding announcement? We can put something in the paper or give it to your public relations person in a few months or so."

"Why? There's no need to waste money on an announcement. We know that we are getting married," Navar countered.

"That makes sense," Tomlin yielded. Tomlin and Navar then sat down to dinner. After dinner, they watched a movie and talked about their future together.

Over the next six months, Navar spent his time between Los Angeles and Miami, Florida. He landed his first action movie role about a Navy Seals officer who runs a for-hire security firm in Miami and, using his expertise, foils a plot to assassinate a government leader. Navar played the role of the Navy Seals officer and planned to perform most of the stunts himself. He went through intensive training for the role.

Seven months after Navar's proposal of marriage, Tomlin's best friend, Deborah Wilcox ("Wilcox") called to surprise her with a trip to Las Vegas for her bachelorette party. "So how's the wedding planning coming along?" Wilcox asked.

"There's no planning really," Tomlin told Wilcox. "We set the date in August and booked the minister. Besides you and Deepak's agent, no one else will be there. He wants it to be small. We're not even sending out announcements or invitations. It's for the best, really. Deepak is rarely here and I would have had to plan a huge wedding all alone. I think he's been home about one weekend each month. He's really busy."

"Well, small wedding or not, we are going to Las Vegas for your bachelorette party," Wilcox said. "We leave next weekend. I'll pick you up."

"That will be great. I'll be ready. Thank you for planning the trip, Deborah," Tomlin replied and hung up the phone.

Later that evening, Tomlin went to the Trader Joe's grocery store to buy some produce and wine. While standing in the checkout line, Tomlin noticed the cover of the latest issue of *In Touch Weekly* magazine. The headline read, "TriniDee: Back in Stride Again." Tomlin opened the magazine and saw pictures of Navar and Morgan holding hands on the beach. One of the picture's caption and cutline read, "Trinity and Deepak: Walking the beach in Tahiti."

"Tahiti? This must be an old picture from the magazine's files," Tomlin thought. "Deepak is in Miami right now shooting his movie. The press will do anything to conjure up a story." She put the magazine back, pulled out her cell phone, and called Navar. The call went straight to voicemail. Tomlin left a voice mail message and sent him a text.

Navar returned Tomlin's call later that evening. "How's Miami?" she asked him.

"Hot, very hot," Navar replied. "But we are making really good progress on the movie. I cannot wait for you to see it."

"What do you think about my coming to Miami to visit?" Tomlin asked.

"I would love to see you but it's not a good time right now," Navar explained. "I need to focus all of my time and energy on getting my lines down and perfecting these stunts. I am going to be working overtime so that I can take a break for our wedding in a couple of weeks. We'll see each other soon."

The next weekend, Tomlin and her best friend, Wilcox, traveled to Las Vegas to celebrate her upcoming nuptials. The two had a wonderful time going from one casino to the next. While roaming through the Forum Shops at Caesar's Palace, Tomlin spotted a beautiful wedding dress in one of the boutique's windows. "That's it, Deborah!" Tomlin exclaimed. "I have found the perfect wedding dress. I had no idea what I was going to wear until now." Before Tomlin and Wilcox headed back to Los Angeles, Tomlin stopped by the boutique to purchase the dress.

The next weekend, Tomlin, Wilcox, Navar's agent, and the officiant all arrived at Navar's house at 6 p.m. for the wedding. Navar and Tomlin met with the officiant briefly in the study before the ceremony. Navar gave the officiant their marriage license, which provided Tomlin's married name as "Lea Tomlin," and explained their decision to file a confidential marriage license.* Tomlin also showed the officiant a poem that she wanted him to read. The ceremony lasted only about fifteen minutes. There was no media representative or paparazzi present. Wilcox took a few pictures on her digital camera. The ceremony was small but moving.

Right after the wedding, Navar surprised Tomlin with a brand new 3,000 square foot home in Woodland Hills, California, a neighborhood in the southwestern area of the San Fernando Valley. He showed her pictures of the house and the deed that listed both Navar and Tomlin as the owners. "This is absolutely beautiful!" Tomlin shouted. "But, what about your house?"

"I am going to sell it. I bought it with Trinity and will give her half of the sale proceeds," Navar explained. "Feel free to decorate this one however you want," Navar said. "I also found a great location for a new business right up the street. You mentioned that you wanted to open a boutique. I have some extra money now to invest and get you started."

"All of my dreams are finally coming true," Tomlin said softly. Within a few days, Tomlin hired an interior decorator and signed the lease on her new business space. She used the money Navar gave her to get started. She named her shop, *Lea's Luxuries*. Tomlin planned to cater to upscale clientele and hoped to make many new industry contacts through Navar's projects.

---

* California law provides for the registration of public and confidential marriage licenses. *See* Cal. Fam. Code § 511 (Deering 2011). To obtain a confidential marriage license, the couple must be living together as spouses at the time they apply for the marriage license, and they must sign an affidavit on the license attesting to that fact. Confidential marriage licenses are filed with the country clerk but remain private records. Only the married couple may purchase a copy of the marriage certificate and they must present valid identification to receive the document. Other persons may obtain a copy of a confidential marriage license only through an official court order, showing good cause for obtaining the information.

Tomlin remained very busy working on their new home and with her new business. She took care of all of the couple's affairs in Los Angeles. She paid the household bills from their joint checking account. She signed all of the checks. She hired maintenance people, groundskeepers, and contractors. Navar spent most of his time in Miami finishing the movie and preparing for its opening night.

Navar's new movie opened in February in Miami. Navar walked the red carpet alone but took several pictures with Morgan, who also attended the star-studded event. Tomlin watched the opening on *Access Hollywood* and saw the paparazzi's shots of Navar and Morgan together. Tomlin had seen an early editor's cut of the new movie during one of Navar's weekend visits to Los Angeles and she knew that Navar's fans would love the movie.

Tomlin did not mind staying at home while Navar took the spotlight. Navar attended many Hollywood events and needed plenty of freedom to interact with key industry people and his fans. Tomlin also did not want her marriage to become a media target. So, she did not attend any industry events with Navar and Navar never asked her to join him. Tomlin had plenty to do around the house and for her new business.

Tomlin's prediction about the movie was correct. Navar's new movie grossed approximately 20 million dollars during its opening weekend. Navar's agent was busy fielding calls about new movie and television projects. Within two weeks, Navar signed with SyFy Television to host a new series called the *Horror Hour*, where the audience votes on old horror movies and selects the next one for the station to air each Friday night. The producers planned to film the series in a studio in New York City. Navar also committed to play the lead role in two new films. He wanted to maintain a constant presence in both film and television and planned to stay very busy.

Over the next six months, Tomlin remained in the San Fernando Valley area while Navar worked in New York City, traveled for his next movie role, and appeared on talk shows throughout the country. A few tabloids reported sightings of Navar with Morgan at "hot spots" in New York City and others documented Navar's outings with other famous Hollywood personalities. Wilcox made sure Tomlin knew about each report.

"I just want to make sure you know," Wilcox explained.

"It's nothing," Tomlin told Wilcox. "It's all media hype."

Tomlin remained in Los Angeles and continued to manage the couple's affairs there and Navar asked his agent and other business contacts to help with any financial matters. For example, Navar's longtime accountant prepared their tax returns. Tomlin and Navar filed separate tax returns and identified themselves as single. Tomlin signed her tax return as "Lea Tomlin." Navar's accountant explained the financial benefits of the separate filings.

Tomlin and Navar spent most of their time apart but this arrangement was nothing new to them. Navar, however, did manage to fly to Los Angeles to be with

Tomlin on their one-year wedding anniversary. Tomlin cooked a romantic dinner at their Woodland Hills home.

Meanwhile, Morgan eventually learned about Navar's relationship with Tomlin and his weekend trips to Los Angeles. "I have been so busy with work that I missed all of the signs," Morgan said. "I know now and you better end it! I will not be made to look like a fool!" Morgan shouted. She also threatened to divorce Navar if he did not end the affair immediately.

The following weekend, about a year and half after their marriage ceremony, Navar flew to Los Angeles to see Tomlin. When Navar arrived at their Woodland Hills home, he sat Tomlin down to talk. Navar proceeded to tell Tomlin that he was very unhappy with their relationship and had been feeling that way for a while. Navar then revealed that he leaving Tomlin and going back to his wife.

"Your wife?" Tomlin answered in shock. "What are you talking about? I'm your wife."

"My real wife, Trinity," Navar stated firmly. "I am moving to New York to be with her." Tomlin, in tears, ran out of the room and Navar left.

Tomlin immediately filed a petition for dissolution of the marriage. The court entered a judgment of nullity, finding that Tomlin and Navar's marriage was illegal since Navar was still married to Morgan at the time he purportedly married Tomlin. Tomlin sought to be declared a putative spouse.

Under California law, does Tomlin have putative spouse status, such that she is entitled to a division of the property acquired during her relationship with Navar (quasi-marital property) as if it were community property? Do not address whether Navar had a valid marriage to Morgan or the laws that prohibit bigamy. Focus on the putative spouse doctrine. Is Tomlin a putative spouse?

The statutory section and cases for this exercise are:

- Cal. Fam. Code § 2251 (Deering 2011)

- *In re Marriage of Sun*, 112 Cal. Rptr. 3d 906 (Ct. App. 2010)

- *In re Domestic P'ship of Ellis*, 76 Cal. Rptr. 3d 401 (Ct. App. 2008)

- *Estate of DePasse*, 118 Cal. Rptr. 2d 143 (Ct. App. 2002)

STATUTORY ANALYSIS FOR SUCCESS

EXERCISE 76

Using the statutory sections and cases listed at the end of this exercise, determine whether Kevin Statham violated the Texas criminal trespass statute.

Background Facts

Kevin Statham ("Statham") lives in Waco, Texas. One Monday, Statham checked his voicemail and listened to a message from his friend, Terry Gutierrez ("Gutierrez"). Gutierrez invited Statham to attend a football-game-watching party on Sunday afternoon and asked guests to bring chips, soda, and beer. Gutierrez promised to provide plenty of nachos and chicken wings and a variety of dips and desserts.

When Sunday arrived, Statham could not wait to leave work and go to the party. He had worked an unusual number of overtime hours, and although he was very tired, he planned to attend the party. Gutierrez lived in Statham's apartment complex, so Statham knew he could get home easily and quickly from the party. Statham left work at 2:00 p.m. and drove to the corner store to buy a case of beer to take to the party.

As Statham approached Gutierrez's apartment, he could hear everyone inside cheering and music coming from the back patio. Gutierrez lived on the first floor of his building and had a spacious patio located off his kitchen. Statham lived in the building at the rear of the complex on the third floor. Statham lived alone, but his girlfriend had a key to his apartment. Occasionally, Statham's girlfriend would drop by his apartment unannounced. In the complex, each apartment's front door opened to the outside and had the apartment number posted below the peephole.

Statham knocked on the door of Gutierrez's apartment and the door flew wide open.

"Hey there, Kevin!" Gutierrez shouted as he greeted Statham. "Man, what took you so long to get here? We have been eating and drinking all afternoon."

"I just got off work," Statham responded. "I'm dead tired but would not miss the game and your party for anything." Statham then handed Gutierrez the case of beer.

"Yes! We were starting to run low. You came just in time," Gutierrez stated.

Statham walked through the door and followed Gutierrez to the kitchen. "You want a cold one?" Gutierrez asked.

"Yeah, that would be great," Statham replied. Statham grabbed the beer and walked to the front room to join the other guests. Statham quickly finished his first beer and went back for a second one and then a third. During halftime, Gutierrez went to the store for more refreshments. When he returned, the half-time show was over and his guests were cheering for their favorite team. A few guests remained on the patio listening to music.

By the end of the game around 10 p.m., Statham had drunk at least nine beers but had eaten very little food. Statham stumbled to the kitchen to find some snacks. He grabbed a handful of chips, about six wings, and another beer, and sat on a stool to eat. A couple of times, Statham lost his balance on the stool and fell to the floor. Onlookers just started laughing when they heard the commotion and saw Statham on the floor. He managed to get back on the stool with some assistance. After a few bites, Statham practically fell asleep on his plate.

"Hey Kevin, are you okay?" Gutierrez asked. "We had a blast today, but you may have had one too many. Why don't you go lie down in the guest room and sleep this off?"

"Nah, man, I'm alright. I can make it to my place. But I will leave my car here," Statham said as he cracked a smile.

Gutierrez propped Statham up and walked him to the front door. "I'll see you later, Terry. Thanks for everything," Statham said as he walked out the door.

Statham walked straight to the back of the complex toward building number 13. When he reached the second floor, Statham stopped, turned right, and started to walk down the balcony. He held on to the railing to prevent falling down. "Man, I feel dizzy. I've got to stop drinking so much," he thought. Statham then reached into his pocket for his keys. "Oh no, I forgot my keys," Statham said. "How will I get into my apartment?"

Statham looked down the balcony and saw an open window. "What luck? My window is open," he thought. Statham took a few more steps, grabbed the window sill, and climbed through the window headfirst. He touched the carpet and instantly fell asleep.

Meanwhile, the tenant of the apartment, Lomasi Begay ("Begay"), was in the kitchen throwing away her burnt meal and washing the dishes. She had opened the window briefly to let the smoke clear out of her apartment. She knew the security officer would be making his rounds at that time. Begay did not hear Statham climb through the window. When Begay finished cleaning, she poured a glass of wine and headed to the living room to close the window. As she turned the corner, Begay immediately spotted Statham on the floor, dropped her wine glass, and screamed, "Get out! Get out!"

Statham raised his arm, waved his hand in Begay's direction, and murmured, "Please stop shouting." He went back to sleep. Begay ran to her bedroom, locked the door, and called 9-1-1.

When the police arrived, they arrested Statham for violating the criminal trespass statute. Once Statham became sober, he explained that he did not know he was in the wrong apartment. He thought he was in his apartment on the third floor.

Did Statham violate the Texas criminal trespass statute? Develop the arguments for the prosecution and Statham and determine which position is stronger. The parties agree that Statham's conduct does not rise to the level of intentional or knowing activity.

The following statutory sections and cases are for use with this exercise:

- Tex. Penal Code Ann. §§ 6.02, 6.03 (West 2011)

- Tex. Penal Code Ann. § 8.04 (West 2011)

- Tex. Penal Code Ann. § 30.05 (West 2011)

- *West v. State*, 567 S.W.2d 515 (Tex. Crim. App. 1978)

- *Banister v. State*, 761 S.W.2d 849 (Tex. App. 1988)

- *Reed v. State*, 762 S.W.2d 640 (Tex. App. 1988)

- *Bustillos v. State*, 832 S.W.2d 668 (Tex. App. 1992)

- *Jones v. State*, 900 S.W.2d 103 (Tex. App. 1995)

- *Griffith v. State*, 315 S.W.3d 648 (Tex. App. 2010)

STATUTORY ANALYSIS FOR SUCCESS

EXERCISE 77

Using the statutory sections and cases listed below for this exercise, determine whether Cassie Davis can recover under Oregon's Workers' Compensation Law for injuries she sustained when the car hit her.

Background Facts

Cassie Davis ("Davis"), a 19-year-old, works at the Pearl District Delicatessen ("Pearl District") in Portland, Oregon. Davis has been employed there for the past eight months. Davis works full time and is one of three clerks at the deli. As a clerk, she waits on customers, prepares and stocks all deli products received, cleans the equipment and cases, and makes sure the shop complies with applicable health standards. Davis's supervisor is Benjamin Delaney ("Delaney").

Davis has an hour for her lunch break and receives two fifteen-minute breaks during her regular shift. Last Wednesday, Davis arrived at work at 7:00 a.m. for her regular shift. The breakfast crowd was large and in a rush to leave for work. All three clerks were on duty at that time, and the checkout line was extremely long. Davis helped with the orders by walking down the line to answer customers' questions and take their orders before they reached the counter. Most customers wanted a bagel or Danish pastry and hot coffee. The coffee orders required the most time to prepare, especially when the customer required special ingredients and varying shots of espresso. Pearl District is known for its fresh bagels and variety of toppings and the deli proudly serves Stumptown Coffee, a Portland original.

At 11:30 a.m., Davis went on her lunch break. As instructed by Delaney, Davis clocked out and walked toward the back of the deli. Davis stored her lunch, a sandwich and a cup of mixed fruit, in the small refrigerator that the employees shared. She quickly ate her sandwich and decided to save her fruit cup to eat during one of her short afternoon breaks. Davis then reappeared on the deli floor and decided to tell her supervisor she planned to ride her bike to Active Culture Frozen Yogurt ("Active Culture") to buy some "YoCream" yogurt, another local Portland product. Active Culture serves fat free yogurt at less than 120 calories per serving. Davis's favorite flavor was Root Beer Float, and she had been craving a taste of YoCream for weeks. Active Culture was only a mile away from the deli shop, and Davis knew she could get there and back to work in about twenty minutes, within her lunch break, and she would still have plenty of time to eat her yogurt in the back room before her lunch break ended.

"Hey, Benjamin, I'm going to ride down to Active Culture to get some yogurt," Davis told Delaney.

"Active Culture? That's a mile away, right?" Delaney asked. "You still have some time on your lunch break, but you may want to just go across the street to

TCBY. They have yogurt too and lots of flavors. It's not your momma's TCBY anymore. Plus, we are pretty busy here now and it's just going to get worse while you are gone as the afternoon crowd starts coming in."

Davis shrugged her shoulders, took off her apron, and walked across the street to TCBY. Davis was disappointed that she would not have her favorite Root Beer YoCream, but she was pleasantly surprised by the variety of flavors offered at TCBY. She read the calorie chart and ordered the coffee flavored yogurt. She paid the cashier, grabbed her to-go cup, and walked out the front door. As Davis walked across the street back to the deli, a car ran the red light, sped through the intersection, and hit her. A young man standing at the curb called 911 and several onlookers ran to Davis's assistance. Not only did the driver run the red light, he also failed to yield for Davis even though she was in the pedestrian crosswalk.

The driver of the car that hit Davis did not stay to help her but fled the scene. The police have not located the driver. Davis suffered major injuries and remained in the hospital for several weeks. She filed a claim for workers' compensation, which Pearl District's insurer rejected. The insurance company concluded that Davis's injuries were not sustained during the course of her employment with Pearl District. Rather, she was on her lunch break, away from the deli.

Oregon's Workers' Compensation Law is an exclusive remedy for workplace injuries and replaces any other liability on the employer's part. Pearl District contends that, because the accident occurred during Davis's lunch break, Davis's injury did not occur in the course of her employment and the Workers' Compensation Law does not apply. Davis, on the other hand, contends that the "special errand" exception to the going and coming rule applies to the facts of this case.

Can Davis recover under Oregon's Workers' Compensation Law for the injuries she sustained when the car hit her? Does the going and coming rule bar Davis's recovery or does the special errand exception apply in this case? Develop the arguments for Pearl District and Davis and determine which position is stronger. The parties agree that none of the other exceptions for the going and coming rule applies in this case.

These are the statutory sections and cases you need for this exercise:

- Or. Rev. Stat. § 656.005(7)(a) (2009)

- Or. Rev. Stat. § 656.017 (2009)

- *Krushwitz v. McDonald's Rests. of Or., Inc.*, 919 P.2d 465 (Or. 1996)

- *Cope v. W. Am. Ins. Co.*, 785 P.2d 1050 (Or. 1990)

- *Barker v. Wagner Mining Equip., Inc.*, 487 P.2d 1162 (Or. Ct. App. 1971)

- *White v. State Indus. Accident Comm'n*, 389 P.2d 310 (Or. 1964)

STATUTORY ANALYSIS FOR SUCCESS
EXERCISE 78

Using the statutory section and cases listed below for this exercise, determine whether the sticker award system used by the teacher, Terry Houston, violates the Family Educational Rights and Privacy Act of 1974, as an unlawful release of confidential student education records.

Background Facts

Terry Houston ("Houston") teaches third grade math at Longfellow Elementary in Baltimore, Maryland. Houston is a very popular teacher at the school. She has received the "Teacher of the Year" Award twice since she started working at Longfellow Elementary five years ago. Houston credits her success at teaching to her ability to motivate and encourage her students to strive for excellence, regardless of the task on which they are working. No assignment or project is too big or too small for her students to perform to the very best of their abilities.

Houston also uses an awards system to recognize those students who perform well each week. She gives each student who receives a perfect score on the week's homework assignments a sticker to wear on his or her cheek. The sticker is in the shape of a star and contains the words, "You are a star!" The following is a picture of the sticker:

Students who did not receive a perfect score on the week's homework assignments do not receive a sticker that week. Houston carefully records her students' scores on each assignment and keeps track of their progress throughout the week. On Fridays, she awards each high-performing student by placing a sticker on his or her cheek. Many other teachers at Longfellow Elementary have adopted similar awards systems to recognize their students' good work.

One day, a group of parents met with the principal of Longfellow Elementary to discuss Houston's third grade math class. One parent explained that her daughter was embarrassed because she had not received a sticker award when several of her friends in the class had received one that week. Another parent stated that his son has never received one of the stickers even though he completes his homework each week and does his best work. Several other parents raised similar examples of how their children did not receive a sticker award and felt humiliated and not as smart as their peers.

The parents have asked the principal to prohibit Houston from using her sticker award system or require her to implement an award system in which every student receives some form of recognition. The parents also have threatened to sue the school and Houston for violating the Family Educational Rights and Privacy Act ("FERPA"). In particular, the parents argue that Houston's award system unlawfully discloses information about her students' "education records."

Does Houston's sticker award system constitute an unlawful release of confidential student education records under FERPA? Provide the arguments for Houston, the teacher, and the parents.

The following statutory section and cases are for this exercise:

- Family Educational Rights and Privacy Act of 1974, 20 U.S.C.S. § 1232g (LexisNexis 2011)

- *Owasso Indep. Sch. Dist. v. Falvo*, 534 U.S. 426 (2002)

- *Risica v. Dumas*, 466 F. Supp. 2d 434 (D. Conn. 2006)

- *C.N. v. Ridgewood Bd. of Educ.*, 146 F. Supp. 2d 528 (D.N.J. 2001)

- *Belanger v. Nashua, N.H., Sch. Dist.*, 856 F. Supp. 40 (D.N.H. 1994)

STATUTORY ANALYSIS FOR SUCCESS
EXERCISE 79

Using the statutory sections and cases listed after this exercise, determine whether there is sufficient evidence to show that Corky Moore actually believed he needed to defend himself against Benjamin "Hurricane" Carver.

Assume the following evidence was admitted at Moore's trial for murder in the second degree.

Background Facts

Corky Moore ("Moore") walked through the front door of the Mahogany Bar and Lounge ("Mahogany") in Tarzana, California and the bartender and owner, Manny Holm ("Manny"), greeted him with a smile. "You're back! This makes four Fridays in a row. You are a regular now," said Manny.

"What can I say? I really like this spot. It reminds me of my favorite bar back home and I do miss home," Moore responded. "Can I get a Jameson on the Rocks?"

"Coming right up," Manny said. Manny prepared Moore's drink and placed it in front of him. "How about I start a tab for you?"

"Yeah, I plan to hang out here for a while," Moore said. He sipped on his drink and looked around the bar. The place was not too crowded that night. The women outnumbered the men by at least two to one. As Moore sat at the bar, he could see the pool tables and small dance floor area. Benjamin "Hurricane" Carver's ("Carver's") girlfriend, Christy Hampton ("Christy"), stood in front of the jukebox looking for a song to select.

"This thing is too old, Manny! When are you going to come into the twenty–first century?" Christy asked Manny.

"Real soon, and remember we will be closing down the bar for a month for renovations. You'll have to get your drinks at home for a bit," Manny chuckled. "When we reopen, this place will have satellite radio, plasma screens all over, real mahogany wood on the bar, and a backroom for parties. How does that sound?"

"That's going to be great, Manny . . . a real improvement," Christy said. Then, a patron who was playing pool walked over to Christy and asked her name.

"Hey pretty lady, what's your name?" the patron asked.

"Christy. What's your name?" she responded.

"Charles. Here's a quarter for the next round of music," the patron said. "What do you want to hear?"

"Something upbeat, something I can dance to," Christy said.

"Pick Maze and Frankie Beverly's *Happy Feelin's*," the patron told Christy. She selected the song and the music started to play. "Wanna dance?" the patron asked Christy as he politely touched her hand. Before Christy could answer, Carver, who stood six feet and four inches tall and weighed 220 pounds, came across the room and hit the patron in the mouth. The patron fell to the floor and Carver continued to hit him.

"Hurricane, stop! He didn't do anything. Stop!" Christy yelled.

Manny reached for the phone to call the police. "Here he goes again. Hopefully, the cops will get here sooner this time," Manny told Moore.

"This has happened before?" Moore asked.

"Unfortunately it has, and I am too old to get between men fighting. I really like Hurricane. He is a very loyal customer. I mean, I practically paid my kids' way through college on his bar tab alone. Nevertheless, he does have a serious anger management problem. He gets in at least one fight a month here. He aggravates easily. Most of the incidents were minor scuffles though, and did not require any police attention. If anyone comes too close to that girlfriend of his, he is just asking for trouble," Manny explained. "I need to make sure they send an ambulance this time."

Moore sat calmly at the bar watching the events unfold. The police arrived and took Carver into custody. Christy cried nonstop. She left the bar right after the police escorted Carver out in handcuffs. The battered patron remained in the hospital for a week recovering from his injuries. The police released Carver the following day. Carver was never charged for this incident.

Over the next few months, Moore frequented Mahogany consistently on Fridays after work. He came to know the other regular bar patrons pretty well. They would sit at the bar and share horror stories about work, debate politics and sports, and comment on happenings at the bar. Occasionally, someone would tell Moore about another argument or fight involving Carver. "He is someone you don't ever want to cross," one patron remarked. Moore added, "Yeah, that guy is nothing but bad news."

The last Friday before the bar closed for renovations, Moore arrived an hour earlier than his usual time. He wanted to make sure his favorite seat at the bar was empty and knew the place would be extra crowded that evening. Moore ordered a Jameson on the Rocks and asked Manny to start a tab.

"This is going to be a great night, Manny! However, I have to say, I am pretty bummed that the place will be closed for four weeks. I guess I'll have to go to the pub around the corner until you reopen," Moore said.

"That's what everyone keeps saying," Manny commented. "I'm not worried though. The renovations will bring everyone back. We will have a big party for the grand reopening."

People filled most of the tables already. They were drinking, talking, laughing, celebrating birthdays and the end of the workweek, and reconnecting with friends.

Everyone was smiling and enjoying the oldies music playing from the jukebox. A few women jumped up and ran to the dance floor when Kool and the Gang's song, *Celebrate Good Times*, started to play. Christy approached the bar and stood next to Moore's seat.

"Manny, can you give me two Gin and Tonics," Christy asked and then turned toward Moore. "Hey, excuse me for getting so close. It is pretty crowded in here. Hey, I've seen you here almost every Friday. I'm Christy," she said.

"Nice to meet you, Christy. I'm Corky," Moore replied, as he anxiously looked over her shoulder to see if Carver was in the vicinity.

"Well, Corky, what do you do for fun?" Christy asked.

"Fun? Come here, I guess. I work long hours at my accounting job. I don't have much time for fun."

"So you are an accountant. How exciting," Christy said sarcastically and grinned. At that moment, Carver walked through the front door. He spotted Christy talking to Moore, balled up his fist, and glared in Moore's direction. Carver's face turned red, and he marched toward Moore. Christy saw Carver approaching, reached out and grabbed Carver's hand, and pulled him to the dance floor.

"I've already ordered our drinks, baby. Let's dance!" Christy told Carver. He reluctantly followed her to the dance floor. Moore quickly finished his drink and left the bar. Moore made sure he left a large tip for Manny.

"See you when we reopen!" Manny shouted after Moore.

While Mahogany was closed for renovations, Moore went to the nearby pub and a lounge closer to his home. He saw a handful of Mahogany's regular patrons during this time but he did not see Carver or Christy. As the renovations neared completion, Manny posted a large sign on Mahogany's door that announced the grand reopening event for the following Friday. The sign read, "After Four Long Weeks, We Are Ready to Reopen. Come and Celebrate Our New Charm! Next Friday Night."

On the Friday of the grand reopening, Moore arrived at the bar just before the Happy Hour ended. "Manny, thank God you are finally open again! This place looks great. Did I miss the drink specials?" Moore asked as he grabbed a seat at the bar.

"You still have plenty of time. We extended the happy hour to celebrate our grand reopening. The usual?" Manny asked.

"Yes, and keep them coming. I had a rough day today." Moore said.

"Oh yeah, Hurricane asked about you a couple of hours ago," Manny revealed.

"He asked about me? Why?" Moore asked nervously. "Is he still here?"

"Yeah, I think so," the bartender stated. "He was checking out the new room and plasma screens that we added in the back. You need to walk around and look at the renovations. Let me know what you think." Before the bartender could finish, Moore placed some money on the bar, quickly grabbed his coat, and headed out the door toward the parking garage.

Moore walked so fast to his car that he practically galloped. Inside the bar, Carver noticed that Moore paid his tab and left before he finished his drink. Carver pushed back his chair and headed toward the front door after Moore. Moore moved so quickly that Carver started jogging after him. When Moore reached his car, Carver called out to him.

"Hey you!" Carver shouted loudly in Moore's direction. Moore, who stood five feet and ten inches tall and weighed 180 pounds, turned around and saw Carver headed in his direction. Carver's face was flushed red and he was sweating. Moore's heart started to pound hard and fast, and his hands began to shake. He found it difficult to breathe.

"Oh no," Moore thought. "He's going to kill me. Think fast!" Moore looked around but could not find a place to hide. He stood with his back to the wall, in between his car, a Ford Focus, and a large truck. The garage had one entrance and exit for cars and a small walkway for pedestrians. Carver was in the path of the only way out of the garage. Moore noticed his backseat window was down and saw his aluminum baseball bat lying on the back seat. He reached through the window and grabbed his baseball bat. He placed the bat down by his side so Carver could not see it.

When Carver came near, Moore closed his eyes and swung his bat with all his might, hitting Carver on the side of his neck. Moore caught Carver off guard. The blow caused Carver to fall and strike his head on the truck parked next to Moore's car. Carver fell to the ground, bleeding profusely from his head. Moore leaped over Carver who lay motionless on the ground and ran back to the bar for help.

When the police asked Moore about the baseball bat, Moore explained that he coaches a softball team and usually keeps the equipment in his car. He then showed the police the equipment in his car. Moore had a couple of baseball gloves and two bags full of baseballs on the floor of the backseat. Moore claimed he reached for the baseball bat to protect himself against Carver. When the police questioned the bartender, Manny, he recounted the many arguments and fights involving Carver and confirmed Carver's bad temper. Manny also told the police that Carver had just asked about Moore. He inquired whether Moore was an accountant. He believed Carver wanted to ask Moore for help with his taxes.

Carver suffered serious injuries to his brain and spinal cord and remained in a coma for months. Carver never regained consciousness and eventually died from his injuries. The prosecution filed a charge against Moore for murder in the second degree. Moore raised his right to self-defense.

At his trial, Moore requested a jury instruction on self-defense and an instruction that specifically explained the relevance to Moore's mental state of Carver's prior assaults and threats. The prosecution objected to both instructions, maintaining, among other things, that Moore had presented no evidence he actually feared imminent injury from Carver. The court requested arguments on whether, under California law, Moore had the requisite subjective belief to apprehend an imminent design by Carver to commit a felony or to do some great bodily injury upon him.

Provide the arguments for Moore and the prosecution. Did Moore actually believe he needed to use self-defense against Carver? Do not focus on the other requirements for justifiable self-defense (such as the existence of an objective and reasonable belief or the amount of force used) unless case law provides that such related evidence can be used to support your arguments. Address Moore's subjective belief in the need to defend himself against Carver.

These are the statutory sections and cases for this exercise:

- Cal. Penal Code §§ 197-199 (Deering 2011)

- *People v. Morales*, No. H026508, 2005 Cal. App. Unpub. LEXIS 367 (Ct. App. Jan. 13, 2005) *

- *People v. Viramontes*, 115 Cal. Rptr. 2d 229 (Ct. App. 2001)

- *People v. Trevino*, 246 Cal. Rptr. 357 (Ct. App. 1988)

- *People v. Davis*, 408 P.2d 129 (Cal. Ct. App. 1965)

---

* For purposes of practicing in the California court system, the *Morales* decision is marked as "not publishable" or "not citable" per the California Rules of Court. However, for this exercise, you can use this case, as needed, for authority.

STATUTORY ANALYSIS FOR SUCCESS

EXERCISE 80

Using the statutory section, regulations, and cases listed below for this exercise, determine whether Linda Paolo will be entitled to claim a tax deduction for each of the expenses identified below.

Background Facts

Linda Paolo ("Paolo") is an assistant professor of law at Roger J. Benton College of Law ("Benton College of Law") in Covington, Kentucky. She has been a member of the law faculty for two years now and teaches several courses including Family Law, Wills, Trusts, and Estates, and Administrative Law. She also serves as the Director of the school's Family Law Clinic (the "Clinic"). In this position, Paolo oversees approximately sixty cases each year. She supervises law students who work in the clinic as they interview new clients, identify their legal issues, conduct research on cases, draft legal memoranda, and appear in court. The Clinic handles several types of cases such as divorce, child custody, and restraining orders and prepares wills and other estate planning documents. For complex legal cases, the Clinic refers people to local counsel.

Paolo enjoys teaching at Benton College of Law and hopes to spend her entire academic career at the school. Every few years, the faculty closely reviews her performance and considers her for the next promotion. In Paolo's fourth year of service, the faculty will consider her for promotion to Associate Professor of Law. The faculty will consider several factors in reaching its decision including Paolo's teaching abilities, scholarly production, and service to the school and community. Paolo's student evaluations and peer reviews of her teaching have been very positive. In addition, Paolo serves on two major university committees, the board of directors for a national charity organization, and as a volunteer judge for student oral advocacy and trial competitions.

As she approached her third academic year, Paolo spent some time preparing a five-year plan. Paolo wants to make sure she remains competitive and continues to develop as a teacher. For this upcoming year, she plans to focus on her scholarly activities and complete her book project on clinical education and at least one journal article on the new probate laws. If time permits, she hopes to write a couple of essays on teaching and directing a law school clinic. All of these writing projects will help her to receive the promotion. Paolo, however, knows that tackling her writing projects and keeping up with her regular teaching load will take much time and commitment. So in order to be fully ready for her promotion next fall, Paolo decided to forgo her usual summer teaching duties and stipend to focus on writing. To accomplish this task, Paolo knows she must cut back on other expenses and find ways to save additional money.

Since Paolo graduated from law school and started working, she has personally completed her federal income tax return and consistently filed the form in a timely manner. Each year, she owes the United States Treasury at least $600.00. One day, while waiting in the lobby of her dentist's office, Paolo flipped through the pages of her Money Magazine and came across an article on maximizing the amount of your federal tax income return. She noted many of the suggestions and even jotted down a few helpful notes. For the upcoming year, considering her decision to focus on writing, Paolo resolved to be more proactive and aggressive as she prepared her federal income tax return form. She planned to keep a detailed log and journal of all her activities, purchases, and receipts, and identify all of the deductions to which she is entitled.

In January, Paolo received her membership dues statement for the Kentucky State Bar. The form provided that she owed $150.00 by her birth date to remain an active member of the bar. Paolo completed the membership form and filled out a check for the amount payable to the Clerk of the Kentucky Supreme Court. She made copies of the form and check and mailed them to the court. She then logged the payment into her journal. She also added several receipts for other purchases.

Later in March, during Spring Break, Paolo took a class in floral design and arrangement through the Leisure Learning Center. The workshop lasted five days, two hours each day. The class cost $70.00 and provided students with a course book, design materials, and silk and fresh flowers for projects. Paolo's family and friends always tell her that she has a "green thumb," and Paolo enjoys visiting nationally recognized gardens and arboretums. She hopes to open a flower shop or floral design business one day so she can remain active during her retirement years.

On the last day of class at Benton College of Law, Paolo treated her class to a pizza party. She paid for ten pizzas and the delivery fee and even bought cookies and drinks. The students appreciated the gesture and thanked her for a wonderful class. Afterwards, Paolo returned to her office and gathered all of the receipts for items she purchased for her class over the semester. She recorded the purchases in her tax journal. At Paolo's previous school, faculty received a budget for class parties and purchases. Faculty simply submitted their receipts and received a reimbursement check within a few weeks. Benton College of Law does not have a similar reimbursement policy.

In April, Paolo went to the Apple Store to browse through the laptop selection. She mainly used her office computer to complete assignments and needed a more reliable computer system at home. The Apple salesperson showed Paolo all the new laptop editions, and Paolo settled on a MacBook Air. The salesperson also identified several software programs that Paolo needed to purchase to take full advantage of her new laptop. When she returned home, Paolo spent the evening loading the programs on her laptop and accessing her LinkedIn page and other social networking websites. Before she went to bed, she placed all of the receipts from her purchases at the Apple Store in her tax files.

The next month, Paolo traveled to Las Vegas to attend the National Wills and Trust Planning Conference ("NWTPC"). She brought her new laptop with her. Paolo had never before visited Las Vegas, and she planned to stay an extra day for sightseeing. Paolo paid the conference registration fee, purchased her flight, and reserved the hotel online. She arrived in Las Vegas on the first day of the conference, a Wednesday. The conference workshops covered recent updates in trust and estate law and proposed legislation that could affect the practice and provided practical solutions to problems legal professionals encounter in trust administration, estate planning, probate, and litigation. A number of conference sessions also addressed client relations and managing a law practice. The conference took place from Wednesday to Friday. On Saturday, Paolo toured the Las Vegas strip and saw a dance performance at the Mirage Hotel. She checked out of the hotel on Sunday morning and returned to Covington. She added copies of the receipts for the registration fee, flight, airfare, and hotel to her tax records.

The following Monday, Paolo went to her office at the school to continue to work on her book project. She checked her mailbox and pulled out the latest issue of Money Magazine and a letter from the Dean of Benton College of Law. The Dean's letter informed the faculty of recent state budget cuts and the school's immediate decision to reduce the faculty travel budget significantly. Paolo sighed and thought to herself, "Well, I guess I won't be reimbursed for my Vegas trip." Still, Paolo submitted her receipts from the conference in Las Vegas to the school accounting department.

Paolo sat in her office reviewing her notes and the articles she printed for her book. Over the next few hours, she read and wrote several pages for her book. She occasionally took a break and walked to the faculty lounge. On her way to the lounge, Paolo would see another professor or a student and chat for a while. Even though Paolo worked to keep distractions to a minimum, people often interrupted her to handle matters related to the clinic. By the end of month, Paolo decided that she needed to isolate herself completely to make any meaningful headway on the book, and she reserved a week's stay at a local hotel. Paolo had read that some of the world's best writers check into hotels to complete their novels. She planned to do the same.

In June, Paolo stayed at a hotel and worked on her book. She brought her new laptop with her so that she could use the word processing program, access her school email account and LinkedIn page, and pay bills online. During her stay, Paolo completed a number of book chapters with minimal interruptions. Only three of her friends stopped by to say hello, and she rented only two movies when she wanted to take a break from writing. She did not leave the room, except to use the elliptical machine in the gym, and she ordered room service and food delivery. She was very pleased with her progress on the book. "I am almost done," she thought to herself. Paolo wanted to stay longer at the hotel but she needed the remaining funds in her savings account to pay for the book editor and proofreader. When she checked out of the hotel, Paolo received a copy of the bill and placed it in her tax files.

The next week, Paolo went to the school to check her mailbox and any messages about the clinic. In her mailbox, she received a check from the school for $364.71. The memo line read, "Airfare Travel to NWTPC." Paolo did not receive any other reimbursements from the school for attending the NWTPC.

Toward the end of July, Paolo started to get ready for the new school year. She went to the Outlet Mall and bought four new designer business suits from the Ann Taylor and Jones New York stores. She purchased two pantsuits and two skirt suits. All of the suits required minor alterations. She took the suits to her tailor and he finished the work in two weeks, just before the school's Orientation week. Paolo wore her new black pantsuit to the Orientation's Opening Session during which she gave a brief presentation on the law school's Clinic services and accomplishments.

On her tax return for this year, Paolo plans to claim business expense deductions in the following amounts:

Wills, Trust, and Estates Conference

> Conference Registration and Materials Fee................... $ 450.00
>
> Conference Airfare... $ 364.71
>
> Conference Meals (for 4 days)............................... $ 284.00
>
> Conference Lodging (for 4 days)............................. $ 516.00

Floral Design Workshop.. $ 70.00

Kentucky State Bar Dues.. $ 150.00

Money Magazine... $ 44.95

Refreshments for Class... $ 53.25

Book Editor and Proofreader.................................. $ 5,500.00

Hotel Stay... $ 725.80

New Suits.. $ 640.23

Alterations.. $ 239.80

Laptop and Software... $ 1,300.00

Can Paolo claim each of these expenditures as a trade or business deduction under the United States Internal Revenue Code? Do not address whether Paolo can substantiate any of her expenses sufficiently by adequate records. Focus on whether the court would permit each planned deduction as a trade or business expense under relevant tax law. Provide the viable arguments for Paolo and the Tax Commissioner. Identify whether you require additional information to make the determination.

The statutory section, regulations, and cases are for this exercise:

- I.R.C. § 162(a) (2011)

- Treas. Reg. § 1.162-5 (2011)

- Treas. Reg. § 1.162-6 (2011)

- *Langer v. Comm'r*, 96 T.C.M. (CCH) 334, 2008 Tax Ct. Memo LEXIS 253 (T.C. Nov. 12, 2008)

- *Nehus v. Comm'r*, 68 T.C.M. (CCH) 1503, 1994 Tax Ct. Memo LEXIS 645 (T.C. Dec. 21, 1994)

- *Gardner v. Comm'r*, 46 T.C.M. (CCH) 1283, 1983 Tax Ct. Memo LEXIS 245 (T.C. Sept. 1, 1983)

STATUTORY ANALYSIS FOR SUCCESS
EXERCISE 81

Using the statutory section and cases listed below for this exercise, determine whether the Good Samaritan statute protects Dr. Kapoor with regard to his treatment of Tim Washington.

Background Facts

Tim ("Tim") Washington was visiting his father, John ("John") Washington, in the hospital. John had been in the hospital for six days, following heart surgery. Tim had been traveling to the hospital during the day and going home at night. On this particular evening, however, John had suffered through a difficult day of tests, and John's doctors were worried that he was not progressing as he should be.

Tim had hoped to return to his home in the evening to help his wife with their three young children. But upon seeing how concerned the doctors were with his father's progress, Tim decided to sleep on the couch in his father's hospital room that night.

Tim and his father watched some television in the evening together, and then they chatted for a bit. "I'm very tired," said John, and he said that he would sleep for a while. Tim went to sleep as well. At about 1:00 a.m., Tim awoke, very hungry. He went out to the nurses' station. "I haven't eaten much today," he said. "Is there anywhere to eat at this hour in the hospital?" The nurses explained that there was a small 24-hour snack bar in the hospital's basement. Tim could not sleep anyway, so he decided to take the elevator down to the basement and eat something.

He climbed aboard the elevator and finally reached the basement. The basement was rather dark, and Tim could not immediately see a snack bar at all. He walked down a dark hallway, past a lab and an X-ray room. "I must be going the wrong way," he thought to himself, becoming frustrated with the maze of hallways. Finally, he smelled fried food, and his pace quickened. He rounded a corner quickly, failing to see an X-ray machine that had been placed just out of sight around the corner. He struck his head hard against the metal machine, passing out immediately and falling onto the hard floor.

Tim started to awaken after about ten minutes. Right at that moment, a young resident walked toward him and stopped. "What happened to you?" he asked. Tim groaned. "I'm actually a resident in oncology, but I'll take your vitals and see what we need to do," said the resident. The resident reached over and quickly straightened Tim's neck. Tim screamed, "Oh my God, that hurts!" The resident returned Tim's head to its previous position and telephoned for help. A team arrived within minutes and moved Tim to a stretcher. The resident's act of straightening Tim's neck had worsened an already-serious injury. Tim eventually recovered, but not

228

before months of therapy. Tim sued for negligence, and the resident asserted the Good Samaritan statute.

You represent the resident, Dr. Kapoor. Based on the following statutory language and cases, what is your best argument that the Florida statute should protect Dr. Kapoor? This is an issue of first impression in Florida.

> Any person, who in good faith gratuitously renders emergency care at the scene of an accident or emergency care to the victim thereof, shall not be liable for any civil damages for any personal injury as a result of any act or omission by such person in rendering the emergency care or as a result of any act or failure to act to provide or arrange for further medical treatment or care for the injured person, except acts or omissions amounting to gross negligence or willful or wanton misconduct.

Fla. Stat. § 111.11 (2011).*

- *Burciaga v. St. John's Hosp.* 232 Cal. Rptr. 75 (Ct. App. 1986)

- *Velazquez v. Jiminez*, 798 A.2d 51 (N.J. 2002)

---

* This language differs from the actual Florida Good Samaritan statute.

STATUTORY ANALYSIS FOR SUCCESS
EXERCISE 82

Using the statutory section, regulation, and cases listed below for this exercise, determine whether Sheila Johnsan's carpal turned syndrome is a "qualifying disability" under the Americans with Disabilities Act?

Background Facts

After graduation from high school, Sheila Johnson ("Johnson") started working for Tia Motors ("Tia") as a welder in the company's manufacturing plant in Louisville, Kentucky. She was excited to start working for Tia, which was known for great benefits and job security. Johnson had studied welding in a shop class at school and she was pleased to be able to use that knowledge.

She attended three days of orientation and then she started her regular responsibilities. On most days, she welded parts onto trucks and other large vehicles. A few weeks after she started work, she started to feel a strange sensation in her hands. She took some over-the-counter pain medications, which stopped the feeling for a few days. Later in the same week, however, she began complaining of pain in her hands, wrists, and fingers. She also felt numbness in her fingertips. She tried to complete her work each day as quickly as possible, but the pain and numbness were holding her back. On a Friday afternoon, about four months after she started at Tia, she was overcome by pain. She finished the shift in tears and sat down in the break room with her head in her hands. Her supervisor saw her there and the two discussed her health problems.

The supervisor told her to take three days off to rest. She did so, and made sure she did nothing at all with her hands when she was off. When she first returned to work, she was able to weld quickly and easily, just as she could before the problems started. But after a day or two, the pain came back and continued. She again fought the pain but was unable to keep up the busy pace at Tia. She then saw an orthopedic surgeon, who diagnosed her with carpal tunnel syndrome. He gave her medication and splints for her arms, and he prescribed physical therapy. He said that she could no longer lift more than twenty pounds, and that she should no longer use vibrating tools. The welding equipment that Johnson used vibrated slightly, and Johnson suspected that it was part of her problem. She made an official request for a non-welding position, but the managers said that welders were in high demand. The company had no one to weld if she could not. "If you want to stay here, you weld," the supervisor reported to her.

The carpal tunnel was not a problem unless she was at work. Even at work, she was able to complete other tasks without difficulty, but the welding was always painful. About forty percent of her day was spent on sweeping, general clean-up, and paperwork. When working on those tasks, her carpal tunnel condition did not bother her. At home, she was able to clean, cook, and take care of her house. She could perform maintenance on her house without any difficulty. Only sustained welding work caused problems.

After another six months of painful days, Johnson requested a light-duty position at Tia, but the manager declined her request. She continued to see doctors and therapists, and she continued her regular position at Tia. After eight months, Johnson was taking about one day off per week, so that her hands could recover. She left early on Mondays and Fridays for physical therapy.

Finally, her supervisor and manager called her into the main office for a discussion. "Look, Sheila. The other welders are getting annoyed. You are gone half the time, and you can't weld very fast when you're here. It's time for you to move on. You have three weeks to find another job, and you have no job here after three weeks. Sorry."

Johnson was devastated. She had difficulty finding another job, and she had to pay extremely high health insurance premiums to continue her coverage. Finally, she found a job as a deli counter assistant in a supermarket. The job paid less than her job at Tia, and it had no health insurance or other benefits. As she slipped into financial difficulties, Johnson decided to meet with a lawyer. "Do I have a claim under the Americans with Disabilities Act?" she asks. "I can't do my job because of my carpal tunnel syndrome. That counts, right?"

You gather some research on the issue. First, you have to determine whether Johnson's carpal tunnel syndrome is a qualifying disability under the Americans with Disabilities Act ("ADA"). Is it? Please explain why, using the following cases, statute, and regulations:

Cases:

- *McKay v. Toyota Motor Mfg.*, 878 F. Supp. 1012 (E.D. Ky. 1995).

- *Lowry v. Cabletron Sys. Inc.*, 973 F. Supp. 77 (D.N.H. 1997).

Statute and Regulations:

The ADA prohibits discrimination against "a qualified individual with a disability because of the disability of such individual in regard to . . . discharge of employees. . . ." 42 U.S.C. § 12112(a) (2011).

A "disability" is defined as "(A) a physical or mental impairment that substantially limits one or more of the major life activities of such individual; (B) a record of such an impairment; or (C) being regarded as having such an impairment." 42 U.S.C. § 12102(2) (2011).

"Major life activities" include "caring for oneself, performing manual tasks, walking, seeing, hearing, speaking, breathing, learning, and working." 29 C.F.R. § 1630.2(i) (2011).

A court deciding whether an impairment substantially limits a major life activity should consider the following factors: "(i) [t]he nature and severity of the impairment; (ii) [t]he duration or expected duration of the impairment; and (iii) [t]he permanent or long term impact, the expected permanent or long term impact, or the expected permanent or long term impact of or resulting from the impairment." *Id.* § 1630.2(j)(2). Furthermore, when a court is determining whether an impairment substantially limits the major life activity of working, it may consider the following additional factors:

(A)   The geographical area to which the individual has reasonable access;

(B)   The job from which the individual has been disqualified because of an impairment, and the number and types of jobs utilizing similar training, knowledge, skills or abilities, within that geographic area, from which the individual is also disqualified because of the impairment (class of jobs); and/or

(C)   The job from which the individual has been disqualified because of an impairment, and the number and types of other jobs not utilizing similar training, knowledge, skills or abilities, within that geographic area, from which the individual is also disqualified because of the impairment (broad range of jobs in various classes).

Id. § 1630.2(j)(3).

PART 3

SKILLED STATUTORY EXERCISES

STATUTORY ANALYSIS FOR SUCCESS

EXERCISE 83

Using the statute and the cases listed after the problem, determine whether Henry and Beverly Walker can be successfully appointed primary custodians of their granddaughter, Allison, under Texas law.

Background Facts

Henry and Beverly Walker (the "Walkers") take care of their two-year-old granddaughter, Allison Marie Walker ("Allison"). The Walkers are both retired. Henry was a licensed therapist, and Beverly was a social studies teacher. They live in Houston in a two-story house with four bedrooms and two bathrooms. The home also has a large backyard. They have owned this home for over 20 years. Allison currently lives with the Walkers. Allison's biological mother, Renée Harris Walker ("Renée"), objects to granting the Walkers permanent custody of Allison and insists that Allison should live with her and Renée should remain Allison's sole guardian. Renée's parental rights have not been terminated, and the Walkers have never sought permanent custody of Allison before now.

Renée married the Walkers' son, Joseph Henry Walker ("Joseph"), two years ago in February. They lived in a small studio apartment with no frills in north Houston. When they met, Renée was a nurse and was studying to be a registered nurse. She worked at Ben Taub Hospital and mainly worked the night shift from about 6:00 p.m. to 3:00 a.m. On occasion, she worked eighteen-hour shifts. During those shifts, she would take sleeping breaks in the lounge, and would have the following two consecutive days off. Joseph's work history was rather inconsistent due to the nature of his work, which was construction. In general, Joseph's assignments lasted about three to four months, after which he was usually out of work for about two or more months until he could get work again. The couple's financial situation worsened during the winter, as construction jobs became scarce. The Walkers occasionally helped the couple with household bills, such as rent, electricity, and water. Renée's parents are deceased, and she has no close family in Texas.

In March, the same year they married, Renée found out she was pregnant. Both Renée and Joseph were excited about the news and started to prepare for their new baby. Unfortunately, about five months later, Joseph was killed in a car accident involving a drunk driver. The driver did not have any insurance or personal assets. Renée received a judgment in her civil suit but could not expect to

233

see any payment from the driver. Criminal charges were filed against the driver. Renée received a small sum from a life insurance policy. The Walkers do not know how much she received.

Renée was devastated by Joseph's untimely death. She took leave from work but returned in about one month. The Walkers helped Renée as much as they could. Henry drove Renée to all of her doctor's appointments, and Beverly stayed at Renée's apartment most of the time as her due date became close. The Walkers even suggested that Renée seek grief counseling and made an appointment for her. Renée met with the grief counselor for only two sessions. She stopped going, claiming she was fine. However, Beverly said she would often hear Renée crying herself to sleep and Renée frequently looked disheveled and distant. Beverly also stated Renée was forgetful. One time, Renée left the stove on for hours.

On December 14, Renée gave birth to Allison by C-section. The Walkers were at the hospital for Allison's birth. Renée remained in the hospital for about three days. The doctor prescribed Renée pain medication, oxycodone, during her recovery. Henry filled the prescription for Renée and booked her follow-up appointments. Upon her discharge from the hospital, the Walkers took Renée home. Beverly stayed with Renée and her new baby for about one week until Renée insisted that she go home to be with Henry. Renée was adamant about taking care of Allison by herself. Beverly called Renée often just to check how she was doing and whether she needed anything.

In late March the following year, Beverly stopped by Renée's apartment, bringing her lunch. She knew Renée had returned to work by then, and she wanted to help. She also missed Allison dearly and wanted to see her granddaughter. Beverly stood outside the door, knocking for over ten minutes. Finally, Renée answered the door. Beverly said that Renée looked as if she had just gotten out of bed, but she initially dismissed this because new mothers often look extremely tired. When she asked Renée how she was doing, Renée indicated she was fine. When Beverly asked about the doctor appointments, Renée appeared confused and admitted that she had forgotten about them. She promised to call the doctor's office in the morning. Beverly also asked who kept Allison while she was at work. Renée told her about the nursery in the basement of the hospital that gave employees priority placement. The hospital deducted the cost from her paycheck.

Although she did thank Beverly for stopping by, Renée was quite abrupt with Beverly and ended her visit rather quickly. Beverly did get to see Allison briefly and did not notice anything wrong with the child. Beverly continued to call Renée, at least once a week. Renée stopped answering or returning Beverly's calls.

In August of the same year, Beverly and Henry went to Renée's home, fearing that something might have happened to her or Allison. The landlord let them into Renée's apartment because he knew they were close relatives. The landlord mentioned that Renée was over two months late in her rent. He had been lenient with her because she had just lost her job and had a new baby. Beverly and Henry were shocked at the news but thankful he told them. Beverly said Renée's apartment was a "pigsty." Dirty clothes were thrown all over the small studio space. The kitchen area was filthy. Dishes were stacked in the sink, and gnats were flying around them. Unopened mail was scattered throughout the place. They found Renée asleep on the couch and the baby crying in her crib. There was no food in the refrigerator, just spoiled milk. Beverly tended to Allison. Henry had a difficult time waking Renée and noticed several pill bottles on the floor in front of her. All of them read "codeine," and many of the bottles were empty. Henry had seen this before and instantly knew Renée was addicted to pain medications.

Once she woke up and after much prodding, Renée eventually told the Walkers about how she lost her job. She also admitted that she was still taking pain medications. The hospital fired her for stealing oxycodone and codeine. The hospital did not file any charges against her because of her years of stellar service, but it ended all of her health benefits. She also told them that she had not paid a number of bills and the electricity would be disconnected in a few days. She had spent all of her savings, mainly on the pain medications. The Walkers asked why she had not called them, and Renée just started to cry.

Henry immediately got on the phone calling rehabilitation centers. He found one in the Memorial area that had an opening. Renée agreed to seek treatment. They packed her a bag, gathered items for the baby, and drove Renée to the treatment facility. Renée remained there for about one month. During this time, Allison stayed with the Walkers, and they paid most of Renée's overdue bills.

When Renée finished the program, she moved back to her apartment and began looking for a new job. She asked the Walkers to keep Allison until "she got back on her feet." Renée finally landed a job as a 911 dispatcher from 3 pm to midnight. At the urging of her doctor at the treatment facility, she also resumed grief counseling, realizing she never healed from Joseph's death. Renée called the Walkers at least once a week to check on Allison. She generally visited with Allison on every other Saturday.

This arrangement continued for about a year. Then, in September, Renée's calls and visits started to lessen. She claimed she was either too busy or had forgotten to call or visit. Renée seemed to forget other things as well. For example, in early December, Renée told the Walkers she wanted to have a birthday party for Allison at her home. The Walkers agreed. When they showed up for the party, Renée looked surprised and asked why they were there. They mentioned the party and Renée said, "What party? I planned to stop by your house later with Allison's gift."

Beverly then asked to come in and use the bathroom. The apartment was a mess, and the dishes were unwashed. In the bathroom, she noticed an empty bottle of codeine on the basin. Beverly confronted Renée about the pill bottle, and Renée said her dentist prescribed it for some recent dental work she had. Beverly did not believe her and pressed the issue. Renée became angry and asked the Walkers to leave. As they gathered their belongings and Allison, Renée shouted, "It's about time for me to start taking care of Allison by myself." The Walkers hurriedly left the apartment.

The Walkers believe Renée may have relapsed into her addiction to pain medications and do not think she is stable or capable of caring for Allison properly.

They also think Renée's home is too small and untidy to accommodate a child. Although Renée has not formally asked for physical custody, the Walkers fear that at any time Renée may insist they return Allison to live with her. The Walkers want to know if they can be Allison's permanent guardians or managing conservators. They do not mind if Renée has visitation rights, but they want to have primary custody and be responsible for Allison's care and upbringing. They have not mentioned any of this to Renée, fearing she will file suit first.

Special rules govern the primary custody of a minor child. Here, the Walkers seek appointment as Allison's managing conservators, the technical term used under Texas law. In general, in reviewing custody disputes, the court will assess what is in the best interest of the child. The Texas Family Code and cases clarify this legal standard and explain how it applies when a non-parent (as opposed to a biological parent) seeks managing conservatorship over a minor child. You may use any part of the statute and cases listed below. The statute, in its edited form, follows the list of authorities.

The statute and cases for this exercise are:

- Tex. Fam. Code Ann. § 153.131 (West 2011) (edited version below)

- *Mumma v. Aguirre*, 364 S.W.2d 220 (Tex. 1963)

- *Lewelling v. Lewelling*, 796 S.W.2d 164 (Tex. 1990)

- *May v. May*, 829 S.W.2d 373 (Tex. App. 1992)

STATUTE FOR EXERCISE 83

Texas Family Code

§ 153.131. Presumption That Parent to be Appointed Managing Conservator

(a) Subject to the prohibition in Section 153.004, unless the court finds that appointment of the parent or parents would not be in the best interest of the child because the appointment would significantly impair the child's physical health or emotional development, a parent shall be appointed sole managing conservator or both parents shall be appointed as joint managing conservators of the child.

(b) It is a rebuttable presumption that the appointment of the parents of a child as joint managing conservators is in the best interest of the child. A finding of a history of family violence involving the parents of a child removes the presumption under this subsection.

Notes:

In 1995, the Texas Legislature recodified Chapter 14 of the Family Code, consisting of §§ 14.01 to 14.983, relating to parents and children and suits affecting the parent-child relationship to the current Chapter 153.

STATUTORY ANALYSIS FOR SUCCESS

EXERCISE 84

We have been retained to represent Mary Ortega ("Ortega") in a continuation of the divorce proceedings between Sam Smith ("Smith") and Ortega. Smith and Ortega (Ortega always kept her maiden name) were divorced on January 4, 2009, after just fourteen months of marriage.

In the early months of their marriage, they shared a love of art and music. Their favorite piece of art was one that they bought on their honeymoon in Las Vegas. It was a modern painting featuring pink and blue horses, painted by an unknown artist. After about eight months of marriage, the two started to drift apart. Smith realized he did not enjoy collecting art very much, and Ortega's two Siamese cats started to annoy him. He began spending large amounts of time watching Ultimate Fighting and playing the video game "World of Witchcraft" on his home computer. Ortega refused to be in the apartment when Ultimate Fighting was on the television, so the two spent less and less time together. Ortega took classes on art appreciation and collection, and she traveled to art conferences. She took a class on German expressionist art, and at that time, she moved the blue and red horse painting to a place of prominence in the apartment. In July 2008, the two realized they no longer had much in common, and they decided to divorce.

The divorce was fairly amicable, although they had some disagreement over the division of property. The two had rented an apartment together, so Ortega simply moved out when the lease ended. The main dispute during the divorce was over the art collection and the computer.

Both parties retained counsel, and the court ordered them to mediate. The mediator strongly encouraged the parties to settle. "This judge doesn't like to see divorce cases go to trial. If I were you, I would settle for sure," he said. During the mediation, Ortega whispered to her attorney, "Make sure I get the horse picture." At the same time, Smith's attorney told Smith she was very busy, and if he did not settle today, she would have to transfer his case to another firm.

Ortega's lawyer argued for the horse painting, and said that Ortega would give up four landscape oil paintings in exchange; Smith agreed. "I just want to remember our good times," Ortega said. "The picture has purely emotional value; no serious artist paints pink and blue horses anyway." After six hours of mediation, the parties resolved all the issues, and they signed a Mediated Settlement Agreement ("MSA") pursuant to the Texas Family Code. Smith and Ortega signed, as did their attorneys, and the agreement contained an underlined statement at the top saying, "This Agreement is Not Revocable." A week after signing the MSA, Smith started to think about the horse painting; he regretted negotiating it away. He decided to withdraw his consent to the MSA and requested that no judgment be entered on it. The judge nevertheless incorporated the MSA into a divorce decree and entered a final judgment.

A week after the divorce was finalized, Smith was watching television. Just before his Ultimate Fighting match was about to start, he saw Ortega on television, holding the horse painting. Apparently, the horse painting was a little-known piece by German expressionist artist Franz Marc—Ortega had just sold it at auction for $3 million.

Smith immediately called his lawyer and moved to have the MSA and divorce decree set aside and a new trial granted. He argues that a new trial should be granted because the MSA was procured by fraud, specifically that Ortega lied about the picture's value. Please set out Ortega's best argument as to why the motion for new trial should be denied.

Please use only the following sources to answer the question:

- Tex. Fam. Code Ann. § 6.602 (West 2011)

- *Boyd v. Boyd*, 67 S.W.3d 398 (Tex. App. 2002)

- *Loehr v. Loehr*, No. 13-08-00380-CV, 2009 Tex. App. LEXIS 6863 (Tex. App. Aug. 28, 2009).

- *Ricks v. Ricks*, 169 S.W.3d 523 (Tex. App. 2005)

STATUTORY ANALYSIS FOR SUCCESS

EXERCISE 85

Using the statutory provisions and the cases listed after the problem, determine whether Springfield Charter School failed to provide Leonora Bolden with a reasonable accommodation for her seasonal affective disorder in accordance with the Americans with Disabilities Act.

Background Facts

Leonora Bolden ("Bolden") moved from Florida to Springfield, Illinois in May. She taught successfully at Springfield Charter School ("SCS") from June through September. Then, in late January of the following year, Bolden requested a move from her fifth grade classroom in the interior of the school to Classroom 5, one that had exterior windows and natural light.

SCS is a private charter school that specializes in math and science education for grades one through six. The sixth grade classes are experimental classes and have a very low student-teacher ratio. The school plans to add more sixth grade classes over the next few years. The school's building is only one floor. Most of the classrooms are arranged in pods, or suites, in the center or interior of the school. Each suite has about three classrooms, and none of these interior rooms has windows. Each pod is comprised of students in the same grade level. For example, all of the first grade classes are located in the same suite. This pod arrangement allows the teachers to collaborate more easily and even share instructional materials. The school uses pods mainly for grades one through four.

The fifth grade classes are positioned in a pod arrangement, but the teachers work more independently. Currently, there is one sixth grade classroom located in the interior of the building and one sixth grade classroom located on the exterior, next to the cafeteria. The exterior classroom is Classroom 5, the only classroom with windows. Ron Beckingham ("Beckingham") currently teaches his sixth grade class in Classroom 5. Beckingham is the most senior teacher in the school. He has been there for seven years. Given his long tenure, the school rewarded Beckingham with a move to Classroom 5 after Marjorie Monroe, who previously taught in that room, retired last year. Beckingham has several more years to teach before he plans to retire from education. Next in line for Classroom 5 is Jonathan Parker, a fifth grade teacher, who has been teaching at SCS for five years.

Also on the perimeter of the school are several administrative offices, the gymnasium, the nurse's office, a newly constructed science lab, and a fully equipped computer room. The science lab has several windows that may be opened easily in case of an emergency. Some science experiments use chemicals, and the school wants emergency personnel to be able to access the lab easily and quickly. The lab is fitted with large counters and stools, workstations, two sinks, and other science equipment. The lab has no traditional classroom desks, tables, and chairs.

The windows in the computer room are tinted dark to protect the equipment from the sun's heat. The school has immediate plans to construct an additional wing with several exterior classrooms. The construction is scheduled to be completed in approximately one year.

In late October, Bolden began experiencing severe fatigue and anxiety. She attributed the tiredness to her huge workload and the anxiety to her lack of sleep. She looked forward to the Thanksgiving break to catch up on her sleep. However, in November, her condition worsened, as she started experiencing hypervigilance, tearfulness, racing thoughts, and trouble organizing tasks. On November 15, Bolden felt so bad that she asked her teaching assistant to cover her class. She went to the nurse's office to lie down on a cot.

While in the office, the nurse asked Bolden what was wrong. "You don't look like your usual self, Leonora. What's going on with you? Do you have a headache or something?" Bolden responded, "I have been feeling really troubled lately. I can't sleep through the night. I get very sad and just cry. I cannot focus. I have racing thoughts all day." "Have you been eating and sleeping at all?" the nurse asked. "No, not really. I can't even focus on the students and their questions. I'm getting really scared," Bolden explained. She then continued, "I tend to feel a bit better while we are at lunch in the cafeteria. I try to spend a few minutes outside."

The nurse listened to Bolden and said, "Leonora, it sounds like you may have some type of depression, but I don't know much about psychology. You should see a doctor. I have read about certain psychological disorders that are connected to the seasons and our ability to receive lots of sunlight. For example, you may feel better when you are outside because you are getting more light. You may even feel better in a different classroom. What about Classroom 5, the one with the windows?" Bolden then replied, "Beckingham's classroom? He's waited forever to receive that room. He'll put up a fight before he's ever moved out of there." The nurse sighed and said, "Well, tell him what's going on and see if he'd be willing to switch rooms with you, at least until the construction is completed. I remember when Marjorie Monroe had that room, she let Samantha Munoz teach there for one whole year, right before Samantha retired. Samantha hadn't taught here that long but was planning to retire soon. Marjorie did a nice thing for her. Just ask Ron or talk to the principal. Talk to someone, Leonora, before you get worse." Bolden did not speak to Beckingham about Classroom 5.

One week later, Bolden sought medical attention. Her condition had worsened. She could no longer concentrate or organize her thoughts, and she had panic attacks and thoughts of suicide. After a couple sessions, Bolden's doctor, Dr. Philip Fremont ("Fremont"), a licensed clinical psychologist, diagnosed her with seasonal affective disorder ("SAD"). As Fremont explained, extensive research has shown that approximately five to ten percent of the population suffers from severe SAD and twenty-five percent have some tendency to become depressed in the winter due to lack of sunlight. Fremont opined that Bolden would likely improve if she had more exposure to natural sunlight. The next day, Bolden met with the principal, explained that she was depressed, and asked if she could move her classroom. The principal did not understand how moving Bolden's classroom would help with her condition and instead offered to give her a few days of medical leave right before the Thanksgiving break. Knowing that she needed some time to rest, she agreed to the medical leave.

During her next doctor's appointment in December, Bolden told Fremont she received a few extra days of vacation. He seemed pleased but told Bolden he was very concerned that Bolden had not improved significantly since her break. When Fremont asked about her classroom, Bolden told her that most of the classrooms at SCS were in the interior of the building, except for one room. Bolden told him she felt it would be difficult for her to be moved to the exterior classroom without a good reason. In response, Fremont wrote a letter to the school principal, stating that Bolden had seasonal affective disorder, a form of depression, and would have difficulty teaching in a room with artificial light and no windows. The principal received the letter that week. The principal contacted the school's nurse and asked if she knew anything about SAD or Bolden's condition. The nurse told the principal her limited understanding of SAD but did suggest that he move Bolden to a classroom with more sunlight, like Classroom 5.

During the winter break, Bolden scheduled additional sessions with Fremont and remained close to home. On January 2, a few days before the school reopened, the principal contacted Bolden and told Bolden he received her doctor's letter and she could use a section of the computer lab for her class the following semester. The principal informed Bolden he would try to place a divider between the area set aside for her class and the remainder of the lab. Bolden explained that the computer lab probably would not help to improve her condition because the windows were tinted. She then asked the principal if she could teach in Classroom 5. The principal explained the school's seniority policy and how it would be unfair to force Beckingham to give up the room. The principal acknowledged that the policy was not in the employee handbook or included in any other written rules. Nevertheless, he emphasized the need to be fair to Beckingham. He also reiterated her doctor's request for a room with windows. "We will have even more classroom availability once the construction is completed next year," he mentioned. Lastly, the principal indicated he would install appropriate light bulbs or any other equipment that would help to relieve her symptoms. Frustrated by the school's response and fearing further decline in her health, Bolden terminated her employment with SCS. She found an adjunct teaching position at the local community college and started to send out her resume for other local teaching positions.

Bolden claims that SCS failed to accommodate her Americans with Disabilities Act ("ADA") claim by refusing to move her to Classroom 5, the one with natural light. SCS contends that Bolden failed in her obligation to engage in an interactive process with the school and that a reassignment to Classroom 5 would have been unreasonable under the circumstances. To allege a claim for disability discrimination under the ADA, the plaintiff must show that: (1) she is a qualified individual with a disability, (2) the employer was aware of her disability, and (3) the employer failed to reasonably accommodate that disability. Please analyze the merits of Bolden's failure-to-accommodate claim. Address the <u>second and third elements only</u>. SCS does not dispute that Bolden may be a "qualified individual with a disability" under the ADA.

You may use any of the following statutes and cases for this exercise:

- 42 U.S.C.S. § 12111 (LexisNexis 2011)

- 42 U.S.C.S. § 12112 (LexisNexis 2011)

- *US Airways, Inc. v. Barnett*, 535 U.S. 391 (2002)

- *King v. City of Madison*, 550 F.3d 598 (7th Cir. 2008)

- *EEOC v. Sears, Roebuck & Co.*, 417 F.3d 789 (7th Cir. 2005)

- *Gile v. United Airlines, Inc.*, 213 F.3d 365 (7th Cir. 2000)

- *Beck v. Univ. of Wis. Bd. of Regents*, 75 F.3d 1130 (7th Cir. 1996)

- *Zamudio v. Patla*, 956 F. Supp. 803 (N.D. Ill. 1997)

STATUTORY ANALYSIS FOR SUCCESS

EXERCISE 86

Using the statutory provisions and the cases listed after the exercise, determine whether the State of Texas can prove beyond a reasonable doubt that Jacoby Patrick unlawfully possessed Alprazolam (or Xanax) in violation of the Texas Controlled Substances Act.

Background Facts

Jacoby Patrick ("Patrick") was arrested for unlawful possession of a controlled substance at the Diamond Homes Apartment Complex ("Diamond Homes") in Texarkana, Texas. Diamond Homes is located at 3260 Pepper Tree Street. The apartment complex is located on the north side of Woodside with its only entry and exit point centrally located on the south side of the property. The apartment complex has "No Trespassing" notices posted intermittently along the exterior perimeter fence, throughout the complex, and on every building in the complex. The complex is known to be a high crime area for violent crimes, drug trafficking, and prostitution.

On the north side of building #4 of the Diamond Homes, at approximately 1800 hours, Officers Ruiz and Wilson conducted security patrol of the complex and noticed a beige 2001 Buick Regal, four-door vehicle. The vehicle bore Texas tag "068 BPK." The officers also observed that two males occupied the front seat of the vehicle. The vehicle was parked in a low light area. Although parked, the vehicle's engine and taillights were turned on. Visibility was poor due to nighttime hours and minimal artificial lighting. The officers only had flashlights.

As the officers continued to make their rounds, they monitored the vehicle and noticed no people entered, exited, or approached the vehicle. After approximately 30 minutes of no one exiting, entering, or approaching the vehicle, the officers initiated contact with the males in the vehicle. As the officers approached the vehicle, they could smell the odor of burned marijuana. Officer Ruiz made contact with the driver of the vehicle, Patrick, and asked why he was waiting in the vehicle. Patrick explained that he was waiting on his cousin. When asked his cousin's name, Patrick responded, "Gregory." When asked what apartment he lived in, Patrick could not provide an apartment number.

Officer Ruiz then advised Patrick of the posted notices throughout the complex and that the officers had observed Patrick and his passenger, Randy Tolliver ("Tolliver"), loitering at the complex. Tolliver appeared to be much younger than Patrick. The officer also told Patrick that, if they did not live on the property, they were considered to be trespassing. Patrick said he understood.

Officer Wilson asked Patrick why the vehicle smelled of burned marijuana. Patrick freely admitted the vehicle belonged to his cousin, Gregory, and explained that Gregory frequently smoked marijuana in it. As Patrick spoke, the officers shone their flashlights into the vehicle and observed marijuana residue (pieces of

244

marijuana leaves and seeds) scattered about the vehicle on the seats and on the floorboards. When the officers asked Patrick and Tolliver if any contraband, drugs, narcotics, or weapons were in the vehicle or on their persons, both males said "No." The men also assured the officers that no illegal substances were in the vehicle.

The officers asked both men to step out of the vehicle and patted them down for the men's and officers' safety. Both men consented to a search. The officers did not find any illegal substances on either Patrick or Tolliver. The officers then received Patrick's consent to search the interior of the vehicle. The officers found a clear plastic bag containing twelve white pills in the center console, behind the cup holder. The center console is located between the two front seats of the vehicle. The officers lifted the console cover to retrieve the bag holding the pills. Officer Ruiz noticed that Patrick had a shocked but uneasy look on his face when they discovered the pills.

The officers recognized the pills in the bag to be Alprazolam (Xanax). Later testing confirmed the officers' conclusions and revealed the drugs weighed approximately 4.1 grams. Both Patrick and Tolliver admitted they did not have a prescription for the pills and denied having any knowledge of the pills being in the vehicle. The officers released Tolliver from the scene with a criminal trespass warning and threatened to arrest him on sight if they observed him on the property again. The officers arrested Patrick for unlawful possession of a controlled substance. During his arrest, Patrick admitted that, many years ago, he had used Xanax without obtaining a prescription.

Please analyze the merits of the State's charge against Patrick for unlawful possession of Alprazolam (or Xanax). Under the Texas Controlled Substances Act, any material that contains substances that have a potential for abuse associated with a depressant effect on the central nervous system, such as Alprazolam (or Xanax), constitutes a substance under "Penalty Group 3." Infractions concerning Penalty Group 3 substances are addressed in section 481.117(a) of the Texas Health and Safety Code. You may use any part of the following statutes and cases for this exercise:

- Tex. Health & Safety Code Ann. § 481.104(2) (West 2011)
- Tex. Health & Safety Code Ann. § 481.117(a), (b) (West 2011)
- Tex. Health & Safety Code Ann. § 481.002(38) (West 2011)
- *McGoldrick v. State*, 682 S.W.2d 573 (Tex. Crim. App. 1985)
- *Utomi v. State*, 243 S.W.3d 75 (Tex. App. 2007)
- *Chisum v. State*, 988 S.W.2d 244 (Tex. App. 1999)
- *Ortiz v. State*, 930 S.W.2d 849 (Tex. App. 1996)
- *Porter v. State*, 873 S.W.2d 729 (Tex. App. 1994)

STATUTORY ANALYSIS FOR SUCCESS

EXERCISE 87

Sue Worthing ("Worthing") buys and sells prize-winning parrots. Three years ago, she purchased a beautiful red Eclectus parrot, whom she named Ted. She chose Ted over other birds because of his beautiful plumage and outgoing personality. She knew that he would be easy to train, and that he would be repeating numerous amusing phrases in no time. She had planned to sell Ted to a favorite client in Brazil. She emailed him the good news: "I have the most wonderful Eclectus for you—smart, handsome, and talkative!" Unfortunately, the Brazilian client purchased another parrot instead. Worthing therefore kept Ted at home until she could find another suitable buyer.

Worthing could not find a suitable buyer right away, so she decided to keep Ted in her home and increase his vocabulary. Clients enjoyed buying birds that already knew plenty of fun words and phrases, so further training would increase Ted's market value. Although parrots were her business, Worthing also enjoyed training birds so she was happy to spend extra time with him. Ted was a quick study, and in no time he was amusing friends and neighbors with his upbeat observations and pithy remarks.

Recently, however, Ted started to behave in a lethargic manner. He usually enjoyed talking with Worthing, but now he would not answer her at all. Upon closer inspection, Worthing saw that Ted had lost weight. He refused to eat even his favorite snacks. She rushed him to the vet, who diagnosed him with Polyoma virus. Polyoma can be fatal to parrots, although there is a vaccination against it. "Didn't Ted get his vaccinations before you bought him?" asked the vet. Worthing thought back over the transaction. "Yes, I thought he did. I have the paper in his file."

Worthing dug through the papers and brought out a record. "Look, here it is. It's on the letterhead of the vet who examined Ted, called Birds To Love Veterinarian. 'Polyoma vaccine, 1 avian dose plus boosters. $25.00. AVA.'" Worthing's vet said he did not know what "AVA" meant, but if Ted had had the vaccinations as written, he would almost certainly not have contracted the disease. Two weeks later, Ted died. Worthing was upset at the loss of her inventory, but also upset that a great parrot had passed away unnecessarily. Furthermore, she felt tricked.

She has come to your office to find out whether she has a claim against Birds To Love Veterinarian for the vet's failure to give the vaccination as represented in Ted's records. You research the claim and the relevant statute of limitations, which is two years in Ohio for injury to personal property:

> An action for bodily injury or injuring personal property shall be brought within two years after the cause thereof accrued.

Ohio Rev. Code Ann. § 2305.10 (LexisNexis 2011).

All parties agree a parrot is "personal property" for purposes of the statute.

You represent Worthing in the lawsuit against Birds To Love Veterinarian. Birds To Love responds with a motion to dismiss, arguing that Birds To Love did not create the medical record in question. In addition, Birds To Love stated that it never provided shots to any birds at all. Rather, the sellers of the birds contracted with Avian Veterinary Associates (noted as "AVA" in the records) to provide vaccinations for all the birds that were about to be sold. Birds To Love stated that if any company was to blame for the missing vaccination, it was AVA.

The court dismissed the lawsuit against Birds To Love, stating that Worthing had sued the wrong defendant. By the time Worthing received the court's judgment, however, a year had passed since the lawsuit against Birds To Love was first filed. Four years and six months have now passed since Ted missed the vaccination that should have saved him from the Polyoma virus.

Is it too late to sue AVA? You find the following cases to help resolve this issue:

- *Brown v. Quimby Material Handling, Inc.*, No. 1999AP110066, 2000 Ohio App. LEXIS 2651 (Ohio Ct. App. June 15, 2000)

- *Reed v. Vickery*, No. 2:09-cv-91, 2009 U.S. Dist. LEXIS 102151 (S.D. Ohio Oct. 9, 2009)

- *O'Stricker v. Jim Walter Corp.*, 447 N.E.2d 727 (Ohio 1983).

Using the statute and these cases, please determine and explain whether the two-year statute of limitations will bar Worthing's lawsuit against AVA.

STATUTORY ANALYSIS FOR SUCCESS
EXERCISE 88

Using the statutory sections and cases for this exercise, determine whether Corky Moore ("Moore") had a reasonable ground or belief to apprehend an imminent design by Benjamin "Hurricane" Carver to commit a felony or to do some great bodily injury upon Moore.

This exercise is based on the background facts for Exercise 79. These same facts are provided here.

Background Facts

Moore walked through the front door of the Mahogany Bar and Lounge ("Mahogany") in Tarzana, California and the bartender and owner, Manny Holm ("Manny"), greeted him with a smile. "You're back! This makes four Fridays in a row. You are a regular now," said Manny.

"What can I say? I really like this spot. It reminds me of my favorite bar back home and I do miss home," Moore responded. "Can I get a Jameson on the Rocks?"

"Coming right up," Manny said. Manny prepared Moore's drink and placed it in front of him. "How about I start a tab for you?"

"Yeah, I plan to hang out here for a while," Moore said. He sipped on his drink and looked around the bar. The place was not too crowded that night. The women outnumbered the men by at least two to one. As Moore sat at the bar, he could see the pool tables and small dance floor area. Benjamin "Hurricane" Carver's ("Carver's") girlfriend, Christy Hampton ("Christy"), stood in front of the jukebox looking for a song to select.

"This thing is too old, Manny! When are you going to come into the 21st century?" Christy asked Manny.

"Real soon, and remember we will be closing down the bar for a month for renovations. You'll have to get your drinks at home for a bit," Manny chuckled. "When we reopen, this place will have satellite radio, plasma screens all over, real mahogany wood on the bar, and a backroom for parties. How does that sound?"

"That's going to be great, Manny . . . a real improvement," Christy said. Then, a patron who was playing pool walked over to Christy and asked her name.

"Hey pretty lady, what's your name?" the patron asked.

"Christy. What's your name?" she responded.

"Charles. Here's a quarter for the next round of music," the patron said. "What do you want to hear?"

"Something upbeat, something I can dance to," Christy said.

"Pick Maze and Frankie Beverly's *Happy Feelin's*," the patron told Christy. She selected the song and the music started to play. "Wanna dance?" the patron asked Christy as he politely touched her hand. Before Christy could answer, Carver, who stood six feet and four inches tall and weighed 220 pounds, came across the room and hit the patron in the mouth. The patron fell to the floor and Carver continued to hit him.

"Hurricane, stop! He didn't do anything. Stop!" Christy yelled.

Manny reached for the phone to call the police. "Here he goes again. Hopefully, the cops will get here sooner this time," Manny told Moore.

"This has happened before?" Moore asked.

"Unfortunately it has, and I am too old to get between men fighting. I really like Hurricane. He's a very loyal customer. I mean, I practically paid my kids' way through college on his bar tab alone. Nevertheless, he does have a serious anger management problem. He gets in at least one fight a month here. He aggravates easily. Most of the incidents were minor scuffles though, and did not require any police attention. If anyone comes too close to that girlfriend of his, he is just asking for trouble," Manny explained. "I need to make sure they send an ambulance this time."

Moore sat calmly at the bar watching the events unfold. The police arrived and took Carver into custody. Christy cried nonstop. She left the bar right after the police escorted Carver out in handcuffs. The battered patron remained in the hospital for a week recovering from his injuries. The police released Carver the following day. Carver was never charged for this incident.

Over the next few months, Moore frequented Mahogany consistently on Fridays after work. He came to know the other regular bar patrons pretty well. They would sit at the bar and share horror stories about work, debate politics and sports, and comment on happenings at the bar. Occasionally, someone would tell Moore about another argument or fight involving Carver. "He is someone you don't ever want to cross," one patron remarked. Moore added, "Yeah, that guy is nothing but bad news."

The last Friday before the bar closed for renovations, Moore arrived an hour earlier than his usual time. He wanted to make sure his favorite seat at the bar was empty and knew the place would be extra crowded that evening. Moore ordered a Jameson on the Rocks and asked Manny to start a tab.

"This is going to be a great night, Manny! However, I have to say, I am pretty bummed that the place will be closed for four weeks. I guess I'll have to go to the pub around the corner until you reopen," Moore said.

"That's what everyone keeps saying," Manny commented. "I'm not worried though. The renovations will bring everyone back. We will have a big party for the grand reopening."

People had filled most of the tables already. They were drinking, talking, laughing, celebrating birthdays and the end of the workweek, and reconnecting with friends. Everyone was smiling and enjoying the oldies music playing from the jukebox. A few women jumped up and ran to the dance floor when Kool and the Gang's song, *Celebrate Good Times*, started to play. Christy approached the bar and stood next to Moore's seat.

"Manny, can you give me two Gin and Tonics," Christy asked and then turned toward Moore. "Hey, excuse me for getting so close. It is pretty crowded in here. Hey, I've seen you here almost every Friday. I'm Christy," she said.

"Nice to meet you, Christy. I'm Corky," Moore replied, as he anxiously looked over her shoulder to see if Carver was in the vicinity.

"Well, Corky, what do you do for fun?" Christy asked.

"Fun? Come here, I guess. I work long hours at my accounting job. I don't have much time for fun."

"So you are an accountant. How exciting," Christy said sarcastically and grinned. At that moment, Carver walked through the front door. He spotted Christy talking to Moore, balled up his fist, and glared in Moore's direction. Carver's face turned red and he marched toward Moore. Christy saw Carver approaching, reached out and grabbed Carver's hand, and pulled him to the dance floor.

"I've already ordered our drinks, baby. Let's dance!" Christy told Carver. He reluctantly followed her to the dance floor. Moore quickly finished his drink and left the bar. Moore made sure he left a large tip for Manny.

"See you when we reopen!" Manny shouted after Moore.

While Mahogany was closed for renovations, Moore went to the nearby pub and a lounge closer to his home. He saw a handful of Mahogany's regular patrons during this time but he did not see Carver or Christy. As the renovations neared completion, Manny posted a large sign on Mahogany's door that announced the grand reopening event for the following Friday. The sign read, "After Four Long Weeks, We Are Ready to Reopen. Come and Celebrate Our New Charm! Next Friday Night."

On the Friday of the grand reopening, Moore arrived at the bar just before the Happy Hour ended. "Manny, thank God you are finally open again! This place looks great. Did I miss the drink specials?" Moore asked as he grabbed a seat at the bar.

"You still have plenty of time. We extended the happy hour to celebrate our grand reopening. The usual?" Manny asked.

"Yes, and keep them coming. I had a rough day today." Moore said.

"Oh yeah, Hurricane asked about you a couple of hours ago," Manny revealed.

"He asked about me? Why?" Moore asked nervously. "Is he still here?"

"Yeah, I think so," the bartender stated. "He was checking out the new room and plasma screens that we added in the back. You need to walk around and look at the renovations. Let me know what you think." Before the bartender could finish, Moore placed some money on the bar, quickly grabbed his coat, and headed out the door toward the parking garage.

Moore walked so fast to his car that he practically galloped. Inside the bar, Carver noticed that Moore paid his tab and left before he finished his drink. Carver pushed back his chair and headed toward the front door after Moore. Moore moved so quickly that Carver started jogging after him. When Moore reached his car, Carver called out to him.

"Hey you!" Carver shouted loudly in Moore's direction. Moore, who stood five feet and ten inches tall and weighed 180 pounds, turned around and saw Carver headed in his direction. Carver's face was flushed red and he was sweating. Moore's heart started to pound hard and fast and his hands began to shake. He found it difficult to breathe.

"Oh no," Moore thought. "He's going to kill me. Think fast!" Moore looked around but could not find a place to hide. He stood with his back to the wall, in between his car, a Ford Focus, and a large truck. The garage had one entrance and exit for cars and a small walkway for pedestrians. Carver was in the path of the only way out of the garage. Moore noticed his backseat window was down and saw his aluminum baseball bat lying on the back seat. He reached through the window and grabbed his baseball bat. He placed the bat down by his side so Carver could not see it.

When Carver came near, Moore closed his eyes and swung his bat with all his might, hitting Carver on the side of his neck. Moore caught Caver off guard. The blow caused Carver to fall and strike his head on the bed of the truck parked next to Moore's car. Carver fell to the ground, bleeding profusely from his head. Moore leaped over Carver who lay motionless on the ground and ran back to the bar for help.

When the police asked Moore about the baseball bat, Moore explained that he coaches a softball team and usually keeps the equipment in his car. He then showed the police the equipment in his car. Moore had a couple of baseball gloves and two bags full of baseballs on the floor of the backseat. Moore claimed he reached for the baseball bat to protect himself against Carver. When the police questioned the bartender, Manny, he recounted the many arguments and fights involving Carver and confirmed Carver's bad temper. Manny also told the police that Carver had just asked about Moore. He inquired whether Moore was an accountant. He believed Carver wanted to ask Moore for help with his taxes.

Carver suffered serious injuries to his brain and spinal cord and remained in a coma for months. Carver never regained consciousness and eventually died from his injuries. The prosecution filed a charge against Moore for involuntary manslaughter. Moore raised his right to self-defense.

Under California law, did Moore have a reasonable ground or belief to apprehend an imminent design by Carver to commit a felony or to do some great bodily injury upon him? Did Moore have a right to use self-defense against Carver? Do not address the other requirements for justifiable self-defense (such as the existence of an honest and subjective belief in the need to defend). Address only the reasonableness of Moore's belief in the need to defend himself against Carver.

These are statutory sections and cases for this exercise:

- Cal. Penal Code §§ 197-199 (Deering 2011)

- *People v. Hickman*, No. E043962, 2008 Cal. App. Unpub. LEXIS 9464 (Ct. App. Nov. 21, 2008)

- *People v. Bayardo*, No. B167682, 2004 Cal. App. Unpub. LEXIS 6952 (Ct. App. July 26, 2004) *

- *People v. Trevino*, 246 Cal. Rptr. 357 (Ct. App. 1988)

- *People v. Clark*, 181 Cal. Rptr. 682 (Ct. App. 1982) **

- *People v. Whitfield*, 66 Cal. Rptr. 438 (Ct. App. 1968)

---

* For purposes of practicing in the California court system, the *Hickman* and *Bayardo* cases are marked as "nonpublishable" or "noncitable" per the California Rules of Court. However, for this exercise, you can use these cases, as needed, for authority.

** Note the *Clark* case was overruled on other grounds in *People v. Blakeley*, 999 P.2d 675, 681 (Cal. 2000) (addressing first impression issue of imperfect self-defense and unlawful killing and expanding the crime of voluntary manslaughter).

STATUTORY ANALYSIS FOR SUCCESS
EXERCISE 89

You are an assistant district attorney in Topeka, Kansas. Using the statute and cases set out below, please determine whether you should charge Mary Sully with felony murder. Assume that all elements of felony murder are met except the following, which you have been asked to analyze. Determine whether (1) the death is within the res gestae of the underlying crime and (2) there was a sufficient causal connection between the underlying felony of sale of cocaine and the death that occurred to support a charge of felony murder.

Fact Pattern:

Roger Fare ("Fare") and Mary Sully ("Sully") are drug dealers in Topeka, Kansas. Fare is a member of the notorious Dips-27 gang, whose members are feared in Topeka and beyond. Sully received a phone call one evening from a regular customer, Milton Rosen ("Rosen"). Rosen placed an order for four grams of cocaine, which he planned to bring to an upscale party that weekend.

Sully did not have the cocaine in her storage facility, so she telephoned Fare, who could obtain almost any drug at any time. Fare said that he could obtain the drugs, and he would give Sully a ten percent cut of the profits. Rosen was a little uncertain about meeting Fare alone, so he asked that Sully come too, as he had bought drugs from Sully on numerous other occasions. He had always been pleased with her prompt and friendly service, and he felt safe when dealing with her.

Sully suggested that the three of them meet that evening behind an apartment complex on the west side of Topeka. Sully and Rosen arrived on time, each in a separate car. Sully had a friend at the complex, Martha Arriba ("Arriba"), who agreed to serve as lookout. Fare had not yet arrived, so Sully and Rosen chatted while standing next to Sully's car. Fare arrived soon afterwards, and he approached Sully and Rosen in his car. "What are you doing, standing in the middle of everything? Are you just trying to attract cops? Do you enjoy federal prison, you bone-heads?" The two jumped into Fare's car, and Fare drove to a nearby parking space. Rosen took out his money, and Fare held up a bag of cocaine. "Enjoy—this is good stuff."

A hooded figure appeared at the side of the car. "OK, Fare, what are you doing in this complex? This is our turf. Stay on your turf. Or else." The figure turned and started to walk away. Fare yelled after him, "Topaz! Get lost. Nobody tells me what to do! Least of all you, Topaz." Fare pulled out a handgun and shot in the figure's direction, backing out of the parking lot at the same time. The plastic bag of drugs fell to the ground. "Can I just get out?" asked Rosen. "I can push back the party date with no problem. Really, it's better if we just do this another day, perhaps." Fare said, "Relax, man, we'll just take this somewhere else. You'll get your stuff. No problem."

Topaz jumped onto a motorcycle and started following Fare's car. "OK, wise guy, what have you got, big guy?" he yelled in Fare's direction. "You want to be bad, let's go!" Fare hit a dead end and then drove back into the parking lot of the same apartment complex. Arriba started yelling, "Police! The police just came through! Run!"

Suddenly, a squad car blocked the way in front of Fare's car. Fare, Sully, and Rosen jumped out of the car and attempted to run behind a large waste bin. Two police officers ran after them, quickly apprehending and handcuffing Sully and Rosen. Fare ran out from behind the bin and started to climb the complex's fence. "Stop!" yelled one of the officers. "Look. He's got Dips-27 tattoos. We've got to get him." They told the other two defendants to stay by the car while they took off after Fare. Rosen started to cry. "This is unreal. This is so not worth it!" Sully stayed quiet and stood by the car.

The officers reached Fare and grabbed him roughly. They brought him back to the car and began to frisk him. Fare spun around, pulled a gun from behind his pants, and started shooting. A bullet made a pinging sound as it hit a car, ricocheted off the car. Rosen dropped to the ground, apparently hit by the ricocheting bullet. The officers completed Fare's arrest, and both Sully and Fare were taken into custody. Rosen died two days later of his wounds.

Should you charge Sully with felony murder for the death of Rosen? It is undisputed that the crime is inherently dangerous as required by the statute.

The statute for this exercise is:

The Kansas felony-murder rule provides that "[m]urder in the first degree is the killing of a human being committed . . . (b) in the commission of, attempt to commit, or flight from an inherently dangerous felony as defined in K.S.A. 21-3436 and amendments thereto." Kan. Stat. Ann. §21-3401(b) (1993).

The cases for this exercise are:

- *State v. Jackson*, 124 P.3d 460 (Kan. 2005)

- *State v. Beach*, 67 P.3d 121 (Kan. 2003)

- *State v. Milam*, 156 N.E.2d 840 (Ohio Ct. App. 1959)

- *State v. LaMae*, 998 P.2d 106 (Kan. 2000)

- *State v. Berry*, 254 P.3d 1276 (Kan. 2011)

- *State v. Sophophone*, 19 P.3d 70 (Kan. 2001)

CHAPTER VI

STATUTES WITH LEGISLATIVE HISTORY

PART 1

BEGINNING STATUTES WITH LEGISLATIVE HISTORY

STATUTES WITH LEGISLATIVE HISTORY
EXERCISE 90

Using the statute and legislative history set out below, determine whether Tom Green's Amazing Snakes display at the July Fourth celebration violated the dangerous snakes statute set out below. Please explain your answer.

Facts Section:

Tom Green ("Green") owns the Amazing Snakes snake farm in Nashville, Tennessee. He developed a love of snakes in early childhood, when he first visited a zoo reptile house. Green earns a living through his snake-control service, which catches and relocates unwanted snakes, and his Amazing Snakes demonstrations. The Amazing Snakes demonstrations are a popular feature at area birthday parties, scout gatherings, and summer camps.

Last July Fourth, the Jones family booked Green to present his Amazing Snakes demonstration at their annual family reunion and Fourth of July picnic. As part of his demonstration, Green brought five snakes with him. Four of the five were non-venomous species, and one was an extremely venomous Black Mamba snake. The Black Mamba is Green's favorite snake, because it is extremely rare and dangerous. Only a skilled handler such as Green can handle a Black Mamba without injury. Even experienced snake handlers are sometimes bitten by this species.

The day of the demonstration for the Jones family, Green packed his snakes and headed to the park for the picnic. He kept the Black Mamba in a special, secure case with a padlock on it. The demonstration went well at first, and most of the Jones family members were pleased with the demonstration. Two elderly aunts wondered aloud why the family was paying to see snakes, but the children in particular were thrilled.

Green allowed the children to stand three feet away from the four non-venomous snakes. A rope barrier kept the children back and away from the snakes. One of the youngest children, a four-year-old boy called Nicholas, ran towards the snakes, reached out, and grabbed the Green Rough snake. Although the snake was not venomous, it let out its trademark defense: a nasty stench. Then Nicholas started wailing, "It bit me! It bit me! Nasty, stinky snake!" The family erupted. "What are you doing to Nicholas?" asked his grandmother. "Please remain calm," said Green, explaining that further panic would lead to scared snakes and more problems.

Then, it was Green's turn to be dismayed. "Where's my Mamba? Where is it? Where?" The Jones family members knew that the Black Mamba was deadly, and several people ran from the site. "This is a nightmare!" exclaimed Grandma Jones, who had arranged the entire event. "I wanted to bring the family together, not terrify them!" Fred Jones called to Green that he had spotted the Black Mamba. "Look, there he is. On the hot dog bun. Wow, it must have been fast to get over there so quickly." The Black Mamba was lying across a hot dog bun, looking like a long, exotic sausage. Green quickly grabbed him and returned him to the secure case. "The Black Mamba is one of the fastest snakes in the world. But who knew he could open locks? I have no idea how he got out. Guess I'll have to be more careful next time."

Green looked behind him and saw a police patrol car. "What's going on here?" said the officer as he got out of his car. Grandma Jones explained, and Green generally agreed with her account. "Yes," said Green. "It was going great until little Nicholas grabbed the Green Rough snake and it bit him, and we all realized the Black Mamba got out. What a crazy day! But everyone learned a lot about snakes, right, Ms. Jones?" Ms. Jones agreed. "Well, sure we did, but it's a risky business you've got going on here, Mr. Green." The officer agreed. He took out a ticket pad and wrote Green a ticket. "Sorry, I know you're living out your passion here, Mr. Green, but I'm giving you a Class C misdemeanor ticket. In fact, you're guilty of two offenses, so here are two tickets. One for the Black Mamba and one for the Green Rough snake. Pay the fines and get your snakes under control."

Green is offended and does not believe that he should have to pay the fines. "The Green Rough snake is a docile, non-venomous snake! OK, the Black Mamba is a deadly, venomous, and fast snake, but how will people learn about them if they never see one?" Upon further investigation, little Nicholas admitted that the snake had not bitten him at all. "I just wanted to trick everyone," he said. "And then I opened the Black Mamba lock! Aren't I clever?" Now Green has come to you, asking whether he has a chance if he fights the tickets. Based on the statute's language and the legislative history below, how do you advise him?

Statute:

Section 39-17-101: Dangerous snakes or reptiles; handling *

(a) It is an offense for a person to display, exhibit, handle, or use a poisonous or dangerous snake or reptile in a manner that threatens the life or health of any person.

(b) An offense under this section is a Class C misdemeanor.

---

* This statute is based on the actual Tennessee statute, but its language differs significantly. The legislative history here is created for this problem.

Legislative History:

The snake statute was passed in 1999 after an incident involving the Tambini Circus. The circus came to town for four shows. The circus was eagerly anticipated each year, and two of the four shows were sold out. On the final night, the snake act ended with an unfortunate incident. The snake handler had planned to walk about the arena with a rattlesnake in each hand, showing the rattlesnakes to the crowd. At one point, two snake handlers threw rattlesnakes to each other. One of the handlers threw the snake a bit short, and it landed on and bit a young girl. She survived the bite, but her arm was badly affected with permanent scars. There was a public outcry at the lack of regulations governing snake shows. The state legislature noted the incident, and passed the snake law four months later.

(1)   In advance of the introduction of bills on the floor, the legislature held hearings on snake laws and best snake practices in general. Here are some excerpts from the hearings:

- Renowned herpetologist Mary Mastoff testified as follows: "Snakes are not a show. Snakes are creatures that have much to teach us. They are fascinating but also dangerous. If we want to protect the public, we need to require that snakes are not shown in conditions that will startle or hurt them. Snakes are mainly docile. But if they feel threatened, they will strike. And that is no more or less than we should expect from wild animals. Anyone who thinks otherwise is simply misinformed."

- Circus manager Roy Rolder testified as follows: "Circuses and other shows involving snakes bring a tremendous positive economic impact to this state. Who do you think benefits from the taxes when the circus comes through town or when people put on a show? You guys. If you box us in and don't let us give the people the kind of show they want, you'll be the ones suffering. If we can put on an exciting—but still safe—show, then that's a win-win. Leave it to the professionals to know what's safe and what isn't."

(2)   State Senator Jo Ann Jiggs introduced a bill entitled "Dangerous Snake and Reptile Ban for Safety." It included a complete ban on shows with venomous snakes and required that in shows with non-venomous snakes, the snake be a distance of at least six feet from any audience member. No audience member was permitted to touch a snake. This bill passed the Senate but did not pass the House.

(3)   The next version of the bill, sponsored by Representative Chuck Johnson, was entitled "Dangerous snakes or reptiles; handling." This bill states that it is an offense "for a person to display, exhibit, handle, or use a poisonous or dangerous snake or reptile in a manner that endangers the life or health of any person." It makes an offense a Class C misdemeanor.

- During the floor debates, senators and representatives made the following statements:

○ Representative Chuck Johnson: "This bill is designed to address the manner in which snake-handling or exhibiting is done. It shouldn't be dangerous. If people are going to display or exhibit these snakes, they're going to do it safely. If they don't, they're going to be committing a misdemeanor crime. Otherwise, we're putting the safety of our communities at risk. We're not trying to discourage educational programs, not at all. But above all, these things have got to be safe. If a snake is poisonous or dangerous, and by dangerous we mean those snakes that squeeze people, you know, those anacondas and such, then this statute will address those snakes."

○ Senator Sylvia Malone: "If we can't protect people from dangerous snake shows, what are we doing here? After all, people need to know that if they go out to watch something fun like an animal show, they're going to be safe. And this language is fair, because under this language, things don't have to be perfect. The show just can't 'endanger the life or health' of anyone. So that's fair. If things are just a bit wrong or someone has a tiny problem, that's not a person's 'life or health' being endangered. So there's some room to maneuver and some proportionality."

○ Representative Todd Stevens: "What I like about this bill is it doesn't micromanage. It doesn't say you've got to stay five feet away, or you've got to keep a snake in a box. No, it leaves the details to the person who knows the snakes—the snake handler. The problem, though, is how do we know when it's not safe? When something happens? Now that just seems like armchair quarterbacking. Can't we add a bit more detail so there's some sort of preventative quality to this? So I like the direction we're headed, but this text as it stands does not work for me."

(4) In a signing statement, the Governor of Tennessee said he was pleased to sign the bill into law: "This is a great day for snake-lovers of Tennessee. Now they can see snakes and be safe. Snake-handlers will need to take care and be careful with those snakes. And if there's a serious problem, then there's a penalty."

STATUTES WITH LEGISLATIVE HISTORY

EXERCISE 91

Using the statute and legislative history below, determine whether Joshua Braxton, defendant's counsel, has an unconditional right to question prospective jurors.

Background Facts

Earlier this year, the defendant's trial for capital murder began in Jefferson City, Missouri. The defendant was on trial for killing a store clerk during the defendant's robbery of the store at gunpoint. Prior to the first day of trial, the court asked counsel for the State of Missouri and the defendant to submit questions they wished to have asked of prospective jurors during voir dire examination. Counsel for the State offered eight questions. The trial judge did not ask each question verbatim as written by State's counsel but did address most of the topics raised by counsel. Joshua Braxton ("Braxton") submitted a list of fifteen questions, nine of which the trial judge asked verbatim. The court did not ask the remaining questions proposed by Braxton.

The remaining questions submitted by Braxton were designed to elicit any biases of prospective jurors or glean their perspectives on the death penalty. For example, one question asked, "As you can see, the defendant, Phillip Thurman, is male. The victim, CiCi Lopez, was female. Will those facts prejudice you against Phillip Thurman or affect your ability to render a fair and impartial verdict based solely on the evidence?" Another question asked, "The defendant, Phillip Thurman, is also unmarried with no children. The victim was a mother of three children. Will those facts prejudice you against Phillip Thurman or affect your ability to render a fair and impartial verdict based solely on the evidence?" In addition, a third asked, "Do you feel that if a person is to be given the death penalty for the unlawful killing of another person, such penalty should be given only if such killing is of the most severe and aggravated nature?" The trial judge did not ask these questions of the prospective jurors.

During voir dire, each prospective juror was required to answer individually at least two questions concerning capital punishment. These questions were: "Do you have any religious or conscientious objections against the imposition of the death penalty?" "Do you feel that in each and every case, regardless of the facts, where a person is convicted of murder he should receive the death penalty?" Those prospective jurors who answered no to both questions were deemed suitable, without further questioning, with respect to their attitude toward the death penalty. On the other hand, those prospective jurors who answered yes to either question were questioned further by the court.

Right before the trial judge concluded voir dire examination, Braxton requested a few minutes to ask the prospective jurors the remaining questions on his list that the court did not address. The trial judge denied Braxton's request, stating that a defendant has no constitutional right to counsel-conducted voir dire. Braxton vehemently, yet respectfully, objected and insisted that the Jury Selection Act of 1980, codified under Missouri Revised Statutes Chapter 494, afforded him an unconditional right to question prospective jurors.

In 1980, the Missouri General Assembly passed the Jury Selection Act, which, among other things, attempted to clarify the procedures for identifying the potential jury pool, selecting the jury members, and conducting voir dire examination. The Missouri General Assembly, which is the formal designation of the state legislature, consists of a Senate and a House of Representatives.*

Braxton maintains that the Jury Selection Act of 1980 provides him with an absolute right to question prospective jurors and participate directly in the voir dire examination process. State's counsel responds that the trial court has discretion in determining whether to permit counsel-conducted voir dire. Please analyze the merits of Braxton's position and address the plain meaning of the statute as well as the applicable legislative history. You may use any part of the following statutory language and legislative history to complete this exercise.

Missouri General Assembly

Public Laws (1980–1981 Session)

Public Law No. 243

"The Jury Selection Act"

§ 100. Title

This Act may be referred to as the "Jury Selection Act."

§ 101. Purpose

This Act will amend chapter 494 of the Revised Statutes of Missouri of 1980, the general provisions as to juries. The Assembly believes the specific procedures relating to jurors must be clarified to ensure the fair and equitable identification of potential jury pool members and selection of jurors to serve as arbitrators of justice in Missouri's court system. The procedures must be balanced and transparent to all those involved in the judicial system. The Assembly therefore believes that clearer guidelines should be enacted that eliminate further ad hoc and informal practices in selecting jurors.

. . . .

---

* Note: Much of the statutory language and legislative history provided here have been invented for this exercise.

§ 105. Voir Dire Examination of Persons Called As Jurors

Section 477 of chapter 494 shall be amended to read as follows: The court and counsel for either party may examine under oath any person who is called as a juror therein and may ask such person or juror directly any relevant question to ascertain whether he is related to either party, or has any interest in the cause, or has expressed or formed any opinion, or is sensible of any bias or prejudice therein; and the party objecting to any juror may introduce any competent evidence in support of the objection.

§ 106. Juror Initiative

A new section 478 shall be added and provide: A juror, knowing anything relative to a fact in issue, shall disclose the same in open court.

§ 107. Juror Removal

A new section 482 shall be added to chapter 494. It shall read: If it shall appear to the court that the juror does not stand indifferent in the cause, another shall be drawn or called and placed in his stead for the trial of that case.

. . . .

§ 110. Court Discretion

A new section 506 shall be added to chapter 494. It shall provide: Notwithstanding the procedures established herein, the court shall have discretion to determine the appropriate content for questions asked during voir dire examination and authority to implement guidelines to supplement these procedures.

. . . .

§ 118. Effective Date

This Act shall be effective immediately.

Notes & History

This Act was introduced and sponsored in the state House of Representatives by Cynthia Nixon on June 14, 1980, as HB 119, and by Evan Lieberman in the state Senate on July 26, 1980, as SB 237. The bills were referred to the House Judiciary Committee and the Senate Judiciary and Civil and Criminal Jurisprudence Committee, respectively.

HB 119 and SB 237 were essentially identical in all respects.

In conference, the Senate and the House emphasized the importance of the legislation, noted the few minor differences in word choice and article use, and adopted HB 119. The bill was passed in its present form.

This Act was passed by the Missouri General Assembly and signed into law on December 12, 1980.

The following documents were excerpted from the records of the Missouri General Assembly:

Prior Related Legislation

Chapter 494 of the Missouri Revised Statutes of 1897 section 477 provided, insofar as is pertinent, that "[t]he court shall, on motion of either party in any suit, examine on oath any person who is called as a juror therein, to ascertain" the juror's qualifications.

Chapter 494, section 477, of the Missouri Revised Statutes was later revised in 1945. This revised section 477 provided, insofar as is pertinent, that "[t]he court shall, on motion of either party in any suit, or may of its own accord," examine any prospective juror.

Report from the House Judiciary Committee on the Jury Selection Act (HB 119) August 3, 1980

The Committee endorses and approves HB 119, the Jury Selection Act. Juries are the backbone of our judicial system and we must work to ensure a fair and balanced approach is taken when identifying and selecting juries. Prior to this Act, the litigants' counsel had no authority whatsoever for directly participating in voir dire examinations. In most courts, litigants' counsel drafted proposed questions and, when requested by the court, submitted them for review and use. But apparently, this procedure was not adopted in all courts in this great state of Missouri, which has made it quite challenging for attorneys to prepare for trial and seek justice on behalf of their clients, whether it be the State of Missouri or a lifelong resident. We must act now to preserve the integrity of the system that we have in place.

Missouri House – Excerpt from Floor Debate, Wednesday, October 8, 1980

MS. CYNTHIA NIXON: I thank Representative Bailey for yielding his time. I would like to speak briefly in support of HB 119 before our vote today. I want to thank everyone who has supported this bill and worked tirelessly to see it in its final form today. Although the statute that is currently in place requires the trial judge alone to ask the questions of prospective jurors, in practice most trial courts permit counsel to ask them directly. This new Act sanctions this deviation and brings our State in line with the procedures in other jurisdictions. It thus authorizes what was already in fact occurring. I urge you to vote for this bill in its current form. Thank you for your time and attention.

Joint Conference Committee Report Regarding the Jury Selection Act (HB 119/SB237) September 27, 1980

The Conference Committee unanimously agreed the procedures for selecting juries require clarification. Given the virtually identical provisions in the HB and SB, the Committee concluded the discussion by reiterating the purpose of the Act and deciding to proceed with HB 119.

STATUTES WITH LEGISLATIVE HISTORY

EXERCISE 92

Using the statute and legislative history set out below, please determine whether the jello wrestling described in the fact pattern is likely to be considered "wrestling" for purposes of the state wrestling statute.*

Statute:

Section 285:1: Definitions

    II.   "Promoter" means any person, club, association or corporation sponsoring a fighting sports competition.

    III. "Fighting sports" means professional boxing, and amateur and professional wrestling, mixed martial arts, kickboxing, or any other form of amateur or professional sport combat in which blows are struck that reasonably may be expected to inflict injury.

Section 285:14: Tax and Report

    I.   Any promoter who sponsors a professional fighting sports competition under this chapter shall, within 72 hours after the competition file with the commission a written report. The report shall include the number of tickets sold, the amount of gross receipts and other facts as the commission may require.

    II. The promoter also shall, at the same time, pay to the commission by certified check a tax of 5 percent of the gross receipts of paid admissions after deduction of any federal taxes.

Fact Pattern:

Joseph Wall ("Wall") is a first-year law student at New Hampshire Memorial University Law School. He is looking for a part-time job that would increase his available spending money. He has found some on-campus jobs, but all of them require too many hours out of his study schedule. He has therefore decided to start sponsoring for-profit jello wrestling events at his apartment complex.

Wall plans to invite other first-year students—men and women—to compete for prizes such as commercial law outlines, bar prep courses, and even cash prizes. He will also provide concessions such as hot dogs, drinks, and popcorn. He hopes that the matches will be light-hearted and safe, and that the events will bring the

---

* The statute set out below is the actual New Hampshire statute; the legislative history is created for this exercise and is not the actual legislative history.

first-year class together. He will provide a professional wrestling judge as well as licensed medical personnel in the event that someone is hurt. His apartment complex has already consented to his holding the events, provided he pays a $200 fee per event. The "jello" will be a glutinous compound made from syrup, gelatin, water, and sugar. The wrestling pool will be three feet deep and eight feet in diameter. He plans to sell tickets for five dollars each. Contestants will compete free of charge. Wall's events will follow these rules, among others:

1.   Contestants may grapple, push, and grip one another—they may not, however, strike or kick one another directly.

2.   One contestant wins when another capitulates either by shouting "done!" or by tapping his or her hand on the jello's surface three times.

3.   Matches are to last twenty minutes at most. If no contestant has prevailed by that time, a winner will be determined by volume of spectators' cheering and clapping when each contestant's name is called.

4.   No more than one hundred students can attend. This is the maximum number who can fit into the quadrangle in Wall's apartment complex.

As a law student, Wall knows that these events might be governed by statutes or other laws. He has come to your office to find out whether his events must be reported to the state in any way, and whether he has to pay taxes on his ticket and concession sales. You and another associate are working on this project—your task is to determine whether the statute set out above will apply to the jello wrestling events. Please base your answer on the statute's text and the legislative history set out below.

Legislative History:

Historical context: The idea for this legislation first arose in response to the growing problem of underground boxing and wrestling rings that were causing excessive injuries.

Committee report: The bill was discussed extensively in committee, where members debated what sort of sports should be included. Several members argued that only truly violent sports should be included.

- Senator Chuck Jones: "This reporting and taxing legislation should just include the professionally-run events, such as ultimate fighting, professional boxing and the like. Who needs to worry about little events and novelty events? If we have to check on every kid with a jello wrestling event or dunking booth, we're going to drive our state regulators nuts, for little to no money. Let's make that clear in the statute."

- Representative Mary Silva: "I have to disagree with Chuck. Let's keep the language as is. Yes, it's broad, but why not keep it broad? If we're more inclusive, more events will be reported, and that leads to safer, better events. If it's any kind of wrestling, let's include it. If it's mixed martial arts, my goodness, we'd better include that stuff, because you know those folks could well end up in the emergency room. What is the down side? That's what I don't see."

In the end, the statutory language remained as initially drafted. In the floor debates, members of the House and Senate debated the bill's merits.

- Representative Mack Richards, who sponsored the bill originally, explained why the bill was so important to him. "My kids have all competed in various fighting sports, and let me tell you, even when these events are for fun, for charity, for whatever, we need to know what's going on, we need to keep tabs on these types of events. People get hurt, even when they don't expect to. And quite frankly, if the taxing ends up discouraging some of them, then so be it. It's not about whether people are free to have these events, because they are, but let's not let them go unnoticed, untaxed, under the radar, whatever you want to call it. This is a safety issue, first and foremost."

- Senator Sue Strang: "Whenever we tax, we need to think twice. Really. Our people are taxed all over the place, with every step they take. And now we're taxing amateur wrestling? What's with that? Folks, you've got to vote against this nonsense. Not in our state."

Governor's signing statement: "Now that fighting sports are reportable and taxable, we will be more aware of the all the varied and interesting sport combat-type events occurring within our state. The events will be brought into the open and conducted in a fair and safe manner. In addition, we will have tax monies available to cover the injuries that so often occur at these events and that end up being treated within our public hospitals and clinics."

STATUTES WITH LEGISLATIVE HISTORY

EXERCISE 93

Using the statute and legislative history set out below, determine whether Jim Domino's teeth are properly considered deadly weapons.

Background Facts

Your client, Jim Domino ("Domino"), has been arrested and needs your help. He tells you that he was outside a bar with a woman he had met a week before. The woman's name was Susan Farida ("Farida"), and Domino had invited her out for dinner and drinks. They had enjoyed dinner together and then headed to a bar. Outside the bar, Domino ran into a former acquaintance, Fred Staley ("Staley"). Staley recognized Domino and called out to him, "Hey, Domino! I guess you think you're a smart-aleck, don't you? You think I don't know what's going on, right?" Domino had no idea what Staley was talking about. Staley went on, "Oh yeah, play dumb, whatever. I know very well what's going on. You and Susan, bold as anything, behind my back."

Domino turned to Farida and asked her what this was about. "Susan, are you dating Fred?" Before Farida could answer, Domino felt a crushing punch against his face. Domino was not a confrontational person and had never been in a fight. He did not know what to do as he felt punch after punch land on his face and neck. "Dude, I'm sorry, I had no idea," Domino said in between punches. Finally, Domino felt Staley's arm against his mouth, and he gave it a big bite. The police soon arrived and arrested both men.

As it turns out, Domino seriously injured Staley's arm. Staley lost some blood, and his arm later became seriously infected. The injury required weeks of treatment and intravenous antibiotics.

Staley was charged with several crimes, and Domino was charged with first-degree assault, based on the theory that his teeth were dangerous weapons as used in this crime. Your law office plans to assert self-defense, and another lawyer is researching that issue. In addition, however, you would like to defeat the first-degree assault charge on the basis that Domino's teeth were not a dangerous weapon. You find no cases on the issue, but you do find the statutory language itself, as well as the legislative history set out below.

Using only the statute's plain language and the legislative history set out below, please decide whether or not Domino's teeth are properly considered deadly weapons. Please explain your answer.

Statutory Language

(1)   A person commits the crime of assault in the first degree if the person:

(a)   Intentionally causes serious physical injury to another by means of a deadly or dangerous weapon. A "dangerous weapon" is any weapon, device, instrument, material or substance which under the circumstances in which it is used, attempted to be used or threatened to be used, is readily capable of causing death or serious physical injury.

Or. Rev. Stat. § 161.015(1) (2011).

Legislative History

1969   The legislature decided to redraft its penal code and hold hearings as to the language of each provision.

1969   During the hearings, testimony was given as follows:

State Representative Nicholas John: "When defendants are charged with an enhanced offense, the enhancement should be based only on serious aggravating factors, such as the presence or use of a deadly or dangerous weapon. But when a person arms himself or herself with something and threatens or hurts a fellow Oregonian, now that's something we need to address with special provisions. We are not going to be weak on crime! We are tough on crime around here."

State Senator Mary Cooley sponsored the bill that amended the first-degree assault provision to include "dangerous" as well as "deadly" weapons. She testified as follows: "This isn't just about guns. It's about anything that causes serious harm. The bill included a broad definition and multiple classes of weapons, because we want to be inclusive. If you're going out there and arming yourself and hurting folks, you are going to be in big trouble in Oregon."

1970   Both houses of the legislature passed a bill with the following language:

"Dangerous weapon" is defined as any weapon, device, instrument, material, substance, object, item, or force that is capable of causing harm or that does cause harm or that could cause harm.

1970   The governor vetoed the bill, stating as follows: "The bill as written actually has the effect of conflating assault with a dangerous weapon with assault without a deadly weapon. Under a definition this broad, every single assault would be assault with a dangerous weapon, and ordinary assault would be surplusage in our penal code. Therefore, I urge the legislature to return to the drawing board, address this issue more carefully, and come back with language that actually addresses the issue of weapons and objects that create a situation and that distinguishes them from that of an unarmed human being assaulting someone."

1971   The legislature began floor debates on a new amendment to the first-degree assault with a deadly or dangerous weapon provision.

State Senator Mary Cooley again sponsored a bill, this time with the following language: "A person commits the crime of assault in the first degree if the person: (a) Intentionally causes serious physical injury to another by means of a deadly or dangerous weapon." The provision included the following definition of dangerous weapon: a "weapon, device, instrument, material, or substance which under the circumstances in which it is used, is readily capable of causing death or serious physical injury."

Senator Cooley explained that the new language "shows that we are tough on crime in Oregon. If you arm yourself and hurt someone, you're going to get more of a punishment than if you hadn't armed yourself."

State Representative Sophia Xuejiao explained her interpretation of the language: "The way I see this provision, if someone gets out there and causes some harm, they've used a dangerous weapon. They shouldn't be trying to get out of that. They should have thought of that beforehand."

The governor signed the provision into law, noting that the language was narrower than the previous version. "This way, there's at least some space between assault with a deadly or dangerous weapon and assault without. Otherwise, we're making nonsense of our own laws."

PART 2

INTERMEDIATE STATUTES WITH LEGISLATIVE HISTORY

STATUTES WITH LEGISLATIVE HISTORY

EXERCISE 94

Using the statute and legislative history set out below, determine whether John Rodriguez's injuries fall within the strict liability provision of the Trans-Alaska Pipeline Authorization Act.

Background facts

John and Maria Rodriguez moved to Alaska to advance their careers in the oil industry. They both worked as engineers near the Trans-Alaska Pipeline. One evening, as they were driving home from work, a large maintenance truck broadsided them, breaking John's arm. They later learned that the maintenance truck was owned by the company running the Trans-Alaska Pipeline—the truck driver was heading to the pipeline when his truck collided with the couple's car.

John sued ABC Inc., which runs the pipeline and holds the right-of-way. John asserts that his injuries fall within the following strict liability provision of the Trans-Alaska Pipeline Authorization Act:

> Except when the holder of the pipeline right-of-way granted pursuant to this chapter can prove that damages in connection with or resulting from activities along or in the vicinity of the proposed Trans-Alaska Pipeline right-of-way were caused solely by an act of war or negligence of the United States, other government entity, or the damaged party, such holder shall be strictly liable to all damaged parties, public or private, without regard to fault for such damages, and without regard to ownership of any affected lands, structures, fish, wildlife, or biotic or other natural resources relied upon by Alaska Natives, Native organizations, or others for subsistence or economic purposes.

43 U.S.C. §1653(a)(1) (2011).

John and ABC Inc. have filed motions asking for a decision on whether the strict liability provision applies to their injuries. You are the trial court judge assigned to their case. As an initial matter, you must decide whether the plain meaning rule applies—in other words, is the plain meaning of the statutory provision clear? That is, can you determine from the provision's words alone whether or not the claim is included within the provision, or must you look to legislative history? Please decide whether the plain meaning rule applies and whether the strict liability provision set out above applies to John's injuries.

Plain Language Rule of Statutory Interpretation

When a statute's language is clear, there is no need to examine legislative history to determine the meaning. Even if the meaning is clear, the legislature's purpose in enacting the statute can guide the statute's meaning.

Legislative History

(1) Excerpts from the 1973 House of Representatives' Conference Report are set out below.

> The Senate bill and the House amendment had different provisions regarding the liability of the owner or operator of an oil pipeline for damages resulting from its construction and operation. The Senate bill had one provision which related to pipelines on rights-of-way granted under the general law and which applied only to damages incurred by the United States. The Senate had another provision which related to damages incurred by Alaska Natives in connection with the Trans-Alaska Pipeline. The House amendment had three provisions which related only to the Trans-Alaska Oil Pipeline. One related to damages to anyone that were caused by the activities of the pipeline owner along the route of the pipeline. A second provision related to damages to anyone from discharges of oil from vessels owned or controlled by the pipeline owner in violation of the Federal Water Pollution Control Act. A third provision related to damages sustained by Alaska Natives.

> The Conferees adopted modified versions of all of these provisions. One provision is of general application and appears in section 28(x). It requires the Secretary or agency head to specify the extent to which the holder of a right-of-way or permit shall be liable to the United States for damage or injury incurred in connection with the right-of-way. Joint regulations by the agencies involved, as authorized in section 28(c), are contemplated by the Conferees. Strict liability without regard to fault may be imposed, but a maximum dollar limitation must be stated, and liability in excess of this amount may be determined under ordinary rules of negligence.

> The second provision is in section 204. It relates only to the Trans-Alaska Pipeline, and is in three parts. Subsection (a) imposes on the holder of the right-of-way or permit strict liability without regard to fault, and without regard to ownership of the land or resource involved if the land or resource is relied upon for subsistence or economic purposes, for damages or injury in connection

with or resulting from activities along or in the vicinity of the pipe-line right-of-way. Strict liability is limited to $50,000,000 for any one incident, and liability for damages in excess of that amount will be determined in accordance with ordinary rules of negligence.

Subsection (b) imposes on the holder of a right-of-way or permit liability for the full cost of control and removal of the pollutant of any area that is polluted by operations of the holder.

Subsection (c) imposes on the owner or operator of a vessel that is loaded with any oil from the Trans-Alaska Pipeline strict liability without regard to fault for damages sustained by any person as the result of discharges of oil from such vessel. Strict liability is limited to $100,000,000 for any one incident. The owner or opera-tor is liable for the first $14,000,000. A Trans-Alaska Pipeline Liability Fund, which is created by the bill, is liable for the balance of the allowed claims up to $100,000,000. The portion of any valid claim not payable by the Fund may be asserted and adjudicated under other applicable Federal or State law.

The Fund will accumulate and maintain not less than $100,000,000 derived from the collection of a fee of five cents per barrel at the time the oil is loaded on the vessel, from income from invested funds, and from borrowed money if needed.

Strict liability under subsection (c) will cease when the oil is first brought ashore at a port under the jurisdiction of the United States, and the subsection applies only to vessels engaged in coastwise transportation, including transportation to and beyond deepwater ports.

* * *

The Conferees concluded that existing maritime law would not provide adequate compensation to all victims, including residents of Canada, in the event of the kind of catastrophe which might occur. Consequently, the Conferees established a rule of strict lia-bility for damages from discharges of the oil transported through the Trans-Alaska Pipeline up to $100,000,000.

Strict liability is primarily a question of insurance. The fundamen-tal reason for the limits placed on liability in the Federal Water Quality Improvement Act stemmed from the availability, or non-availability, of marine insurance. Without a readily available com-mercial source of insurance, liability without a dollar limitation would be meaningless and many independent owners could not operate their vessels. Since the world-wide maritime insurance industry claimed $14 million was the limit of the risk they would assume, this was the limit provided for in the Federal Water Quality Improvement Act. There has been no indication that this level has since increased.

Accordingly, the Conferees adopted a liability plan which would make the owner or operator strictly liable for all claims (for both clean-up costs and damages to public and private parties) up to $14 million. This limit would provide an incentive to the owner or operator to operate the vessel with due care and would not create too heavy an insurance burden for independent vessel owners lacking the means to self-insure.

H.R. Rep. No. 93-624, at 28 (1973) (Conf. Rep.).

(2)   Letter from Rogers C.B. Morton, Secretary of the Interior to the Congress, dated April 4, 1973:

The environmental risks involved in the Alaska route are not insurmountable. They can be guarded against. . . . Moreover, we are insisting that operation of the maritime leg be safer than any other maritime oil transport system now in operation. If our West Coast markets don't receive their oil from Alaska in U.S. tankers that comply with the requirements we are imposing, their oil will probably be imported in foreign flag tankers that are built and operated to much lower standards.

S. Rep. No. 207, 93d Cong., 1st Sess. 102 (1973), *reprinted in* 1973 U.S.C.C.A.N. 2508, 2509-10.

STATUTES WITH LEGISLATIVE HISTORY

EXERCISE 95

Using the statute and legislative history set out below, determine whether Sam Smith's gun would result in an enhanced sentence.

Background Facts

Sam Smith ("Smith") was convicted of a drug trafficking offense and received a ten-year sentence. His sentence was increased by five years, based on the firearms provision of the federal drug trafficking statute, excerpted below. The weapon (a handgun) was on Smith's kitchen table when Smith was arrested. Smith is not alleged to have picked up or fired the gun during his trafficking offense. The evidence showed that the gun simply rested on the kitchen table while he bought and sold drugs.

At the time of his arrest, Smith had one hundred kilos of cocaine in boxes under the kitchen table; these drugs are the basis of his trafficking conviction. Smith did not touch, fire, brandish, or otherwise use the gun during his arrest.

Does the statutory provision below include Smith's gun? Why or why not? Some legislative history, precedent, and other potentially useful information are set out below.

Statute:

Section 924 (c)(1)(A) Except to the extent that a greater minimum sentence is otherwise provided by this subsection or by any other provision of law, any person who, during and in relation to any crime of violence or drug trafficking crime (including a crime of violence or drug trafficking crime that provides for an enhanced punishment if committed by the use of a deadly or dangerous weapon or device) for which the person may be prosecuted in a court of the United States, uses or carries a firearm, or who, in furtherance of any such crime, possesses a firearm, shall, in addition to the punishment provided for such crime of violence or drug trafficking crime—

(i) be sentenced to a term of imprisonment of not less than 5 years;

(ii) if the firearm is brandished, be sentenced to a term of imprisonment of not less than 7 years; and

(iii) if the firearm is discharged, be sentenced to a term of imprisonment of not less than 10 years.

Legislative History

(1)   The report on the bill to amend the statute by the House Committee on the Judiciary begins by reciting the dictionary definition of the term "furtherance." H.R. Rep. No. 105–344 (1997), at 11 (1997). The report then points out that "mere presence" of a firearm at the scene is insufficient to convict. *Id.*

(2)   "The purpose of adding the 'in furtherance' language is to assure that someone who possesses a gun that has nothing to do with the crime does not fall under 924(c). I believe that the 'in furtherance' language is a slightly higher standard that encompasses 'during and in relation to' language, by requiring an indication of helping forward, promote, or advance a crime. This provision applies equally to the individual simply exercising his or her right to own a firearm, as well as the prosecutor who would bring a 924(c) action where there is, arguably, an insufficient nexus between the crime and the gun."

144 Cong. Rec. S16270-71 (1968) (Statement of Senator DeWine).

Dictionary Definition

"The act of furthering: advancement." Merriam-Webster's Dictionary, http://www.merriam-webster.com/dictionary/furtherance, (September 29, 2011).

Case Excerpt

This excerpt is from a case construing a similar – but not identical – criminal statute involving a gun enhancement provision.

> The word "use" in the statute must be given its "ordinary or natural" meaning, a meaning variously defined as "to convert to one's service," "to employ," "to avail oneself of," and "to carry out a purpose or action by means of."

> Judges should hesitate . . . to treat [as surplusage] statutory terms in any setting, and resistance should be heightened when the words describe an element of a criminal offense. *Id.* at 145.

Bailey v. United States, 516 U.S. 137 (1995).

STATUTES WITH LEGISLATIVE HISTORY

EXERCISE 96

Using the dictionary definition and legislative history set out below, decide how the Endangered Species Act will affect your client's commercial real estate development project:

Fact Pattern:

Emilio Marcos ("Marcos") is a commercial real estate developer in Houston, Texas. Two years ago, he started developing a project that would create an outdoor space for Houstonians where they could listen to live music, shop, and dine. The project was called "Bayou Bridges," because it would contain numerous ornamental bridges and attractive arches over Houston's bayou system.

The initial phases of construction had just begun when Marcos learned that the site is home to the Blue Lizard. The Blue Lizard was recently placed on the endangered species list. Marcos has a plan to collect and relocate each and every Blue Lizard on the site. In fact, he has hired twenty-five workers whose sole task is to find Blue Lizards, place them in aquariums, and drive them to another location that the rare lizards enjoy. The other location is much smaller, however.

Marcos has heard from the Environmental Protection Agency ("EPA") that his lizard relocation plan is insufficient under the Endangered Species Act (the "Act"). The EPA states that even though Marcos's development is not actually directly injuring any Blue Lizards, the destruction of the Blue Lizard's habitat is forbidden by the Act.

Marcos has reviewed the text of the Act, but he does not believe that the Act prohibits destruction of habitats. He noticed that Section 9 of the Endangered Species Act simply states that no one may "take" any threatened or endangered species. 16 U.S.C. § 1531 (2011).

In the Act, the word "take" means "to harass, harm, pursue, hunt, shoot, wound, kill, trap, capture, or collect, or to attempt to engage in any such conduct." 16 U.S.C. § 1532(19) (2011).

The EPA's regulation, however, states that the word "harm" includes a prohibition on "significant habitat modification or degradation where it actually kills or injures wildlife by significantly impairing essential behavioral patterns, including breeding, feeding, or sheltering." 50 C.F.R. § 17.3 (2011). All parties agree that the Bayou Bridges project would destroy the Blue Lizard's main habitat in Houston.

Marcos completed two years of law school before leaving law school to become a successful developer. He remembers from law school that an agency's regulations can be challenged if they are not in keeping with Congress's intentions.

He wants to know whether you believe there is a basis on which to challenge the agency's regulation, and if so, how that challenge might turn out. Marcos suggests an argument that "harm" means only the direct application of force to an animal, such that the lizard relocation program would satisfy the Act.

You perform some initial research, which includes a dictionary definition of "harm" and some legislative history. Based only on the definition and legislative history below, how do you answer Marcos?

Dictionary Definition:

The dictionary definition of the verb form of "harm" is "to cause hurt or damage to; injure." *Webster's Third New International Dictionary* 1034 (1966)

Legislative History:

The 1966 version of the Act gave the EPA power to identify species "of native fish and wildlife threatened with extinction" and directed federal agencies to protect those species "insofar as is practicable and consistent with the[ir] primary purposes" and "preserve the habitats of such threatened species on lands under their jurisdiction." 80 Stat. 926.

The 1969 version of the Act featured a broadened approach to conservation, in that it continued the 1966 version's provisions and also gave the EPA power to list species "threatened with worldwide extinction." 83 Stat. 275. The transportation and sale of wildlife taken in violation of any federal, state, or foreign law was prohibited. *Id.*

In 1973, Congress held hearings on conservation. The hearings included the following statements:

> Stephen R. Seater, for Defenders of Wildlife, stated that species are disappearing at the pace of about one per year, and "the pace of disappearance of species" appeared to be "accelerating."

H.R. Rep.No.93-412, p. 4 (1973).

> The Assistant Secretary of the Interior stated as follows:

> "[M]an and his technology ... continued at an ever-increasing rate to disrupt the natural ecosystem. This has resulted in a dramatic rise in the number and severity of the threats faced by the world's wildlife. The truth in this is apparent when one realizes that half of the recorded extinctions of mammals over the past 2,000 years have occurred in the most recent 50-year period."

> Assistant Secretary of the Interior further stated as follows:

> "As we homogenize the habitats in which these plants and animals evolved, and as we increase the pressure for products that they are

in a position to supply (usually unwillingly) we threaten their—and our own—genetic heritage.

"The value of this genetic heritage is, quite literally, incalculable.

* * *

"From the most narrow possible point of view, it is in the best interests of mankind to minimize the losses of genetic variations. The reason is simple: they are potential resources. They are keys to puzzles which we cannot solve, and may provide answers to questions which we have not yet learned to ask.

"Who knows, or can say, what potential cures for cancer or other scourges, present or future, may lie locked up in the structures of plants which may yet be undiscovered, much less analyzed? . . . Sheer self-interest impels us to be cautious.

" The institutionalization of that caution lies at the heart of H.R. 37. . . ."

H.R. Rep. No.93-412, pp. 4–5 (1973).

Congress found that "[t]he two major causes of extinction are hunting and destruction of natural habitat." S. Rep. No.93-307, p. 2 (1973). The Associate Deputy Chief for the National Forest System stated that the destruction of natural habitats is the greater of these two threats. Id.

An earlier Senate draft of the 1973 Act included language that defined "take" as including "destruction, modification, or curtailment of [the] habitat or range" of fish or wildlife but that language was deleted before enactment.

STATUTES WITH LEGISLATIVE HISTORY

EXERCISE 97

Using the statute and legislative history set out below, determine whether the Sullivans' payments to their daughter are deductable from the Sullivans' income.

Fact pattern:

Miranda Sullivan ("Miranda") has devoted her life to the homeless people of New York. She works every day for the homeless, and she is well known to the staff of the local shelters and ministries. She receives her volunteer assignments from her church, but she is not paid by the church at all. Miranda lives with her parents, who give her a stipend and living expenses. Sometimes Miranda stays at a hotel downtown, because her parents live in the suburbs, far from the homeless population. Miranda's parents, Joan and Arthur Sullivan, give Miranda money to pay for hotel expenses. The Sullivans' money goes directly to Miranda, and it does not go to the church. The church has no power over the money and cannot access it.

When Miranda receives money from her parents, she only spends it on her work with the homeless. She uses other funds that she inherited from her grandmother to meet her daily expenses that are not related to her volunteer work.

Mr. and Mrs. Sullivan are proud of Miranda's work with the homeless and they are happy to pay her expenses. The Sullivans are not, however, wealthy, and they look for every cost savings. They prepare their own taxes, and they assume that the expenses they pay for Miranda are deductible as charitable donations. They are surprised, then, when they receive a notice from the Internal Revenue Service ("IRS") that the payments are not deductible as charitable donations. With interest and penalties added, the total is far higher than anything the Sullivans can currently pay.

The Sullivans have come to your office to ask whether the IRS is correct, or whether they may be able to challenge the IRS's position. A partner in your office asks you to look into whether the Sullivans' contributions can be considered "for the use of" the church, under the statutory language below. You find no cases on the matter, but you quickly locate the statute and legislative history that are set out below. Using only the statutory language and this legislative history, how do you advise the Sullivans?

Statutory language

(a) Allowance of deduction.

(1) General rule. There shall be allowed as a deduction any charitable contribution. . . .

(c) Charitable contribution defined. For purposes of this section, the term "charitable contribution" means a contribution or gift to or for the use of . . . a corporation, trust, or community fund or foundation . . . (B) organized and operated exclusively for religious, charitable, scientific, literary, or educational purposes." 26 U.S.C. §170 (1980).

Legislative history *

1962   Congress passes a version of the provision that allows a deduction for contributions "to a corporation, trust, or community fund or foundation . . . organized and operated exclusively for religious, charitable, scientific, literary, or educational purposes."

1967:   Congress holds hearings on the issue of how to increase charitable contributions without permitting potential fraud in taxpayers' deductions. In the hearings, the Commissioner of the IRS testifies as follows: "I'm not sure it's wise to amend the provision too broadly. We have to make sure that the charity keeps the control. After all, what's to stop a donor from donating to a third party, when the charity may never see the money? It's all very well to encourage donations, but let's not open the door too much to donor temptation to defraud."

1968:   Congress holds floor debates over the draft amendment. In the debates, Congressmen and Congresswomen spoke on the floor as follows:

"I certainly want to increase giving. But we are hardly increasing charitable giving if the charities receiving the money do not have control over the funds. After all, if someone can just give the money to someone else, and that third party can do as he or she pleases with the money, what good is that? It's nothing more than tax fraud." (Bill Sponsor Senator Terrance Brown of New York)

"What's important here is that charities get more money. In these tough times, we need to encourage donors to give. And the best way to do that is to help the donor as broadly as possible." (Representative Sarah Summers of Pennsylvania)

"Of course, we're all here to encourage charitable giving. But I'm not sure what 'for the use of' means, quite frankly. It's confusing, and we'd be better off going back to square one on this amendment." (Representative Karen Cole of Nebraska)

"'For the use of' could mean that the funds are given in trust for the charity, that much is clear, anyway." (Virginia Senator Christopher Alan of Virginia)

1969:   Congress amends the provision so that it allows a deduction for contributions "to *or for the use* of a corporation, trust, or community fund or foundation." (Emphasis added.)

---

* This legislative history is not the actual legislative history but has been created here for purposes of this exercise.

1969: At the signing ceremony for the amendment, the President made the following statement: "Through this amendment, we expand the ability of donors to receive tax deductions, without paving the way for fraud. This is an important day for all those who labor on behalf of the less fortunate among us."

PART 3

SKILLED STATUTES WITH LEGISLATIVE HISTORY

STATUTES WITH LEGISLATIVE HISTORY
EXERCISE 98

Using the statute and legislative history below, determine whether the Good Samaritan statute will apply to Dr. Mary Smith's treatment of Sandra Simmons.

Fact Pattern:

Sandra Simmons ("Simmons") went to sleep one evening feeling a little tired. She had spent a busy day at work, and she did not feel very well. She hoped that an early night and a good night's sleep would cure her.

She woke up on a Saturday at 2:00 a.m. with a severe pain in her chest. Her chest hurt when she breathed, and she felt weak and extremely tired. Simmons had a good friend who was also her family practice physician, so Simmons immediately thought of calling her. Simmons knew it was not Dr. Mary Smith's night to be on call, so Simmons called Dr. Smith's personal cell phone number. "I'm in pain, Mary," said Simmons. "I know this is not a work night for you, but I need your help. I have never felt this bad in all my life." Dr. Smith lived nearby, and she said that she would come to Simmons's house immediately and examine her. "I can't let a friend be in pain," Dr. Smith said.

When Dr. Smith arrived, Simmons was lying on the bed, moaning. "Mary, I'm in pain," she said. "Please help me." Dr. Smith examined Simmons and took her vital signs. "You seem OK overall," Dr. Smith said. "Let me listen to your heart again." Dr. Smith listened carefully. She told Simmons that she most likely had pleurisy, a painful disease of the pleural (lung) cavity's lining. "The best thing to do is rest." Dr. Smith told Simmons that she should be checked out in the morning by the on-call doctor, just to make sure. "Shall I give you my co-pay?" Simmons asked sleepily. "Sandra, don't worry about that. Just get the rest you need. There's no bill or anything for this—you're a friend, not just a patient."

In the morning, however, Simmons felt even worse. She got up and staggered slightly as she tried to cross the room. She felt excruciating pain, and she reached out to call 911. As she began to talk to the 911 operator, she slumped down and passed away. As it turns out, Simmons had suffered a massive heart attack, and she did not have pleurisy at all. Her earlier symptoms had been early signs of a massive heart attack.

Simmons's estate sued Dr. Smith for negligence. Dr. Smith responded by asserting the Indiana Good Samaritan statute, the text of which follows:

> Any person who gratuitously or without obligation renders emergency care at the scene of an accident or emergency care to the victim thereof, shall not be liable for any civil damages for any personal injury as a result of any act or omission by such person in rendering the emergency care or as a result of any act or failure to act to provide or arrange for further medical treatment or care for the injured person, except acts or omissions amounting to gross negligence or willful or wanton misconduct.

Ind. Code § 34-4-12-1 (2011).

You represent Dr. Smith. You have found no cases addressing the issue of whether the Good Samaritan statute applies to sudden illnesses rather than exclusively to car accidents, falls, and the like. In addition, you're not sure whether Dr. Smith's status as Simmons's regular physician changes the analysis. You have, however, found legislative history, dictionary definitions, and other information that could help. You also checked Good Samaritan statutes in other states, to see if they will help you interpret Indiana's Good Samaritan statute.

Using the information set out below, please explain whether you believe the Good Samarian statute will apply to Simmons's estate's lawsuit against Dr. Smith, and why.

Legislative History and Background:

California

California's Good Samaritan statute protects those who render "emergency care at the scene of an emergency." Cal. Bus. & Prof. Code § 2395 (Deering 2011). A previous version of the California Good Samaritan statute used the phrase "at the scene of an accident" instead of the current term, "emergency." After intense lobbying by medical professionals, the provision was revised in 1990 to its current form.

Georgia

Georgia's Good Samaritan statute protects "any person who provides emergency care to a person who is a victim of an accident or emergency." Ga. Code Ann. § 31-11-8 (2011). A previous version of the Georgia Code provision used the language "a victim of an accident or calamity."

Medical professionals lobbied for a revision, after a physician on an airplane was held liable for injuries to a baby that she delivered in mid-flight. In floor debates, several state senators observed that medical professionals should be encouraged to help and thanked, rather than sued, when they help out in any sort of emergency. "The good doctors, nurses, and other Good Samarians of this state are there for us—let's be there for them too," urged one. The revision was made in 1992.

Indiana

The current Indiana Good Samaritan statute was enacted in 1971. The 1971 version provided immunity where "any person renders aid at the scene of a potentially fatal Act of God or other calamity, without payment or promise of any kind."

The provision was revised in 1993, after a number of states revised their own provisions to expand protection of Good Samaritans. The 1993 revision was passed by both houses of the legislature, but was vetoed by the governor. The vetoed revision read as follows:

> Any person who renders emergency care at the scene of a serious medical situation shall not be liable for any civil damages for any personal injury as a result of any act or omission by such person in rendering the emergency care or as a result of any act or failure to act to provide or arrange for further medical treatment or care for the injured person, except acts or omissions amounting to gross negligence or willful or wanton misconduct.

In his veto statement, the governor stated that the language was overly broad: "Folks in the legislature, I know you all have a number of very active doctors and nurses back home, and they are watching this discussion closely. And you are doing your best to make everyone happy. This has been a tough legislative session, so I hate to do this to you. But the way this thing is written, ambulance personnel, the entire emergency room staff—well, they're all off the hook, always! This is too broad. Try again. We're not looking for some sort of blanket immunity, much as I think highly of doctors and such, but this is too much."

In the renewed discussion over the revisions, the legislature delved into the reasons behind the statute and the possible changes it could undergo.

- "This is the time to support our medical professionals and other people who step in at the drop of a hat, when they're on vacation, or they're having fun, or they're just minding their own business. Who are we to criticize, second-guess, and sue? We should be sending them a bouquet of roses. The least we can do is get this statute sorted out so it's clear that they are protected. Not against their own patients, of course, but against the helpless stranger, the lost traveler, the injured person on the airplane, or the woman suddenly giving birth away from her own doctor. Let's get this revision done, folks." Floor Debate Statement of Representative John Garcia.

- "I guess what I'm worried about is that doctors and nurses who see an accident are going to have to think first about their own liability. And that's not right. If we are asking a doctor or nurse or other person to do the right thing, to set aside their own concerns and problems, and step into a tough situation and help, we've got to take care of them." Floor Debate Statement of Senator Susan Simone.

- "When I sponsored this bill, I was thinking about the innocent victims of accidents and the like, and getting them more help. What we don't want to do is have people stop and help and wish they never had. Because those stories get around, and then maybe people don't want to help. And that's not what this state is about. We're about doing the neighborly thing and saying, 'Thanks.' And of course we have some other protections for doctors in terms of their own patients and medical malpractice caps and so forth, and that is not what this bill is about. It's about that moment when a member of the public is needing help, and there's a person with training—or maybe even without—who can help. And we just need to encourage those folks to get together and get through the accidents and those types of things that can happen out there." Bill Sponsor and Representative Tammy Washington.

- During the debates on the possible revisions, the legislature heard from an expert on Good Samaritan laws. He testified as follows: "In recent years, other states have revised their Good Samaritan laws significantly. The trend is more protection for Good Samaritans. Do you want to be behind this national trend?" Dr. Roderick Malone, General Counsel of Memorial Hospital.

- The legislature also heard from an Indiana resident, Vivian Smith, whose daughter went into childbirth on an emergency basis, while she was in the hospital for a broken arm. The doctor, who worked at the hospital but was an eye doctor, made some serious mistakes in the delivery, and the baby spent months recovering. "If that negligence claim had been barred by some sort of statute, I wouldn't have been able to give little Jessica the care she deserved. Today, she's running around and happy, despite all that St. Cecelia's Hospital and its careless doctor did to harm us."

- After Vivian Smith's statement to the legislature, a state senator, Robert Giles, spoke up as well: "If we're looking to relieve all doctors and nurses of doing their jobs right, then forget it, I'm not going along with anything that does that. I don't think this language does. Just remember, there's no lobby for the people who are going to need this kind of care, because who knows when a person is going to be in an accident? I don't know, it could be me. It could be you."

The legislature passed the 1993 version. The governor signed it into law. It grants immunity as follows: "Any person, who gratuitously or without obligation renders emergency care at the scene of an accident or emergency care to the victim thereof, shall not be liable for any civil damages for any personal injury as a result of any act or omission by such person in rendering the emergency care or as a result of any act or failure to act to provide or arrange for further medical treatment or care for the injured person, except acts or omissions amounting to gross negligence or willful or wanton misconduct."

Ind. Code § 34-4-12-1 (2011).

Ballentine's Law Dictionary defines an accident as "[a]n occurrence by chance or not as expected . . . an occurrence which could not have been foreseen by the exercise of reasonable prudence, one which happens from the uncontrollable operations of nature alone, without human agent." *Ballentine's Law Dictionary* (3d ed. 2010).

STATUTES WITH LEGISLATIVE HISTORY
EXERCISE 99

Using the statute and legislative history set out below, determine whether Suzy Smith Watson's refusal to have her photograph taken upon booking and processing constitutes obstruction of justice.

Fact pattern

Carina Smith ("Smith") was shopping in a Woods Department Store when she saw a beautiful baby dress that would be perfect for her new baby girl. She looked at the price tag: $120. Smith could not afford that much money for a single baby dress, so she walked on and paid for the shoes she had chosen. Later that evening, she told her sister about the dress. "It was gorgeous! Pink ribbons and white satin. Just lovely." Her sister hugged her. "Look, we'll find a way to get it!" she said.

The following day, Smith's sister, Suzy Smith Watson ("Watson"), came home with the dress. "Look at it! I have it! Little Jessica is going to look gorgeous in it." Smith was delighted, but she knew Watson could not have bought the dress—Watson never had much money at all. "How did you get this?" Watson smiled. "Well, never mind. Don't you worry." The following weekend, the two women were shopping together in the local Woods Department Store. "Hey, Carina, did you see the baby shoes that match the dress we have?" said Watson. Smith looked at the shoes. "Those are cute, but too expensive. Let's go." Watson told Smith she would be right behind her. When Watson walked out of the store, an alarm went off. Watson started to run, but a guard yelled at her to stop. The guard held Watson by the arm as he opened her purse. The shoes fell out onto the mall's tiled floor. Watson hung her head and started to cry. The guard walked Watson to a small office and called the police. The police soon arrived and arrested Watson.

Watson had never been arrested before, and she was terrified as the police drove her away. When she arrived at the police station, the police told her that she would be booked and photographed. Watson said that she would not be photographed. "I don't trust you!" she screamed. "Back off!" The officer was surprised. "You're refusing even to be photographed? No one does that. The prosecutors are going to be pretty mad." Watson could not stop crying. "So what? I'm a big old thief! I'm guessing they're going to be pretty darned mad ANYWAY!" In a few hours, the officer came back. "Ready to have your photo taken now?" the officer asked. "Sure," said Watson. But when the officer asked her to face the camera, Watson instead turned her back on the camera. She started crying again. "I don't want my photo all over the internet! I don't trust you! I want a lawyer!"

The following day, Watson met with a lawyer. The lawyer explained that Watson was charged with misdemeanor theft. Watson had expected this. The lawyer explained that this was Watson's first offense, and the circumstances were somewhat sympathetic. "We can probably get you probation, or maybe just community service," the lawyer explained. "There's something sort of strange, though.

You've been charged with obstruction of justice. What did you do, exactly?" Watson wasn't sure. "Are they talking about the photo thing?" The lawyer asked what "photo thing" Watson was referring to. Watson explained that she had not wanted to be photographed. "That's not optional, you know," explained the lawyer. Watson explained that she was afraid, and she didn't want anything to do with the process. "I realize now I should have cooperated. What's going to happen?" The lawyer said that he would return the following day with more information. "I'm going to have our summer associate work on this."

You are the summer associate. The lawyer who is representing Watson has asked you to look into the issue of whether a person can obstruct justice under the statute by refusing to have her photograph taken upon booking and processing. You find the following statutes, legislative history, and cases. Please draft an answer for the lawyer, who is eager to hear your assessment.

The prosecution has charged Watson under the following statute:

> A person obstructs the administration of justice or hinders the administration of law if the person intentionally obstructs, impairs or hinders the administration of law or governmental or judicial function by means of intimidation, force, physical interference or obstacle.

Or. Rev. Stat. § 162.235(1) (2011).

For help in interpreting the statute, you may use the following sources:

(1) The following are two other Oregon statutes:

> A person commits the crime of interfering with a peace officer . . . if the person refuses to obey a lawful order by the peace officer.

Or. Rev. Stat. § 162.247 (2011).

> A person commits the crime of resisting arrest if the person intentionally resists a person known to be a peace officer or parole and probation officer in making an arrest.

Or. Rev. Stat. § 162.315 (2011).

(2) An earlier draft of the bill that ultimately was passed to become section 162.235 read as follows:

> A person obstructs the administration of justice or hinders the administration of law if the person intentionally obstructs, impairs or hinders the administration of law or governmental or judicial function by means of any action or inaction, gesture or statement.

This draft passed both houses of the Oregon legislature, but was vetoed by the governor with the following statement: "Oregonians are fiercely independent. They are not going to tolerate a law that makes it a crime to just sit and do nothing. They're not going to go for that, and I'm not going to put up with it either. Make this the seventeenth veto as governor for me! Go back, members of the House and Senate, and give me something with the specificity you know is required. Forget this mushy, feel-good, tough-on-crime nonsense. It's not going to cut it in Oregon."

(3)   The current provision (the one Watson was charged with) was drafted as part of the 1971 revision of Oregon's penal code. Following are excerpts from the legislative history leading up to the passage of the current section 162.235(1).*

Statement of bill sponsor Representative Shania Smith:

> We have to have a way of punishing those whose aim is to prevent our public servants from carrying out their duties. Let's make sure we point out in this bill that anyone who would physically stop our representatives from carrying out their duties will be punished!

Statement in floor debates of Senator John Samuels:

> It's fine to punish those who would stand in the way of our public servants, but let's figure out what this means. After all, what in this world is not physical? Are we including everything? Or just actual actions? It's not clear to me at all. My constituents are interested in knowing what they have to do and not do in order to obey the law. I'm not sure that this does it. Let's go back to the drawing board and figure out something better.

Statement in floor debates of Senator Leslie Lane:

> What I don't like about this bill is that it seems to criminalize doing nothing. Is it criminal to do nothing? Should it be criminal to do nothing? We can certainly think of situations in which it should be criminal to do nothing—consider an evacuation, when a person stands in front of an officer and does nothing. Shouldn't that be criminalized? Is it criminalized in this statute? I'm not so sure. I think it should be, but I'm not so sure that it is.

(4)   Following is an Oregon statute that describes how legislative history is to be treated by Oregon courts:

> (1)(a)   In the construction of a statute, a court shall pursue the intention of the legislature if possible.
>
> (b)   To assist a court in its construction of a statute, a party may offer the legislative history of the statute.
>
> (2)   When a general and particular provision are inconsistent, the latter is paramount to the former so that a particular intent controls a general intent that is inconsistent with the particular intent.
>
> (3)   A court may limit its consideration of legislative history to the information that the parties provide to the court. A court shall give the weight to the legislative history that the court considers to be appropriate.

Or. Rev. Stat. § 174.020 (2011).

---

* This legislative history was created for this exercise and is not the actual legislative history of this provision.

STATUTES WITH LEGISLATIVE HISTORY

EXERCISE 100

Using the statute and legislative history below, determine whether Betty Wang's interpretation of the putative spouse statute applies.

Background Facts

Six years ago, Betty Wang ("Wang") married Jeff Landry ("Landry") in a private ceremony in Cleveland, Ohio. At the time of their marriage ceremony, and unbeknownst to Wang, Landry was still married to Cynthia Landry. During Wang and Landry's time together, the couple opened a shoe repair business and a customized belt store. Both businesses were located in the Flats, a mixed-use industrial, entertainment, and residential area of Cleveland. On her own, Wang purchased several income-producing properties in and around the downtown area, taking title only in her name. The couple had a number of assets in their portfolio.

Then, a month before Wang's fiftieth birthday, she received a letter in the mail from Cynthia Landry ("Cynthia"), who claimed to be Landry's wife. Wang confronted Landry about Cynthia. Landry explained he had filed the documents for legal separation from Cynthia, and Cynthia told him she had filed for divorce. Landry assumed their divorce was final.

Devastated by this discovery, Wang filed for divorce, seeking a judgment of nullity of the marriage. She also requested that the court confirm all property in her possession as her separate property. Landry filed a petition seeking putative spouse status. He claimed that he in good faith believed his marriage to Wang was valid and, as putative spouse, he is entitled to an equitable division of their marital or quasi-marital property. Wang did not seek status as a putative spouse.

At the hearing, only Wang testified. Wang stated she did not know that Landry was still married to Cynthia. She further explained that Landry told her he was divorced and Wang did not discover the truth until she received Cynthia's letter. Prior to that time, Wang admittedly believed she was lawfully married to Landry.

The court determined that the marriage was void because Landry was already married. The court entered a judgment of nullity. The court also found that since either party (here, specifically Wang) or both parties believed in good faith that the marriage was valid, the court was statutorily required under Section 3105.91 of the Ohio Revised Statutes (1) to declare them to have putative status and (2) to find that their property was quasi-marital property subject to division.

Wang maintains that the court erred in applying the putative spouse statute to her divorce action. She argues that Section 3105.91 should be applied only at the request of the putative or innocent spouse or in cases in which both parties constitute putative spouses (i.e. innocent parties). Landry disagrees, contending that if either party achieves putative spouse status, marital property principles should apply to the division of any quasi-property at issue, regardless of a party's fault in the divorce.

Please analyze the merits of Wang's position and address the plain meaning of the statute as well as the applicable legislative history. Can a party, who is the bad actor in a divorce, benefit from putative spouse status and receive a share of the quasi-marital property? You may use any part of the following statutory language, legislative history, and related statutes to complete this exercise.[*]

Also, consider the applicability of the following maxim or canon of construction to your analysis: *expressio unius est exclusio alterius*. The Latin term *"expressio unius est exclusio alterius"* means "the expression of one thing is the exclusion of the other."[**] Stated another way, under this maxim, the mention of one thing implies the exclusion of another.[***] Thus, for example, "'if a statute specifies one exception to a general rule or assumes to specify the effects of a certain provision, other exceptions or effects are excluded [under this maxim].'"[****] "[T]he maxim *expressio unius est expressio alterius* is not a rule of law but, rather, is a rule of construction and requires caution in its application."[*****]

Page's Ohio Revised Code Annotated (codification of the Putative Spouse Act)

XXXI. Domestic Relations

3100. Divorce, Legal Separation, Annulment, Nullity, Dissolution of Marriage; Division of Property; Alimony

    3105.91   Status of putative spouse; division of quasi-marital property; separate property

(a) If a determination is made that a marriage is void or voidable and the court finds that either party or both parties believed in good faith that the marriage was valid, the court shall:

    (1)   Declare the party or parties to have status of a putative spouse.

---

[*] Note: The statutory language and legislative history provided here have been adopted, in part, and invented for this exercise based in Ohio.

[**] *Thomas v. Freeman*, 680 N.E.2d 997, 1000 (Ohio 1997).

[***] *Bd. of Educ., Erie Cnty. Sch. Dist. v. Rhodes*, 477 N.E.2d 1171, 1175 (Ohio Ct. App. 1984).

[****] *Thomas*, 680 N.E.2d at 1000 (quoting *Black's Law Dictionary* 581 (6th ed.1990)).

[*****] *Rhodes*, 477 N.E.2d at 1175.

(2)   If the division of property is in issue, divide, in accordance with Section 3105.171(B) (requiring equitable division of marital property), that property acquired during the union which would have been marital property if the union had not been void or voidable. This property is known as "quasi-marital property."

(b)   If the court expressly reserves jurisdiction, it may make the property division at a time after the judgment.

Notes and History

The Putative Spouse Act was introduced and sponsored in the state House of Representatives by Eleanor Murray on February 12, 1986, as HB 3, and by Bryan Rivers in the state Senate on March 3, 1986, as SB 5. The bills were referred to the House Judiciary and Ethics Committee and the Senate Judiciary Committee on Civil Justice, respectively, for discussion.

HB 3 and SB 5 were essentially identical in all respects.

In conference, the Senate and the House emphasized the importance of the legislation, noted the few minor differences in word choice and article use, and adopted HB 3. The Act was passed by the Ohio General Assembly and signed into law on October 20, 1986, and later codified as section 3105.91 of the Ohio Revised Code.

The following documents were excerpted from the records of the Ohio General Assembly:

Report from the House Judiciary and Ethics Committee on the Putative Spouse Act (HB 3) April 16, 1986

The Committee endorses and approves HB 3, the Putative Spouse Act. Our judiciary has recognized time and time again the need to protect innocent spouses from the negative consequences of an invalid or illegal marriage that was no fault of their own. In the *Simon* case, a woman who believed she was lawfully married to her husband for ten years worked nonstop to put her husband through medical school and raised five children. After her husband graduated from medical school, she learned he had never divorced his first wife. Distraught and fearing for her family's future, she requested putative spouse status. The court granted her request and awarded her an equal share of the marital property. Later, in the *Resendez* case, the court found that a professed husband did not have putative spouse status because, under the circumstances, no reasonable person in his position would harbor a good faith belief that his marriage was lawful. Because he lacked a marriage license, and knew of the licensing requirement in our state, the purported husband knowingly went forward with the ceremony without one of the prerequisites. He therefore could not avail himself of putative spouse status because he was not an innocent party. He did not receive a share of his deceased wife's estate. We must act now to codify the common law, preserve the integrity and sanctity of marriage, and protect innocent spouses.

Ohio House – Excerpt from Floor Debate, Tuesday, April 22, 1986

MS. ELEANOR MURRAY: I thank Representative Harris for yielding his time. I would like to speak briefly in support of HB 3 before our vote today. I want to thank everyone who has supported this bill and worked tirelessly to see it in its final form today. Although the putative spouse doctrine has been applied in our courts for many years now, this new Act memorializes and codifies this equitable doctrine and makes it possible for the law to develop from one unifying legislation. With this legislation, we should have a more consistent application of the rules and division of marital property that reflects the expectations of the parties in the relationship. In a marriage, parties arrange their economic affairs with the expectation that, if there is a dissolution or end to the marriage, the marital property will be divided equally. The putative spouse doctrine embodies that expectation. It thus authorizes what was already in fact occurring. I urge you to vote for this bill in its current form. When a party believes in good faith that a valid marriage exists, that marriage should be validated. Thank you for your time and attention.

Ohio House – Excerpt from Floor Debate, Tuesday, April 22, 1986

MR. JOSHUA ERIC: I too support our efforts here today to continue to protect the rights of innocent spouses. The determination of a person's status as a putative spouse is a fact intensive review and has very important consequences on various legal rights, including the right to share in property accumulated in the name of the other party during the putative marriage, the grant of attorney's fees and costs, and standing to sue in wrongful death actions. We cannot leave such determinations up to chance.

Joint Conference Committee Report Regarding the Putative Spouse Act (HB 3/SB 5) October 3, 1986

The Conference Committee unanimously agreed the equitable putative spouse doctrine recognized by the judiciary should be a part of our legislative acts to ensure the even application of property division rules upon the dissolution of marriage. Given the virtually identical provisions in the HB and SB, the Committee concluded the discussion by reiterating the purpose of the Act and deciding to proceed with HB 3.

Related Ohio Statutes

XXXI.   Domestic Relations

3100   Divorce, Legal Separation, Annulment, Nullity, Dissolution of Marriage; Division of Property; Alimony

    3106. Order for support; putative spouse

The court, may, during the pendency of a proceeding for nullity of marriage or upon judgment of nullity of marriage, order a party to pay for the support of the other party in the same manner as if the marriage had not been void or voidable if the party for whose benefit the order is made is found to be a putative spouse.

. . . .

3107. Grant of attorney's fees and costs

The court may grant attorney's fees and costs in proceedings to have the marriage adjudged void and in those proceedings based upon voidable marriages in which the party applying for attorney's fees and costs is found to be innocent of fraud or wrongdoing in inducing or entering into the marriage, and free from knowledge of the then existence of any prior marriage or impediment to the contracting of the marriage for which a judgment of nullity is sought.

XXIII.　Civil Actions and Judgments

2300.　Civil Actions, Wrongful Death

2330.161 Persons with standing

A cause of action for the death of a person caused by the wrongful act or neglect of another may be asserted by any of the following persons or by the decedent's personal representative on their behalf:

(a)　The decedent's surviving spouse, domestic partner, children, and issue of deceased children. . . .

(b)　If they were dependent on the decedent, the putative spouse, children of the putative spouse, stepchildren, or parents. As used in this subdivision, "putative spouse" means the surviving spouse of a void or voidable marriage who is found by the court to have believed in good faith that the marriage to the decedent was valid.

CHAPTER VII

WRITTEN SAMPLE ANSWERS WITH ANNOTATIONS

EXERCISE 2

SAMPLE ANSWER

Leads with clear thesis sentence identifying the legal issue presented by the facts.

A court will likely find that Jefferson violated the City Ordinance for texting her friend but did not violate the ordinance for viewing the directions on her phone or calling to check her voicemail messages. The City Ordinance for Cell Phone Usage or Text Messaging provides that it is a moving violation and unlawful to use a wireless communication device to talk or listen to another person on the telephone or to view, send, or compose an electronic message or engage other application software while operating a motor vehicle.

Next, provides the relevant rules for the identified legal issue.

Explains the general rule prohibiting cell phone use and text messaging while operating a vehicle.

Texting

Addresses each of the violations separately. Provides a clear conclusion, relevant rule, and application for each alleged violation.

Jefferson likely violated the ordinance by texting her friend. The ordinance prohibits the driver from composing or sending an electronic message while operating a motor vehicle. Here, while waiting at a crosswalk, Jefferson picked up her cell phone, typed, and sent a message to her friend. She violated the letter of the law. Further, cities enacted such rules prohibiting texting while driving to prevent driver distractions. People are often involved in car accidents when they take their focus off the road while operating a car. Jefferson risked causing an accident by taking her eyes off the road and concentrating on her text message.

Presents affirmative arguments. Provides the relevant facts and explains how those particular facts support the conclusion that Jefferson violated the ordinance.

Applies the rules to the client's facts.

On the other hand, Jefferson will argue that she was not operating her car when she sent the text. In particular, she will maintain that she was stopped at the crosswalk (waiting for the children to cross the street) when she sent the text. She was not driving the car when she sent the text. Consequently, Jefferson will contend she did not violate the ordinance and she presented no danger to pedestrians or drivers.

Explains how Jefferson can challenge the officer's position.

Jefferson's argument will likely fail given that her conduct violated not only the language of the rule but also the spirit behind anti-cell phone use rules. Even though she was stopped at the crosswalk, typing a text to her friend while in a car presented a distraction to her and risk to pedestrians and other drivers. Jefferson could have accidentally pulled her foot off the brake or hit the gas

Rebuts Jefferson's argument by challenging the inferences raised in the counter-argument.

pedal. She would have been slow to react given that her attention was on the text message. Therefore, a court will likely find that she violated the City Ordinance for texting her friend while waiting at the crosswalk.

Directions

Unlike the texting situation, a court likely will conclude that Jefferson did not violate the ordinance when she viewed the directions to the restaurant on her phone. The City Ordinance makes it unlawful to engage other application software while operating a motor vehicle. Clearly, Jefferson did not send a text message or make a call in this situation. She merely picked up her phone to see and read the directions. She did not start any application to view the directions, as they were already visible on her phone.

Officer Talbot will probably emphasize the policies behind the City Ordinance to prevent distractions while driving and encourage drivers to focus on the road. According to Officer Talbot, by picking up and reading the directions on her cell phone, Jefferson used one of the applications and risked the safety of civilians and drivers. However, Officer Talbot's position likely will be unsuccessful. Jefferson's conduct was tantamount to reading directions printed from MapQuest or written by hand. She did not manipulate any of the keys on her phone to view the directions. She merely picked up the phone and read the directions. Therefore, she did not violate the City Ordinance by viewing the directions on her phone.

Voicemail

A court will probably find that Jefferson did not violate the ordinance when she checked her voicemail message. The City Ordinance provides that, while operating a motor vehicle, a driver cannot use her cell phone to talk or listen to another person on the telephone. Here, while driving the car, Jefferson picked up her cell phone to check her voicemail. She hit the "call voicemail" option on her phone and heard the recorded voice. The message stated that Jefferson did not have any messages. She did not call, speak, or talk to another person on the phone. She simply heard a recorded electronic voice and, therefore, did not violate the ordinance.

Conversely, Officer Talbot will argue that the recorded voice constitutes another person under the rule and Jefferson unlawfully used her phone to check her messages. Jefferson, however, will successfully counter the officer's position. A recording is not a person, a live human being. Further, the rule likely seeks to prevent driving distractions that are inherent in engaging in a conversation with another person on the phone, such as a friend who can respond or prolong a conversation. Jefferson did not talk to another person on the phone. Moreover, her call was short, as she did not have any messages. Thus, she did not break the law by checking her voicemail messages.

Based on the foregoing, a court will likely find that Jefferson violated the City Ordinance for texting her friend but did not violate the ordinance for viewing the directions on her phone or calling to check her voicemail messages.

Follows with Officer Talbot's brief counter-argument to Jefferson's position. Then provides a rebuttal to Officer Talbot's argument.

Ends with summary conclusion.

ORIENTATION TO CRITICAL THINKING

EXERCISE 4

SAMPLE ANSWER

<u>Jordan did not violate the mall's policy</u>: Jordan will maintain that he did not violate the mall's anti-smoking policy. In particular, Jordan will emphasize that he was not using a real cigarette and that he was not emitting actual smoke from his device. Although the vapor may have contained a small quantity of nicotine, the vapor did not present any potential harmful effects to other patrons. He essentially released a water vapor into the air. Therefore, since he was using a mock electronic cigarette, Jordan did not violate the mall's anti-smoking policy.

Begins with a straightforward thesis sentence; identifies key factual support and the legal relevance (inference) for the fact.

Ends with a clear conclusion.

<u>Jordan did violate the mall's policy</u>: On the other hand, the mall owners and the security guard would maintain that Jordan violated the policy against smoking in the common area. The policy arguably exists to prevent patrons from experiencing the negative effects of second-hand smoke and to encourage a family-friendly atmo-sphere. Although Jordan was not inhaling from an actual cigarette, his conduct closely resembled that which the notice on the sign prohibited. He held a cigarette-looking device to his mouth, inhaled, and released a smoke-like vapor. Said vapor may have even contained some nicotine, and the vapor could have distributed allergens in the air. In addition, some parents may have found his conduct troublesome given the children playing in the area and their tendency to mimic adult behavior. Using the e-cigarette to smoke rather than a real cigarette is not completely harmless. Although there is no tobacco smoke involved, the device allows users to mimic the act of smoking. Thus, Jordan violated the mall's anti-smoking policy.

Begins with a straightforward thesis sentence; identifies key factual support and the legal relevance (inference) for the fact.

Elaborates on policy behind the rule and explains how Jordan's conduct might have violated the spirit of the rule.

Ends with a clear conclusion.

ORIENTATION TO CRITICAL THINKING

EXERCISE 6

SAMPLE ANSWER

Keith Washington violated the policy:

Begins with a straightforward thesis sentence and then sets out the policy.

Washington did violate the exact words of the policy. The policy states that no resident should contact another after he or she has been told to stop. Washington did contact another student after she asked not to be contacted— she told him not to call her because she had a boyfriend. Washington then contacted her again almost two years later. Despite the lapse of time between contacts, he still violated the policy. The policy does not mention any time restrictions, however, so Washington would have violated the policy even if the contact had been ten years apart. Washington therefore violated the policy and should be expelled from the residence halls.

Applies the policy to the present facts; mentions nuances of the policy that would result in its application as written.

The policy should be revised:

Begins with a straightforward thesis sentence; sets out the policy.

The policy should be revised because it is not serving its stated purpose and its strict enforcement here would lead to an injustice. The policy states that no resident should contact another after he or she has been told to stop; Washington did contact another student after she had asked not to be contacted. If the policy were applied as written, however, Washington would be expelled even though he has not placed anyone in fear. The council established this policy to prevent students from being placed in fear from unwanted contacts. Here, Washington's contact did not place the complainant in fear. The complainant was not in fear, nor was she ever unsafe. However, as you apply this policy, consider whether the policy is serving its stated purpose: Was the complainant unsafe or placed in fear? Should pretext charges be permitted? Should Washington's behavior be punished with expulsion from the residence halls?

Examines the broader effects of enforcing the policy as written.

ORIENTATION TO CRITICAL THINKING

EXERCISE 8

SAMPLE ANSWER

The parents will probably tell the children to wait and swim later. Although there is no clear family swimming rule that applies to the current weather conditions, the family's overall rule is to put safety first and swim only when there is no severe weather or risk of severe weather.

Leads with clear thesis sentence.

Although there is no clear overall rule, the rule is inferred from the family's past situations.

The parents' rule is that swimming is prohibited if there is any thunder or lighting. When it comes to other weather conditions, alone or in combination, the rules are less clear. Swimming is permitted in rain, so long as there are no other signs of inclement weather, such as thunder, dark clouds, or strong winds. Clouds alone do not seem to be a sufficient reason to forbid swimming, but the parents have not yet made a clear decision on clouds alone.

Analyzes specific facts and draws conclusions.

In addition, the parents have forbidden swimming where otherwise benign weather conditions have appeared in combination. When there was a strong wind and gray clouds, for example, the mother forbade swimming until later.

One overarching theme is that when the parents are in doubt, they ask the children to wait rather than risk swimming in potentially dangerous weather. In each decision, the parents have reiterated their policy on safety, placing safety above all.

Because there is no clear parental decision on swimming when the weather is cloudy, rainy, and slightly windy, the parents will probably ask the children to wait until the weather has passed before swimming. In addition, the parents are particularly concerned with thunder and lightning, and there had been thunder just hours before. Just as the mother asked the children to wait when a strong wind and gray clouds appeared in combination, today's combination of wind, rain, and clouds is sufficient reason to ask the children to wait.

Articulates clear inferences explaining how the facts support the overall rule/ conclusion.

Moreover, the parents have been clear that if the weather is potentially threatening, the family's policy is to wait until the weather has passed. If there is any doubt, there is to be no swimming. Therefore, the parents will likely follow this policy and ask the children to wait.

Ends with clear conclusion.

RULE-BASED REASONING FOR MASTERY

EXERCISE 10

SAMPLE ANSWER

The covenant probably is unreasonable in terms of geography. The covenant's geographical coverage area should be limited. A covenant not to compete is valid provided that the employer and the employee make certain binding promises in the agreement and that the covenant itself is reasonable in terms of time, geography, and scope of activity. With respect to geography, courts have found that non-compete clauses that cover areas where the employee did not actually work for the employer are overly broad and unenforceable. A covenant's terms are unreasonable if they are greater than what is required to protect the employer's goodwill or business interests or impose an undue hardship on the employee.*

Here, JPC proposes to prevent Brooks from working for any other publishing company, presumably in any location, for at least two years. For example, Brooks could be prohibited from working for a publishing company located in California or even Maine. Without any set geographical limitation, this restraint is overly broad and unenforceable. Assuming that Brooks will work mainly in Texas, Arkansas, Louisiana and New Mexico, a reasonable covenant would be limited to these states (and, more specifically, to cities within these states). Any broader scope would be more than necessary to protect JPC's legitimate business interests in the absence of any supporting evidence. To enforce this restrictive term, JPC would need to show how the company has business concerns in the affected areas outside of Brooks's covered territory.

Therefore, as proposed, the covenant's term regarding geography is unreasonable and should be limited to the specific areas in which Brooks actually will work.

> Leads with clear thesis sentence identifying the legal issue presented by the facts.

> Applies the rules to the client's facts.

> Articulates clear inference explaining how these facts support the conclusion.

> Lastly, links analysis back to the applicable rule and provides clear conclusion.

> Next, provides the relevant rules for the identified legal issue.

> Explains the general rule requiring the covenant's geographical coverage area to be reasonable. Then, explains how reasonableness is determined. Rule begins with the general terms and then provides specific guidelines.

> Presents affirmative arguments. Provides the relevant facts and explains how those particular facts support the conclusion that the geographical provision is overly broad and unreasonable.

> Explains how JPC can challenge Brooks's position.

---

* The legal aspects of this answer are based on several sources addressing geographical restrictions. *See generally* Tex. Bus. & Com. Code Ann. § 15.50 (West 2011); *Zep Mfg. Co. v. Harthcock*, 824 S.W.2d 654, 660–61 (Tex. App. 1992); *Rimkus Consulting Grp., Inc. v. Cammarata*, 255 F.R.D. 417, 435–37 (S.D. Tex. 2008).

RULE-BASED REASONING FOR MASTERY

EXERCISE 12 [*]

SAMPLE ANSWER

Begins with a clear conclusion with a brief summary of the reasoning.

Rick Harridan ("Harridan") probably has a claim against the Hills Hotel for the rat bite injury he received. Hotel employees knew of numerous rat incidents so the hotel should have taken steps to prevent further problems.

The governing rule requires hotels and other structures that house people to be "kept in good repair and condition." The rule does not, however, provide for strict liability. A property owner is not liable unless the owner "knew or had reason to know" that the dangerous condition was on the premises.

Provides the rule and quotes particularly critical language.

Uses specific facts from the fact pattern; places strongest facts in support of thesis first; links rule to fact with connections.

The Hills Hotel experienced several problems with rats before the Harridan biting incident, so the hotel probably should have known that it had a dangerous rat problem. As an initial matter, the hotel stands next to a rat-infested alley. The trash that attracted the rats to the alley did not come from the hotel, but the hotel was close to the alley. The alley rat problem was common knowledge among hotel personnel, so the hotel cannot reasonably state that it was unaware of the problem.

In addition, a hotel porter literally fell over a rat two weeks before the Harridan incident. The rat that the porter fell over was at the hotel's threshold. The fact that a rat was found in a relatively open and busy area should have signaled that further attention to the rat problem was required.

The incident with the hotel maid quitting because she found a rat under a bed should not be considered in determining the hotel's reaction, because it took place after the Harridan incident. This could not have put the hotel on notice for purposes of the Harridan incident, because it did not occur in time to do so.

The hotel could argue that it did not have reason to suspect a rat problem, because it put down rat poison two

---

[*] This problem is based loosely on the facts and law of *DeLuce v. Fort Wayne Hotel*, 311 F.2d 853 (6th Cir. 1962).

years ago, and the poison was all eaten. This suggests that the rats consumed the bait and died. A hotel's personnel may not want to put down additional bait for fear of creating a safety hazard to visiting children and pets. Knowing that the poison was gone, the hotel's conservative approach to poison was arguably the safer option under the circumstances.

> Provides the strongest counter-argument and makes the argument with specific facts.

This argument will likely fail, however, because the bait was laid so long ago and so many rat sightings have happened since that time. That fact that the rat bait was eaten cuts both ways—the rats could have eaten it and died, or the rats could have died and been replaced by other rats. In addition, the rats could have eaten the poison and simply been resistant to that particular poison. Regardless of which of these scenarios actually took place, the hotel was still on notice that it had a rat problem, because it put down poison. In addition, it appears to have known that the problem remained unsolved, due to all the rat sightings by hotel employees.

> Provides a full rebuttal of the argument rather than mere conclusory statements.

The hotel experienced numerous rat sightings and did not take action, and the only efforts to put down poison took place years ago. Therefore, Harridan probably does have a viable claim against the hotel.

> Provides clear conclusion.

RULE-BASED REASONING FOR MASTERY

EXERCISE 14

SAMPLE ANSWER

Provides a clear conclusion that references the reasoning to follow.

The Good Samaritan law does not appear to apply, because it applies only to care rendered "at the scene of an accident" or emergency care given to an accident victim. An illness—no matter how sudden—is not usually considered an accident.

The Indiana Good Samaritan law protects from liability people who render "emergency care," except in the case of gross negligence. The care must, however, take place at the scene of an accident or be rendered to the victim of an accident.

Sets out the rule language to be applied. Uses language such as "must" to emphasize aspects of the rule that will be significant in the analysis to follow.

Simmons suffered from an illness, specifically a heart attack, which is not generally considered an accident. An accident is most often understood to be a sudden occurrence more like a car crash or a fall. An illness, even if it has a sudden onset, is not generally referred to as an "accident." It may be called a "sudden illness" or other term that suggests a health problem. Furthermore, the statute goes on to refer to the person receiving aid as an "injured person," which, again, is not generally the term assigned to people suffering from health problems. The latter are most often referred to as "patients" or people with illnesses rather than "injured" people.

Uses specific facts to explain the issue's outcome.

Dr. Smith could argue that because the most severe part of the heart attack came on suddenly, that the condition had the characteristics of a sudden accident, rather than a protracted illness. Therefore, the Good Samaritan law arguably should apply. This argument will likely fail. Whether an illness develops slowly or quickly, it is not generally referred to as an "accident." The statute's plain language, including its use of terms such as "accident," "scene of an accident," and "injured person," indicates that the people intended to be protected are those who come upon an accident as normally understood. This might include a car accident or accidental fall, or the like.

The Indiana Good Samaritan law therefore will probably not protect Dr. Smith against any liability for her care of Simmons.

RULE-BASED REASONING FOR MASTERY

EXERCISE 16
SAMPLE ANSWER

A court will find that the agreement between Taylor Michel ("Michel") and Felipe Arribe ("Arribe"), the leasing agent, is invalid since it is not supported by sufficient consideration, only an illusory promise. A legally enforceable agreement or contract must have valid consideration—mutuality of obligation. Consideration is a bargained-for exchange of promises. A promise for a promise is sufficient consideration to support a contract but, if a promise is *illusory*, there is no valid consideration offered and, therefore, no enforceable contract between the parties. A promise is illusory if it fails to bind the promisor, such as when the promisor retains the option of discontinuing performance. An illusory promise is no promise at all. If there is no binding promise or obligation between the parties, there is no legally enforceable agreement or contract.*

There is no valid contract between Michel and Arribe. The key weakness in this case is that Arribe based his performance on his mood during the time that an office on the first floor becomes vacant. In particular, Arribe told Michel that he would give her "first dibs" on a vacant office space if he was "in an especially giving spirit" at that time. He essentially said, "If I am so inclined or so moved to do so." His promise is hollow or ineffective, as it fails to bind the promisor, here Arribe. Arribe has the option of refusing to give Michel the vacant office simply because he was not in a "giving spirit" that season. Further, Arribe based his purported promise on something that is completely within his control or discretion. He has no binding obligation to perform and may only do so if it pleases him.

Michel may try to argue that her gift of a free Valentine's basket serves as sufficient consideration to support the contract. However, there needs to be a promise in exchange for another promise. Since Arribe's promise gives him the choice of performance or nonperformance, it is illusory and ineffective even though Michel delivered the requested basket to him.

---

* For a summary of the rules related to illusory promises, see *Interchange Association v. Interchange, Inc.*, 557 P.2d 357 (Wash. Ct. App. 1976) and *Devine v. Notter*, 753 N.W.2d 557 (Wis. Ct. App. 2008).

Ends with
summary
conclusion.

Based on the foregoing, a court will likely find Arribe's promise is illusory and, therefore, does not provide sufficient consideration for the agreement between Arribe and Michel.

RULE-BASED REASONING FOR MASTERY

EXERCISE 18

SAMPLE ANSWER

An upfront conclusion previews the reasoning to follow.

Smith and Green probably do not have a claim of assault against Elliott. While the surrounding circumstances may have made Smith and Green nervous, Elliott's words and actions probably should not have put a reasonable person in an imminent apprehension of physical harm.

To establish a claim of assault, the plaintiff must show that the defendant's conduct gave her the reasonable belief that the defendant was presently able to inflict "serious bodily harm" upon her. The plaintiff need only have the reasonable belief that this is true—the actual ability is not required. Words can be the basis of an assault claim, but they must be combined with the circumstances and defendant's acts to create a reasonable belief of an imminent harm.

Explains the rule in easy-to-understand terms. Makes sure to include portions of the rule—such as that concerning words—as the basis of an assault claim—that are particularly relevant here.

Uses specific facts from the fact pattern and analyzes them in light of specific portions of the rule.

In the case at hand, Green and Smith evidently felt threatened by Elliott, as they both handed over their wallets to him. To be the basis of an assault claim, however, their feeling must not just be present, but be reasonably attributable to Elliott's words and actions. Smith's and Green's feelings probably were not reasonably attributable to Elliott's words and actions. When he first encountered Smith and Green, Elliott stepped out from behind a hedge. This might have surprised the two women, but it alone should not put one in fear of harm.

He then said the following: "You know what? I'm a thug. What do you think of that?" This statement refers to Elliott's own assessment of himself, but was not an overt threat toward Smith and Green. In addition, the rule states that if words are the basis of the claim, they must be combined with actions to create the belief that imminent harm is about to occur. Elliot's only action was to stand close to Smith and Green. This might have been awkward and made Smith and Green wonder what might happen next, but people commonly stand close to one another without a threat of harm.

In addition, Elliott was dressed in workout clothes and carried a gym back. This suggests that he was a fellow gym member who might have been trying to strike up a conversation.

The fact that Elliott could not have actually harmed the two women due to his back injury is not relevant to the analysis—no actual ability to harm is required, just the reasonable belief of imminent harm.

Green and Smith could argue that the circumstances surrounding their contact with Elliott lead to a reasonable apprehension of immediate harm, because the parking lot was dark, the hour was late, and they encountered Elliott in a remote part of a parking lot. This argument will likely fail, though, because Elliott's words and actions were insufficiently threatening. Green and Smith were nervous about their environment before they ever encountered Elliott, thereby showing that their fear is more attributable to the setting than to Elliott's actions.

Because Elliott did not behave in a manner that would put a reasonable individual in fear of an imminent harm, Smith and Green probably do not have an assault claim against Elliott.

Explains the most valid counter-argument and refutes it using specific facts and arguments.

Provides clear conclusion.

RULE-BASED REASONING FOR MASTERY

EXERCISE 20

SAMPLE ANSWER

Leads with clear thesis sentence identifying the legal issues presented by the facts.

Gina Rhoades's ("Rhoades") statements about Mike Weatherly ("Weatherly") were clearly and directly communicated to Pamela Chavis ("Chavis"). It is unclear, however, whether the custodian and Freda Higgins ("Higgins") both heard and understood Rhoades's comments. Slander law provides that an aggrieved party may bring a slander suit against a speaker for false and defamatory statements about him that are published or communicated to a third party without any legal excuse or permission to do so under the law. The speaker's statements must be about the aggrieved party. The speaker need not specifically name the aggrieved party if those who heard the statements know him, are acquainted with him, and understood that the defamatory publication referred to him. Further, the statement must be communicated to and heard by someone (other than the aggrieved party) who is capable of understanding, and did so understand, the comment's allegedly harmful meaning. Also, the speaker may be held responsible for remarks that she actually did not intend to make to other people where she created such an unreasonable risk that the comments would be overheard by others.*

Next, provides the relevant rules for the identified legal issue.

Explains the general rule for slander. Then, explains guidelines for determining whether statements have been communicated to a third party. Rule begins with the general terms and then provides specific guidelines.

Rhoades's statements were clearly heard and understood by Chavis. Chavis responded appropriately and even identified the subject of Rhoades's remarks as Weatherly by using his nickname "Big Mike." The custodian cleaning the restroom and Higgins, who was in the adjoining lounge area, also may have heard Rhoades's statements. However, it still needs to be determined whether the custodian and Higgins understood the meaning of her comments and knew they specifically referred to Weatherly.

Applies the rules to the client's facts.

Applies rules to Chavis's situation.

Presents affirmative arguments. Provides the relevant facts and explains how those particular facts support the conclusion that the comments were communicated to Chavis but may not have been fully communicated to the custodian and Higgins.

The custodian's and Higgins's situations require further analysis. Both situations require additional investigation.

Although the custodian may have heard Rhoades's conversation, she likely did not know that Rhoades was talking about Weatherly. The custodian does not work in

---

* For background on the slander element that requires communication to a third party, see generally *Thomas-Smith v. Mackin*, 238 S.W.3d 503, 507–08 (Tex. App. 2007), *Reeves v. Western Co. of North America*, 867 S.W.2d 385, 393–96 (Tex. App. 1993), and *R.T. Marshall v. Mahaffey*, 974 S.W.2d 942, 949–50 (Tex. App. 1998).

the Document Logistics Department or closely with any of the employees. In fact, many custodians are independent contractors and only deal with human resources personnel. Further, the custodian may have been too busy cleaning the stall to really focus on what Rhoades and Chavis were discussing.

With respect to Higgins, Rhoades potentially could be held responsible for any information that she overheard in the restroom. Even though Rhoades did not intend for Higgins to be privy to her bathroom conversation, Higgins easily could have heard Rhoades's statements since Rhoades spoke openly in a public restroom that is used by employees from all departments of the company. Plus, the door separating the lounge area from the rest of the restroom was ajar. There is no mention that Rhoades took any effort to keep her conversation a secret, such as by whispering or closing the door. Consequently, if Higgins heard the remarks and understood what Rhoades was implying about Weatherly then, under the law, Rhoades may have effectively communicated the statements to Higgins.

Based on the foregoing, Rhoades clearly communicated her statements about Weatherly to Chavis but may not have published them to the custodian or Higgins. Further investigation is required to determine whether the custodian and Higgins both heard and understood Rhoades's comments.

Identifies factual support and inferences for argument that the custodian likely did not hear and understand Rhoades's comments.

Identifies factual support and inferences for argument that Higgins may have heard and understood Rhoades's comments.

Lastly, links analysis back to the applicable rule and provides clear conclusion. Also identifies unresolved issues requiring further investigation.

RULE-BASED REASONING FOR MASTERY

EXERCISE 22

SAMPLE ANSWER

Begins with a forthright conclusion that references the reasoning behind the conclusion.

LeGrand and Townsend probably have a contract to convey the nail salon. Although LeGrand was in an emotional state, her words and actions were those of someone who wanted to sell her property.

With regard to contract formation, a person's behavior and intentions are judged by an objective standard. That is, the person's intentions are judged by a reasonable interpretation of what those words and actions would normally mean. A person's inner intentions are not relevant. Furthermore, intoxication does not invalidate a contract unless the intoxication is so great that the intoxicated person does not understand the effect of the document in question.

Sets out the applicable rule before turning to the facts at hand.

Begins the application section with a statement that summarizes the reasoning to follow.

Although LeGrand and Townsend formed their contract in a bar setting, LeGrand's words and actions indicated both that she wanted to sell the salon and that she understood she had done so. Initially, she stated explicitly that she wanted to sell the salon. Although LeGrand spoke in an emotionally-charged fashion, her message was clear that she wanted to sell the salon. She repeatedly stated she was finished with wanting to own a salon. The objective understanding of this statement would be that she intended to sell the salon, and this objective understanding supports the valid formation of a contract.

Furthermore, the two women executed a written contract regarding the sale. Although the writing was somewhat informal, in that it was written on a napkin, it still contained specific terms, a price, and a time frame for closing. It was signed by both parties to the contract. This writing is also a clear sign that LeGrand intended to sell the salon; she expressed in writing her intent to do so.

Uses explicit linking words to guide the reader from one argument to the next.

Uses very specific facts and reasoning to make the point.

After LeGrand executed the contract, she stated, "Done! I sold it, and I feel so good." This statement constitutes additional outward expression supporting an objective belief on the listener's part that LeGrand intended to sell and did sell her salon. This statement also shows that LeGrand herself understood she had sold her salon.

Townsend's reactions confirm that LeGrand's actions and words were reasonably understood as reflecting her intention to sell her salon. Townsend understood throughout the interactions that LeGrand intended to sell the salon, and that she had done so by specifying the contractual terms on the napkin. In addition, Townsend transferred money and arranged for an inspection of the property, further showing Townsend's understanding that LeGrand had sold the salon to her.

The reaction of Mary Granger, another member of the group of friends out that evening, showed she also understood that a sale had taken place. She remarked to LeGrand that she would feel happier without the salon, thereby indicating Granger understood that LeGrand would not have the salon from then on.

LeGrand could argue she was somewhat intoxicated, and also that the entire setting of the purported business deal suggested she was simply venting her frustrations rather than actually trying to sell her salon. This argument will likely fail, however, because LeGrand drank only one martini, which she ordered two hours before the two women discussed the salon sale. LeGrand likely further reduced any effects of that drink by dancing for a while before returning from the dance floor with all the terms and her signature on the napkin, which she then offered to Townsend. Intoxication does not invalidate a contract unless the person is so intoxicated she cannot understand the effect of the documents she signed. In LeGrand's case, she consumed only one martini two hours before signing the contract, and her statements directly following the contract signing indicate she did understand the import of the document she had signed, and she was happy to have signed it. Only the following day did she start to have reservations about the sale. Nor should LeGrand's asthma invalidate the contract—by the time she felt ill from her asthma, she had already signed the contract and indicated she fully understood its effect.

> Brings up a valid counterargument and rebuts it using specific facts.

LeGrand may not have intended to sell the salon, but her objectively-understood words and actions suggested otherwise. If she had had any intent just to joke around with Townsend about selling the salon, the joke was not revealed to Townsend, and LeGrand's unexpressed intentions are immaterial. Because a person's actions are understood by their objective meaning rather than any inner, hidden intent, Townsend could rely on LeGrand's words and actions to form a valid contract to sell her salon to Townsend.

> Ends with a brief summary in support of the conclusion.

RULE-BASED REASONING FOR MASTERY

EXERCISE 24

SAMPLE ANSWER

The Gomezes probably do have a claim against the manager (and through his employment, against the bar). Although the manager was under no duty to help Remy, once he did so, he should have taken care not to cause harm. He did cause harm by permitting a visibly drunk person to drive a car that otherwise was undrivable.

Generally, a person has no duty to help a stranger. If, however, a person voluntarily undertakes to assist another and the other relies upon the assistance, the person must use reasonable care in helping the stranger.* Furthermore, a person who takes affirmative steps, even those that were not required or repaid, must use reasonable care not to cause harm arising out of the act.**

In Remy's case, the manager could have left Remy alone and suffered no liability. However, he chose to intervene and take the affirmative act of helping Remy start his car. The manager did perform the act without negligence in one sense, which is that he started the car without hurting the car.

However, a reasonable person would have seen that Remy was visibly intoxicated and that he could well cause harm by driving the car, as he in fact did. In taking the affirmative step of starting the car despite this knowledge, the manager failed to exercise reasonable care and was negligent. The manager could have left Remy better off if he had simply left him alone or even called him a taxi. Instead, however, the manager took the affirmative step of starting the car, which directly caused Remy to be able to drive his car and hit the Gomez family's car.

While the manager in a sense did no more than to place the car in the same drivable position that it had been before its battery ran out, the manager did take affirmative steps to make the car drivable. In addition, he

---

* *Stelts v. Epperson*, 411 S.E.2d 281, 282 (Ga. Ct. App. 1991).

** Restatement (Second) of Torts § 320 cmt. a (1965).

took those steps in the full knowledge of the number of drinks Remy had consumed and the intoxicated state that he was in.

The manager could argue that his actions alone did not cause the accident, but instead that Remy was the intoxicated person who directly caused the harm. While this is true to the extent that Remy's intoxicated driving most directly caused the harm, Remy would not have been able to drive at all if the manager had not jump-started his car.

Provides a counter-argument based on problem facts.

Moves to a clear conclusion.

The Gomezes probably do have a viable negligence claim against the manager for starting Remy's car when he was clearly intoxicated.

RULE-BASED REASONING FOR MASTERY

EXERCISE 26[*]

SAMPLE ANSWER

An upfront conclusion previews the reasoning to follow.

The Sweeneys probably will be held strictly liable for the injuries cause by Duke's rushing at Hilda Storey ("Hilda"). The Sweeneys knew of previous incidents involving Duke's aggressive behavior, so they probably will be strictly liable for Duke's rushing incident that injured Hilda.

A dog's owner can be held strictly liable for injuries caused by his dog if the owner is on notice of the dog's tendencies to cause the same sort of harm that the plaintiff claims. The owner must have actually known, or have information such that the owner should have known, of the dog's tendencies. The information need not be from the owner's direct observation—knowledge from other people is also considered. The information must pertain to the particular dog at hand; information pertaining to a dog's breed alone is not considered.

Sets out the rule, focusing on the portions that are particularly relevant to the facts at hand.

Begins the application section with a topic sentence that explains the argument to follow.

The Sweeneys had sufficient knowledge that they should have known that Duke had the tendency to break open the gate and rush passersby. As an initial matter, the Sweeneys had direct knowledge of Duke's behavior toward the new mailman last year. In that incident, Duke escaped through the gate and rushed the mailman, barking all the while. This is very similar to the type of behavior that he exhibited toward Hilda.

Uses specific details from the fact pattern to build the argument.

In addition, the Sweeneys had direct knowledge of the Fedex company's refusal to deliver packages to their house because of Duke's behavior. The neighbor testified that Mary Sweeney ("Mary") had to pick packages up at the main distribution center because of Duke's rushing a Fedex delivery person. The Sweeneys can hardly state that they did not know of the incident, because it resulted in their having to pick up packages instead of having them delivered. Indeed, Mary hinted at knowledge of Duke's aggressive tendencies when she said that Duke was a gentle dog with family but "so tough with outsiders."

---

[*] This problem is based on the court's opinion in *Slack v. Villari*, 476 A.2d 227 (Md. Ct. Spec. App. 1984).

Neighbor Jack Swan's testimony that Duke "look[ed]" vicious to him, based on Duke's appearance and breed, will not be considered. Mere conclusory statements by a neighbor based on a dog's appearance do not indicate any greater or lesser knowledge on the Sweeneys' part. In addition, the mere fact that a dog belongs to a certain breed is not considered—the information must pertain to the particular dog in question.

> Explains why some of the facts do not show knowledge on the defendants' part.

Nor do Duke's actions toward rats—aggressively shredding them—add to the case for strict liability. Knowledge of the animal's aggressive tendencies must be knowledge of the same type of harm that the dog caused in the case at hand. Here, Duke rushed and barked at Hilda, actions that are quite different from attacking rats. This knowledge therefore does not advance the Sweeneys' knowledge of the type of harm caused to Hilda.

Based, however, on the Sweeneys' direct knowledge of Duke's actions toward a mailman and a Fedex delivery person, they knew of Duke's tendency to rush and bark at strangers, as well as his ability to leave through the gate. The Sweeneys will therefore likely be held strictly liable for Duke's injuries to Hilda.

> Ends with clear conclusion.

RULE-BASED REASONING FOR MASTERY

EXERCISE 28

SAMPLE ANSWER

A clear conclusion that gives a brief preview of the reasoning to come; conclusion is not too categorical.

Campbell's silence following Lory's statement regarding the auto theft will probably be considered an adoptive admission and therefore admissible as an exception to the hearsay rule.

Sets out rule in clear and complete terms; makes clear shift to application.

Generally, statements made out of court are inadmissible at trial as hearsay, if the statement is offered to establish the truth of the matter. There are exceptions to the hearsay rule, however, where the statement has some other indications of reliability. Where such a statement is offered against a party, it is not hearsay if the party adopts the statement. A party adopts a statement if (1) the statement is made in the party's presence, (2) the party understands the statement, and (3) the party does not deny the statement, even though the party could have done so.*

Provides the exact statement for full reader understanding.

When Lory and Campbell were awaiting booking, Lory made the following statement to Campbell: "Well, I guess that's our first car theft. We did it, didn't we?" At that, Campbell looked away and brushed away a tear but said nothing except, "I wish those college students would be quiet." Because Campbell did not deny Lory's statement about the theft, the statement probably meets the requirements to be admissible under the adopted admission exception to the hearsay rule.

Analyzes the requirements in turn, in the same order they are set out in the initial rule statement.

As an initial matter, the statement was made in Campbell's presence, so the first requirement is satisfied. As to the next requirement—whether Campbell understood the statement—the result is less clear but is probably in favor of admissibility. Campbell and Lory were surrounded by noisy college students at the time Lory made the statement about the car theft, so Campbell might have had problems hearing Lory. When Lory made the statement, however, Campbell was sitting right next to her. Even in a noisy room, a person can usually hear and understand another person who is sitting close by.

---

* *See* Fed. R. Evid. 801(d)(2)(B).

In addition, Campbell seemed to acknowledge the statement by turning away and crying a little, thereby showing that she understood the statement. Given this physical reaction and Campbell's proximity to Lory, a court would probably find that Campbell heard and understood the statement.

Uses specific facts from fact pattern to make the argument; points out weaknesses in the argument and explains which argument will likely prevail.

The final requirement—that Campbell did not deny the statement although she could have done so—is probably satisfied as well. When Lory said that the two had just completed their "first car theft" and that "we did it," Campbell did not deny the statements. She appears to have had the opportunity to do so, in that she and Lory were sitting together and Campbell was not prevented from speaking in any way. Campbell did, however, appear to be overwhelmed with emotion, and she noted the presence of the noisy college students. Campbell could argue that she was too emotional to respond or that she did not want to do so in the presence of the college students.

Provides rebuttal to counter-argument.

This argument will likely fail, however, because a person who is confronted with the statement that she committed a car theft would reasonably deny it rather than simply leave the statement unchallenged. In addition, Campbell was not too emotional to comment on the noisy college students, and she gave an audible sigh upon hearing the statement. She was engaged with Lory's statements, and she did not take the opportunity to disagree with them.

Ends with clear conclusion.

Because Lory's statements and Campbell's lack of a response likely meet the standard for adoptive admissions, they will probably be admitted under an exception to the hearsay rule.

RULE-BASED REASONING FOR MASTERY

EXERCISE 30

SAMPLE ANSWER

The agreement between Flores and Walker to share their winnings is probably supported by consideration and is probably not subject to the statute of frauds.

(1) Consideration

Flores's agreement to share her winnings is supported by consideration, because the two friends exchanged promises with each other. An agreement is not an enforceable contract unless it is supported by consideration. Mutual obligations can, however, serve as consideration.

Walker is suing on Flores's agreement to share her winnings with Walker, and there is no separate consideration for that promise. One promise, however, can be supported by the return promise as consideration. That is, the two women made the same agreement to each other regarding their winnings. When they arrived in Las Vegas, Walker said to Flores, "Anything we win, we split, right?" In response, Flores laughed and said, "Whatever you say; sounds good to me." In addition, when Walker said that the two would share their winnings, Flores also stated, "OK, we'll do this together. One for all and all for one, I'm there for you. If I win, we win. If you win, we win." Thus, the two women made the same promise to each other regarding their winnings, and those mutual promises can serve as consideration for one another.

Flores's promise is therefore supported by consideration.

(2) Statute of Frauds

The agreement between Flores and Walker is probably not subject to the statute of frauds because the agreement could conceivably have been performed within one year.

The statute of frauds makes certain promises or agreements unenforceable unless (1) reduced to writing; and (2) signed by the person to be charged with the promise or agreement. One of the agreements governed by the statute of frauds is one that is not to be performed within one year from the date of its making.

When no time for performance is given, a reasonable time for performance can be read into the contract. If the implied time is less than one year, then the contract does not fall within the statute of frauds, and it does not have to be in writing or signed by the parties to be enforceable. The length of time to be implied is judged according to the circumstances existing at the time of contracting, specifically, "a reasonable time as viewed by the parties at the time the agreement was made, rather than any circumstances or facts that might have arisen afterwards."

Also, if no time for performance is given and a particular act is to be performed under the contract, the contract does not fall within the statute of frauds so long as the act *could* be performed within a year. The contract need not be one that is always or obviously performed within a year in order to fall outside the statute of frauds.

Makes a clear shift from rule explanation to application.

Flores and Walker mutually agreed to share their winnings from the Las Vegas gambling trip. At the time, they did not specify a time for performance of this agreement. Nothing indicates the payout had to be on a twenty-year schedule—on the contrary, Flores stated that after the win, the casino personnel specifically asked her whether she preferred a one-time payout or a longer payout. After considering the options, she selected a twenty-year payout.

Takes a position without being too categorical—understands that a court could decide differently.

The court will likely view the contract as one that calls for the completion of a specific, definable act, namely the splitting of the winnings. The court would imply a reasonable term for completion, and could read in a reasonable time that is less than one year. The casino's payout options make feasible a split of winnings almost immediately after the win. Flores's choice of a twenty-year payout does not preempt or control the court's assessment of the circumstances existing at the time of contracting and determination of the possible completion time on the contract. If the court determines that the act of splitting the winnings *could* have been completed in under a year, then the contract would not be subject to the statute of frauds.

However, the court also could imply a reasonable term of more than a year, taking into account the circumstances existing at the time the contract was formed. At that time, the two women had debated whether they would opt for an immediate payout—Walker's suggestion—or a long-term payout, which was Flores's. Inasmuch as Flores's agreement to share her winnings is the one that become applicable because Flores won the money, the court could imply a term of twenty years, based on the circumstances existing at the time. If the court takes this approach, the contract would be subject to the statute of frauds, and would not be enforceable because it is not in writing. This approach is less likely to be the court's choice, however, because the contract calls for the gambling winnings to be split, which is one specific, definable act rather than an ongoing relationship or process. The women's agreement to share the winnings, therefore, will likely be considered to have a term of less than one year and to not be governed by the statute of frauds.

Thus, the agreement between Flores and Walker to share their winnings is probably supported by consideration and is probably not subject to the statute of frauds.

Entertains another possible outcome and explains why this outcome is less likely.

Concludes with a clear thesis that addresses both points in the problem.

RULE-BASED REASONING FOR MASTERY

EXERCISE 32

SAMPLE ANSWER

Provides a brief conclusion, followed by the overall rule.

The scent-lineup evidence against Fournace probably should not be admitted, because the lineup was not conducted in a scientifically reliable manner.*

To be admitted at trial, scientific evidence must be reliable. When, as here, science is based on training rather than the scientific method, three questions determine whether the field produces reliable scientific evidence: (1) whether the particular area of expertise is a legitimate one, (2) whether the expert will testify on matters within that field of expertise, and (3) whether the expert correctly uses the principles involved in the field. It is undisputed that Downs's proposed testimony would be within this field of expertise, so this analysis focuses on the first and third elements.

Sets out the overall rule in the same order that it is discussed below; divides up the elements with headings.

(1) Whether the area of expertise is a legitimate one

The field of identifying suspects through scent lineup is probably a legitimate area of expertise, although it is not as accepted by courts as the field of dog-tracking evidence. Scent-lineup evidence has never been addressed or admitted in courts in this state. Dog-tracking evidence, in contrast, has been admitted to establish probable cause to search a building, and evidence of a dog's reaction to drugs has been admitted to establish probable cause to detain a suspect.

Because much of the rule and the facts focus on dog tracking evidence, the analysis makes a distinction between tracking and scent lineups.

The FBI has used scent-lineup evidence to rule out suspects in significant national security cases, suggesting that evidence from a scent lineup carries weight with law enforcement and the procedure is a legitimate field of expertise. In addition, courts in thirty-seven states have admitted scent-lineup evidence, and courts in four states have prohibited it.

Significantly, the prosecution's own expert recognized the limitations of scent-lineup evidence—she suggested

---

* This problem and its answer are based on the facts and opinion in the following case: *Winston v. State*, 78 S.W.3d 522 (Tex. App. 2002).

that such evidence be used only in conjunction with other evidence. In addition, she testified that scent-lineup evidence should be used to exclude suspects rather than positively identify suspects.

On balance, scent lineup evidence probably has sufficient respect and weight that it is a legitimate field of expertise, but expert testimony indicates it should be used with caution.

(2) Whether the witness will testify within his area of expertise. This element is undisputed and is therefore established.

(3) Whether the expert correctly uses the principles involved in the field

Downs probably did not use the principles of this field correctly, because he used leashed dogs; selected, stored and transported his samples incorrectly; and used dogs with experience in tracking but not in scent lineups.

Courts in other jurisdictions admit scent-lineup evidence when a showing is made that both owner and dog are trained properly and respected inside and outside the courtroom. In addition, the particular tracking or lineup must be objective.

(a) Qualifications and training of the dog

Based on the requirements for dog qualification, Downs's dogs are qualified to identify human scents.

A dog is said to be qualified if (1) it is a member of a breed of dog known for its acute sense of smell, (2) the dog has been trained in discerning one human scent from another, (3) the dog has a history of being reliable in identifying and discerning scents, (4) the dog was given the suspect's scent, and (5) the scent was given to the dog while the scent was still effective.

Downs's dogs are bloodhounds, which are known for their strong sense of smell and ability to differentiate one human scent from another. Downs's dogs received two years of training with the FBI, and the two dogs have worked full time with Downs for the police department for at least eight years. They therefore have the requisite training for an admissible scent lineup. Downs's dogs have a successful history in tracking, although they lack experience in successful scent lineups. They do, however, have experience discerning scents and differentiating one scent

[margin annotation: Sets out the conclusion with some details as to the reasons supporting the conclusion.]

[margin annotation: States the specific details that support the conclusion and also gives the reason the fact matters to the rule.]

from another. It is undisputed that the dogs were given the suspect's scent. As a consideration apart from the actual procedure used in this lineup, Downs's dogs are qualified to identify and differentiate one human scent from another.

(b)   Qualifications and training of the trainer

Downs has fairly weak qualifications in the field of dog training and scent lineups. He is self-taught and does not have formal training in scent lineups. Downs has a bachelor's degree in marketing, which is not relevant to the fields of scent lineups or dog handling. He has, however, worked with the K-9 unit in the police department for over twenty-five years. His publications are all concerned with police dog work, although they are for a police union health magazine called "Police Today," which is a wellness publication rather than a scientific or other peer-reviewed journal.

> Points out the strengths and weaknesses in Downs's qualifications.

With regard to the special field of scent lineups, Downs does not have specific training or experience. He is, however, well known in the local area for his tracking work with his dogs—the dogs have tracked down escaped convicts, even tracking one with a trail that was a week old. As to scent lineups, though, Downs's experience and training are not extensive.

(c)   Particular application of the scent evidence must be fair and objective.

Downs's application of the scent lineup evidence in this case was flawed and not objective—Downs did not attempt either to maximize reliability or to minimize the risks of trainer influence and sample contamination—so the evidence should not be admitted.

To be fair and objective, a scent lineup must be conducted according to guidelines particular to that field and should minimize the risks of trainer influence, sample contamination, and unreliability.

Downs's lineup lacks several important indicia of accuracy. The lineup did follow some guidelines, in that Downs used multiple samples placed more than six feet apart. The alerts, however, were apparent to no one but Downs, and he testified that because the dogs provided no observable physical reaction in the alerts, he could not record them.

> Uses specific facts from the fact pattern to show why the necessary reliability is lacking.

The lineup suffers from some additional indications that it lacks reliability. First, Downs kept the dogs on leashes during the test, and a leash increases the risk of trainer influence in that the dogs could have felt a suggestion through the leashes of when to alert, particularly because Downs knew which sample was Fournace's. The leashes were objectionable to Fournace's expert because of a possibility of unobservable and even unintended communication between trainer and animal.

Second, the containers Downs used could have increased the risks of contamination of the samples. Downs kept the samples in plastic baggies rather than the recommended glass containers, suggesting that the samples could have been contaminated. Even worse, Downs kept all his samples in his workout bag, which is a location generally characterized by strong human smells. The gym bag raises the risk of contamination considerably.

Third, the age disparity in the samples presented to the dogs could have affected the reliability of the identification. Fournace's sample was ten days old, while the foil samples were four weeks old. Scent fades over time, suggesting that a dog would be more attracted to stronger, fresher scent.

Additional possibilities affecting reliability exist in Downs's use of multiple dogs and his failure to use a "negative lineup." The procedure of multiple dogs identifying samples in a single lineup is not used in this country; however, the prosecution's expert testified that experts in other countries do use multiple dogs in lineups. This alone, then, may not be a definitive indication of unreliability; however Fournace's expert testified the use of multiple dogs increases the chances of one dog copying another and reinforcing a mistake.

Absence of a "negative lineup" would not make the lineup here unreliable, but using a negative lineup could have increased the reliability of the lineup conducted. According to Fournace's expert, a negative lineup is one in which the defendant's scent would have been excluded altogether. Negative lineups test the accuracy of the initial lineup, so that the handler can see whether the dog is simply alerting out of habit or guesswork.

The final concern affecting the scent lineup's reliability is testimony from the prosecution's expert that scent-lineup evidence has limitations and that it should be used to exclude suspects rather than to positively identify them. Given this concern and the weaknesses in the process as described above, the scent-lineup evidence should not be admitted in this case.

RULE-BASED REASONING FOR MASTERY

EXERCISE 34 *

SAMPLE ANSWER

Provides a brief conclusion, followed by the overall rule.

The court's certification of a class for purposes of the class action lawsuit was very likely correct with regard to the requirements of numerosity, commonality, typicality, and adequacy of the lead plaintiffs to represent the class. As to the adequacy of class representation, however, the Montgomery Firm's lack of class action experience indicates that certification of the class with the Montgomery Firm as class counsel may well have been an abuse of discretion.

To be certified properly as a class, the class must meet the requiments of numerosity, commonality, typicality, and adequacy of representation.

(1) Numerosity

The numerosity requirement is satisfied here, because thousands and thousands of people purchased the Hot Mamba lipstick; their joinder would be impracticable.

To be certified, a class must be so numerous that "joinder of all members is impracticable." Joinder need not be impossible, but must be difficult and inconvenient so that joining all members would not be practical. The rule is not driven by any particular number—the number differs according to each case and circumstance. Generally, the court will need to approximate the number of class members and make common sense assumptions.

Details the reasons why the numerosity requirement is established here.

Here, the class meets the numerosity requirement, because the class consists of thousands of women who purchased the Hot Mamba lipstick. Joinder of all the class members would be impracticable, because the women live all over the country, and most of them are not yet aware of any legal action against Reptile Cosmetics. A class action would be the most efficient way to bring forth each person's claims without joining each and every one separately.

---

* The question and its answer are based on the court's opinion in *Cheminova America Corp. v. Corker*, 779 So. 2d 1175 (Ala. 2000).

(2) Commonality

The commonality requirement is met, because common issues of law and fact predominate—each woman bought the Hot Mamba lipstick and claims to be equally deceived regarding the safety of the Mamba venom.

The commonality requirement calls for a "common nucleus of operative facts" such that there are common issues of law or fact. Some factual variation among class members does not defeat certification—it is sufficient that the common issues predominate over individual issues that the plaintiffs may have. Also, certification is not defeated simply because the facts fluctuate throughtout the class period.

Here, there are multiple common issues of law and fact. With regard to common facts, each purchaser of the Hot Mamba lipstick bought a product with the following notice on the box: "Contains Safe Mamba Extract for Extra Shimmer and Shine." Each lipstick did not contain safe Mamba extract but instead contained significant amounts of Mamba venom. Upon applying the lipstick, each woman felt a stinging sensation that was not harmful. Upon feeling that stinging, the known plaintiffs threw away or returned the lipstick—there are no recorded instances of women ingesting the venom or falling ill. These issues were common to all of the women who purchased the lipstick: the alleged deception regarding the safety of Mamba "extract," the loss of the lipstick's value, because it could not be used, and the brief stinging pain suffered upon applying the lipstick.

With regard to legal issues, Uniform Commercial Code ("UCC") principles can be applied class wide to a dangerous product. The statement regarding saftey is alleged to be affixed to all Hot Mamba lipsticks. Plaintiffs allege that this statement created an express warranty under the UCC. In addition, plaintiffs allege that the product was not fit for use, so that its sale would violate the implied warranty of merchantability that the product is fit for its intended use; this warranty applies to any sale of a product under the UCC.

Reptile Cosmetics could argue that common issues of law or fact do not predominate, because each claim involves a variety of damages, thereby defeating commonality. In addition, a few women were given the lipstick as a gift, indicating varying levels of privity between Reptile Cosmetics and the plaintiffs. This argument will likely

Quotes exact rule language sparingly, and only where a paraphrase would be less effective.

Sets out all the specific reasons why the case contains common issues of law and fact.

Includes a viable counter-argument where one can be made.

fail, however, because there are so many common issues in the case. The lipsticks were all packaged in the same box with the same statement regarding safety, the women identified to date all suffered the same harm, and the loss of the lipstick's value was approximately the same. While the issue of privity may vary among plaintiffs, common issues predominate in that the factual issues are similar and most of the legal issues are the same. The commonality requirement is therefore satisfied.

(3) Typicality

The typicality requirement is satisfied, because the named plaintiffs' claims are for the most part similar to those of the remaining women who purchased the lipstick.

The typicality requirement means that the named plaintiffs' claims should have essentially the same features as the claims of the rest of the class. To be typical, the named plaintiffs' claims should arise out of the same conduct or events as the other class members' claims.

Here, the named plaintiffs each bought a Hot Mamba lipstick in a department store. Each one took the lipstick home and wore it at some later time—one applied the lipstick in the car on her way home. Each one suffered the same tingling, stinging sensation that the other women felt. Although Smith threw the lipstick away while some of the other proposed class members returned theirs for a refund, this is a minor issue that does not predominate. The issues that predominate will be the consumer decepetive trade practices act claims, the issue of the statement regarding safety of the Mamba "extract." The commonality requirement is therefore likely satisfied.

(4) Adequacy of representation

The lead plaintiffs are likely adequate, because they have no apparent interests antagonistic to the other class members; the class counsel are less likely adequate, because they lack class action experience.

The last requirement—adequacy of representation—requires that the named plaintiffs properly represent the class numbers. This requirement has two parts: (1) whether the named plaintiffs' interests are antagonistic to the those of the rest of the class and (2) whether plaintiffs' counsel will adequately represent the class.

> Uses transition words to move from one topic to another, so the reader can understand the shifts from one section to the next.

As to the first consideration, the named plaintiffs do not have any interests antagonistic to the other potential class members. The named plaintiffs are therefore proper class representatives.

As to the second consideration, the ability of class counsel to represent the class adequately, the issue is less clear. The Alabama Rules of Civil Procedure require a plaintiff to show that class counsel has sufficient qualifications, experience, and ability to represent the plaintiff class in the litigation. In making this determination, the court can look to the firm's reputation, experience, and conduct in litigation.

The Montgomery Firm's lawyers seem to be beloved by their clients, and they have worked on the Hot Mamba litigation for over a year without any compensation to date. The Montgomery Firm's lawyers have conducted themselves well, and their court filings have been exemplary. On the other hand, the firm has been disciplined by the state bar, and they have no experience in class action litigation.

Once those considerations are taken into account, the Montgomery Firm may not be the best choice to represent a nationwide class. However, the class certification is reviewed for abuse of discretion. In order for the decision to amount to an abuse of discretion, it must be unreasonable. The decision has some reason behind it because the firm has conducted itself correctly to date in the litigation. It could be argued, however, that the litigation is at an early stage, and the court could thus conclude that the firm's inexperience has yet to show.

The certification of a class represented by very inexperienced counsel could, therefore, be viewed as an abuse of discretion.

ANALOGICAL REASONING WITH DEPTH

EXERCISE 36

SAMPLE ANSWER

Begins with a clear thesis statement that serves as the conclusion.

The prosecution likely will be unable to show that Antonio Garza ("Garza") possessed the authority to consent to the officer's search of Sylvia Trenton's ("Trenton") business premises. The Fourth Amendment provides that "[t]he right of the people to be secure in their persons, houses, and effects, against unreasonable search and seizures, shall not be violated." This Fourth Amendment protection extends to private businesses. *United States v. Sandoval-Vasquez*, 435 F.3d 739, 742 (7th Cir. 2006). "'A warrantless search does not violate the Fourth Amendment if a person . . . *reasonably believed* to possess . . . authority over the premises voluntarily consents to the search.'" *United States v. King*, 627 F.3d 641, 647–48 (7th Cir. 2010) (quoting *United States v. Groves*, 530 F.3d 506, 509 (7th Cir. 2008) (emphasis added)). Such reasonable belief or "[a]pparent authority turns on whether the facts available to the officer at the time would allow a person of reasonable caution to believe that the consenting party had authority over the premises." *Id.* at 648.

Provides the starting point for analysis of an officer's search—the Fourth Amendment.

Sets out the test or legal standard for determining whether there was authority to consent to search of business premises.

Notwithstanding the foregoing, an officer's entry into an open business does not violate the Fourth Amendment. *Sandoval-Vasquez*, 435 F.3d at 743 (upholding officers' search when they entered business where the garage and customer doors were open, persons had just entered and left the premises, and the establishment was still open for business). As the Seventh Circuit has stated, "[a]n open gate invites entry." *Id.* (quoting *United States v. Tolar*, 268 F.3d 530, 532 (7th Cir. 2005)). "'What a person knowingly exposes to the public, even in his . . . office, is not a subject of Fourth Amendment protection.'" *Id.* (quoting *Katz v. United States*, 389 U.S. 347, 351 (1967)).

Derives a specific rule about "open" business premises.

In *King*, the police arranged a sham drug purchase at the defendant's small taco restaurant using a secret government informant. 627 F.2d at 644. After the defendant received the drugs he purchased, he hid them in piping above the refrigerator in the back of his restaurant. *Id.* at 645. The next day, the police arrested the defendant and searched his home. *Id.* at 646. Later that same day, at about 9:00 a.m., an ATF agent and two police officers, wearing plainclothes, bulletproof vests, and badges, arrived at the defendant's restaurant to search the premises. *Id.* The restaurant was not scheduled to open for business until 11:00 a.m. *Id.* After about 45 minutes, a cook arrived and opened the door. *Id.* The officers followed the cook inside the building. *Id.* An alarm was activated, and the cook used a code to disable it. *Id.* Since the cook could not speak English very well, the ATF agent waited for a Spanish-speaking agent to arrive. *Id.* The second agent learned that the cook was not the restaurant owner. *Id.* The cook, however, orally consented to the search of the premises but did not sign a consent form since it was written in English. *Id.* The officers found the drugs in the piping above the refrigerator. *Id.*

The defendant filed a motion to suppress the seized drugs and maintained that the cook did not have the authority to consent to a search of the restaurant. *Id.* The Seventh Circuit disagreed, holding that the cook had sufficient apparent authority to consent to the search. *Id.* at 648. The officers entered the restaurant with the cook only after the cook first unlocked the door and disabled the alarm. *Id.* at 647–48. The cook had not only keys to the restaurant but also the code to deactivate the alarm. *Id.* at 648. He also opened the restaurant alone, and it was a small establishment. *Id.* Furthermore, the cook never objected to the officers' entry. *Id.* Thus, the court concluded, the cook's "actions clearly justified the officers' belief that he had full control over the premises, including the authority to grant access to others." *Id.* As the district court had determined, "because [the defendant] gave [the cook] the keys to the restaurant and full control over the premises (including the code to deactivate the alarm), [the defendant] assumed the risk that [the cook] might permit others to enter while [the defendant] was absent." *Id.* at 646. Notably, the Seventh Circuit also disagreed with the defendant's contention "that simply because the restaurant was not 'open for business,' any entry was automatically illegal[.]" *Id.* The court found no merit in this argument since a regular customer conceivably could have entered the business in the same manner (as done by the officers) to place a special order. *Id.* at 648.

Trenton will maintain that the officer's search of her paint business was unreasonable under the Fourth Amendment given that Garza lacked apparent authority to grant access. Unlike the ATF agent and police officers

Provides a clear explanation of the legal standard from precedent. Includes the key facts, holding and reasoning from this case so that the reader can clearly understand how the court applies the test in a real-world scenario.

Provides the court's reasoning for its decision.

in *King*, Officer Ada Lee ("Officer Lee") did not reasonably believe that Garza possessed the authority to consent to entry and search. In *King*, the cook showed up to a closed business and opened the door using a key that he had in his possession. In addition, the cook knew the owner's private code to disable the security alarm. There is no similar evidence in this case to suggest the appearance of authority to consent. Officer Lee did not see Garza with a key to Trenton's business, which reasonably indicated his lack of authority to control the premises. Furthermore, Garza, who admitted to Officer Lee that he heard her knock at the front door, did not open the front door for her. Garza's admission that he heard a knock should have prompted Officer Lee that Garza may not have possessed (or had access to) a key to unlock the front door of the business. In turn, the officer should have realized that Garza did not have control over the premises or owner-ship of the business or, at least, that his authority was questionable. Additionally, the lack of any definitive evidence that Garza was an employee of the store, that he made extensive use of the premises, or that he stayed there for an extended period of time all prove that the prosecution cannot show that Garza had apparent authority to consent to Officer Lee's request to enter the store. The circumstances faced by Officer Lee lacked credible indicia of Garza's apparent authority.

Moreover, when Officer Lee approached the building, Garza stood outside the business with the door propped open, not inside with the door locked. Anyone can stand outside a business loitering and this possibility should have caused Officer Lee to inquire further about Garza's authority. Further, a propped door suggests that Garza did not have independent access to the store. He had to make sure the door would not close and prevent his entry. Lastly, at the time that Officer Lee arrived, Trenton's paint business was closed. Unlike the situation in *Sandoval-Vasquez*, Officer Lee did not have free access to enter. There was no "open gate" here. The lights were turned off, and the door was barely open. From the outside, Officer Lee could not view the store's contents, and she did not observe any people coming to or leaving from the store. This "closed access" prevented the officer's entry, and the overwhelming evidence removed any reasonable belief that Garza had apparent authority to provide consent.

On the other hand, the prosecution will argue that the facts available to Officer Lee at the time would allow a

---

Follows with the affirmative argument that distinguishes the precedent case.

Also distinguishes *Sandoval-Vasquez* based on the parenthetical information explaining the relevance of an "open" business.

Author decides to rely mainly on the case illustration of the *King* case, as it deals with a closed business.

person of reasonable caution to believe that Garza, the consenting party, had authority over the premises. Officer Lee's situation is analogous to the circumstances confronted by the officers in *King*. Garza stood right outside the business leisurely smoking a cigarette, which suggested he was taking a brief break from work or the business. It was reasonable for Officer Lee to assume that Garza went outside to avoid filling the building with cigarette smoke and that he was connected directly to the paint business, whether as its owner or employee. Furthermore, Garza's smock (worn to protect his clothes) projected his aura of authority to Officer Lee. One could reasonably assume that he wore a smock to protect against the paint he mixed and sold at the store.

> Next, provides the prosecution's counterargument. Analogizes to *King*. Identifies specific factual support and reasons for why those facts support its argument.

Additional evidence supports Garza's appearance of authority over the business. Garza was the only person guarding the open door. Further, when Officer Lee requested to enter the shop, Garza immediately and unequivocally granted access. He led her through the door, stopped to turn on the lights (which were on the far side of the room), and went to the restroom. He showed signs of someone who was very familiar and comfortable with the layout of the store. In addition, Garza's wallet was located inside the shop. Officer Lee reasonably relied on the fact that Garza's personal belonging was in the store to conclude he had authority to consent. Moreover, as he entered the premises, Garza did not communicate with anyone else inside the building to ask whether he could invite the officer inside. Garza did not display any suspicious speech or mannerisms that suggested he needed to obtain someone else's approval to permit entry or that he was exceeding his authority. Based on the evidence, it reasonably appeared to Officer Lee that Garza had uncontrolled or unlimited access to the premises. As such, similar to the defendant in *King*, Trenton assumed the risk that Garza might grant access to others. Nothing about the interaction between Officer Lee and Garza could have undermined a reasonable person's belief that Garza had the authority to allow whomever he pleased into the store.

Despite these arguments, the prosecution's position likely will be unsuccessful. There is no evidence that Garza had a key to the store or that he could obtain access to the building had all the doors been closed and locked. The propped open door clearly suggested to a person of reasonable caution that Garza lacked independent access. At a minimum, the propped door should have prompted

Provides rebuttal as to why the prosecution's argument will likely fail.

the officer to ask Garza more questions. Any random person, unconnected to the business, could have been smoking outside and behind the shop. Garza was not standing in the front of the store and did not open the front door. The evidence fails to present any reasonable indication of Garza's authority or control over the premises. Further, the smock that Garza wore logically suggested that he worked at the deli located just a few doors down. Further inquiry or a more conscientious investigation of nearby businesses by Officer Lee would have resolved the reasonable doubt as to Garza's authority to control the premises.

Consequently, a court will probably find that Garza did not have apparent authority to grant Officer Lee's request to enter Trenton's paint business.

ANALOGICAL REASONING WITH DEPTH

EXERCISE 38

SAMPLE ANSWER

Begins with a clear thesis statement that identifies the issue and briefly explains why the outcome turns out as it does.

Samuel Waters ("Waters") will likely establish that All About Kids negligently hired Javier Thomas ("Thomas") to work as an installation and repair person for its company given the lack of inquiry into Thomas's background. Under California law, an employer may be held liable for negligent hiring if he knows or has reason to know that an employee hired is incompetent or unfit to perform the duties required of the job, or if he fails to use reasonable care to discover the employee's incompetence or unfitness before hiring him. *SeaRiver Maritime, Inc. v. Indus. Med. Servs., Inc.*, 983 F. Supp. 1287, 1297 (N.D. Cal. 1997).

Sets out the test or legal standard for a negligent hiring claim under California law.

In *SeaRiver Maritime, Inc.*, the court held that the employer company failed to use reasonable care to discover the hired employee's unfitness. *Id.* IMS, the employer company, hired Dr. Smith ("Smith") as a temporary physician through a physicians' registry service known at that time as Western Physicians Registry (WPR). *Id.* at 1292. WPR interviewed Smith, received his resume and references from two physicians, and determined that Smith met the criteria set forth by IMS. *Id.*

Provides a clear explanation of the legal standard from precedent. Includes the key facts, holding and reasoning from this case so that the reader can clearly understand how the court applies the test in a real-world scenario.

Smith graduated from medical school and received his medical license. *Id.* at 1291. However, after completing two years of a seven to nine year residency, members of the program's review committee dismissed Smith from the program. *Id.* The committee investigated several incidents that raised concerns about Smith's honesty, trustworthiness, communication and interpersonal skills and his ability to handle the stress of a general surgery practice. *Id.* The committee determined that Smith could only practice medicine under close supervision and that he could not work late hours or without sufficient sleep. *Id.* at 1292. WPR contacted the references provided by Smith but did not contact anyone from his residency program to inquire about his dismissal from the program. *Id.* WPR referred Smith to IMS and provided IMS with verification of his medical license, his curriculum vitae, and his references. *Id.* IMS hired Smith and relied entirely on the screening of his credentials performed by WPR. *Id.*

Continues to provide the relevant factual background on which the court based its decision.

SeaRiver regularly referred its employees in need of medical treatment to IMS. *Id.* at 1291. During his employment, Smith treated Christopher Richards, a SeaRiver employee referred to IMS. *Id.* at 1293. Smith negligently treated Richards by administering a steroid greatly in excess of the recommended and appropriate dosage. *Id.* at 1293–94. Richards suffered permanent injuries and sued SeaRiver for damages. *Id.* at 1295. In turn, SeaRiver sued IMS for negligently hiring Smith. *Id.*

> Note the parties to this present case. SeaRiver seeks indemnification from IMS for the negligent acts.

> Identifies the court's reasoning for its decision.

The court concluded that IMS's failure to interview Smith, check his references or request any information from his residency program constituted a failure to employ reasonable care to discover Smith's unfitness to practice as a temporary physician for the company. *Id.* at 1297. Even though WPR provided IMS with Smith's documentation and references, IMS did not complete its own investigation into Smith's qualifications and experience before hiring him. *Id.* Further, IMS failed to contact the residency program and ask about his early departure. *Id.* IMS did not even verify the information on Smith's CV. *Id.* Had IMS made such inquiries, it would have discovered the many limitations on Smith's ability to practice medicine. *Id.* Such information would have given IMS reason to suspect or at least question his ability to perform competently as a temporary physician. *Id.* Consequently, the court held IMS liable to SeaRiver for negligently hiring Smith. *Id.*

> Begins with the affirmative argument (for Waters). Leads with a clear analogy to the precedent case and incorporates the legal standard in this leading analogy. Serves as a clear thesis for the section.

Like the many omissions made by IMS in *SeaRiver Maritime, Inc.*, All About Kids failed to make sufficient inquiry into Thomas's background. In particular, Andrew Scavo ("Scavo"), Thomas's supervisor, merely chatted with Thomas before hiring him to work as an installation/repair person. During that brief conversation, Scavo did not ask Thomas about his specific duties at The Home Store, accomplishments, or supervisor information. When Thomas spoke about his personal side business, Scavo failed to ask specific questions about the closing of his business. He simply assumed Thomas's explanation about the downturn in the economy was true. He also did not ask about the details of the jobs that he performed under his business, or for references from specific customers or clients. Scavo relied on Thomas's word that he was a great employee, worthy of the position with All About Kids.

> Provides specific factual support for Waters's position that All About Kids did not exercise reasonable care in hiring Thomas.

A conversation with Thomas's past employer at The Home Store, a more thorough search on the Internet, or a call to the Better Business Bureau could have uncovered much more relevant information about Thomas's fitness to work at All About Kids. Had Scavo done any of these things, he would have learned about the various customer complaints about Thomas's work or business dealings. In particular, he would have easily discovered that customers at The Home Store complained about his unsatisfactory work. Even a minimal search or inquiry by Scavo would have uncovered valuable information. Consequently, given that Thomas failed to use even the slightest reasonable care to discover Thomas's incompetence, All About Kids will be held liable to Waters for negligently hiring Thomas.

> **Shows why these particular facts lead to the conclusion that All About Kids negligently hired Thomas.**

All About Kids will attempt to argue that its situation is distinguishable from the events of *SeaRiver Maritime, Inc.* In particular, All About Kids will maintain that unlike the employer's actions in *SeaRiver Maritime*, Scavo made an effort to interview Thomas. He spoke with Thomas in person for at least 25 minutes. He asked questions about his home business and learned about his employment with The Home Store. He spent more than enough time with Thomas to gather information about his interpersonal skills, knowledge and experience with the industry, and eagerness to work. He even conducted a search on the Internet for Thomas's business. And he required Thomas to complete a standard employment application.

> **Next, provides All About Kids's counterargument. Distinguishes the precedent case from All About Kids's situation with Thomas. Identifies specific factual support and reasons for why those facts support the company's argument.**

Even though Waters claims that Scavo's investigation could have been more thorough, Scavo did rely on good recommendations for his decision to hire Thomas. For example, Oscar Martinez ("Martinez"), a veteran employee of the company, walked over while Scavo was interviewing Thomas and spoke very highly of Thomas's talent. He mentioned that Thomas was a "good worker." Scavo did not solicit Martinez's opinion. Martinez volunteered this information, which would lead someone to think that Thomas is a good applicant. Moreover, Martinez knows the demands and expectations of the company and presumably would recommend only someone who would be a good asset to the company and team.

In addition, Scavo heard a long-time customer of All About Kids show support for Thomas's application to work there and this customer apparently knew that Thomas had worked previously at The Home Store. Coupled with the company's long-time and trusted employee, Scavo relied on this customer's show of support as a positive recommendation for Thomas. Thus, All About Kids used reasonable care to gauge and assess Thomas's work background and competency level.

All About Kids's arguments will likely fail. Even though Scavo briefly spoke with Thomas, Scavo really relied only on Martinez as a reference for Thomas. Normally, Scavo required at least two work-related references for employment. Here, he relied on just one and there was no indication that Martinez ever worked with Thomas. Martinez served as a personal reference, not a work-related reference. Plus, since Scavo chose to rely solely on Martinez's judgment, Scavo should have spoken to Martinez again out of Thomas's presence to ensure that a frank and honest discussion took place. Having decided to forego seeking any other opinions about Thomas's fitness or competency, Scavo (and All About Kids) did an extremely poor investigation into Thomas's background. Consequently, a court will likely find that All About Kids is liable to Waters for the negligent hiring of Thomas.

Provides an additional argument, a rebuttal argument, as to why Scavo's efforts were insufficient. Identifies key facts and the relevance of those facts to the argument.

ANALOGICAL REASONING WITH DEPTH

EXERCISE 40

SAMPLE ANSWER

Beginning lays out clear conclusion.

Home Stuff will very likely be able to set up a meritorious defense as part of its motion for new trial.

Sets out the rule.

In order to have a default judgment set aside, a defendant must establish a meritorious defense. *State Farm Life Ins. Co. v. Mosharaf*, 794 S.W.2d 578, 581 (Tex. App. 1990). The defendant need not prove such a defense; rather, it must allege facts that would constitute a defense to the cause of action alleged by plaintiff. *Id*. The defendant's motion must be supported by affidavits or other prima facie evidence that the defendant has such a defense. *Id*. The defendant should be able to establish that if the lawsuit is tried again, the result would be different from the result established by the default judgment. *Id*.

Applies the rule to caselaw by extracting key factors in the court's opinion which were decisional.

For example, a defendant established such a defense where the plaintiff alleged that the defendant hired a roofer, and the roofer negligently caused a fire that burned down an apartment complex owned by the plaintiff. *Id*. at 585. The defendant, as part of its motion for new trial, pled as a defense that the third-party roofer caused the fire, rather than the defaulting defendant who hired him. *Id*. An affidavit with these facts was sufficient to set up the required meritorious defense. *Id*.

Analogizes present case with precedent case to illustrate why a court will likely rule just as precedent court.

Summarizes key points for coming to conclusion and clearly states conclusion one last time.

Like the defendant in *State Farm*, Home Stuff will be able to present evidence showing that another party—namely the customer herself—was responsible for any injuries she suffered by lying on the store's floor. The in-store video shows the customer carefully lying down on the floor, rather than slipping as her petition alleges. Because the facts indicate a meritorious defense, Home Stuff can plead this defense in its motion for new trial and therefore satisfy the second prong of the test for a motion for new trial after default.

ANALOGICAL REASONING WITH DEPTH

EXERCISE 42

SAMPLE ANSWER

Johnson probably has no viable claim of battery against Washington because Washington's attempted "high five" lacks the required element of offensiveness. A battery is a harmful or offensive contact "upon another with the intent to cause such contact or the apprehension that such contact is imminent." *Paul v. Holbrook*, 696 So. 2d 1311, 1312 (Fla. Dist. Ct. App. 1997). The context of the contact and the relationship between the parties affects the analysis, and there is no battery unless the contact was offensive. *Id.*

Where, for example, a store employee touched a suspected shoplifter as the employee attempted to retrieve suspected stolen merchandise, there was no battery. *Gatto v. Publix Supermarket, Inc.*, 387 So. 2d 377, 379 (Fla. Dist. Ct. App. 1980). The court found that while the parties did touch, the touching was not offensive and the suspected shoplifter's dignity was not offended by the touching. *Id.* The touching was no more than a casual touching as the employee attempted to grasp property that he believed was stolen. *Id.* Based on these facts, the court affirmed the claim's dismissal. *Id.*

On the other hand, where an employee approached a co-worker from behind on two occasions and tried to massage her shoulders, the court found that the defendant had a claim of battery. *Paul*, 696 So. 2d at 1312. Each time, the victim pulled away and told the defendant to leave. *Id.* at 1311. The defendant had also harassed the victim and made unwelcome advances toward her. *Id.* The court noted that while intent to commit battery is seldom proved directly, a jury could infer that the defendant here intended to touch the plaintiff in an offensive manner. *Id.* at 1312. The court noted that the relationship's context and the time and place of any contact also influences the analysis. *Id.* "A stranger is not to be expected to tolerate liberties which would be allowed by an intimate friend," the court explained. *Id.*

When Washington touched Johnson in the course of a celebratory high five, Washington did so as a friend. Just

Uses precedential
cases to make
comparisons with
case at hand.
Applies present
facts to illustrate
how precedential
facts are similar
and/or dissimilar

Rounds up
analysis with
clear and concise
conclusion.

as in *Gatto*, where the employee touched the suspect without any indication of ill will or intent to offend, so did Washington touch Johnson with the intent to congratulate rather than hurt. While Johnson was in fact hurt, this was more as a result of the accidentally missed high five rather than of any intent to hurt Johnson. In addition, the two were friends. Even though the two were going through a difficult patch in their relationship, their history of golfing together indicates that a high five would have been a normal part of their relationship, unlike the unwelcome shoulder rubbing in *Paul*. Therefore, Johnson probably does not have a valid claim of battery against Washington.

ANALOGICAL REASONING WITH DEPTH

EXERCISE 44

SAMPLE ANSWER

Begins with a clear thesis statement that serves as the conclusion.

A court will likely find that Culinary Delights had a reasonable business expectancy in securing the food services contract with Samuel Bennett University ("SB University"). Under Virginia law, the requirements for tortious interference with business expectancy are: (1) the existence of a business expectancy with a probability of future economic benefit; (2) the defendant's knowledge of the business expectancy; (3) a reasonable certainty that absent the defendant's intentional misconduct, the plaintiff would have realized the expectancy; and (4) damages. *Muir v. Navy Fed. Credit Union*, 744 F. Supp. 2d 145, 148 (D.D.C. 2010); *Levine v. McLeskey*, 881 F. Supp. 1030, 1057 (E.D. Va. 1995). With respect to the first element, "Virginia law protects only specific expectancies." *Muir*, 744 F. Supp. 2d at 148. "Thus, the *mere expectation* to engage in business is not sufficient to sustain a claim of tortious interference." *Id.* (emphasis added). Furthermore, "continuing to do business . . . is not the type of expectancy protected by Virginia law[,]" as it is too general. *Am. Tel. & Tel. Co. v. E. Pay Phones, Inc.*, 767 F. Supp. 1335, 1340 (E.D. Va. 1991).

Leads the law section with the requirements for tortious interference.

Provides the legal standard under Virginia law for determining whether a business expectancy existed.

Virginia law safeguards a specific business expectancy "only when there is a reasonable probability of future economic benefit[.]" *Muir*, F. Supp. 2d at 148. In other words, "there must be a particular expectancy which it is reasonably certain will be realized." *Am. Tel. & Tel. Co.*, 767 F. Supp. at 1340. Proof of a "possibility" that a future benefit will accrue will not sustain a tortious interference claim. *Muir*, 744 F. Supp. 2d at 148.

For example, in *Levine*, the court held that the plaintiff presented sufficient evidence to support a business expectancy with a probability of future economic benefit. 881 F. Supp. at 1058. In *Levine*, the defendant filed a *lis pendens* (litigation) on the property the plaintiff owned and planned to develop. *Id.* at 1038. The plaintiff maintained that the defendant's *lis pendens* interfered with her business prospect of securing a capital loan from GE Capital ("GE") and, in turn, prevented her from building an apartment complex on the subject property.

Id. at 1057. To assist her in obtaining financing for the construction project, the plaintiff had hired a specialist, who had considerable experience and knowledge of investment mortgage financing. *Id.* at 1057–58. The specialist found two interested lenders, one of which was GE. *Id.* at 1058. The specialist testified he had extensive knowledge of GE's loan practices and stated he believed "one, and perhaps both, of the interested firms would have extended financing for the project," except for the pending litigation regarding the property. *Id.* Because of the pending litigation, the specialist recommended to the plaintiff that she delay her financing efforts "until the litigation picture became clearer." *Id.* The specialist's testimony supported the plaintiff's claim of a specific business expectancy. *Id.*

On the other hand, the court in *Muir* concluded that the plaintiff set forth no evidence that he had a probability of future economic benefit. 744 F. Supp. 2d at 149. The plaintiff claimed the defendant's misconduct precluded him from investing in at least three properties. *Id.* The defendant credit union had applied funds held in the plaintiff's joint account with his father to satisfy a debt incurred by his father. *Id.* at 147. The plaintiff, therefore, did not have access to these funds to make investments. *Id.* at 149-50. The court disagreed with the plaintiff's position and found there was insufficient evidence showing an investment from which the plaintiff would derive future profits. *Id.* at 149.

With respect to the plaintiff's first real estate investment, the property owner stated, "she could not recall what agreement, if any, she had with [the] plaintiff." *Id.* As for the second investment opportunity, the plaintiff could not even remember the property owner's name. *Id.* at 150. In addition, the plaintiff provided no evidence regarding the prices for which he expected to buy or could sell the property. *Id.* The court stated, "No reasonable jury could find that [the] plaintiff could strike a deal with the owner, let alone turn a profit on the property." *Id.* With the third property, the plaintiff claimed he would have invested *alone* (the specific business expectancy) if he had access to the funds in his joint account. *Id.* However, the plaintiff's co-investor testified that she offered the investment opportunity to the plaintiff because she needed a partner to manage repairs on the house. *Id.* Thus, the court reasoned the plaintiff failed to provide sufficient evidence that he could have invested in the property

Provides a clear explanation of the legal standard from precedent. Includes the key facts, holding and reasoning from this case so that the reader can clearly understand how the court applies the test in a real-world scenario.

Describes the facts and reasoning in another case where the court reaches the opposite conclusion.

without his partner. *Id*. The plaintiff's claims of specific investment opportunities were simply "based on evidence which hardly present[ed] a possibility, let alone a probability, of future profits." *Id*. at 149.

Culinary Delights will maintain that, like the plaintiff in *Levine*, the company had a business expectancy with a reasonable probability of future economic benefit. There is substantial evidence that Culinary Delights's expectation in winning the bid for the food service contract with SB University was valid. Ukwu informed Culinary Delights that the University ranked its bid for the contract second among the five proposals and that the company's bid was "very close" to Tasty Cuisine's winning submission.* Both proposals had similar projected costs and meal plans and food options. Culinary Delights can show more than a proof of a "possibility" that a benefit would have accrued in its favor.

> Note the analysis focuses on the first element, business expectancy with probability of future economic benefit, and does not discuss Bowen's alleged interference.

Furthermore, the company's experience and industry recognitions would have been attractive to the University. Culinary Delights currently services two colleges in Virginia, one with a student body and faculty totaling about 4,970 people. The company is accustomed to working with a large number of patrons. In addition, one of its clients, Bates College, has three full-service dining halls and two cafes. Culinary Delights has substantial experience that would have assisted the company in servicing SB University's large campus population. Moreover, Culinary Delights has been recognized as a "Rising Star" in the food services industry. The company also received the Bronze Award for a catered special event and an Honorable Mention for its Mardi-Gras themed dinner. In addition, the head chef won third place in a culinary competition. These unique features of Culinary Delights serve as additional evidence that the company was well positioned to secure the food services contract with SB University. Like the plaintiff in *Levine*, Culinary Delights had more than a general expectancy to continue to do business.

> Next, provides Bowen's counterargument. Identifies specific factual support and reasons for why those facts support her argument.

Bowen will contend that there is insufficient evidence to support the notion that Culinary Delights had a chance to acquire the contract with SB University. In particular, Bowen will maintain that, similar to the situation in *Muir*,

---

* Some of the key facts for this exercise are from the opinion in *Western Blue Print Co. v. Roberts*, No. WD 72025, 2011 Mo. App. LEXIS 606, *32 (Ct. App. Apr. 29, 2011).

Culinary Delights bases its position on evidence that hardly presents a possibility, let alone a probability, of future profits. Bowen will emphasize the highly competitive nature of submitting a successful bid and Culinary Delights's shortfalls. Although the companies' submissions shared some similarities, Culinary Delights did not have the experience to service a large university. SB University has almost 9,000 patrons for its food service program. The University has six dining halls and a number of other eating locations throughout the campus. Culinary Delights's largest college client has only about 4,900 students and faculty members and one dining hall on campus. Thus, Culinary Delights was not prepared to handle such a dramatic increase in required service. Moreover, there is no evidence that Culinary Delights has ever secured a food services contract with SB University and thus, the company cannot offer a prior relationship with the University as support for its position. Culinary Delights's evidence is attenuated at best. Culinary Delights merely had a hope to continue to do business, more business, in Virginia, not a reasonable expectancy in securing the contract with SB University.

Bowen's arguments, however, will likely fail. Although Culinary Delights did not have a prior contract with SB University or a prior relationship with the school, the company submitted a very promising bid for the food services contract. Unlike the lack of supporting evidence in *Muir*, Ukwu's favorable statements about Culinary Delights's bid, and the company's current accounts and industry recognitions support Culinary Delights's position that it could successfully compete. Similar to the plaintiff in *Levine* who did not have an existing or prior contract but strong evidence indicating likely success, Culinary Delights identified a specific business expectancy with a reasonable probability of future economic benefit.

> Leads with clear transition to the rebuttal.

> Challenges the counter-argument by distinguishing *Muir*.

Therefore, given the circumstances suggesting that it could successfully compete, a court will likely find that Culinary Delights had a reasonable business expectancy in acquiring the food services contract with SB University.

> Ends with clear and concise conclusion.

ANALOGICAL REASONING WITH DEPTH

EXERCISE 46

SAMPLE ANSWER

Begins with clear conclusion that identifies the issue and briefly explains why the outcome turns out as it does.

Smith's eighty-minute detention was likely too long to be considered reasonable for purposes of the shopkeeper's privilege; the longest permissible detention in the applicable authority was just over an hour. Smith is very elderly, so her detention may well be viewed more strictly than that of an average adult.

Sets out the rule and states the elements. Explains how to satisfy the rule, using specific examples.

Describes how courts assess whether a detention is reasonable in length or not.

The shopkeeper's privilege gives shopkeepers legal authority to detain a customer to investigate ownership of property. *Willard Dep't. Stores, Inc. v. Silva.** To qualify for this privilege, the merchant must show: (1) the merchant's suspicion of theft was reasonable, (2) the detention was reasonable in length, and (3) the detention was reasonable in manner. *Id.* To assert the shopkeeper's privilege, the merchant must hold the suspect only as long as is reasonable under the circumstances. *Id.* In one case, the detention lasted a little over one hour while employees questioned the customer and employees, and spoke to police. *Id.* Without determining the outer boundaries of a detention's length, the court held that this detention was reasonable under those circumstances. *Id.*

Explains further additional considerations that will drive the court's decision.

Courts in this jurisdiction will also take into account how efficient and organized the store's procedures were, as well as any protests on the part of the detainee. *Guijosa v. Qwik-Mart Stores, Inc.*** Where, for example, a store detained for twenty to thirty minutes two customers suspected of stealing hats, the court noted that the length of time was reasonable to investigate the possible theft. *Id.* In addition, the court noted the store's efficient investigation procedures and the fact that the customers did not protest their confinement. *Id.*

Uses specifics to compare with the present case with precedent

At eighty minutes, Smith's detention was longer than either of those noted in the authority. Wow held Smith while employees reviewed the video and while the store

---

* This case is fictitious and/or adopted, in part, from an actual case.

** This case is fictitious and/or adopted, in part, from an actual case.

Brings in additional considerations that the court mentioned; considers the context of the present case's facts.

television was being repaired. It was unreasonable for Smith to wait while the television was repaired; in *Willard,* the delay was due to speaking with police, whereas here, the lengthy detention was the store's fault alone. Wow's inability to find a substitute television suggests that the store did not have the efficient procedures noted in *Guijosa.* In addition, Smith protested her confinement, and she is elderly, which places her in the class of people that the *Guijosa* court said should be detained with "special concern." Furthermore, Smith missed taking her medication, although she asked to go home and take it. Because she is an elderly person needing her medication, Smith's detention arguably should have been shorter, not longer, than that of an average adult.

Makes a distinct shift to counter-argument; develops counter-argument using specifics from precedent.

Wow could argue that review of the videotapes was necessary to investigate the property's ownership, which is the goal of the shopkeeper's privilege. Nevertheless, the fact that this detention involves an elderly person and is longer than any other detention in the available case authority may well result in this detention being held unreasonable in length. In addition, the fact that the electronics store—which has numerous televisions in stock—could not quickly substitute another television for the broken one suggests that the procedures were inefficient.

Rebuts counter-argument with specific facts.

Sets out final conclusion to round out the analysis.

Thus, Wow's detention of Smith was not reasonable in length and Wow will not be able to assert the shopkeeper's privilege successfully.

ANALOGICAL REASONING WITH DEPTH

EXERCISE 48

SAMPLE ANSWER

Jossery's office probably is not an "inhabited dwelling house" for purposes of first-degree burglary, because the office is not a structure where people ordinarily live.

In this jurisdiction, burglary of an inhabited dwelling house is a first-degree burglary. *Fond.** A structure is an inhabited dwelling house if it is a structure "where people ordinarily live, and . . . is currently being used for dwelling purposes." *Id.* The structure need not be the person's primary residence, but must be a place expected to be free from unwanted intrusions. *Id.*

For example, a motel room was an inhabited dwelling house because it was a "temporary place of abode" and its resident had a reasonable expectation of privacy from unauthorized intrusions. *Villalobos.*** The court noted that other temporary abodes, such as a weekend fishing retreat or a jail cell could also qualify. *Id.* If the motel room had been occupied for purposes other than as a temporary dwelling, such as for business, the room would not have been "inhabited" for purposes of the definition. *Id.* Burglaries in buildings that are not intended for habitation, such as a warehouse, the court explained, do not raise the same safety and confrontation concerns that arise with regard to an inhabited building. *Id.*

Likewise, a patient's room in a psychiatric hospital was an inhabited dwelling house because it was a place in which the patient stayed overnight and was staying at the time of a burglary. *Fond.* Although the hospital staff had access to the room, the patient still had a reasonable expectation of privacy from intruders. *Id.*

Here, Jossery's office is probably not an inhabited dwelling house, because it was designed for his professional activities, not for habitation. Unlike the other structures that were found to be inhabited dwelling houses—a hospital room, a jail cell, and a motel room—an office is not designed to be used as an abode and generally is not used

---

* This case is fictitious and/or adopted, in part, from an actual case.

** This case is fictitious and/or adopted, in part, from an actual case.

for that purpose. Burglary of a downtown office outside of business hours would not normally implicate the safety concerns described in *Villalobos* that underlie the common law of burglary, because an office is not designed for sleeping and would not normally be occupied outside business hours. This enhanced category of burglary is meant to punish particularly those crimes aimed at threats to people's place of repose; places such as offices where one might sleep only under unusual circumstances are generally not included.

> **Brings in policy concerns underlying the court's reasoning and applies those concerns to the case at hand.**

> **Takes into consideration the reasons behind the law at issue.**

The prosecution will likely argue that Jossery's office was locked each night, indicating that he had an expectation of privacy, just like the resident of a motel room or hospital room. But while an expectation of privacy is part of the "inhabited dwelling house" analysis, an expectation of privacy alone is not sufficient. As the *Villalobos* court observed, a motel room used for business would not be "inhabited" for purposes of burglary law, even though the motel room could be locked. Likewise, Jossery's office was designed for a business purpose and used for a business purpose, and it had fewer features of an abode than the motel room cited in *Villalobos*. If Jossery's office were included within the term "inhabited dwelling house," then practically every place would be brought within that term, if a person simply fell asleep there from time to time.

> **Transitions overtly to counter-argument and sets out an argument based on precedent cases.**

> **Rebuts counter-argument using specific facts from precedent and from the fact pattern.**

Because Jossery's office was designed for business purposes and was not a place of abode, it will not be considered an "inhabited dwelling house" for purposes of first-degree burglary.

> **Links back to rule and gives clear conclusion.**

ANALOGICAL REASONING WITH DEPTH

EXERCISE 50

SAMPLE ANSWER

Begins with a clear thesis statement that identifies the issue and briefly explains why the outcome turns out as it does.

A court will likely find that, given Beth Cohen's ("Cohen's") level of awareness and subsequent inaction, both equitable estoppel and equitable tolling are inappropriate in this case. Thus, Adrian Lucas ("Lucas") is not estopped from asserting the statute of limitations as a defense and the limitations period of one-year did not toll for any period.

Sets out the tests or legal standard for asserting equitable estoppel or tolling under NY law.

Note the fully developed explanation of the legal requirements derived and synthesized from the precedent cases.

Note the law section leads with a brief background about the policy behind statutes of limitations and the need to apply equity in certain cases.

Note the facts of the exercise require focus on Cohen's conduct. There need not be much legal discussion about the difference between estoppel and tolling here.

Although the purpose of statutes of limitations is to protect individuals from stale claims, the law recognizes that it would be unjust to allow a defendant to raise a limitations defense in certain circumstances. *Zumpano v. Quinn*, 849 N.E.2d 926, 929 (N.Y. 2006). The doctrines of equitable estoppel and equitable tolling can prevent a defendant from pleading limitations as a defense where, by fraud, misrepresentation, or deception, the defendant had induced the plaintiff to refrain from filing a timely action. *Zumpano*, 849 N.E.2d at 929; *Kotlyarsky v. New York Post*, 757 N.Y.S.2d 703, 706 (App. Div. 2003). These doctrines embrace the truism "that a wrongdoer should not be able to take refuge behind the shield of his own wrong[.]" *Gen. Stencils, Inc, v. Chiappa*, 219 N.E.2d 169, 170 (N.Y. 1966).

Even though the court applies each doctrine in different circumstances, a defendant is not estopped from asserting a statute of limitations defense, nor is the limitations period tolled if the plaintiff possesses timely knowledge sufficient to place her under a duty to make an inquiry and ascertain all the relevant facts prior to the expiration of the applicable statute of limitations. *Kotlyarsky*, 757 N.Y.S.2d at 707. Further, even if the plaintiff arguably did not possess timely knowledge of the actionable conduct, the plaintiff must show that her failure to timely commence the lawsuit is not attributable to a lack of diligence on her part. *Id*. at 707–08. The degree of due diligence needed varies with the circumstances of each case. *Id*. at 708. A plaintiff who unreasonably relies on the assurances of a wrongdoer has not satisfied the obligation of due diligence. *Id*. A plaintiff is held to have "discovered" a wrong at the point where the facts could have been ascertained by using reasonable diligence. *Id*.

For example, in *Kotlyarsky*, the court held that the facts did not warrant the equitable estoppel or tolling of the limitations period. *Id.* The plaintiff's suit against a newspaper for libel was barred by the one-year period. *Id.* at 706. In December 2000, the newspaper reported that plaintiff's company was set up to defraud insurance companies. *Id.* at 705. The plaintiff gathered evidence showing the falsity of the paper's comments and sought a retraction. *Id.* Apparently, during an April 2001 meeting, the plaintiff received a promise from the newspaper that it would use the documentation in the retraction. *Id.* Later, the plaintiff was convicted, and while he was in prison, the plaintiff did not receive any news about the retraction. *Id.* at 705–06. He wrote a letter to the newspaper and eventually received a response in February 2002 that the newspaper had withdrawn the requested retraction article. *Id.* at 706. In August, the plaintiff filed suit against the newspaper for libel. *Id.*

> Follows the legal standard with case illustrations. The first case exemplifies a situation where the plaintiff could not use the doctrines of estoppel or tolling.

> Provides sufficient detail for the reader to fully understand the application of the precedent case to the client's facts.

Although the one-year limitations period ended in December 2001 after the paper published the article, the plaintiff claimed that the doctrines of equitable tolling or estoppel prevented the newspaper from asserting statute of limitations as a defense. *Id.* The court disagreed, holding that the plaintiff not only had timely knowledge of the article and the grounds for a defamation suit but also failed to show due diligence on his part. *Id.* at 707–08. In particular, the plaintiff waited many months before he wrote the newspaper to ask about the promised retraction. *Id.* at 708. Had the plaintiff exercised some effort, he could have easily discovered that the retraction was not going to be printed. *Id.* Even while in prison, the plaintiff could have made a simple phone call to the paper, or asked his attorney to inquire about the retraction much sooner. *Id.* Therefore, the court concluded that the plaintiff did not exercise reasonable due diligence to justify application of estoppel or tolling. *Id.*

> Provides the court's holding and reasoning.

On the other hand, in *General Stencils*, the court found that a defendant might be equitably estopped from asserting a limitations defense because her affirmative conduct in concealing the crime at issue prevented the plaintiff from timely bringing its action. 219 N.E.2d at 171. In *General Stencils*, the plaintiff's bookkeeper stole petty cash funds from the company and concealed her misappropriations, causing the plaintiff to file suit after the limitations period. *Id.* at 170. The court determined that the defendant's admitted thievery entitled the plaintiff to

> Nicely transitions to a precedent case illustration where the court allowed plaintiff to litigate the doctrine of equitable estoppel.

litigate the issue of equitable estoppel. *Id.* at 171. The defendant's admitted wrongdoing—a carefully concealed crime—produced the long delay between the accrual of the cause of action and the plaintiff's filing suit. *Id.* She, therefore, could not be allowed to "take refuge behind the shield" of her own wrongdoing. *Id.* at 170.

Lucas will compare Cohen's inactivity to that of the plaintiff in *Kotlyarsky* and argue that she did not use reasonable diligence in discovering the purported misconduct. Cohen clearly had timely knowledge imposing a duty on her to investigate the facts further prior to the expiration of the limitations period. In February, the same month that Lucas sent the email at issue, Cohen overheard employees discussing a sordid affair between a supervisor and a call center employee named Reginald. Cohen knew that she had an employee named Reginald in her department. Moreover, she often went to lunch with Reginald outside of the office. This connection should have spurred Cohen to inquire about the email or at least ask the employees about their conversation. In addition, the employees' conduct should have drawn much suspicion. When they noticed Cohen, they immediately stopped talking about the affair. Any reasonable person would have suspected that she might have been the topic of conversation. Again, this incident put Cohen on notice that she may have been the subject of the office gossip.

In addition, like the plaintiff in *Kotlyarsky*, Cohen waited far too long to take action. She waited about three months to ask Lucas about the rumor and then did nothing for about nine months until the Director confirmed that she was the subject of Lucas's rumor mill. Had Cohen exercised even the slightest effort, she would have easily discovered that Lucas had sent an email around the office claiming that she was having an inappropriate relationship with one of her employees. In fact, she knew Lucas well—he was the office gossiper. She could have inquired whether any other employees named Reginald worked in the call center. She could have pressed Lucas further about her suspicions. She knew his history and inclination to spread gossip around the office. In addition, she could have asked her secretary about Lucas's email asking everyone to delete messages about "B." She could have contacted the company's network department herself to start an investigation. However, Cohen took little to no action. She merely asked Lucas, the wrongdoer, whether he knew anything about the rumor. This was not enough.

Begins the affirmative argument by leading with a clear analogy to the precedent case.

Provides specific factual support for Lucas's position that Cohen cannot rely on either doctrine to prevent his limitations defense. Explains the relevance of the factual support to his argument.

Fully develops the affirmative argument.

Cohen did not exercise reasonable due diligence to ascertain or discover the facts surrounding Lucas's misconduct and, therefore, cannot rely on the doctrines of estoppel or tolling in this case.

Cohen will likely contend that, like the defendant in *General Stencils*, Lucas cannot be permitted to benefit from his own wrongdoing. Cohen will maintain that Lucas's steps to remove his original email from the company's server constituted affirmative acts designed to conceal his misconduct. Lucas not only contacted Raymond, the Network System Director, but also sent a request to the recipients asking them to delete the email. As such, he delayed her knowledge about the email spreading the rumor that she had an affair with her underling. In addition, Cohen will show that she did attempt to find out more about the rumor when she mentioned the incident to Lucas and specifically asked him what he knew. Cohen will maintain that by telling her that he did not know anything about the rumor, Lucas continued to actively conceal his wrongdoing. Consequently, he cannot claim limitations as a defense.

Cohen's argument will likely fail. Arguably, the bookkeeper in *General Stencils* had a unique fiduciary relationship to the plaintiff whereas Lucas had no obligation to admit or disclose his purported misconduct. Further, like the court mentioned in *Zumpano*, "[a] wrongdoer is not legally obligated to make a public confession, or to alert people who may have a claim against it, to get the benefit of a statute of limitations." 849 N.E.2d at 929. Moreover, Lucas's attempt to remove his email from the company's server did not prevent Cohen from investigating or discovering the facts giving rise to her libel suit prior to the end of the one-year limitations period. She simply could have asked another employee or her secretary about the rumor or email. Therefore, the court will likely find that Cohen cannot avail herself of the doctrines of equitable estoppel or tolling given her lack of due diligence.

Transitions to Cohen's argument, the counter-argument, with a leading analogy to precedent.

Challenges Cohen's position with a clear distinction from the precedent case relied on in the counter-argument. Challenges the inferences and conclusions raised in the counter-argument.

ANALOGICAL REASONING WITH DEPTH

EXERCISE 52

SAMPLE ANSWER

Begins with a clear thesis statement that identifies the issue and briefly explains why the outcome turns out as it does.

A court will likely find that, given the lack of a natural catastrophe constituting an act of God and GasPro's continuing ability to perform despite the failure of one of its suppliers, GasPro cannot excuse its performance under the force majeure clause. Thus, GasPro's failure to perform will probably constitute a breach of the contract.

Synthesizes the rule from the precedent cases. Identifies what the courts consider when examining the applicability of a force majeure provision in a contract.

Courts generally have treated contractors as responsible for the performance of their suppliers and subcontractors, especially when the contract at issue is silent on the source of supply. *Hutton Contracting Co. v. City of Coffeyville*, 487 F.3d 772, 779 (10th Cir. 2007). Further, a delay by a subcontractor is not itself a force majeure. *Id.* Nor does the fact that an endeavor has turned less profitable constitute a force majeure event. *Benson Mineral Grp. Inc. v. N. Natural Gas Co.*, No. 86-1903, 1988 U.S. Dist. LEXIS 17581, at *17 (D. Kan. Apr. 28, 1988); *City of Topeka v. Indus. Gas Co.*, 11 P.2d 1034, 1036 (Kan. 1932). "When several specific contingencies which will excuse nonperformance are named in a contract, only the named contingencies will excuse nonperformance." *Benson*, 1988 U.S. Dist. LEXIS, at *19.

Follows the legal standard with case illustrations. The first case exemplifies a situation in which the plaintiff could not avail itself of the force majeure provision because of sub-contractor's untimely delivery.

For example, in *Hutton*, the contractor, Hutton Contracting ("Hutton") claimed that a force majeure provision relieved the company of its responsibility for delays caused by its supplier. *Id.* at 777. The city contracted with Hutton to construct a power line and fiber-optic line. *Id.* at 774. The contract provided specific due dates for completion of the project and included a force majeure clause that gave Hutton more time to complete the project in exceptional circumstances. *Id.* at 775. The contract defined such exceptional circumstances as those when the reasonable delay was due exclusively to causes beyond the control or without the fault of Hutton, including acts of God, fires, floods, and acts or omission of the city. *Id.* at 778. As part of the first step in the process, the company began to clear the construction site, but Hutton had to suspend its work once it learned that the delivery of needed steel utility poles would be delayed. *Id.* at 776. Hutton requested several extensions caused by its pole supplier. *Id.* at 776–77. Consequently, the city sought damages for the delay of the project. *Id.* at 777.

The court concluded the force majeure clause did not assist Hutton in the particular circumstances. *Id.* at 778. In particular, the court determined a supplier's delay was not itself a force majeure for the company, remarking that Hutton did not suggest the supplier's failure was caused by a natural catastrophe or anything similar. *Id.* at 779. Explaining it was not making new contract law, the court held Hutton "responsible to the City for its supplier's delays when those delays [were] not themselves excused by a force majeure." *Id.*

> Provides sufficient detail for the reader to fully understand the application of the precedent to case to the client's facts.

Observing that it could locate no Kansas decision on point, the court nevertheless concluded on the basis of law in other jurisdictions that Hutton assumed the risk of its supplier's delay inasmuch as the contract with the city did not call for a specific supplier to complete the task: "Courts have been more inclined to bind the middleman of the contract if the contract is silent on the source of supply, and more likely to release the middleman if the source is referenced in the agreement." *Id.* Thus, in the absence of a force majeure, the company was liable to the city for its supplier's delays and the project's postponement. *Id.* at 780.

> Provides a second case illustration that explains another component of the rule—lack of profitability.

Similarly, the *Benson* court concluded that the defendant gas company was not excused from performance by reliance on a force majeure clause. 1998 U.S. Dist. LEXIS, at *19. The defendant failed to comply with the "take or pay" provision in the contract, that is, the defendant was either to take gas supplied under the contract by the plaintiff or, in the alternative, to pay for the gas not taken, but did neither. *Id.* at *1, *16–17. The defendant claimed that the collapse of its natural gas market constituted a force majeure and excused it from performance. *Id.* at *19. The court disagreed and noted that the collapse of the natural gas market did not fit within the specific contingencies identified in the clause: "When several specific contingencies which will excuse nonperformance are named in a contract, only the named contingencies will excuse nonperformance." *Id.* (citing *City of Topeka v. Indus. Gas Co.*, 11 P.2d 1034 (1932)). The court also rejected lack of profitability of an endeavor as a viable force majeure event. *Id.* The court explained that because the defendant could complete its performance under the contract in an alternative manner, the defendant was not entitled to suspend its performance. *Id.* at *17.

> Note that the sample answer does not include an additional illustration of the *Industrial Gas Co.* case given that similar information is provided in the *Benson* case illustration.

Leads the affirmative argument with an analogy to precedent.

Natural One will maintain that, as with the defendant in *Hutton*, GasPro may not avail itself of the force majeure clause in the contract because the specific contingencies provided in the force majeure clause do not include failure of GasPro's supplier to produce sufficient product, and specificity in listing contingencies excludes contingencies not listed. The *Hutton* decision also would deny relief to GasPro because GasPro did not identify the third party provider in the written contract. The contract between Natural One and GasPro provides that performance will be excused if such failure is due to "force majeure," which is defined to mean such incidents as acts of God, fires, floods, or any other cause beyond the seller's control. A decline in natural gas production from a well is not a natural catastrophe but rather a foreseeable consequence of doing business in the energy industry. There is not a limitless supply of minerals and natural resources. Further, a decline in gas production does not equal a flood, fire, or any other disastrous event or act of God.

Provides the exact language from the contract, as that is the starting point for this particular discussion.

Continues to detail specific facts from the exercise that support Natural One's position.

Also, similarly to the defendant in *Benson*, GasPro can meet its obligations under the contract. The decrease in supply from the Yearlings' well does not prevent GasPro from performing. GasPro simply could contact other raw natural gas suppliers in the area to fulfill its obligations. Consequently, as with the defendant in *Benson*, who had opted not to "take" additional product under the "take or pay" clause, but still had available the option to "pay" for the product not taken, GasPro is not without an option that would allow it to perform. Even if the court were to conclude that the decline in natural gas production from the Yearlings' well constituted a natural catastrophe, GasPro's lack of performance under the contract was not due to this event but rather to its inaction. With gas available from various suppliers, a seller's obtaining adequate volumes of gas to meet its needs is not something beyond the seller's control in the way that acts of God or other generally accepted force majeure events would be. GasPro could further examine its options. The drawback to GasPro is that securing the supply from a supplier other than the Yearlings could be unprofitable as GasPro could risk purchasing gas at a higher price. GasPro's lack of a profit margin does not constitute a force majeure event that excuses GasPro's nonperformance.

GasPro will assert that the decline in production from the gas well constitutes a force majeure under the contract and excuses the company from performance.

Challenges Natural One's position by developing GasPro's counterargument. Counterargument distinguishes the precedent.

The contract between GasPro and Natural One defines force majeure in terms of a few specific contingencies, and GasPro will assert that, unlike the situations in *Hutton* and *Benson*, the reason for GasPro's inability to perform falls within the specific language of the clause. GasPro is unable to provide Natural One with sufficient raw natural gas because the Yearlings' well production has declined. This decline is a natural occurrence, just like other acts of God, and beyond the control of GasPro. Furthermore, GasPro typically receives its raw natural gas supply from the Yearling well and would have to incur increased costs to secure a suitable replacement to fulfill its obligations under the contract. Moreover, Natural One was aware of GasPro's arrangement with the Yearlings and the company's plan to use the family-owned well as the source of its supply. Flores specifically mentioned the Yearlings to Lombardi during their meeting to sign the contract. Thus, given an unforeseeable and natural decline in gas production and reliance on the Yearlings' supply, GasPro is entitled to terminate its performance under the force majeure clause.

GasPro's arguments will likely fail. GasPro did not specifically identify the Yearlings in the contract with Natural One and thus, assumed the risk that its subcontractor or supplier would fail. In addition, GasPro purportedly inspected the Yearlings' well for readiness and cannot now claim that its performance is excusable for an event that was well within its control to remedy. Although it may have cost GasPro more money, the company can work with other suppliers to complete its obligations under the contract. As the *Benson* court made clear, "A change in cost does not, in itself, excuse performance. . . . Neither is a rise or a collapse in the market in itself a justification, for that is exactly the type of business risk which business contracts made at fixed prices are intended to cover." 1988 U.S. Dist. LEXIS 17581, at *14–15. Therefore, the court will likely find that the force majeure clause does not excuse GasPro's performance.

Challenges the inferences and conclusions raised in GasPro's counter-argument.

ANALOGICAL REASONING WITH DEPTH

EXERCISE 54

SAMPLE ANSWER

Begins with a clear thesis statement that identifies the issue.

The court will likely find that Marisol Martinez ("Martinez") did not abandon the leased premises in a reasonable amount of time after her last complaint to Ready Realty LLC ("Ready") and therefore waived her claim of constructive eviction.

Provides the legal standard and factors to consider in determining whether the tenant vacated in a reasonable amount of time.

When a landlord is guilty of a breach of his duty to his tenant so that the tenant would be justified in vacating the premises, the tenant "is not obliged to vacate immediately, but is entitled to a reasonable time in which to do so." *Auto. Supply Co. v. Scene-in-Action Corp.*, 172 N.E. 35, 38 (Ill. 1930); *Shaker & Assocs., Inc. v. Med. Techs. Grp. Ltd.*, 733 N.E.2d 865, 873 (Ill. App. Ct. 2000). "A tenant who does not vacate within a reasonable time, however, is considered to have waived the landlord's breach." *Shaker & Assocs. Inc.*, 733 N.E.2d at 873. What constitutes a reasonable amount of time "is usually a question of fact, though under the circumstances of a particular case it may become a question of law." *Auto. Supply Co.*, 172 N.E. at 38. When determining the reasonableness of the tenant's delay as a question of law, courts consider factors such as the condition of the premises, the tenant's reliance on the landlord's promises to repair, and the tenant's time taken to locate new premises. *Shaker & Assocs., Inc.*, 733 N.E.2d at 872–73. The tenant has the burden of proving the time taken was reasonable under the circumstances after the landlord's breach of duty. *Auto. Supply Co.*, 172 N.E. at 38.

Provides a clear explanation of the legal standard from precedent. Includes the key facts, holding and reasoning from this case so that the reader can clearly understand how the court applies the test in a real-life case.

In *Automobile Supply*, the court held that the tenant did not vacate the leased premises within a reasonable time after the landlord's breach of its covenant under the lease to furnish heat. 172 N.E. at 38–39. The landlord failed to provide the tenant with heat during ordinary business hours of the winter season. *Id.* at 37. Starting in November 1927, the tenant's office, which was located on the sixth floor of a building, was without heat for two to five hours on several days, and the temperature was below fifty degrees. *Id.* The tenant's staff could not complete their work, do it accurately, or even stay a full work-day at times during November, December, February, March, and

April because of the lack of steam heat in the leased premises. *Id.* A number of employees suffered colds because of the office temperature and were unable to remain at work, causing the tenant loss of production. *Id.*

On February 20, 1928, the tenant notified the landlord that, given the untenantable conditions of the premises, the tenant would terminate and cancel the lease effective April 30 and vacate the premises on that same day. *Id.* On April 30, the tenant moved his business out of the office. *Id.* The tenant made his last complaint to the landlord on April 9. *Id.* at 38. The court concluded that if the tenant had the right on several dates to vacate the premises because of the landlord's breaches, the tenant waived those breaches because each time the tenant complained about the lack of heat, it did not vacate the premises. *Id.* at 38. Vacating the premises within a reasonable time is a requirement for proof of constructive eviction. *Id.* The court found the tenant's delay of two months from his February 20 notice was unreasonable under the circumstances; the tenant should and could have acted much sooner to remove itself from such oppressive conditions and acquire a new office space for its business and staff. *Id.* The court further found that the last complaint was made on April 9, and it could not take judicial notice that the tenant's delay of three weeks before vacating was reasonable, nor was there evidence that could have been submitted to a jury on that issue. *Id.*

Similarly, in *Shaker & Associates,* the court concluded that the tenant failed to abandon the leased premises within a reasonable amount of time of the landlord's breach of its duty to provide adequate heat. 733 N.E.2d at 873. The landlord contended that the tenant, a medical claims review company, had waived any claim of constructive eviction because it remained on the premises for many months after learning that the heating and cooling systems were not functioning properly. *Id.* The court agreed and found that the tenant's purported need for more time to locate specially customized office space did not justify a delay of ten months. *Id.*

In Martinez's abandonment of the leased premises, Ready will maintain that Martinez waived any claim of constructive eviction because she remained on the premises for several months. Like the tenants in *Automobile Supply* and *Shaker & Associates,* Martinez took too long to find a new location and vacate the premises. Martinez's last complaint to Ready was in May, and she did not leave the

[Margin annotation] Provides another case illustration showing how a different set of facts warrant the same conclusion. In this case, the tenant allegedly required customized office space.

Follows with the affirmative argument and an analogy to precedent. Leading analogy serves as a thesis for the argument.

premises and find a new space until October, more than four months later. During that extended period, Ready could have assumed that the company handled the problems raised by Martinez to her satisfaction. She remained silent and did not display any dissatisfaction. Of the factors relied upon by the courts—the condition of the premises, the tenant's reliance on landlord's promises to repair, and the tenant's time taken to locate new premises, *Shaker & Assocs., Inc.*, 733 N.E.2d at 872–73—only the condition and Martinez's delay are relevant considerations, and neither favors Martinez. Martinez complained once of loud noise and once each of meat smells and inadequate parking for her clients. In contrast, the tenant in *Automobile Supply* complained of lack of heat in the office on many occasions during a Chicago winter, making it uncomfortable and sometimes impossible for his staff to work. 172 N.E. at 37–39. In *Automobile Supply* the tenant gave two months' notice of vacation after the February 20 complaint, and the court found that delay unreasonable. *Id.* The court even declined to judicially notice that vacating on April 30 was reasonable after the last complaint on April 9. *Id.* The conditions of which Martinez complained and her delay of four months, both failing to match the circumstances in *Automobile Supply*, suggest a court likely will find she did not vacate in a reasonable time and waived any breach. She should have taken action sooner.

Further, Martinez worked in an office space with a simple, uncomplicated arrangement. To find a comparable location, she merely needed enough square footage to have a yoga studio for instruction, a separate room for massage services, and sufficient parking. Martinez's business did not require special security, equipment or technology to service her clients. She just needed a noise-controlled environment, which she or the landlord could achieve through soundproofing. She did not need customized office space and used her own money to design her current space. Even in *Shaker & Associates,* in which a tenant claimed its business required specially customized office space, the court found a delay of several months to secure a new location and vacate the leased premises unreasonable under the circumstances. Martinez's inaction for several months was also unreasonable.

Martinez, however, will maintain that her situation is different from the tenants' positions in *Automobile Supply* and *Shaker & Associates.* Unlike those tenants, Martinez's delay in vacating the premises was reasonable under the

Next, provides
Martinez's
counterargument.
Identifies specific
factual support
and reasons for
why those facts
support her
argument

circumstances because she had very specific requirements for a suitable space for her yoga studio. She could not risk a second relocation and had to make sure the premises provided not only enough space and a separate room for her massage services and aromatherapy but also the serenity and tranquility required for her yoga sessions. To maximize visibility for her business, she searched for available storefronts in strip centers where a passerby could spot her studio easily and possibly enter to inquire about services. Office space in an enclosed building, which was prevalent throughout the city, would not have served her business and marketing needs.

In addition, Martinez will argue she had to thoroughly examine each location for any business that might undermine her studio setting and often had to pass on centers that housed restaurants. She searched extensively for strip centers that did not have a competing business like a Bikram Hot Yoga Studio and worked to find a center with businesses that provided services from which she could draw new clients such as a nail spa or vegan or vegetarian restaurant. Under these circumstances, Martinez will assert she vacated the premises in a reasonable amount of time and did not delay in finding a suitable location.

Provides an
additional
argument, a
rebuttal
argument, as to
why Martinez did
not leave in a
reasonable
amount of time.

Martinez's arguments will likely fail. Despite the laundry list of requirements for her new location, Martinez could have secured a suitable space in less time. There were plenty of available spaces in the city, but Martinez allowed her detailed list of must-haves to delay her move unreasonably. Martinez claimed that her studio space was untenantable given the loud noise, awful smell of meat, and limited parking space. She even suggested that she lost business due to these problems. Under such circumstances, months of waiting served only to exacerbate her situation, and the unique needs for her studio space fail to justify the delay. If a delay of two months was too long for a tenant who did not have any heat, then a delay of almost five months was too long for the allegedly unbearable conditions that Martinez faced each day. Further, Martinez's business did not require specially customized office space. She simply needed a large space for yoga instruction and a smaller space for a massage room. Given her complaints and the ease in moving a yoga studio, Martinez should have vacated the premises sooner.

Thus, the court will likely conclude that she did not abandon the premises in a reasonable amount of time and waived any claim of constructive eviction.

ANALOGICAL REASONING WITH DEPTH

EXERCISE 56

SAMPLE ANSWER

Starts with the overall conclusion and briefly states why the issue turns out as it does.

Brian and Anita Cooper probably can satisfy the elements of adverse possession for the disputed strip of land inside Ladelle Standish's property. The Coopers' use of the land for a wedding business and then a paintball business satisfies all the elements of adverse possession because for more than twenty years, the Coopers used the Standish land as if it were their own, excluding others and operating their businesses on the land visibly and adversely to Standish's title.

Conclusion statement clearly identifies the legal issue and references the rule.

Sets out the claim's elements in a roadmap paragraph, so the reader understands the claim's scope and content.

To establish adverse possession under the common law of Maine, the claimant must show that the possession was (1) actual, (2) open, (3) visible, (4) notorious, (5) hostile, (6) under a claim of right, (7) continuous, (8) exclusive, and (9) for a period exceeding twenty years. *Striefel v. Charles-Keyt-Leaman P'ship*, 733 A.2d 984, 989 (Me. 1999). Because transfer of land by adverse possession is disfavored by the law, the elements of adverse possession must be "established by clear proof of acts and conduct sufficient to put a person of ordinary prudence, and particularly the true owner, on notice that the land in question is actually, visibly and exclusively held by a claimant in antagonistic purpose. *Weeks v. Krysa*, 955 A.2d 234, 238 (Me. 2008); *Striefel*, 733 A.2d at 988. The presumption is that the occupancy "is in subordination to the true title, and if the possession is claimed to be adverse the acts of the wrong-doer must be strictly construed and the character of the possession clearly shown." *Striefel*, 733 A.2d at 988.

Adds policy considerations that drive Maine courts' analysis of adverse possession issues.

A claim of adverse possession is evaluated in light of the "nature of the land, the uses to which it can be put, its surroundings, and various other circumstances." *Id.* In Maine, recreational use of unposted open fields is considered permissive and cannot ripen into title. *Weeks*, 955 A.2d at 238. Wilderness land is particularly difficult to obtain through adverse possession in Maine. *McMullen v. Dowley*, 418 A. 1147, 1153 (Me. 1980). Standish concedes that the Coopers' use was exclusive, so that element will not be addressed here.

A. Actual

The Coopers' use of the land was "actual" because they entered onto the disputed land and used the land for their business; while their use of the land for a wedding business was unusual on the island, their use was one reasonable and possible use of the land—other businesses existed on the island. Likewise, when the Coopers used the land for a paintball business, they and their customers physically entered onto the land and used it, just as a true owner would.

> Each element has its own self-contained analysis, with a conclusion, rule, explanation of the rule, application of the rule to fact, and conclusion for that element.

"Actual" possession and use requires that an occupant have "immediate occupancy and physical control" of the land. *Striefel*, 733 A.2d at 989 (citing *Black's Law Dictionary* 1163 (6th ed. 1991)). The occupation must be literal and physical, and there must be an ability to control the land together with the intent to exclude other people. *Id.* Adverse possession generally extends only to the land occupied and used, rather than to an entire tract. *Id.* The purpose of this element, therefore, is to give a person of ordinary prudence, and the true owner in particular, notice of the trespass's extent. *Id.* The question of whether a property was "actually" occupied is considered in light of the possible uses for the land and the kind of enjoyment that would be typical of a true owner of that property. *Id.* at 990.

> Explains how a claimant satisfies this element and sets out the broader concerns that drive courts' analysis.

For example, the *Striefel* court found the use was "actual" for purposes of adverse possession when a family used a portion of the property adjacent to their own for walking their dog, gardening, and storage of items including a sailboat. 733 A.2d at 990 & n. 4. The family skated on the land in winter, and the children played on it with neighborhood children in the summer. *Id.* In addition, the family stored wood and building materials and kept a picnic table on the land. *Id.* These uses, the court found, were typical of the kind of residential uses in the neighborhood and were of the "kind and degree" of a property's true owner. *Id.* These uses were therefore sufficient to put the true owner on notice of the extent of the trespass.

> Explains the law with specific illustrations that show the reader how the case was decided. Describes the relevant facts in detail so the reader can fully understand the land's use.

On the other hand, when a claimant's children merely played on an abutting lot, and the claimant cut trees and cleared brush after storms, the use was insufficient to ripen into title. *Weeks*, 955 A.2d at 239. The claimant had paid taxes at one time on the property and some testimony suggested the claimant's garden had encroached onto the disputed property. *Id.* One neighbor even called the

> Sets out two cases that show what does—and does not—satisfy the element. Transitions clearly so the reader can follow the arguments.

claimant to report a trespasser on the disputed property. *Id.* at 237. The court found that these uses were not sufficient to put the true owner on notice of a hostile intent, due to Maine's tradition of permissive recreational use of open fields or woodlands. *Id.* A claimant's use of disputed land must, the court found, "show disregard of the owner's claim entirely" and the claimant's use must be "as though the claimant owned the property." *Id.* (citing *Lyon v. Baptist Sch. of Christian Training*, 804 A.2d 369, 370 (Me. 2002)).

Just as the family in *Striefel* physically entered onto the disputed property and used it for recreational and storage purposes as a true owner would, so did the Coopers enter onto the land and use it as their own, to run two separate businesses as a true owner might. The Coopers' use of the disputed property for a wedding business constitutes "actual" possession, because they entered onto the land, erected a shell-encrusted arch, and controlled access to the land, just as a true owner would. As part of the wedding business, the Coopers maintained the land by mowing and clearing branches after storms, as well as applying bright, white ant-killing powder. They also permitted their tame deer to graze on the property. Mowing and grazing cannot, without more, constitute actual possession. *See, e.g., Webber v. Barker Lumber Co.*, 116 A. 586, 587–88 (Me. 1922) (interpreting adverse possession statute to find the combination of claimants' erecting a partial brush fence on the disputed property to keep their cattle from straying and occasionally cutting timber on that land, and the "unrestricted meandering" of claimants' cattle onto disputed land were insufficient to prove actual possession). However, the maintenance and mowing here were part of a larger business enterprise that involved customers' entry onto the land as well. And, as the *Weeks* court required, the Coopers' use of the land did not take the true owner into account, but was in complete disregard of the true owner's claim. 955 A.2d at 238–39.

The Coopers' use of the land for paintball is a closer case, because the paintball called for less extensive uses of the land, such as the entry onto the land from time to time of paintball players and erection of a tent, while the wedding business called for the entry onto the land of guests and vendors as well as the placement of a prominent shell-encrusted arch, and mowing and applying ant-killing powder. Still, at the time of the paintball business, the Coopers permitted their tame deer to graze on the disputed

---

Sidebar annotations (left margin):

- Makes close comparisons between precedent and the present case, so the reader understands the argument and conclusion.

- Uses all the details of each use involved in the wedding business.

- Uses specific factual details and compares with precedent cases.

Sidebar annotations (right margin):

- Analogizes to precedent cases that have the same outcome predicted here.

- Does not overstate the argument but admits that grazing alone cannot ripen into possession in Maine.

- Selects an analytical structure (here, the wedding and paintball businesses discussed in turn) and uses the structure consistently to avoid reader confusion.

Recalls a theme running through adverse possession—that the adverse use must be akin to that of a true owner.

lot, and the paintball activities also resulted in red paint landing on the trees and ground. These multiple uses are akin to the *Striefel* family's use of the disputed property in that case for a variety of activities. The Coopers' use reflects a disregard for the true owner's title and indicates that the Coopers used the land as if it were their own, as required by *Weeks*.

Includes a specific counter-argument—the best argument against the stated conclusion.

Standish could argue that the Coopers' use of the land would appear, to a reasonably prudent true owner, to be recreational and occasional uses that are permissive and therefore not hostile under Maine law. *See Weeks*, 955 A.2d at 238. As such, these uses would not put Standish on notice of a threat to her title. In *Weeks*, the claimant family's playing and cutting trees on the land was merely occasional and recreational, exactly the sort of use that the court described as permissive within Maine's traditions. *Id.* The Coopers' adverse possession claim is likewise based in part on recreational use, exactly the kind of use that failed to establish adverse possession in *Weeks*. This argument will likely fail, however, because the paintball was not merely for the Coopers' own recreation but was a business enterprise. As such, numerous teams would enter the land and play at various times—the games were not simply for the family's recreation. In addition, the use of land for business enterprises was typical of some true owners' uses, because Islesboro did have businesses such as the café where Anita worked. Repeated weddings and paintball games on a piece of land should put a true owner on notice of a threat to her title.

Counter-argument includes a case analogy and supporting facts; counter-argument is rebutted with specifics.

Each element has its own final conclusion to the analysis.

The Coopers' possession of the disputed property was therefore "actual" for purposes of adverse possession.

B. Open, visible, and notorious

The Coopers' possession will most likely be considered open, visible, and notorious, because the couple did not attempt to hide either of their two businesses and any person could see the weddings or paintball games taking place on the disputed lot. To be open, a possession must be without concealment; to be visible, it must be capable of being seen by someone who views the property; to be notorious, it must be known to someone who might reasonably be expected to communicate the knowledge to an owner maintaining a reasonable degree of supervision over the property. *Striefel*, 733 A.2d at 990. These elements are often considered together, because together they make up

Analyzes each element distinctly, with a clear heading to show the shift to a new topic.

Explains what is required to establish this element.

the requirement that the true owner have actual or constructive knowledge of an adverse use. *Id.*

For example, where adverse claimants' children played openly on the disputed property, and the claimants also gardened and stored a boat on the property, the possession was considered open and visible. *Id.* The claimants did not try to hide their use of the land and passersby were able to view clearly the claimants' recreational and storage activities on the disputed land. *Id.* The use also satisfied the notoriousness element, because the children who were permitted to play on the property could have told a true owner about the claimants' use of the property. *Id.* An encroachment would not satisfy the "visible" element, however, if it were not visible to the naked eye. *Id.* Likewise, hostile uses that are secret or furtive would not satisfy the "open" and "visible" elements of adverse possession. *McMullen,* 418 A.2d at 1153.

The Coopers' use of the land for their wedding business was open, visible, and notorious, because the weddings attracted a large number of people to the property. Just as the logging operation in *McMullen* was deemed open and visible due to the logging equipment and stacked logs on the property, so would the Coopers' shell-encrusted arch and mowed ceremony area be considered open and visible. In addition, the Coopers' tame, collared deer roamed the Standish property, while vendors and potential clients visited frequently. The business was notorious as well because of the national advertising campaign that pictured the Standish property's grassy area and stream.

The paintball business was less visible than the wedding business, because the paintball players dressed in camouflage gear and part of the game involved hiding. The paintball business would still more likely than not be deemed to put a true owner on notice of a hostile use, however, because the game involved firing red paint at different objects and the red paint often fell on different parts of the Standish land. In addition, the use was notorious, because the Coopers used an aggressive marketing campaign on the island, and customers were from the island's community of celebrity residents. Like the children in *Striefel,* who could reasonably have been expected to inform the true owner of the hostile use, so could the paintball customers here have informed Standish of the encroachment because Standish was part of the island's community of celebrities. In addition, the use was visible because the tame, collared deer roamed around the Standish property throughout the time that the business encroached upon the land. So even if a true owner did not see paintball players, she could have seen red paint and collared deer.

Rebuts the counter-argument using specific facts and law.

Standish will likely argue that a paintball business with camouflaged players is not sufficiently open and visible to ripen into title superior to that of a true owner. This argument will likely fail, however, because Maine law does not require that every aspect of the claimant's use be visible, only that enough of the use be visible so that the true owner would be put on notice. *Striefel*, 733 A.2d at 990–91. A reasonably diligent true owner is put on notice of a hostile claim by uses such as logging operations or recreational uses even if every aspect of the use is not visible. *Id*. at 991; *Mullen*, 418 A.2d at 1154. Assuming a true owner did not see any paintball players at all, the true owner could still see the Army surplus tent and hear the noise of people shooting and playing. The Coopers' claim to title by adverse possession is weakest with regard to the paintball use, though, because by its nature, the use was partially hidden. Due to the visible portions of the paintball use, however, the claim will likely be satisfied with regard to this element.

Transitions clearly to counter-argument.

Sets out the counter-argument and then rebuts it, using specific problem facts and details from case.

Admits weaknesses in argument and does not overstate—important in predictive writing mode.

The Coopers will therefore likely satisfy the open, visible, and notorious elements of adverse possession.

Ends with a clear conclusion for these elements.

C. Hostile

The Coopers' use of the Standish land will be considered hostile, because they used the land in multiple ways for their own benefit, without regard for the true owner's title. For an encroachment to be considered hostile, it must be without the true owner's permission. *Striefel*, 733 A.2d at 991. "Hostile" does not refer to ill intent or argument. *Id*. A true owner's express or implied permission negates an adverse possession claim. *Id*. Furthermore, Maine has a tradition of permissive access to wild land, so that wild land is particularly difficult to possess adversely due to the implied consent. *McMullen*, 418 A.2d at 1154. To qualify for the heightened standard for wild lands, however, the land must be truly wild and devoid of features that are not found on wild land such as fences. *Id*. at 1153. If a true owner has a tradition of permissive use, the true owner's

Explains what is required to satisfy the element of hostility.

Addresses the permissive use argument suggested by precedent and problem facts.

373

implied consent may even extend to an entire community, so that adverse possession is particularly difficult to establish. *Falvo v. Pejepscot Indus. Park*, 691 A.2d 1240, 1243 (Me. 1997).

For example, when a company owning a company town permitted residents to use company land surrounding their own land, the court found that hostile intent must be demonstrated by "unusual" acts. *Id*. The family claiming adverse possession had kept the company land surrounding their own land mowed, and they used the company land for a septic tank and drain, as well as a horseshoe pitching area, hen house, and storage shed. *Id*. at 1242. Because the company permitted residents to use the company property surrounding their own, the court held that hostile intent would have to be shown by acts beyond those typical of other residents' permissive uses. *Id*. Otherwise, the court reasoned, the company would not be put on notice of a threat to its title. *Id*. These "unusual" acts, the court explained, could consist of posting the land, building a fence, or giving written notice. *Id*. at 1243.

> Quotes sparingly, and only if the court uses particularly pertinent language.

The celebrity residents of Islesboro, like the company town in *Falvo*, permitted other residents to use the celebrities' land for recreational and grazing purposes. But the Coopers' uses of the land went beyond those uses more typical in the area, and extended to running two businesses. The wedding business in particular would satisfy the court's requirement that the use be "unusual" and beyond typical local permissive uses. The paintball business should also satisfy this standard, because the use was not simply for recreation, but involved groups of people paying to play paintball over months. This business use went beyond other residents' recreational and occasional use of other celebrities' property.

> Distinguishes the permissive use in *Falvo* from the uses in the present case.

> Uses specific facts from the fact pattern to show why the use at hand is not a permissive use.

Moreover, the Standish land would not be considered "wild" and therefore more difficult to adversely possess, as it had features that were inconsistent with wild land. The disputed land contains a rock birdbath, which, like the fence in *McMullen,* is inconsistent with land that is kept wild.

> Notes specific details that remove this case from the "wild lands" doctrine.

Standish could argue that a celebrity owner in Islesboro would not be put on notice of a hostile use when a local resident simply organized paintball games, as that use could be perceived as recreational of the same kind enjoyed permissively by other residents on other celebrities' property. From simply viewing such a game, a true owner had no way to know that the game was in fact a business. Similarly, the Coopers' use of the land for grazing their tame deer was arguably no different from the grazing enjoyed permissively by other residents. Standish has a fairly strong argument on this point, but a court would likely find that the Coopers' systematic use for paintball, the erection of a tent, the business signage, and the repeated gathering of different groups for games would indicate a use beyond the permissive uses of a typical Islesboro resident. In addition, the wedding business extended well beyond a resident's typical permissive use, creating an overall pattern of hostile use.

Thus, the Coopers' use of the property is likely to satisfy the "hostile" element of adverse possession.

D. Under a claim of right

[margin note: Does not dwell on elements that are easily satisfied.]

The Coopers' use of the Standish land was under a claim of right: the Coopers did not occupy the land under any mistake of boundary—they used the disputed property as if they owned it. A claimant uses land under a claim of right if the claimant intends to claim the property as the claimant's own, and not in any recognition of the true owner's title. *Striefel*, 733 A.2d at 991. The Coopers even went so far as to express that they were the "real residents" of Islesboro, such that they should have a superior right to the land. There is no indication in the facts that the Coopers' use of the land was by mistake or in subordination to Standish's title. The Coopers therefore satisfy the "under a claim of right" element of adverse possession.

[margin note: Provides the applicable rule and quickly applies the standard to problem facts, showing element is met.]

E. Continuous for more than twenty years

[margin note: Considers facts not in isolation but within the context in which they take place.]

The Coopers' use of the land will likely be considered continuous. The Coopers' use was partially interrupted when each of their two businesses declined, but these interruptions were within an overall context of constant use akin to that of a true owner, for over twenty years. To establish continuous use, a claimant must show occupancy of the land as a true owner would for over twenty years. *See Striefel*, 733 A.2d at 993. Abandonment of the property interrupts continuous occupation, but absence does not necessarily constitute abandonment. *Clewley v. McTigue Farms, Inc.*, 389 A.2d 849, 851 (Me. 1978). To maintain continuity, the claimant need not be physically present on the land at all times. *Id.* The occupation's continuity is determined in view of possible uses for the land, the land's

[margin note: Provides the rule for continuous use.]

nature, and the reason for any interruption in the claimant's use. *Id.*

Claimants satisfied the continuousness requirement, for example, when absent from the disputed property for eighteen months after the house on the property burned down. *Id.* After the fire, the property was unoccupied except for the claimant's occasional visits to determine where a new house could be built. *Id.* The Supreme Judicial Court affirmed the trial court's finding of continuousness, noting that the adverse claimant need not keep a constant presence on the property. *Id.* Rather, the claimant's continuousness of occupancy is assessed in light of the property's nature, the uses to which it could be put, and the reason for the claimant's absence. *Id.*

Just as the claimant in *Clewley* left the land because of a fire that made residential use at the time impracticable, so did the Coopers leave the land temporarily because of business conditions, which equally rendered the Coopers' occupation of the land impracticable for their business uses. Even when their businesses were not in operation, the Coopers still grazed their tame, collared deer on the Standish property. Although animal grazing alone cannot ripen into adverse possession in Maine, grazing can be considered part of a larger adverse use and as evidence of the claimant's intent. *See, e.g., Webber*, 116 A. at 588 (noting that unrestricted meandering of cattle over neighboring premises does not amount to adverse possession). Thus, the Coopers' use of the land for business purposes was no different from that of a true owner, and the waxing and waning of each business was no different from the business conditions that would have affected a true owner. The Coopers' grazing of tame deer on the Standish property only confirms that the Coopers intended to continue their possession of the land and use it as a true owner would. They used the land from 1987 to 2010, well in excess of the required twenty years.

Standish can argue, on the other hand, that the Coopers left the property for considerable periods of time, in excess of the eighteen total months' absence in *Clewley*. The occupation was interrupted from 1993 to 1998, when the weddings slowed to one every eight weeks or so, and again in 1999, when there was just one wedding all year. In all of 2002 and part of 2003, there was just one paintball game and grazing of deer in 2002. Even when the businesses were doing better, the occupation was sporadic, with paintball and weddings both taking place from time to time

---

Illustrates the rule with factual detail from precedent cases; describes the court's reasoning.

Uses the court's reasoning in Clewley, *in addition to the facts, to argue that the problem facts warrant the same outcome.*

Makes clear shift to counter-argument and uses specific facts to make a strong counter-argument.

Provides counter-argument with specific facts distinguishing present case from precedent.

rather than constantly. The Coopers' occupation arguably was too inconsistent to satisfy the continuousness element.

This argument will likely fail because the Coopers' time away from the disputed land was within a context of constant business use of the land. There is no indication that the Coopers ever altered their position that they were the "real residents" and that they were claiming the land as their own. When the Coopers were absent from the land, their intent to continue using it is evidenced by the continued grazing of their tame deer and the presence of the shell-encrusted arch. In addition, when their use of the land was less intensive due to business conditions, they always returned with a new plan to use the land. The Coopers will therefore probably satisfy the requirement that an adverse possessor's use of the land be continuous for at least twenty years.

> Rebuts the counter-argument using factual details. Places the Coopers' actions within the context of their overall use of the land, as a court might.

In conclusion, the Coopers' use of the disputed Standish land for a period in excess of twenty years will most likely satisfy the elements of adverse possession. The Coopers' wedding and paintball businesses involved physical occupation of the land, with a variety of accompanying uses, such as the application of bright white ant-killing power, the presence of clients, the grazing of deer, and the installation of a shell-encrusted arch and then a tent. These uses satisfy the requirements of adverse possession, because they demonstrate the character of use that a true owner would have, and they put a true owner on at least constructive notice of the hostile claim. The Coopers will most likely be found to have established superior title to the disputed land through adverse possession.

> Sums up the argument with a conclusion that states how the issues will turn out and, briefly, why.

ANALOGICAL REASONING WITH DEPTH

EXERCISE 58

SAMPLE ANSWER*

Napoli's case should be remanded, because language quite similar to the language in Napoli's employment contract (the "Contract") has been construed as a clear waiver of removal. The waiver clause is similar to one the United States Court of Appeals for the Fifth Circuit identified as unambiguously reflecting the defendant's agreement to submit to trial in any court plaintiff chose, and to waive removal. *City of Rose City v. Nutmeg Ins. Co.*, 931 F.2d 13, 15 (5th Cir. 1991). In the *Nutmeg* endorsement, the following language was at issue:

"[W]e, at your request agree to submit to the jurisdiction of any Court of Competent jurisdiction within the United States and will comply with all requirements necessary to give such Court jurisdiction and all matters arising hereunder shall be determined in accordance with the law and practice of such Court . . . [I]n any suit instituted against us upon this contract, we will abide by the final decision of such Court or any Appellate Court in the event of any appeal." *Id.* at 14.

Observing that the defendant could have reserved a right to remove a case to federal court after plaintiff filed suit in state court but failed to do so, the *Nutmeg* court remanded the case to state court. *Id.* at 15. Explicit reference to removal was not required; defendant agreed to resolve disputes with plaintiff in the forum of plaintiff's choosing : "[W]hile the provision does not specifically mention the right of a defendant to remove an action from state to federal court, the language of the clause makes clear that the [plaintiff] shall enjoy the right to choose the forum in which any dispute will be heard." *Id.*

In Napoli's Contract, Carefree's waiver of removal is unambiguous and calls for the same result as in *Nutmeg*:

"Carefree irrevocably (i) agrees that any such suit, action, or legal proceeding may be brought in the courts of such state or the courts of the United States for such state,

---

* This problem is based on the case of *Waters v. Browning-Ferris Indus.*, 252 F.3d 796 (5th Cir. 2001).

(ii) *consents to the jurisdiction of each such court in any such suit, action or legal proceeding* and (iii) waives any objection it may have to the laying of venue in any such suit, action or legal proceeding in any of such courts."

Just as in *Nutmeg*, Carefree's statement that it "irrevocably . . . consents to the jurisdiction of each such court in any suit" leaves no doubt it intended Napoli to have his choice of forum. And, had Carefree wished to preserve any right to remove an action filed against it in state court, it could easily have said so in the contract. *See Nutmeg*, 931 F.2d at 15.

A waiver of removal, however, need not say "removal" on its face to be effective. The *Nutmeg* court was clear the endorsement gave "to [Rose City] . . . the right to select the forum, foreclosing [the insurance company's] right to remove th[e] action to federal court." *Id.* at 16. Although *Nutmeg* involved an insurance company, its reasoning is not limited to the insurer/policyholder context. The court based its reasoning on the plain language of the provision, without resort to principles of contract interpretation. *Id.* (finding that "on its face" the provision was "unambiguous" and plainly gave the plaintiff the right to choose the forum).

Finally, the drafter principle applies in Napoli's favor. The drafter principle is the "principle that ambiguities in contracts of insurance are to be construed against the drafter of the policy." *Rose City*, 931 F.2d at 15. Carefree's contracts were drafted by its lawyers, and clauses such as the one in Napoli's Contract have consistently had the same meaning since *Nutmeg* was decided twenty years ago. Even courts before the decision in *Nutmeg* found waiver of removal based on similar language. *Perini Corp. v. Orion Ins. Co.*, 331 F. Supp. 453, 457 (E.D. Cal. 1971) (remanding pursuant to clause stating submission "to the jurisdiction of any Court of competent jurisdiction").

As the author of the disputed provision, Carefree cannot be permitted to commit to a clause during contract negotiations, and then reject the clause's established meaning when the clause actually is to be applied to Carefree's disadvantage. Carefree is in the same position as was Lloyd's of London in *Perini*, 331 F. Supp. at 455: "If the courts have misconstrued the clause, Lloyd's has had ample opportunity to invoke the ultimate remedy, the drafter's pen. Until the clause is changed, therefore, the parties are entitled to expect that the clause now means

[Annotation: Moves cleanly to application, bringing precedent and the present case facts side by side.]

[Annotation: Begins each paragraph with a strong topic sentence that leaves no doubt as to the paragraph's direction.]

what it has always meant-that "submission" to a state tribunal precludes removal to a federal court." *Id.*

Instead of revising its contracts, Carefree used the same language repeatedly, showing that it purposely selected and remained committed to the language of this clause, all the while knowing its meaning.

> Anticipates counter-argument and refutes it. Makes specific distinctions—not conclusory statements—about how that case is different from this one.

Nor does *McDermott* govern this case. *McDermott Int'l, Inc. v. Lloyds Underwriters*, 944 F.2d 1199 (5th Cir. 1991). In *McDermott*, the court considered the intended roles of a service-of-suit clause and an arbitration clause as to the insured's right to select the forum in which the policy disputes would be decided. *McDermott*, 944 F.2d at 1204. *McDermott* turned on the defendant's foreign citizenship, principles of arbitration, and the Convention on the Recognition and Enforcement of Foreign Arbitral Awards— issues that are absent from Napoli's dispute with Carefree. While the *McDermott* court reiterated the *Nutmeg* holding but chose not to apply it, none of the facts resulting in the *McDermott* decision are present here:

- Foreign defendant: In *McDermott*, the fact that the defendant was foreign made the meaning of the service-of-suit clause ambiguous, in that the service-of-suit clause could have been a mere waiver of personal jurisdiction and not a waiver of removal. *Id.* at 1207. Carefree is a domestic defendant.

- Dueling forum selection clauses: *McDermott* involved both a service-of-suit clause and an arbitration clause, raising the issue of whether both were forum selection clauses, the service-of-suit clause applying to enforcement of arbitration awards and the arbitration clause applying to all disputes arising out of the policy. *Id.* at 1205. The court explained that "the service-of-suit clause does not necessarily apply here because a suit to determine arbitrability is not necessarily a suit for failure to pay a claim." *Id.* at 1207. Only one unambiguous clause is at issue in Napoli's case against Carefree.

- The drafter principle that ambiguities in contracts are to be construed against the drafter: Although Lloyd's agents originally drafted the language of the service-of-suit clause, McDermott chose the clause for its policy, so the language was construed against it. *Id.* at 1207. But here, Carefree has used the same language in its contracts for the past twenty years, and Napoli did not select the clause as one to be included in the Contract, as McDermott did for its policy. The drafter principle should apply against Carefree.

The *McDermott* court acknowledged that the *Nutmeg* court did not have to consider the above factors, and because it was "[f]aced with no alternative meaning for the service-of-suit clause [and] language strongly implying waiver of removal rights . . . the court naturally held that Nutmeg waived its removal rights." *Id.* at 1206. The *McDermott* court in fact reaffirmed the *Nutmeg* reasoning that "where a service of suit clause applies, its probable effect is to waive . . . removal rights." *Id.* at 1204. *McDermott* thus provides no basis for disregarding Carefree's waiver of removal.

The endorsement provision in *Nutmeg* was straightforward, unambiguous, and waived the insurer's right to remove a case from state court once Rose City had brought suit there. *Nutmeg*, 931 F.2d at 15. In the case before this Court, Carefree also unambiguously waived its right to remove a case filed by Napoli in a forum of his choice. Remand of this case is required by Carefree's contract with Napoli. The applicable provision in the Contract reflects both Carefree's agreement that in any dispute with Napoli it would submit to the jurisdiction of any court selected by Napoli and its explicit waiver of the right to removal. Carefree's removal of this case violated its contractual agreement, and the case should be remanded.

ANALOGICAL REASONING WITH DEPTH

EXERCISE 60

SAMPLE ANSWER

Starts with a brief statement of the conclusion with a short statement of why the issue turns out as it does.

Carefree's motion to stay the state court lawsuit while the federal appeal proceeds will probably be denied because there is no irreparable injury if the stay is not granted, the granting of a stay would injure Napoli, and no particular public interest weighs in favor of granting a stay.

Sets out the rule in a succinct, easy-to-understand manner. Makes clear the criteria for a stay.

The requirements for obtaining a stay are (1) whether the movant has made a showing of likelihood of success on the merits, (2) whether the movant has made a showing of irreparable injury if the stay is not granted, (3) whether the granting of the stay would serve the public interest, and (4) whether the granting of the stay would substantially harm the other parties. *Ruiz v. Estelle*, 666 F.2d 854, 856 (5th Cir. 1982). The movant bears the burden of proving entitlement to the extraordinary relief of a stay pending appeal. *Id.*; *Belcher v. Birmingham Trust Nat'l Bank*, 395 F.2d 685, 685 (5th Cir. 1968) (noting that a stay pending appeal is an "extraordinary remedy"). The first requirement, success on the merits, is not addressed here. The remaining requirements are analyzed in their numerical order.

Discusses precedent case, bringing up issues that will be important in the application section and avoiding irrelevant background material.

(A) Irreparable Injury:

Uses headings to make clear the transition from overall discussion to individual element.

Applies law to fact succinctly, starting each paragraph with a strong topic sentence.

Even if the state court lawsuit results in Carefree's paying additional legal fees or duplicating effort, neither is a basis for the extraordinary relief of a stay pending appeal. Monetary damages, without more, are insufficient to constitute irreparable injury. *Wildmon v. Berwick Univ. Pictures*, 983 F.2d 21 (5th Cir. 1992) (denying stay and noting that "[b]y definition, 'irreparable injury' is that for which compensatory damages are unsuitable"). As to litigation costs in particular, the Supreme Court held in reversing a grant of injunction that "[m]ere litigation expense, even substantial and unrecoupable cost, does not constitute irreparable injury." *Renegotiation Bd. v. Bannercroft Clothing Co.*, 415 U.S. 1, 23 (1974).

In *Lightbourn*, the court issued a remand order, and defendants appealed and filed a motion to stay the remand pending appeal. *Lightbourn Equip. Co. v. Perkins Engines,*

Inc., 39 F. Supp. 2d 785, 785–86 (N.D. Tex 1999). The court denied the motion to stay, observing that defendants had presented no reason a stay was necessary and had alleged no resulting harm or prejudice if the remand was allowed to proceed while appeal was pending. *Id.* at 786. The court reasoned that, assuming the remand order was appealable, whether the case was returned to the federal court or remained in the state court, the parties would have the same duties, "to comply with a scheduling order and move forward with the filing of responsive pleadings and discovery." *Id.* That reasoning is equally applicable to Carefree's claims. Because the parties have essentially the same procedural preparations in state or federal court, Carefree's claims about wasted money and effort seem disingenuous at best.

Also, courts are particularly reluctant to grant a stay based on purely financial harms when the harm results from a contract of the movant's own making. The *Wildmon* court lifted a stay pending appeal and vacated an injunction prohibiting distribution and exhibition of a documentary film in a case brought by movants against the film producers for breach of the contract covering the distribution and exhibition of the film. 983 F.2d at 22–23. The movants, who had drafted the contract, were denied all relief in the breach of contract suit. *Id.* at 22. However, in seeking the stay, they made no showing of irreparable injury, and alleged only the harm of liquidated damages— the same relief they had been denied in the contract suit they lost. *Wildmon*, 983 F.2d at 23–24. The court noted the absence of an irreparable injury, adding that "[w]hen parties such as [movants], who have drafted their own agreement, expressly advert to the possibility of a breach and specify the remedy as liquidated monetary damages— with no mention of injunction—injunctive relief is virtually waived. By definition, 'irreparable injury' is that for which compensatory damages are unsuitable, yet compensatory damages is precisely the remedy prescribed by [movants] in [their] contract." *Id.* at 24.

> Points out relevant facts that make this case particularly unlikely to be stayed.

Thus, even if Carefree could show that it would suffer monetary loss if the stay of the state court lawsuit were denied, that loss is not an "irreparable injury" that could justify a stay pending appeal. Just as the court in *Lightbourn* decided the remand should proceed, Napoli's suit should proceed because a scheduling order, discovery, and other routine trial preparation matters would be required in either court. And, even though Carefree is contractually required to pay Napoli's legal fees, this obligation does not amount to the requisite irreparable injury. As in the *Wildmon* case, any financial harm here is of the movant's—here, Carefree's—own making and cannot be the basis for Carefree's allegation of irreparable injury. Carefree's allegation of financial harm is an insufficient basis for a stay pending appeal.

(B) Public interest:

There is no public stake in this private contractual dispute that would justify a stay. Cases in which the courts have recognized that granting a stay would serve the public interest have a decidedly different flavor from this procedural dispute in the context of one man's claim for increased retirement payments.

> States a forthright conclusion while succinctly giving a basis for the conclusion.

The public interest was naturally at stake in cases such as the *Ruiz* Texas prison reform litigation, in which a stay pending appeal was granted. *See, e.g., Ruiz v. Estelle,* 666 F.2d 854 (5th Cir. 1982). The pending appeal of a remand order in a private contractual dispute does not, however, concern the public interest and justify a stay. *See, e.g., McDermott Int'l, Inc. v. Lloyds Underwriters*, Nos. 91-0841, 91-0871, 1991 U.S. Dist. LEXIS 8776, at *5 (E.D. La. June 21, 1991), *remand order vacated*, 944 F.2d 1199 (5th Cir. 1991) (denying motion to stay pending appeal of remand of a contractual matter and noting that "whether or not the stay will serve public interest is a neutral factor in this case"); *Lightbourn Equip.*, 39 F. Supp. 2d at 786 (denying motion to stay appeal of remand of a private contractual matter and finding "no sufficient reason to stay this action").

> Compares and contrasts different cases in which stays were or were not granted.

Thus, the private contract removal dispute at issue here does not concern the public interest and does not justify a stay. The public interest, if any, is in having this dispute decided promptly and without delay.

(C) Prejudice to the other parties:

Napoli is in retirement and would be prejudiced by a delay. Case law supports the principle that "litigants themselves owe a duty not to delay litigation unduly, nor to stretch out the proceeding to its utmost." *Gulf Cent. Pipeline Co. v. Motor Vessel Lake Placid*, 315 F. Supp. 974, 974 (E.D. La. 1970) (denying motion to stay arbitration).

Any unnecessary delay is prejudicial to Napoli and denies him his established right to litigate in the forum of his choice as his contract provides.

Because none of the requirements to obtain a stay of the state court lawsuit pending appeal to the federal appellate court likely will be resolved in Carefree's favor, the stay should be denied. Thus, Napoli's suit in the state court should proceed without further delay.

ANALOGICAL REASONING WITH DEPTH

EXERCISE 62

SAMPLE ANSWER

<table>
<tr>
<td>

Begins with a clear thesis statement that identifies the issue and briefly explains why the outcome turns out as it does.

</td>
<td>

The court will likely find that Errol Isadore ("Isadore") cannot prove the elements of battery under Rhode Island law because Mohamed Noor's ("Noor's") contact with Isadore's seat did not "in its ordinary course" cause Isadore injury.

Rhode Island law defines battery as:

</td>
<td></td>
</tr>
<tr>
<td>

Sets out the overall or umbrella rule for civil battery under Rhode Island law.

</td>
<td>

an act that was intended to cause, and in fact did cause, "an offensive contact with or unconsented touching of or trauma upon the body of another. . . . An intent to injure plaintiff, however, is unnecessary in a situation in which a defendant willfully sets in motion a force that in its ordinary course causes the injury."

</td>
<td></td>
</tr>
<tr>
<td>

Identifies two main ideas at issue in this situation given the case law: (1) unconsented touching and (2) intent to injure. Addresses each concept separately.

</td>
<td>

Picard v. Barry Pontiac-Buick, Inc., 654 A.2d 690, 694 (R.I. 1995) (quoting *Proffitt v. Ricci*, 463 A.2d 514, 517 (R.I. 1983)); *Lee v. Gelineau*, Nos. Civ.A.93-3466, Civ.A.93-3468, 2001 Super. Ct. LEXIS 69 (Super. Ct. June 28, 2001).

1. Nonconsensual Touching

Isadore can show that Noor committed a "touching" of his person under Rhode Island law. A defendant's nonconsensual contact with an "object attached to or identified with plaintiff's body" is sufficient to constitute a battery. *Picard*, 654 A.2d at 694.

</td>
<td>

Note other organizational schemes may work just as well for this problem. Just make sure the response addresses the main issues in a clear manner. Review the analysis structure adopted in the opinions.

</td>
</tr>
<tr>
<td>

Provides case illustrations for when the defendant commits an unlawful touching. The holding in *Picard* supports Isadore's position whereas Noor may try to argue that there was no contact whatsoever similar to the situation in *Gelineau*.

</td>
<td>

In *Picard*, the plaintiff wanted to document suspicious activity that she encountered at two car inspection sites. *Id.* at 691–92. She took a camera to one site and began to take pictures of the defendant as he began to inspect the brakes. *Id.* Although the plaintiff and defendant gave different versions of what happened next, a photograph the plaintiff took showed the defendant facing the camera, standing upright, and pointing his finger at the plaintiff. *Id.* at 692. The defendant then told the plaintiff not to take his picture. *Id.* A witness testified that he saw the defendant reach for the camera and touch it, but he saw no contact between the plaintiff and the defendant. *Id.* The witness also stated he did not see the defendant lift

</td>
<td></td>
</tr>
</table>

the plaintiff. *Id.* The defendant admitted he placed his index finger on the camera but denied grabbing her or touching her body. *Id.* In the plaintiff's suit for battery, the defendant argued that her claim failed because he did not intend to touch or injure her; he intended only to touch her camera. *Id.* at 691, 694.

The court disagreed, finding that even if he intended only to touch her camera, he had committed a battery because his actions were intentional, not accidental or involuntary. *Id.* He admittedly touched "an object attached to or identified with" the plaintiff's body. *Id.* The court reasoned, in accordance with Restatement (Second) Torts § 18, comment c at 31 (1965), that such "[u]npermitted and intentional contacts" were offensive and sufficient to constitute battery. *Id.*

When no contact at all was made between the parties, the court will find no battery was committed. *See Gelineau,* 2001 R.I. Super. LEXIS 69, at *44. The *Gelineau* court found in favor of the defendant because the plaintiff offered no evidence of any contact between himself and the defendant. *Id.*

Leads with the stronger argument for this issue. Provides an analogy to *Picard.* Identifies specific facts supporting Isadore's position.

Isadore will rely on *Picard*, maintaining that like the defendant, Noor touched an object intimately related to the plaintiff's person. Noor grabbed the back of Isadore's seat to provide himself with leverage to stand. At that moment, Isadore was in the seat, and he did not give Noor permission to touch or use his seat for leverage. Moreover, Noor does not claim that he accidentally or involuntarily touched Isadore's seat. To the contrary, Noor apparently plans to use this incident as an indictment of the lack of space between seats on a plane. Noor does not dispute that he grabbed Isadore's seat and released it, causing the seat-back to spring forward. Such unpermitted and intentional contact with Isadore's seat—something so connected with Isadore's body—is actionable as a non-consensual touching of his person. *Picard*, 654 A.2d at 694.

Noor may attempt to argue that like the situation in *Gelineau*, there is no evidence of any contact whatsoever between himself and Isadore and thus, no battery. However, the holding in *Picard* would severely weaken Noor's position. Although Noor did not touch Isadore's physical body directly, he did in fact make contact with Isadore's chair. *Gelineau* is therefore distinguishable on its facts. A plaintiff may base his battery claim on a nonconsensual touching of his person accomplished by the touching of any object so intimately connected to the plaintiff that it may serve as an extension of the plaintiff, such as a chair he is sitting in, a hat on his head, or a paper in his hand. *Picard*, 654 A.2d at 694. Therefore, Noor committed a non-consensual touching of Isadore's person.

2. Intent to Injure or Action in Its Ordinary Course Causes Injury

Although a court will find that Noor did "touch" an object attached to Isadore's person, it will probably hold that Noor's act did not "in its ordinary course" cause Isadore injury. To constitute battery, "[i]t is not necessary that defendant intend to injure plaintiff." *Proffitt v. Ricci*, 463 A.2d 514, 518 (R.I. 1983)); *see also Ghassemieh v. Schafer*, 447 A.2d 84, 88 (Md. Ct. Spec. App. 1982) ("[I]ntent to do harm is not essential to battery. The gist of the action is not hostile intent on the part of the defendant, but the absence of consent to the contact on the plaintiff's part."). Simply stated, "[i]t is enough to set in motion willfully a force that in its ordinary course causes an injury." *Proffitt*, 463 A.2d at 518.

The Rhode Island courts have defined "in its ordinary course." *See, e.g., Hennessey v. Pyne*, 694 A.2d 691, 694 (R.I. 1997). In *Hennessey,* an errant golf ball hit by the defendant struck the plaintiff on her head. *Id.* The defendant was playing on a golf course adjacent to her condominium complex. *Id.* at 693–94. The plaintiff filed suit for battery, arguing that the defendant intentionally hit the golf ball, thus causing "an offensive contact or unconsented touching" required for battery. *Id.* at 696.

The court disagreed with the plaintiff's position, emphasizing that no evidence suggested the defendant intended to cause such contact with the plaintiff or any other person. *Id.* He merely hit a golf ball that happened to "veer slightly left." *Id.* at 694, 696. Furthermore, the court reasoned that, although the defendant's teeing off on the ball willfully set in motion a force, that force did not in its ordinary course cause the plaintiff injury. *Id.* at 696. Had the ball traveled in its ordinary course, one could assume that it would have headed for the fairway rather than the plaintiff's head. *Id.* Therefore, the plaintiff failed to show the requisite intent to cause the offensive contact or a force set in motion by the defendant that in its ordinary course caused injury. *Id.*

Begins to address the next issue—intent to injure.

Provides a clear conclusion for this issue. Then explains the legal standard.

Provides explanations of precedent cases that shed light on phrase "in its ordinary course."

In contrast, the *Proffitt* court concluded the defendant willfully set in motion forces that in their ordinary course cause injury. 463 A.2d at 518. The defendant sat in the driver's seat of his truck while the plaintiff, attempting to execute a search warrant, stood on the running board outside his window. *Id.* at 516. When the defendant started to drive away, the plaintiff attempted to stop him by reaching for the keys in the ignition. *Id.* The defendant accelerated the truck and pushed the plaintiff with his elbow, and the plaintiff fell to the ground and suffered injuries. *Id.* The court commented that either the defendant's act of accelerating his truck with the plaintiff on the running board or sriking the plaintiff with his elbow was the force initiated by the defendant that naturally caused injury. *Id.* at 518.

Noor will maintain he did not intend to injure Isadore and his touching of the seat did not set in motion a force that would in its ordinary course cause injury. As in *Hennessey*, no evidence here suggests that Noor harbored any intention to cause offensive contact with or unconsented touching of anyone. Noor did not know that Isadore held a lidless cup of hot coffee in his hands. Also, Noor did not grab the seat to cause injury to Isadore but needed it as leverage to get up from his seat. Moreover, by using the seatback for leverage, Noor willfully set in motion a force, but that force did not in its ordinary course cause injury, just as the golf ball in *Hennessey* did not cause injury in its ordinary course. Noor admittedly touched and pulled on Isadore's seat and thereby, purposefully put in motion a force (the rebound of the seat). However, that force did not in its ordinary course cause injury to Isadore. In its ordinary course, the rebound would merely push Isadore forward slightly or shake him somewhat, but the force ordinarily would not cause him to suffer injury from spilled hot coffee. This scenario presents a rare occurrence that does not warrant liability for battery.

Isadore will equate his situation to that of the plaintiff in *Proffitt*, and argue that Noor willfully set in motion a force that in its ordinary course would cause injury. Even though Noor claims he did not know specifically that Isadore was drinking coffee at the time, one passenger could easily assume that another was engaged in any number of activities while seated. Injury from spilled coffee, a bruised back, or even a sprained neck could result from the force (pushing of the Isadore's seat) that Noor set in motion. Unlike the situation in *Hennessey*, in which the

[Annotation] Clear thesis for affirmative argument.

[Annotation] Leads with Noor's argument that there was no intent to injure and the force set in motion did not ordinarily result in injury. Analogizes to *Hennessey*.

[Annotation] Provides specific facts and inferences supporting Noor's position.

[Annotation] Next, provides Isadore's counter-argument. Analogizes to *Proffitt*. Identifies specific factual support and reasons for why those facts support his argument.

389

force did not reach its customary destination or take its logical path, the force in this case remained on its ordinary course. When Noor pulled the seat as leverage and released it, the resulting thrust set a chain of events in motion that led to Isadore's coffee spilling in his lap. Such an event or injury is a natural and anticipated consequence of Noor's purposeful force and sufficiently establishes a battery.

Isadore's argument will likely fail. There is no evidence that Noor intended to injure Isadore by pulling on his seat. Noor simply had difficulty getting up and needed some leverage. Although intent to injure Isadore would not be required if Noor willfully had set a force in motion that would cause injury in its ordinary course, the seat-back's rebound would not cause injury in its ordinary course. Movement from the seatback would naturally push Isadore forward but would not typically cause burns from spilled coffee. Thus, a court will probably find that Isadore cannot establish the elements for battery under the law of Rhode Island.

ANALOGICAL REASONING WITH DEPTH

EXERCISE 64

SAMPLE ANSWER

Begins with a clear thesis statement that serves as the conclusion.

Identifies the likely conclusion that the court will reach.

The United States District Court will likely find that Brian Clemens ("Clemens") has standing to challenge the search of the car that he was driving. "A defendant has standing to challenge the admission of evidence only if the defendant's own constitutional rights have been violated." *United States v. Whitehead*, 428 F. Supp. 2d 447, 450 (E.D. Va. 2006). In cases involving searches that allegedly violate the Fourth Amendment, the court must determine "whether the defendant in question had a reasonable expectation of privacy in the area searched. . . ." *United States v. Rusher*, 966 F.2d 868, 873–74 (4th Cir. 1992). More specifically, the court will examine whether the defendant can establish "a possessory interest sufficient to entitle him to a reasonable expectation of privacy in the place searched." *Whitehead*, 428 F. Supp. 2d at 450–51. The defendant bears the burden of proving he had such a reasonable expectation of privacy. *Id.*; *Rusher*, 966 F.2d at 874.

Sets out the test or legal standard for standing to contest a search.

The trial court here is bound by the decisions of the United States Court of Appeals for the Fourth Circuit. The Fourth Circuit has identified certain factors to consider in determining whether a defendant has a reasonable expectation of privacy in property held by another. *Whitehead*, 428 F. Supp. 2d at 451. These factors are "whether that person claims an ownership or possessory interest in the property, and whether he has established a right or taken precautions to exclude other[s] from the property." *Id.* (quoting *Rusher*, 966 F.2d at 875).

Provides specific factors from the 4th Circuit for analysis.

Shows similar guidelines adopted by other circuit courts that assist with the reader's understanding of the law.

Other circuits have adopted similar factors to determine whether a defendant has a reasonable expectation of privacy. For example, the First Circuit examines several factors including ownership, possession, control, historical use of the property searched, ability to regulate access, the totality of the circumstances, the subjective anticipation of privacy, and the objective reasonableness of such expectancy. *United States v. Sanchez*, 943 F.2d 110, 113 (1st Cir. 1991); *Whitehead*, 428 F. Supp. 2d at 451 (listing the factors considered by the First Circuit).

The Tenth Circuit considers whether the defendant had lawful possession of the item searched, thereby giving rise to a legitimate expectation of privacy. *See United States v. Obregon*, 748 F.2d 1371, 1375 (10th Cir. 1984) (holding that defendant had no standing to contest search of aircraft when defendant failed to show he had anything to do with the owner or that he was authorized to use, possess, or fly the aircraft).

In the Fourth Circuit, when contesting a vehicle search and proving standing, the defendant must show he or she had legitimate possession of, continuous access to and unlimited use of the vehicle, and the ability to exclude others from the vehicle. *See Rusher*, 966 F.2d at 874; *Whitehead*, 428 F. Supp. 2d at 451. The provision of regular maintenance on the vehicle also favors a defendant's position on standing. *Whitehead*, 428 F. Supp. 2d at 451.

Provides a clear explanation of the legal standard from precedent. Includes the key facts, holding and reasoning from this case so that the reader can clearly understand how the court applies the test in a real-world scenario.

In *Whitehead*, the federal district court determined that the defendant had standing to challenge the search of his wife's car. 428 F. Supp. 2d at 450. The officers responded to a report of two men fighting. *Id.* at 449. Witnesses told the officers that Whitehead had a gun in a car parked nearby and that he had attempted to retrieve the weapon during the fight. *Id.* The officers located the car, and Officer Mojica asked Whitehead to consent to a search. *Id.* Whitehead told the officer his wife owned the car, and the officer verified her ownership through the vehicle registration. 428 F. Supp. 2d at 449. Whitehead's wife was present at the scene because she had been driving Whitehead in the car at issue because he had no driver's license. *Id.* Mrs. Whitehead initially refused consent for the search but later yielded and gave the officer the car keys. *Id.* The officers discovered marijuana and a firearm. *Id.* Whitehead admitted he had purchased the gun. *Id.* Prior to trial, Whitehead moved to suppress the evidence seized during the search. *Id.*

Leads with the best cases that support the defendant's position that he has standing to contest the search. The position mirrors the author's prediction for this exercise.

Explains the court's reasoning for why these particular facts support a finding of standing.

In ruling Whitehead had standing to contest the search even though he was not the owner, or even the driver, the court concluded that Whitehead had a "possessory interest sufficient to entitle him to a reasonable expectation of privacy" in the car. *Id.* at 450–51. Although not the owner, "he had continuous access to the vehicle, unlimited use of the vehicle, and the ability to exclude others from it." *Id.* at 451. In addition, he provided regular maintenance on the vehicle and money for fuel. *Id.* He kept personal items in the vehicle and used it as his primary mode of transportation. *Id.* Whitehead was married to the owner, and he had the authority to have others drive him places in the vehicle. *Id.* The court considered the totality of the circumstances and concluded the defendant had a reasonable expectation of privacy in the vehicle, which, in turn, gave him standing to challenge the validity of the search. *Id.*

Likewise, in *Rusher*, the Fourth Circuit held James Flannery, one of the defendants and the driver of the vehicle that had been searched, had standing to contest the officer's search given Flannery's legitimate possession of the vehicle. 966 F.2d at 874. A North Carolina state trooper stopped a truck driven by Flannery and occupied as well by David and Sarah Rusher, codefendants. *Id.* at 871. Flannery produced an Arizona driver's license in the name of an alias and an Arizona registration for the truck in another person's name. *Id.* at 872. The trooper asked questions about the truck and their trip. *Id.* Flannery stated the truck belonged to a friend in Arizona and he had borrowed it to deliver welding supplies to friends he had been staying with in North Carolina. *Id.* The trooper gave Flannery a ticket for driving without proper registration and handed back his license. *Id.* After further discussions, the officer eventually asked Flannery for permission to search the truck, and he consented. *Id.* The officer's search uncovered marijuana, hallucinogenic mushrooms, ice, cash, and handguns. *Id.* Flannery and the Rushers were arrested. *Id.* At trial, Flannery moved to suppress the items seized during the officer's search. *Id.*

Even though Flannery did not own the truck he was driving, the Court reasoned he had a reasonable expectation of privacy in the truck because he was its driver and no evidence showed he was illegitimately in possession of it. *Id.* at 874. In addition, Flannery's ownership or possessory interest in the particular seized goods was relevant to determining whether he had a reasonable expectation of privacy. *Id.* Flannery later claimed to own the drugs and firearms that the officer seized. *Id.*

A contrary result was reached in *Sanchez*, in which the First Circuit held that the defendant lacked sufficient expectation of privacy in the car he was driving to challenge its search. *Sanchez*, 943 F.2d at 113–14. A state trooper stopped Sanchez for speeding as the defendant drove along the interstate in Rhode Island. *Id.* at 111. Sanchez claimed he was traveling to the Dartmouth, Massachusetts area to meet some friends. *Id.* The trooper questioned Sanchez about the car and he explained that a friend loaned it to him in New York and that the car

Provides another case example from the Fourth Circuit in which the court determined the defendant had standing. Further illustrates the circumstances under which a defendant has a legitimate expectation of privacy in a searched vehicle. In this case, the defendant was the driver.

Sanchez provides the best fact scenario to which the Commonwealth can analogize. *Carter*, a Fourth Circuit case, has the holding sought by the Commonwealth but the facts are very different. In *Carter*, the defendant lacked standing because he had no idea whose car he was in at the time he was pulled over by the officer. Thus, *Carter* is not the ideal case to illustrate here.

belonged to his friend's girlfriend. *Id.* at 112. The defendant did not know his friend's or the car owner's full name, address, or telephone number. *Id.* The only luggage in the car was a bag in the back. *Id.* Although the trooper claimed the defendant appeared extremely nervous, computer checks on the defendant's license and the car registration revealed nothing suspicious. *Id.* With the defendant's consent, the trooper searched the car. *Id.* The defendant willingly showed the trooper the bag of items stored in the back area. *Id.* at 114. The trooper discovered cocaine hidden behind a rear panel, and arrested Sanchez. *Id.* at 112. He sought to suppress the cocaine on the ground that the trooper's search violated his rights. *Id.*

> Explains the court's reasoning in this case and identifies the various factors it considered for this standing issue.

The court considered this a close case on the issue of standing to contest the search but concluded Sanchez had no legitimate expectation of privacy. 943 F.2d at 113. He had only a casual possession of the car and did not own it. *Id.* at 113–14. Further, no evidence indicated he had used the car on other occasions. *Id.* at 114. In addition, the defendant gained possession of the car from a friend about whom he knew very little—not even his last name. *Id.* The fact that Sanchez was driving alone in the car tipped in his favor, but the factor was offset by his lack of direct authority from the owner to use the car. *Id.* Had the defendant had a closer relationship with the car's owner or a pattern of using the car, the court could have presumed permission to use the car on this excursion. *Id.* In addition to lack of permission, the defendant did not claim any interest in the drugs contained in the car nor did he exhibit an expectation of privacy in the bag stored in the back area. *Id.* Thus, the court reasoned that the "informal and temporary nature of this specific acquisition" along with the lack of an "intimate relationship with the car's owner or a history of regular use" of the car undermined Sanchez's standing to challenge the search. *Id.* The totality of the circumstances failed to establish a legitimate expectation of privacy in the car. *Id.*

> Follows with the affirmative argument that analogizes Clemens's situation to *Whitehead* and then *Rusher*.

Clemens will maintain he had a reasonable expectation of privacy in the Mazda searched by the state troopers. Like the defendant in *Whitehead*, who had access to the vehicle owned by his wife, provided maintenance and money for fuel, and kept personal items in the vehicle, Clemens had access to the car that is owned by his girlfriend's mother, provided money for its maintenance, insurance, and fuel, and filled it and had it washed for his trip to Virginia beach. They have the mother's car because

Kelly's car needs to be repaired before they can drive it, and they have not yet saved enough money for the repairs. Clemens has no car, and Kelly drove him to work when her car was working or let him use her car to drive to work, about once a week. He simply had to ask Kelly to use her car, and she offered her mother's car for his Virginia Beach trip because hers was still inoperable. Further, as the sole driver of the car on the day of the search, Clemens had the authority to prevent others from using it.

Moreover, similarly to the defendants in *Whitehead* and *Rusher*, Clemens legitimately possessed the car. Clemens did not steal the car, and one could presume easily that he had the owner's permission to use it. Kelly borrowed the car from her mother, and Kelly specifically allowed Clemens to use her mother's car to drive to Virginia Beach. Kelly's mother, the car's owner, knows that Kelly lives with Clemens and she presumably would not object to his driving the car. It is also reasonable to assume that Kelly's mother knew Clemens would have access to her car. Even knowing this, she did not place any restrictions on who could drive her car.

Clemens's legitimate possession of the car supports his standing to challenge the search. Also, although not dispositive, the fact that Clemens claimed ownership in some of the seized goods is relevant to determining his expectation of privacy. Just as Flannery acknowledged in *Rusher* that the seized drugs and firearms were his, Clemens admitted to owning the drugs found in the car's console, which supports his possessory interest. Consequently, given the totality of the circumstances, the court will likely find that Clemens had a reasonable expectation of privacy in the car he was driving.

Next, provides the government's counterargument. Identifies specific factual support and reasons for why those facts support its argument.

The government will contend that Clemens did not have a reasonable expectation of privacy or possessory interest in the car to support a finding of standing. First, Clemens did not take any precautions to exclude others from the car and did not have the opportunity to do so. Second, Clemens did not have legitimate possession of the car. Like the defendant in *Sanchez*, who was driving his friend's girlfriend's car and knew neither of their last names, Clemens had only a casual possession of the car belonging to Kelly's mother. Neither Sanchez nor Clemens had direct authority from the owner to use the car at issue, and there was no indication of regular use. Here, there is no evidence that Roberta Peterson ("Peterson"), the car's

Analogizes to *Sanchez* case, in which the First Circuit concludes the defendant did not have standing.

owner, gave Clemens permission to drive her car or that she knew Clemens was using her car. Further, as in *Sanchez*, permission to drive the car cannot be presumed in this case because Clemens's relationship to the car is too attenuated. Unlike the spousal relationship in *Whitehead*, Clemens lacks a sufficiently close relationship with the car's owner to substantiate a possessory interest in the car. His girlfriend's mother owns the car. Clemens and Kelly are not married or even engaged. They have been living together for just two months. Moreover, Clemens admitted that Peterson does not like the idea that Clemens and her daughter live together. The lack of an intimate, or even friendly, relationship between Clemens and the car's owner weighs against Clemens's possessory interest and reasonable expectation of privacy in the car.

Furthermore, unlike the defendant in *Whitehead*, Clemens cannot show such continuous access and unlimited use of the car so as to justify his standing to contest the search. Clemens had only a casual possession of the car and a one-time limited use of it to drive to Virginia Beach. He was not a regular driver of the car and did not have free rein to drive it. At a minimum, he had to ask his girlfriend, Kelly, to borrow the car, and should have asked her mother to use the car. In addition, he did not provide regular maintenance for the car, only limited car insurance and loan contributions and gas for his particular trip. In addition, unlike Flannery's situation in *Rusher*, there is evidence in this case that Clemens illegitimately possessed the car. Although there is no suggestion or indication that Clemens stole the car, Clemens did not have specific permission from the owner to use it. In addition, Clemens was driving the car with a suspended license. He not only lacked explicit permission to drive the car but also could not operate the car legally. Thus, Clemens did not have legitimate possession of the car to support his claim of standing.

To counter the government's position, Clemens will argue that the Fourth Circuit's holding in *Rusher* compels a finding of standing in this case. Flannery, the defendant in *Rusher*, drove the car at issue, gave the officer a driver's license in the name of an alias and improper proof of registration, and had "lost" the license plate so had handmade a cardboard replacement, but Flannery still had standing to contest the search. Here, Clemens was the car's driver and he had a suspended license. As occurred

[margin note:] Also distinguishes the cases relied on by Clemens.

[margin note:] Includes a rebuttal and a distinction from *Sanchez*.

in *Rusher*, any problems with documentation should not undermine the fact that Clemens has standing to challenge the search of the car. Further, at a minimum, Kelly bestowed a possessory interest in the car to Clemens when she allowed him to drive the car to Virginia Beach. Clemens did not receive permission from a stranger or from someone whose last name he did not know. Compared to the defendant in *Sanchez*, Clemens has a closer connection to or nexus with the car's owner, from which a presumption of permission and a legitimate expectation of privacy could be drawn. In addition, Clemens claimed interest in at least some of the drugs discovered in the car. The defendant in *Sanchez* claimed no ownership of the items seized from the car, and he willingly displayed other items to the officers. When asked whether there were other drugs in the car, Clemens merely shrugged his shoulders. He did not show the items to the officers on his own initiative. Unlike the defendant in *Sanchez*, Clemens exhibited an expectation of privacy in the car.

Ends with a concise conclusion.

Therefore, given Clemens's possessory interest and legitimate expectation of privacy in the car, the court will probably find that Clemens has standing to challenge the search.

STATUTORY ANALYSIS FOR SUCCESS

EXERCISE 66

SAMPLE ANSWER

<table>
<tr>
<td>Begins with a clear conclusion sentence predicting the likely outcome of this case.</td>
<td>A court will probably find that Brett Cullen ("Cullen") is not entitled to a charge on mistake of fact as a defense.* Georgia law provides that "[a] person shall not be found guilty of a crime if the act or omission to act constituting the crime was induced by a misapprehension of fact which, if true, would have justified the act or omission." Ga. Code Ann. § 16-3-5 (2011). Generally, however, "ignorance or mistake of fact constitutes a defense to a criminal charge only if it is not superinduced by the fault or negligence of the party doing the wrongful act." *Crawford v. State*, 480 S.E.2d 573, 575 (Ga. 1997). Furthermore, in order for the defense to be available, the belief must be both honest and real. *Clark v. State*, 386 S.E.2d 378, 379 (Ga. Ct. App. 1989).</td>
<td>Starts the law section with the relevant statutory language. Provides the operative rule from the statute.</td>
</tr>
<tr>
<td>Follows with language from relevant cases that expand on the requirement in the statute.</td>
<td></td>
<td></td>
</tr>
<tr>
<td>Includes case example that illustrates the application of the test in a comparable situation.

Shows how the defense is unavailable where incident was superinduced by the defendant's own fault or negligence.</td>
<td>In *Crawford*, the jury convicted the defendant of felony murder for shooting his wife and the defendant claimed the trial court erred in failing to give his requested charge on his mistake of fact defense. 480 S.E.2d at 574–75. The defendant's wife had asked her son and two of his friends to protect her while she moved out of the house. *Id*. at 575. The defendant became angry, shot at the three men, and they fled. *Id*. He then dragged his struggling wife back inside the house. *Id*. The defendant claimed the men had assaulted him in his home and that his stepson had a knife. *Id*. After the men fled, the defendant was unsure whether they had left the premises. *Id*. The defendant closed and locked the front door. *Id*. He then heard a noise in the direction of the family room and turned, pointed his gun, and fired. *Id*. The defendant fired his gun before realizing his wife stood there and had made the noise. *Id*. The defendant purportedly believed he was repelling a renewed attack by his wife's son and mistakenly shot his wife. *Id*.</td>
<td></td>
</tr>
<tr>
<td>Provides the relevant facts from the case.</td>
<td></td>
<td></td>
</tr>
</table>

At his trial for felony murder, the court denied the defendant's request for a charge on the defense of mistake of fact. *Id*. The Supreme Court of Georgia upheld the trial court's decision, finding that any mistake on the defendant's

---

* The facts used in this exercise are based, in large part, on *Hines v. State*, 578 S.E.2d 868 (Ga. 2003).

part "as to the identity of his intended target was solely the result of his own failure to identify the source of the noise before he fired." *Id.* The defendant turned and fired blindly at an unidentified noise in an occupied house. *Id.* He may have been unaware of the exact location of his wife's son but he definitely knew his wife and small child remained in the home. *Id.* The defendant did not attempt to determine at whom he was shooting and, therefore, the shooting of his wife was his own fault or negligence. *Id.* The evidence did not warrant a charge on the defense of mistake of fact. *Id.*

> **Identifies the court's reasoning.**

Cullen's mistaken belief that his cousin, Miller, was a turkey was due to his own fault and negligence. Like the defendant in *Crawford*, the fatality was superinduced by the shooter's own neglect and wrongdoing. Cullen took an unsafe shot under unsafe conditions at a target that he had not positively identified as legal game. Both Cullen's vision and judgment were impaired. Cullen claimed to have heard a turkey gobble and seen it "fan out" but he did not see the entire turkey and the target was at least fifty feet away. Another hunter could have been making the gobbler call using a decoy device or holding a turkey fan decoy. He knew that another group of hunters was also using the hunting grounds. They could have been in the area. Moreover, Cullen's apparent turkey sighting was in very heavy foliage. Cullen could not see clearly through the trees to ascertain whether he was shooting at a turkey, let alone a gobbler or a hen. In addition, since it was growing dark and misty, Cullen could not have been certain that he was shooting at a turkey and not another hunter. He did not have the benefit of daylight to improve his accuracy. Furthermore, Cullen had been drinking alcohol the evening before the trip at his barbeque party and had at least two beers while hunting. Additionally, he set out on the hunting trip after sleeping only about five hours. The alcohol and lack of a full night's sleep more than likely impaired Cullen's cognitive abilities and judgment. Thus, as compared to the situation in *Crawford*, Cullen's predicament presents an even more compelling case where a charge on the mistake of fact defense should be unavailable. Cullen's impatience and eagerness to bag a turkey caused his cousin's death. Hunting may be a dangerous sport but, by taking certain precautions, a hunter can prevent shooting fatalities. Cullen's actions endangered all hunters using the grounds that day. Accordingly, Cullen is not entitled to a mistake of fact defense.

> **Provides the affirmative argument—the likely stronger argument given the facts of this case. Compares Cullen's case to the facts in *Crawford* and argues for the same outcome.**

> **Identifies specific supporting facts for this argument and the legal relevance or significance of those facts. Avoids making conclusory statements.**

Provides the argument for the opposing party, Cullen.

Identifies key ways in which Cullen's situation differs from the defendant's in *Crawford*. Argues that, given these facts, a mistake of fact defense charge is warranted.

On the other hand, Cullen will maintain that he accidentally shot his cousin in the mistaken belief that he was shooting at a turkey. Unlike the defendant in *Crawford* who knew his wife and child were in the house, Cullen did not know his cousin's exact location and had no reason to think that Miller and his family would be near his hunting area. When they arrived at Big Oak, Cullen and Miller discussed their hunting route and plans. Miller indicated that he and his group would be hunting on the far side of the grounds, an area known as the "grove." Cullen and his team planned to hunt in the "timber fields" area. These two areas are roughly a half mile apart. Cullen would have never suspected Miller or his family to be in the "timber fields" area. The defendant in *Crawford* knew his wife and child's exact location within a confined area of their home whereas Cullen believed his cousin was in a location far away from him. Moreover, unlike the defendant in *Crawford* who shot blindly at his wife, Cullen heard a turkey gobble and thought he saw a turkey "fan out." Cullen did not fire blindly; he shot only after first hearing and seeing signs that a turkey was in the foliage. Therefore, he is entitled to his requested charge on mistake of fact as a defense.

Provides a rebuttal argument as to why Cullen's argument is insufficient. Identifies key facts and the relevance of those facts to the argument.

Ends with clear conclusion.

Although Cullen claimed to believe that Miller and his family were on the far side of the grounds, he knew that other hunters could have been in the "timber fields" area. Further, Miller and his group could have changed their minds and moved to an area closer to Cullen's location. Cullen should have taken better precautions to ensure everyone's safety. Similar to the defendant in *Crawford*, Cullen's act of firing merely because he heard a noise in a wooded area potentially occupied and used by other hunters, without any attempt to determine at what or whom he was shooting, was unacceptable. In essence, Cullen admittedly fired blindly through heavy foliage, while it was becoming dark and misty, at an unidentified noise. His conduct mirrors the defendant's actions in *Crawford* exactly. Any mistake on Cullen's part as to the identity of his intended target was solely the result of his own failure to identify the source of the noise accurately before he fired. Thus, Cullen likely cannot avail himself of the mistake of fact defense and should not receive the requested charge.

STATUTORY ANALYSIS FOR SUCCESS

EXERCISE 68

SAMPLE ANSWER

Begins with concise conclusion and reasons for arriving at it by incorporating law.

The State of Florida could bring a charge of battery against the librarian, because the librarian touched an object intimately connected with Mary Seville's person, and the touching could be interpreted as offensive. The applicable Florida statute states that a "[b]attery occurs when a person either actually and intentionally touches or strikes another person against the will of the other." Fla. Stat. § 784.03 (2001). The term "person" includes not just the actual body of the victim, but also objects that are generally regarded as a part of the person. *Clark v. State*, 746 So. 2d 1237, 1239 (Fla. Dist. Ct. App. 1999). With regard to battery, the damage is "in the offense to the dignity involved in the unpermitted and intentional invasion of the inviolability of his person and not in any physical harm done to his body." *Id*. at 1240 (citing the Restatement (2d) of Torts).

Lays out rule of law pertinent to deciding likely outcome of case.

A court affirmed a battery conviction where a defendant stabbed a money bag that a grocery store employee was holding. *Malczewski v. State*, 444 So. 2d 1096, 1099 (Fla. Dist. Ct. App. 1984). The defendant followed the victim to a bank as the victim sought to deposit a money bag from the grocery store. *Id*. The victim did not relinquish the bag, but clutched it to his stomach. *Id*. The defendant stabbed the bag with a knife, but the knife did not touch the victim's person. *Id*. The defendant argued that without any actual touching of the person, the conviction should be reversed. *Id*. The court affirmed the conviction, noting that the term "person" in the statute includes "anything intimately connected with the person." *Id*. The court concluded that because the victim had held the bag against himself to protect against an attack, a stabbing of the bag was contact with something intimately connected with the person and was included within the statute. *Id*.

Lays out case law by first stating court's finding to guide reader and then breaking down holding into its determinative facts.

Similarly, where a defendant crashed his pick-up truck into the victim's pick-up truck, the defendant's battery conviction was likewise affirmed. *Clark*, 746 So. 2d at 1240. The defendant and victim had an altercation concerning materials in the victim's pick-up truck, and then the defendant's vehicle hit the victim's vehicle, spun it around, and pulled off the bumper. *Id*. at 1239. In affirming the conviction, the court emphasized that battery turned not on whether the victim's actual body was disturbed, but on whether the defendant had contacted something "so connected with the body as to be customarily regarded as part of the other's person . . . such as clothing or a cane or, indeed, anything directly grasped by the hand." *Id*. (citing the Restatement (2d) of Torts). The court noted that battery is a harm to personal dignity, and that no injury is required. *Id*. The court went on to note that even if a personal disturbance were required, the victim here suffered such a disturbance by being in a pick-up truck that was struck by another truck at thirty-five miles per hour. *Id*.

On the other hand, where a suspect bumped a police officer's car with his own car after a high-speed chase, the court reversed a battery conviction, holding that the necessary contact with the person did not exist. *Williamson v. State*, 510 So. 2d 335, 338 (Fla. Dist. Ct. App. 1987). The court noted that the officer was not even jostled within the car, and that the car lacked the intimate connection with the person that is necessary for a battery conviction. *Id*.

Just as the defendant in *Malczewski* touched the victim's person by stabbing the money bag he was holding, so did the librarian touch Seville's person by grabbing the book she was holding. The money bag that the victim held was part of his person, because he held it next to himself; the defendant violently stabbed it. Seville held the books in her arms, so the books were in contact with her body and part of those things that she would not expect others to grab. Even though the librarian did not touch Seville's body, the *Clark* court emphasized that no contact to the body is necessary. *Clark*, 746 So. 2d at 1240. Given that the crime of battery is concerned with the dignity and inviolability of the person, the librarian's humiliating attitude and the public nature of the incident increase the likelihood that the incident would be considered a battery. Seville was embarrassed in front of friends and the community, and the librarian had no right to take any of the steps that she did since she admitted that the rule was not the library's but her own. Therefore, the librarian contacted an object associated with Seville's person in a manner that was humiliating and interfered with Seville's dignity. The librarian can therefore be charged with battery.

The librarian could argue that even though contact with a book held in a person's hand might amount to

---

Margin annotations:

Provides further precedent to show how the law has been applied to similar facts on more than one occasion.

Sets out more precedential support with a contrary finding to provide reader with case law to distinguish or analogize with.

Analogizes to precedent case.

Emphasizes the law that was used in precedent case to determine outcome.

Offers a counter-argument that could be made with the law and facts given. Also does this by tying in precedent case with similar facts. However, quickly diminishes weight of counter-argument by distinguishing key facts from precedent case.

battery, here, the book sat on top of a stack of books, such that the contact was further attenuated to the point that no battery occurred. As in *Williamson*, the contact was arguably with an object that was not intimately associated with the victim. And, as the *Williamson* court noted in that case, here, there was no physical disturbance of the person. This argument will likely fail. In *Williamson*, the court did not note any dignitary harm, which is a pivotal question where battery is concerned. *Williamson*, 510 So. 2d at 338. The contact in that case was not noted as offensive. In Seville's case, on the other hand, the contact with the book on the stack came with an insulting lecture, all designed to humiliate Seville.

Provides clear and concise outcome once again to hammer in overall argument of analysis.

The librarian therefore can be charged with battery of Seville.

STATUTORY ANALYSIS FOR SUCCESS

EXERCISE 70

SAMPLE ANSWER

The Alabama court will probably find that Joshua Mantegna ("Joshua") has been a bona fide resident of the state for six months before he filed for divorce, and in turn, that the court has jurisdiction over the proceeding. Alabama law provides that, in a divorce proceeding, "[w]hen the defendant is a nonresident, the other party to the marriage must have been a bona fide resident of th[e] state for six months next before the filing of the [divorce] complaint[.]" Ala. Code § 30-2-5 (LexisNexis 2011). If the residency requirements are not met, the trial court does not have jurisdiction over the proceedings. *Fuller v. Fuller*, 991 So. 2d 285, 290 (Ala. Civ. App. 2008). For purposes of this rule, "residence is the same thing as domicile" and "[d]omicile is defined as residence at a particular place accompanied by an intention to stay there permanently or for an indefinite length of time." *Id.* Furthermore, a domicile once acquired continues until a new one is established. *Id.* Essentially, a change of domicile is shown by both an act and an intention, which consists of "'physical presence in the new domicile and the requisite intent to remain there for an indefinite length of time.'" *Id.* (quoting *Nora v. Nora*, 494 So. 2d 16, 18 (Ala. 1986)). Notably, the person's intention is usually the controlling consideration. *Id.* Moreover, if a person lives at a particular place, there is a presumption that such place is his domicile. *Id.* This presumption, however, may be rebutted by facts showing that the contrary is actually true. *Id.*

In *Fuller*, in November 2006, the husband sued his wife for divorce in an Alabama trial court and the wife did not file an answer or otherwise respond. *Id.* at 286. When the court entered a default judgment against the wife, she filed a motion to set aside the order. *Id.* at 287. In particular, the wife argued, among other things, that the court lacked proper jurisdiction over the case since she and her husband were nonresidents of the state. *Id.* at 289. The wife was a resident of Mississippi. *Id.* Further, the evidence revealed that the husband had renewed his Mississippi driver's license and vehicle tag and that he claimed to be a Mississippi resident in order to do so. *Id.* In addition, the husband had maintained his Mississippi driver's license since 2001 and had only applied for his Alabama license in November of 2006, just days before he filed the divorce action. *Id*. The husband also admitted that he stayed in Alabama for at least fifteen days from January 2006 to November 2006. *Id*. He could not remember whether he had stayed in Alabama more than twenty days during that time. *Id*. Lastly, the wife and her mother testified that both the wife and her husband had lived in Mississippi at the mother's home until August 2006. *Id*.

Identifies the court's holding and reasoning.	Based on the evidence, the court determined that the wife made a meritorious showing that neither party was an Alabama resident when the complaint was filed. *Id*. at 290. There was sufficient evidence to show that the husband was a nonresident six months before the filing, namely, the husband's out-of-state license and tags and the very limited time he spent in Alabama. *Id*. Although not explicitly stated by the court, it reasoned that, given his conduct or lack thereof, the husband had not shown the requisite intent to remain in Alabama for an indefinite length of time. *See id*.

Identifies the court's holding and reasoning.

Based on the evidence, the court determined that the wife made a meritorious showing that neither party was an Alabama resident when the complaint was filed. *Id*. at 290. There was sufficient evidence to show that the husband was a nonresident six months before the filing, namely, the husband's out-of-state license and tags and the very limited time he spent in Alabama. *Id*. Although not explicitly stated by the court, it reasoned that, given his conduct or lack thereof, the husband had not shown the requisite intent to remain in Alabama for an indefinite length of time. *See id*.

Notice the legal standard or test applied in this precedent case and provided in the law section above.

Provides the affirmative argument—the likely stronger argument given the facts of this case. Distinguishes Joshua's situation from the facts in *Fuller* and argues for the opposite outcome.

In this case, Joshua will maintain that he was a bona fide resident of Alabama for six months before he filed his complaint (namely, from April to October). Unlike the husband in *Fuller*, Joshua not only had a physical presence in Alabama but also displayed a clear intention to remain in Alabama permanently or for an indefinite time. Joshua is in his third year at the University of Alabama School of Law in Tuscaloosa, Alabama and has an apartment in the city. He moved to Tuscaloosa about two and one-half years ago to start school and, since his second year of law school, made significant efforts to remain in Alabama. Since starting law school, Joshua has kept all his household furniture and personal effects in his apartment in Alabama. All of his paperwork at the law school indicates that his permanent address is his apartment in Alabama. Furthermore, during his second year of law school, Joshua submitted a change of address form with the United States Postal Service, placing his new address at his apartment in Tuscaloosa. Further, this past April, Joshua filed both his federal and state income taxes (married filing separately) in Alabama and again provided his apartment address in Tuscaloosa as his place of residence and mailing address. Additionally, he opened and maintains both a checking and money market account at the Alabama Credit Union. Moreover, for the past two and

Identifies key ways in which Joshua's situation differs from the husband's case in *Fuller*. Argues that, given these facts, jurisdiction has been established here.

one-half years, Joshua has spent all of his holidays, except for one Thanksgiving, in Alabama. These facts all indicate that Joshua intended to remain in Alabama and change his domicile accordingly.

In addition to these activities, Joshua made several strides to obtain permanent employment in Alabama. In his second year of law school, he applied for the Alabama state bar exam and paid a down payment for a bar study course for the Alabama bar exam. Both of these decisions show Joshua's significant commitment to the state and his willingness to make a financial investment in his future in Alabama. Furthermore, since his second year of law school, Joshua has applied for numerous positions in Alabama with law firms, public interest organizations, and judges. He focused mainly on positions in Alabama and continued his search during his third year of law school. Joshua's resume provides his apartment address for his contact information. Lastly, in August of his third year of law school, Joshua contacted a real estate agent to discuss properties for purchase in the Tuscaloosa area. He has already viewed a number of listings on the agent's website and, once he receives an offer of permanent employment, Joshua plans to purchase a home in Alabama. Thus, unlike the husband in *Fuller*, Joshua's conduct six months before the filing date indicates that he intended to abandon his domicile in Maryland and acquire a new domicile in Alabama.

Provides the argument for the opposing party, Joshua's wife, Alexis.

On the other hand, Joshua's wife, Alexis, will argue that, just like the husband in *Fuller*, Joshua showed little intention to remain in Alabama. In fact, Joshua's temporary residence in Alabama simply served his needs for law school study and did not rise to the level of a change in domicile. Joshua applied to several law schools but received an acceptance letter and substantial scholarship to attend law school at the University of Alabama. And, given the intensity of needed study, Joshua made plans to spend most of his time close to the school and its resources, such as the library and computer lab. However, Joshua's limited contact with Maryland was not a statement of his intent to change domicile but rather was a practical and strategic decision to best help him perform well in law school. His domicile remained in Maryland. He owned a house with his wife in Baltimore, Maryland and, while he worked in Washington, D.C., he lived at his Maryland home. These facts show that his domicile remained in Maryland.

Identifies specific evidence that shows Joshua lacked the intent to change his domicile to Alabama. Note that Alexis cannot dispute Joshua's physical presence in Alabama. Her argument will focus on his intent to remain there.

Further, even though Joshua temporarily resided in Alabama, he did not own real property in Alabama, never acquired an Alabama driver's license or license tags, and never registered to vote in Alabama. He maintained his license and registration tags in Maryland. Moreover, he voted in the past September and November elections, by absentee ballot, in Maryland. Further, Joshua has maintained a joint checking and savings account with his wife at the Harbor Bank of Maryland. Joshua has not expressed a sufficient intent to remain in Alabama permanently or for an indefinite period of time. Therefore, Joshua's domicile in Maryland at the start of their marriage continued to be his domicile when he filed for divorce. He had not effectively changed his domicile to Alabama and, thus, neither party was a bona fide Alabama resident when the complaint was filed. In turn, the Alabama court lacks jurisdiction over the divorce case.

Alexis's position will likely fail. Joshua has shown both the requisite act and intent to remain in Alabama. Joshua may still have an out-of-state license and tags, but he has a physical presence and plans to stay in Alabama. Joshua moved to Alabama to start law school and, although his initial move may have been for study, he eventually decided to make Alabama his home. Joshua's residence in Alabama before he filed the complaint creates the presumption that his domicile had changed. At no time did he ship his personal belongings back to Maryland. Rather, he applied for the Alabama state bar examination, interviewed for legal positions in Alabama, and began discussions with a local realtor. When he went to Washington, D.C. to intern briefly for a judge during the summer after his second year of law school, he returned to Alabama immediately once the internship ended. He spent only seven weeks in Washington, D.C. (not Maryland) to gain legal experience.

> Provides a rebuttal argument as to why Alexis's argument is insufficient. Challenges the arguments raised in the counter-argument and identifies key facts and the relevance of those facts to the argument.

Moreover, Joshua's Alabama driver's license, tags, and voter registration do not serve to rebut the presumption of his changed domicile to Alabama. At most, these items only show Joshua's absentmindedness or delay in notifying various authorities of his changed residence and decision to remain in Alabama. Such oversight could have been committed by anyone and does not necessarily equate to intent to be a Maryland resident. Furthermore, Joshua is not scheduled to renew his license or tags until November, a month after the filing date, and he plans to apply for an Alabama license and registration at that time. Joshua has demonstrated that, at the time the complaint for divorce was filed, he intended to remain in Alabama permanently or for an indefinite period of time.

> Restates the legal standard here in the conclusion sentence.

Therefore, given his physical presence in Alabama and clear intention to remain in Alabama for an indefinite length of time, the court will likely find that Joshua is a bona fide resident of Alabama, which gives the court jurisdiction over the parties' divorce proceeding.

> Ends with clear conclusion.

STATUTORY ANALYSIS FOR SUCCESS

EXERCISE 72

SAMPLE ANSWER

A court will probably find that Stellar Meats Company ("Stellar") did not breach the implied covenant of good faith and fair dealing in its contract with Matsui's Meat Market ("MMM"). Colorado law provides that "[e]very contract or duty . . . imposes an obligation of good faith in its performance and enforcement." Colo. Rev. Stat. § 4-1-304 (2011); *Amoco Oil Co. v. Ervin*, 908 P.2d 493, 498 (Colo. 1995).* This statutory language creates a duty or an implied covenant of good faith and fair dealing when one party retains discretionary authority to determine certain open terms of a contract, such as quantity, price, or time. *Amoco Oil Co.*, 908 P.2d at 498-99. "The covenant may be relied upon only when the manner of performance under a specific contract term allows for discretion on the part of either party." *Id.* at 498. "Good faith performance of a contract involves 'faithfulness to an agreed common purpose and consistency with the justified expectations of the other party.'" *Id.* (quoting *Wells Fargo Realty Advisors Funding, Inc. v. Uioli, Inc.*, 872 P.2d 1359, 1363 (Colo. App. 1994)). Notwithstanding this "justified or reasonable expectations doctrine," the covenant of good faith and fair dealing will not contradict the terms or conditions for which a party has bargained. *Id.* Further, "[w]hether a party acted in good faith is a question of fact which must be determined on a case by case basis." *Id.* at 499. In determining if a party has breached the covenant, the court will examine whether the disputing party would have signed the contract had it known about the term at issue. *Id.*

In *Amoco Oil Co.*, Amoco, a nationwide manufacturer of petroleum products, sold its products to Amoco brand retail service station dealers located throughout Colorado, who in turn resold the same products to the public. *Id.* at 495. Amoco entered into lease and supply agreements with these independent dealers that provided for monthly rental payments for the service station facilities and real property. *Id.* The agreements had terms of one to three

---

* The corresponding provision in the Uniform Commercial Code is U.C.C. § 1-304 (2011).

years and included specific dollar amounts for rent but gave Amoco discretion to modify station rentals, among other things. *Id.* at 495, 497. Under these agreements, Amoco internally calculated the amount of rent it could collect from each dealer for its service station. *Id.* Amoco used a valuation program that considered capital improvements, average maintenance cost, taxes, and service bay charges to calculate the rent for a particular location. *Id.* at 496. Amoco also applied a uniform charge for each automotive service bay despite its inclusion in the capital improvements portion of rent calculations. *Id.* The dealers argued that Amoco's valuation program for the internal calculation of rents resulted in redundant service bay charges—double charging—and violated the implied covenant of good faith and fair dealing. *Id.* at 497.

Identifies the court's holding and reasoning.

Notes the legal standard or test derived from this precedent case.

The court agreed and determined that Amoco breached the covenant. *Id.* at 499. Since Amoco retained discretion to modify the monthly rental amounts, the company had a duty of good faith and fair dealing. *Id.* By duplicating the charge for service bays, Amoco did not perform the contract in accordance with the dealers' reasonable expectations. *Id.* Further, Amoco was aware of the double charging and never disclosed the implications of its valuation program until years later. *Id.* "The dealers were justified in expecting that, in determining the appropriate rent, Amoco would not charge double for any one element of the calculation." *Id.* Presumably, the dealers would not have signed the agreements had they known Amoco would charge a duplicate amount for the service bays. *Id.* Therefore, by double charging the dealers, Amoco breached the covenant of good faith and fair dealing. *Id.*

Provides the affirmative argument—the likely stronger argument given the facts of this case. Distinguishes Stellar's situation from the facts in *Amoco Oil Co.* and argues for the opposite outcome.

Stellar, however, did not breach the covenant of good faith and fair dealing given that the company performed in accordance with a purchaser's reasonable expectations. Under the contract, Stellar retained the discretion to change the sales price for turkey products at the start of each calendar quarter. Having retained this power or discretion to set an open term in the contract, Stellar had a duty to act in good faith and the company's actions complied with this requirement fully. Unlike the plaintiffs in *Amoco Oil Co.*, MMM and Jiro Matsui ("Matsui") cannot reasonably claim that they would not have signed the contract with Stellar had they known the exact amount of the price increase for fresh turkey products. Stellar did not calculate the price of its products under the agreement using a valuation program that would apply double charges

Identifies specific supporting facts for this argument and the legal relevance or significance of those facts. Avoids making conclusory statements.

Identifies key ways in which Stellar's situation differs from the defendant's in *Amoco Oil Co.* Argues that on these facts the covenant has not been breached here.

or other questionable procedures. Rather, the company's new price, although higher, was based on sound economic principles considering the market supply and demand. Given the recent outbreak of "mad cow" disease, the demand for turkey products increased dramatically. Naturally, Stellar could benefit from its unique position as a seller of high-quality meats and increase its wholesale price for turkey products, thereby, remaining a leader in a competitive marketplace. Further, MMM and Matsui should have expected such a price increase given the national news about "mad cow," the increase in product demand, and the few manufacturers of turkey meat products located in the Colorado-area. There were no surprises here. Stellar did not act inappropriately or take advantage of MMM. Thus, Stellar did not breach the covenant.

Provides the argument for the opposing party, MMM.

On the other hand, MMM will maintain that Stellar's performance under the agreement violated the covenant of good faith and fair dealing. In particular, MMM will argue that the new price for turkey meat products far exceeded the company's original price by over fifty percent. Further, the new price was higher than the wholesale price offered by Stellar's competitors. Similar to the disputing party in *Amoco Oil Co.*, MMM and Matsui would not have signed the sales agreement with Stellar had they known Stellar would charge such a high price for its fresh turkey meat products. Stellar retained discretion to modify the sales price each quarter and MMM relied upon the good faith of Stellar in setting the price term. Stellar acted in bad faith by taking advantage of a terrible epidemic that was sweeping the country. Given the market study conducted by its research team, Stellar was obviously aware of the rates of its competitors and the challenges that retailers and restaurants faced given the outbreak. Rather than gouging its loyal customers, Stellar should have set terms that were reasonable and consistent with MMM's justified expectations.

Provides a rebuttal argument as to why MMM's argument is insufficient. Identifies key facts and the relevance of those facts to the argument.

MMM's position will likely fail. MMM may not agree or be happy with Stellar's price increase given the circumstances, but MMM cannot identify any way in which Stellar acted in bad faith. Stellar based its decision on sound economic principles and evaluated what price the market could stand. Furthermore, Matsui would have signed the contract had he known about the new term given the many other intangible benefits provided to MMM under the contract. Stellar is the only producer and manufacturer of turkey products in Colorado and fits well with MMM's commitment to use locally grown products. In addition, given Stellar's close location to MMM (only forty-five miles), MMM does not have to pay egregious shipping costs for products and can even drive to Stellar's manufacturing plant in Longmont for last minute purchases. MMM may be able to obtain a lower price for turkey products from one of Stellar's competitors, but MMM also would have to pay shipping costs and forego the convenient delivery terms and pick-up procedures with Stellar. Thus, the record shows that any expectation by Matsui or MMM that, in determining the appropriate price, Stellar would not consider the current market conditions, supply and demand, its competitor's prices, and adjust its price accordingly (even if it results in an increase) was unreasonable.

Ends with clear conclusion.

Therefore, Stellar likely did not breach the covenant of fair dealing and good faith when the company increased the price for its fresh turkey product under the agreement with MMM.

STATUTORY ANALYSIS FOR SUCCESS

EXERCISE 74

SAMPLE ANSWER

Begins with a clear conclusion sentence predicting the likely outcome of this case.

After introducing the statutory section, provides the relevant statutory language. Includes the operative rule from the statute and then provides the legal standard from the regulation that serves to interpret or expand the understanding of the statutory provision.

Author must synthesize and use the substantiation requirements under both the treasury regulations and the temporary treasury regulations.

The court will probably conclude that, except for his hotel expense, Randy Valladolid ("Valladolid") failed to substantiate the remaining costs he claimed as travel expense deductions with "adequate records" as required under the law. Section 274(d) of the United States Internal Revenue Code "imposes substantiation requirements upon the deductibility of expenses incurred for travel aware from home in pursuit of a trade or business." *Gardner v. Comm'r*, 46 T.C.M. (CCH) 1283, 1983 Tax Ct. Memo LEXIS 245, at *13 (T.C. Sept. 1, 1983); I.R.C. § 274(d) (2011). Under Section 274(d), no deduction is allowed under Section 162 (business expenses) for any travel expense "unless the taxpayer substantiates by *adequate records* or by sufficient *evidence corroborating* the taxpayer's own statement (A) the amount of such expense or other item, (B) the time and place of the travel . . . (C) the business purpose of the expense or other item. . . ." I.R.C. § 274(d)(4) (emphasis added). Travel expenses include meals and lodging while away from home. *Id.* § 274(d)(1).

To substantiate a deduction by adequate records, a taxpayer must maintain an account book, diary, statement of expense, or similar record and such document must be "prepared contemporaneously with the expenditure and documentary evidence, such as receipts or paid bills." *Gardner*, 1983 Tax Ct. Memo LEXIS 245, at *14; Treas. Reg. § 1.274-5T(c)(2) (2011). Furthermore, these records must be sufficient to establish each element of the expenditure or use—amount, time, place, and business purpose. Treas. Reg. § 1.274-5(c)(2)(iii)(B) (2011); *Gardner*, 1983 Tax Ct. Memo LEXIS 245, at *13; *Wilson v. Comm'r*, 82 T.C.M. (CCH) 899, 2001 Tax Ct. Memo LEXIS 339, at *17 (T.C. Nov. 14, 2001). "In enacting section 274(d), the intent of Congress was to 'insure that no deduction is allowed solely on the basis of . . . [a taxpayer's] own unsupported, self-serving testimony.'" *Gardner*, 1983 Tax Ct. Memo LEXIS 245, at *15 (quoting S. Rep. No. 1881, 1962 IRB LEXIS 1203, at *93 (1962)).

The Treasury Regulations do provide a limited exception for lost records. Treas. Reg. § 1.274-5T(c)(5). Where the taxpayer can show that his failure to produce adequate records is due to the loss of such records "through circumstances beyond the taxpayer's control, such as destruction by fire, flood, or other casualty," the taxpayer can reconstruct his expenditures to substantiate a deduction. *Id.*

In *Wilson*, the court determined that the taxpayer did not satisfy the substantiation requirements under Section 274(d). 2001 Tax Ct. Memo LEXIS 339, at *16. The taxpayer worked on several constructions projects throughout California and claimed his travel expenses to those sites, including mileage for his vehicle, occasional overnight stays in motels, and meals on his tax return. *Id.* at *3-8. The Commissioner disallowed the taxpayer's deductions, in part, given the lack of substantiation. *Id.* at *9. The court agreed with the Commissioner's decision. *Id.* at *16. The taxpayer did not produce any records for his travels and did not maintain a log for mileage deductions claims. *Id.* at *17. Furthermore, he did not offer any statement of expense or receipts for his trips. *Id.* The taxpayer's uncorroborated testimony as to his claimed travel expenses failed to meet the strict substantiation requirements under the Code. *Id.* In addition, the taxpayer did not satisfy the limited exception for lost records since he did not present any evidence as to how the records were in fact lost or that the loss was due to "circumstances beyond" his control. *Id.* at *18 (quoting Treas. Reg. § 1.274-5T(c)(5)).

On the other hand, in *Gardner*, the court concluded that the taxpayer substantiated by sufficient evidence part of her business travel expenditures. 1983 Tax Ct. Memo LEXIS 245, at *16. The taxpayer, a university professor of education, claimed deductions for an interterm taken at an out-of-state university. *Id.* at *6. The interterm consisted of a course on Mexico and a trip to the country. *Id.* The taxpayer listed, among other things, the registration fee as a business deduction. *Id.* She testified that she paid $594 to attend the course. *Id.* at *16. She also produced a receipt acknowledging both her payment of that amount and her attendance at the interterm. *Id.* However, she only produced checks payable to the school for $585. *Id.* Given that the Commissioner conceded the business purpose of the expense, *see id.* at *17, the court held that the taxpayer was entitled to a deduction for the substantiated registration fee of $585. *Id.*

Provides a clear explanation of the legal standard from precedent. Includes the key facts, holding, and reasoning from this case so that the reader can clearly understand how the court applies the test in a real-world scenario.

Presents affirmative argument (stronger argument) that Valladolid did not sufficiently substantiate all his expenditures.

With the exception of the hotel expense, Valladolid has failed to corroborate his other expenses. As done by the taxpayer in *Wilson*, Valladolid did not substantiate all his business travel expenditures with adequate records. He did not maintain a log or offer any statement of expense or receipts (except for the hotel bill). He apparently paid cash for meals but did not submit any receipts. As for his cab fare, he produced a couple of questionable receipts that included notations all in the same handwriting. Additionally, the cab receipts did not show the place of purchase, as they did not provide the company's address. Yellow Cab is a popular cab company that is located in many areas. Thus, his documentation does not sufficiently establish the place of the expenditure.

In addition, Valladolid paid the conference fee with a money order and somehow lost or misplaced the carbon copy. Without the receipt or a confirmation from the conference organizer, he cannot prove that he paid the fee and that the organization received it. Further, like the taxpayer in *Wilson*, Valladolid is not entitled to substantiate his expenses by reconstructing his payments since he did not offer a legitimate excuse for the lost records. He simply indicated that he could not locate the duplicate money order. He did not claim that it was lost in a fire or some other natural disaster. Had Valladolid paid the registration fee with a check or cashier's check, he could have contacted his bank to request documents to verify the payment. Moreover, he could have contacted the conference organizer to obtain a payment confirmation document. However, Valladolid did not take any of these simple steps to prove his expenditures. His uncorroborated account of his travel to Dallas for the conference will not satisfy the strict substantiation requirements of Section 274(d).

Valladolid will attempt to compare his situation to the taxpayer in *Gardner* and argue that he has met the substantiation requirements for all his expenses. Similar to the taxpayer in *Gardner*, Valladolid submitted evidence of his business travel expenses. At trial, he testified that he attended the Annual Collective Artists' Business Conference in Dallas, Texas for three days (Wednesday to Friday). He returned to New Mexico on Saturday. During his stay in Dallas, he incurred a number of costs for meals and transportation. Valladolid estimated his food expenses at a total of $117.00. He also emphasized that he traveled only by taxicabs and public buses.

Follows with counter-argument in support of Valladolid's position.

He submitted cab receipts totaling $55.00. He also produced a copy of the program for the conference, detailing each day of the conference and the content for the workshop sessions. In addition, he submitted a copy of his hotel bill. Unlike the taxpayer in *Wilson* who failed to produce any records, Valladolid offered far more than uncorroborated testimony.

Valladolid's arguments likely will fail. Except for the hotel bill, Valladolid did very little to confirm any payments made for this business travel. For example, the cab receipts did not include the company's address for the cab services, or readily identify the cab service as being located in Dallas, Texas. The notations on the cab receipts seemed to be in the same handwriting. Consequently, these documents do not adequately substantiate the amounts he purportedly spent on cab fare. Moreover, unlike the taxpayer in *Gardner* who produced a receipt acknowledging her payment of the deducted amount and confirming her attendance at the event, Valladolid did not submit any other documents to validate his testimony. He used cash for most payments and apparently did not always ask for a receipt. His unsupported testimony cannot satisfy the strict requirements of Section 274(d).

Thus, under the circumstances, a court will likely find that, except for his hotel bill for $620.71, Valladolid has failed to substantiate any of his travel expenses by adequate records or sufficient evidence corroborating his own testimony.

> Challenges the factual support and inferences raised in the counterargument.

> Ends with clear conclusion.

STATUTORY ANALYSIS FOR SUCCESS

EXERCISE 76

SAMPLE ANSWER

Begins with a clear conclusion sentence predicting the likely outcome of this case.

The court will probably find that Kevin Statham ("Statham") violated the Texas criminal trespass statute because he unlawfully entered Lomasi Begay's ("Begay's") apartment without her consent and did not leave when directed to do so. Under Texas law, a person commits criminal trespass "if the person enters or remains on . . . [the] property of another . . . without effective consent and the person: (1) had notice that the entry was forbidden; or (2) received notice to depart but failed to do so." Tex. Penal Code Ann. § 30.05(a) (West 2011). Notice includes both oral and written communication from the property owner or someone acting with authority of the owner. *Id.* § 30.05(b)(2).

Starts the law section with the relevant statutory language. Provides the operative rule from the statute.

Requires references to other statutory sections to determine the applicable mental state. Must carefully read the Notes of Decisions after the statutory language and the cited cases to realize there must be a culpable mental state and to understand how various sections are interrelated. The section about the requirement of culpability is not listed in the Cross References for the criminal trespass statute.

(1)   The relationship between sections 6.02 and 30.05 requires the trespasser to have acted with intent, knowledge, or recklessness in a volitional refusal to leave when asked to do so.

Although the statute defines the term "notice," the statutory language does not prescribe a culpable mental state. *West v. State*, 567 S.W.2d 515, 516 (Tex. Crim. App. 1978). Because section 30.05(a) of the Penal Code dispenses with culpable mental state, Section 6.02(b) requires proof of intent, knowledge, or recklessness. Tex. Penal Code Ann. § 6.02 (West 2011)*; *West*, 567 S.W.2d at 516; *Bustillos v. State*, 832 S.W.2d 668, 674 (Tex. App. 1992). Thus, "[i]t is the volitional refusal to depart from the property when requested which gives rise to a criminal trespass prosecution." *Bustillos*, 832 S.W.2d at 675; *Reed v. State*, 762 S.W.2d 640, 646 (Tex. App. 1988) ("No culpable mental state is required for conviction under this statute, other than a volitional refusal to leave when requested."). Texas courts, therefore, have found that a "defendant

Notice criminal negligence is not a viable culpable mental state for criminal trespass.

---

* In particular, Section 6.02(b) provides that "[i]f the definition of an offense does not prescribe a culpable mental state, a culpable mental state is nevertheless required unless the definition plainly dispenses with any mental element." Tex. Penal Code Ann. § 6.02(b) (West 2011). Under Section 6.02(c), "[i]f the definition of an offense does not prescribe a culpable mental state, but one is nevertheless required under Subsection (b), intent, knowledge, or recklessness suffices to establish criminal responsibility." *Id.* § 6.02(c).

could be properly convicted of criminal trespass even though the entry upon the property was by either accident or mistake, upon subsequent proof that defendant then intentionally, knowingly or recklessly refused to leave after receiving proper notice to depart." *Bustillos*, 832 S.W.2d at 675; *Reed*, 762 S.W.2d at 646 (finding defendant guilty of criminal trespass when he refused repeated requests to leave because he honestly believed he was entitled to be on property).

(2)   A volitional refusal to leave when asked can be reckless when the trespasser truly but mistakenly believes he is rightfully on the property or otherwise voluntarily creates a substantial and unjustifiable risk that he subsequently disregards.

Section 6.03(c) of the Penal Code defines recklessness as follows:

> A person acts recklessly, or is reckless, with respect to circumstances surrounding his conduct or the result of his conduct when he is aware of but consciously disregards a substantial and unjustifiable risk that the circumstances exist or the result will occur. The risk must be of such a nature and degree that its disregard constitutes a gross deviation from the standard of care that an ordinary person would exercise under all the circumstances as viewed from the actor's standpoint.

Tex. Penal Code Ann. § 6.03(c) (West 2011); *Jones v. State*, 900 S.W.2d 103, 105 (Tex. App. 1995). Thus, under the criminal trespass statute, a defendant recklessly refuses a request to leave the premises when he "consciously disregards a risk created by his conduct." *Jones*, 900 S.W.2d at 105. When analyzing a defendant's conduct, "[m]ental culpability is of such a nature that it generally must be inferred from the circumstances under which the prohibited act occurred. A culpable mental state may be inferred by the trier of facts from the acts, words, and conduct of the accused." *Griffith v. State*, 315 S.W.3d 648, 651 (Tex. App. 2010). Notably, voluntary intoxication does not constitute a defense to the crime of trespass. Tex. Penal Code Ann. § 8.04(a) (West 2011); *Griffith*, 315 S.W.3d at 652.

In *Reed*, the court found there was sufficient evidence to support the defendant's conviction for criminal trespass when the defendant, Reed, was on the property by accident or mistake. 762 S.W.2d at 646. The defendant and several

Sidebar notes (left margin):

Continues to define terms relevant to the operative rule. Begins with the statute and provides statutory definition of "recklessness."

Follows with language from relevant cases that expand on the terms/concepts included in the statute.

Sidebar notes (right margin):

Author selects recklessness as the relevant culpable mental state given the facts of Statham's case. "Recklessness" requires the lowest degree of culpability. "Intent" requires the highest level.

Includes case illustrations that address the refusal to leave requirement and then the concept of "recklessness."

others were distributing anti-abortion booklets to high school students as the students got off their school buses. *Id*. at 642. The defendant was standing on a sidewalk inside the school campus. *Id*. The school administrator asked them to leave, and the group's leader gave her an opinion letter from a lawyer that stated the group had a right to distribute booklets on a public sidewalk. *Id*. After conferring with the school's lawyer, the administrator told the group they were on private property and insisted they leave. *Id*. The group, including the defendant, refused to leave. *Id*. They were arrested and convicted of criminal trespass. *Id*.

The defendant appealed his conviction, arguing he did not have the requisite criminal intent since he believed he was lawfully entitled to be on the sidewalk. *Id*. at 646. However, the undisputed evidence supported his conviction. *Id*. The defendant violated the criminal trespass statute, despite his honest mistake, by remaining on school property after the administrator requested that he leave. *See id*.

The *Griffith* court illustrated the type of circumstances by which reckless conduct can be proved. *Griffith*, 315 S.W.3d at 652. The defendant drove a van despite being intoxicated at the time, hit the victim soon after she excited the van, and killed her. *Id*. The defendant did not keep a proper lookout and failed to control the van in a safe manner, jumping a curb and crashing into a fence. *Id*. The court concluded that the evidence showed, beyond a reasonable doubt, that the defendant acted recklessly when he voluntarily created a substantial and unjustifiable risk that he disregarded when he struck the victim with the van. *Id*. Additionally, ample evidence permitted an inference that the defendant should have known where the victim was located in relation to the van. *Id*.; *see also Banister v. State*, 761 S.W.2d 849 (Tex. App. 1988) (finding that defendant acted recklessly when he drove his truck in reverse on a road during foggy conditions, hitting another driver).

(3) The prosecution's argument that Statham violated the criminal trespass statute is stronger than Statham's defense against the statute.

The prosecution will argue that Statham is guilty of criminal trespass because he entered Begay's apartment without her consent and then recklessly refused to leave. As with the defendant in *Reed*, Statham's accident or

Provides the affirmative argument—the likely stronger argument given the facts of this case.

mistake, even if honest, will not serve as a defense to his unlawful conduct. Statham drank so much alcohol at his friend's gathering that he became intoxicated and accidentally went to the second floor of his apartment building rather the third floor where his apartment was located. He even incorrectly assumed that the open window on the second floor apartment belonged to his third floor apartment. Statham entered Begay's apartment without her consent, and he wrongfully believed he was lawfully entitled to enter the apartment through the window. However, as was the case in *Reed*, this mistake or accident will not save Statham from a conviction for criminal trespass. Statham may have unknowingly entered the window of the wrong apartment, but he also refused to leave when the rightful tenant forcibly ordered him to do so.

Statham's subsequent conduct was reckless, as *Griffith* defines that term, and its character can be inferred from the surrounding circumstances. He exhibited a conscious disregard of an unjustifiable risk created by his conduct. When Begay encountered Statham lying on her floor, she dropped her wine glass, screamed, and shouted, "Get out! Get out!" Her directive was clear and definitive. She wanted Statham to leave her apartment at once, and she was terrified by his presence there. Statham clearly heard Begay's cry and order to leave her apartment, but he did not comply. In response, he merely raised his hand and waved her off, saying, "Please stop shouting." At no time did Statham get up and leave. He consciously disregarded Begay's demands that he leave and created the circumstances in which he found himself that day. Statham risked having a lapse in judgment and compromised perception because he had been drinking excessively. He consciously disregarded these risks, heard Begay's orders, and still recklessly refused to leave. Statham, therefore, violated the criminal trespass statute.

Provides the argument for the opposing party, Statham.

Statham will maintain that he did not have the requisite culpable mental state for a criminal trespass violation, *i.e.* that he did not consciously disregard a risk created by his conduct. Unlike the defendants in *Reed* and *Griffith*, Statham did not commit any volitional refusal to leave when requested or create an unjustifiable risk that he disregarded. Statham vaguely recalled hearing noises, but he did not decipher the sounds as the tenant's requests to leave the apartment. He did not move and likely assumed the female voice belonged to his girlfriend.

He lay in a drunken stupor on the floor of the apartment he mistakenly believed belonged to him. He motioned to someone to stop making noise and immediately went back to sleep. He did not recklessly refuse to the leave the apartment. Furthermore, he may acknowledge the ample evidence that indicates he ought to have been aware of the risk, but he will assert his conduct does not rise to level of conscious disregard, which is required by the Texas Penal Code. *See Banister*, 761 S.W.2d at 850-51 (Burgess, J., dissenting opinion) (stating that defendant's act of driving in reverse during a heavy fog presented a risk of which he should have been aware rather than a conscious disregard of that risk).

Provides a rebuttal argument as to why Statham's argument is insufficient. Identifies key facts and the relevance of those facts to the argument.

Statham's argument will likely fail. He acted recklessly when he voluntarily created a substantial and unjustifiable risk that he then disregarded when he climbed through the window and ignored Begay's screams to leave. He was not unconscious or in a coma but was merely asleep, as he waved Begay away and asked her to stop yelling. Thus, as decided by the *Reed* court, a court here will likely find beyond a reasonable doubt that, despite his honest mistake, Statham violated the criminal trespass statute by remaining in Begay's apartment after she clearly requested that he leave. Statham was aware of the risk when he walked home in such an intoxicated state, climbed through an open window, and ignored the rightful tenant's orders to leave.

Ends with clear conclusion.

STATUTORY ANALYSIS FOR SUCCESS

EXERCISE 78

SAMPLE ANSWER

A court will likely determine that the sticker award system used by the teacher, Terry Houston ("Houston"), does not violate the Family Educational Rights and Privacy Act of 1974 ("FERPA"), as an unlawful release of confidential student education records. FERPA provides that any educational agency or institution that receives federal financial assistance must comply with certain conditions. 20 U.S.C.S. § 1232g (LexisNexis 2011). For example, such schools may not release sensitive information about their students without first obtaining parental consent. *Id.* § 1232g(b)(1). FERPA states that federal funds should be withheld from any school that has "a policy or practice of permitting the release of educational records (or other personally identifiable information contained therein . . .) of students without the written consent of their parents. . . ." *Id.* FERPA defines "educational records" as "records, files, documents, and other materials which . . . (i) contain information directly related to a student; and (ii) are maintained by an educational agency or institution or by a person acting for such agency or institution." *Id.* § 1232g(a)(4)(A). FERPA provides certain exceptions that are inapplicable to Houston's case.

1. Policy or Practice

The parties do not dispute that Houston's act of awarding students with the "You are a star!" sticker for their perfect homework grades is a practice or policy of her classroom. "FERPA is violated only when there is a 'policy or practice' . . . by which student education information is disclosed without parental or student authorization." *C.N. v. Ridgewood Bd. of Educ.*, 146 F. Supp. 2d 528, 538 (D.N.J. 2001). Here, the parents do not contest individual violations of student privacy but rather the systematic disclosure of a group of students' educational records with a sticker reward system. It remains debatable as to whether this class award system rises to the level of a practice of the educational agency or the entire school. Other teachers at the school employ similar means of recognizing high-performing students. For purposes of this analysis, the requisite policy or practice will be assumed.

2. Information Directly Related to a Student

The court will probably conclude that Houston's award system did not involve information directly related to a student. In *Risica*, a former middle school student filed suit against school officials, claiming they wrongfully disclosed his "hit list." *Risica v. Dumas*, 466 F. Supp. 2d 434, 436 (D. Conn. 2006). A janitor at the school found the student's geography book that contained his "hit list." *Id.* at 437. The court determined that the student had no expectation of privacy in the existence of the hit list and that it "simply [was] not an 'education record' which FERPA seeks to protect." *Id.* at 441. Although not explicitly stated, the *Risica* court apparently reasoned that the list did not satisfy the first requirement for an educational record as it did not contain information directly related to a student, such as his name, grade, or disciplinary record. *See id.*

In contrast, another court found a student's juvenile count records in question were directly related to the student as defined in FERPA. *Belanger v. Nashua, N.H., Sch. Dt.*, 856 F. Supp. 40, 50 (D.N.H. 1994). The records came from juvenile proceedings at Nashua District Court, and the school district's attorney used these records and other files to evaluate the student's individual educational plan, educational placement, and services. *Id.* at 41. Thus, the *Belanger* court found the juvenile files fit squarely into the "directly related to a student" part of FERPA's "education records" definition. *Id.* at 48, 50; *see also Owasso Indep. Sch. Dist. v. Falvo*, 534 U.S. 426, 431 (2002) (stating without analysis that the students' peer-graded papers contained information directly related to a student, such as his name, work product, and grade).

Houston will maintain that her award system is not an educational record covered by FERPA because the system does not contain or reveal information directly related to a student. In fact, the sticker does not state anything about the student. Like the hit list in *Risica*, the sticker does not provide any sensitive information about a student, such as final course grades, grade point average, standardized test scores, or attendance, counseling or disciplinary records. The face of the sticker just provides the statement, "You are a star!" and allows the student to feel good and confident about his or her academic performance that week. Although the star sticker announces to the

[Margin annotation:] Gives two case illustrations, which show how "directly related to a student" applies in this case. Each situation involves straightforward application with little or no explanation from the court as to its rationale.

[Margin annotation:] Provides the affirmative argument then the counter-argument.

class that a recipient received a perfect score on home-work, the sticker states nothing about the other students who do not have a sticker. Many teachers use this and similar forms of encouragement to inspire their students.

The aggrieved parents in this case will argue that Houston's award system provides information directly related to the students. Similar to the juvenile records in *Belanger* and the peer-graded papers in *Falvo*, the placement of a sticker on the cheek of a student reveals information directly about that student. The sticker tells other students in the school that the recipient received a perfect score on his or her homework for the week. Further, the class knew that those students who did not have a sticker were not high performers that week. The parents, therefore, will assert that the sticker system does not merely suggest the students' scores but readily provides information about the recipients' academic performance to all who can view the sticker award.

The parents' argument likely will not succeed. Even though their children may have experienced slight embarrassment by not receiving an award sticker, their discontent does not transform the sticker into an educational record. The sticker does not provide the student's name, grade, work product, or academic information. It merely states, "You are a star!" and communicates the recipient performed highly that week. Moreover, for those students without a sticker, no information is communicated about that particular student's score, work product, or academic performance. The award sticker is not a record, file, document, or other material that contains information directly related to a student. Nothing is printed on the face of the sticker that provides sensitive information. The sticker is no more than a pat on the back reaffirming that the student did a good job. Therefore, the sticker cannot satisfy the requirement to become an educational record.

3. Maintained by an Educational Agency or Person Acting for Such Agency

Even if the stickers were found to "contain information directly related to a student," the stickers are not "maintained by an educational agency or institution or by a person acting for such agency or institution." 20 U.S.C.S. § 1232g(a)(4)(A). Neither an educational agency nor Houston, a teacher at the school, "maintained" the stickers

Provides a rebuttal argument as to why the parents' argument is insufficient. Identifies key facts and the relevance of those facts to the argument.

The Court's decision in *Falvo* turns on the concept of "maintained." The Court readily accepted that the peer-graded assignments contained information directly related to a student.	at issue in this case. "The word 'maintain' suggests FERPA records will be kept in a filing cabinet in a records room at the school or on a permanent secure database, perhaps even after the student is no longer enrolled." *Falvo*, 534 U.S. at 433. "The ordinary meaning of the word 'maintain' is to 'keep in existence or continuance; preserve; retain.'" *Id.* (quoting *Random House Dictionary of the English Language* 1160 (2d ed. 1987)). In *Falvo*, the Court determined the students' papers that were peer-graded by the class were not maintained within the meaning of
Provides a brief illustration from the *Falvo* case as to what is meant by "maintained."	FERPA. *Id.* The teacher did not maintain the grade while the students corrected their peers' papers or called out their own scores. *Id.* In addition, the Court continued, the student graders handled the assignments only for a few minutes as the teacher called out the correct answers and they scored the papers. *Id.* Thus, "[i]t [wa]s fanciful to say they maintain[ed] the papers in the same way as the registrar maintain[ed] a student's folder in a permanent file." *Id.* As with the assignments in *Falvo*, the stickers given to each high-performing student in Houston's class are not "maintained" by Houston or the school. The stickers were not placed in a filing cabinet in a records room or on a permanent secure database. Houston identifies all students who received a perfect score on their homework
Provides the only viable argument given the facts. The affirmative argument is an analogy to *Falvo*.	assignments for the week, awards each with a sticker, and places it on each student's cheek. The sticker awards leave the classroom and the school with the students; they are not retained by the school or by Houston. Thus, the sticker awards are not "maintained" within the meaning of FERPA.
Ends with clear conclusion.	A court will likely find that Houston's award system of providing stickers to high-performing students does not violate FERPA. The stickers do not constitute "educational records" under the Act because first, the stickers do not "contain information directly related to a student," and second, they are not "maintained by an educational agency or institution or by a person acting for such agency or institution." 20 U.S.C.S. § 1232g(a)(4)(A).

STATUTORY ANALYSIS FOR SUCCESS

EXERCISE 80

SAMPLE ANSWER

Begins with a clear conclusion sentence predicting the likely outcome of this case.

Lynn Paolo ("Paolo") likely will be able to deduct several of her business expenses on her tax return, but she cannot deduct those that do not constitute "ordinary and necessary" expenses under the law. "Deductions are a matter of 'legislative grace', and 'a taxpayer seeking a deduction must be able to point to an applicable statute and show that [s]he comes within its terms.'" *Langer v. Comm'r*, 96 T.C.M. (CCH) 334, 2008 Tax Ct. Memo LEXIS 253, at *4 (T.C. Nov. 12, 2008) (quoting *New Colonial Ice Co. v. Helvering*, 292 U.S. 435, 440 (1943)). Thus, the taxpayer "bears the burden of proving that he is entitled to any deductions claimed." *Nehus v. Comm'r*, 68 T.C.M. (CCH) 1503, 1994 Tax Ct. Memo LEXIS 645, at *16 (T.C. Dec. 21, 1994).

Starts the law section with the relevant statutory language. Provides the operative rule from the statute. Then provides the legal standard from the cases that serve to interpret or expand the understanding of the statutory provisions.

Note: This response will address each of the expenses separately by category and will provide the relevant rules relating to that particular type of expense.

Section 162(a) of the United States Internal Revenue Code allows a deduction for ordinary and necessary business expenses paid or incurred during the taxable year in carrying on any trade or business. I.R.C. § 162(a) (2011). For an expense to be necessary, it must be "appropriate and helpful" to the taxpayer's business. *Langer*, 2008 Tax Ct. Memo LEXIS 253, at *5. An expense will be ordinary if it is "normal or customary" in the type of business in which the taxpayer is involved. *Id.* at *5.

1. Law Conference

Provides the law and relevant evidence for determining when the educational pursuits are deductible as a business expense.

The business portion of Paolo's travel to Las Vegas for the law conference, which her employer has not reimbursed, will be deductible. Regulations promulgated pursuant to the statute provide that a taxpayer may deduct amounts spent on her education as ordinary and necessary business expenses if the education maintains or improves skills required by the taxpayer in his employment or business. Treas. Reg. § 1.162-5(a)(1); Treas. Reg. § 1.162-5(c); *Nehus*, 1994 Tax Ct. Memo LEXIS 645, at *20. The taxpayer cannot deduct any expense that her employer has reimbursed. *Gardner v. Comm'r*, 46 T.C.M. (CCH) 1283, 1983 Tax Ct. Memo LEXIS 245, at *17 (T.C.

Sept. 1, 1983). If the taxpayer "travels away from home primarily to obtain education the expenses which are deductible are the expenditures for travel, meals, and lodging while away from home." *Nehus*, 1994 Tax Ct. Memo LEXIS 645, at *21. However, if the taxpayer's "travel away from home is primarily personal," the taxpayer's "expenditures for travel, meals and lodging (other than meals and lodging during the time spent in participating in deductible education pursuits) are not deductible." Treas. Reg. § 1.162-5(e)(1). In determining whether travel is primarily personal or for business, the court will examine the facts and circumstances of the particular case and will consider "the relative amount of time devoted to the personal activity as compared with the time devoted to educational pursuits." *Nehus*, 1994 Tax Ct. Memo LEXIS 645, at *21; Treas. Reg. § 1.162-5(e)(1).

In *Gardner*, the taxpayer, a university professor of education, claimed deductions for an interterm taken at an out-of-state university. 1983 Tax Ct. Memo LEXIS 245, at *6. The interterm consisted of a course on Mexico and a trip to the country. *Id.* The taxpayer listed, among other things, the registration fee as a business deduction. *Id.* The Commissioner conceded the business purpose of the expense, presumably given its connection to the field of teaching. *See id.* at *17. The court, therefore, held that the taxpayer was entitled to deduction for the substantiated registration fee. *Id.*

Here, as with the taxpayer in *Gardner*, Paolo's expenditures on continuing education clearly serve a legitimate business purpose. Paolo attended a conference on updates in trust law in Las Vegas, Nevada. She received continuing legal education credit for this course and reported her attendance to the state bar. Given that the conference relates to the subject matter of her law school courses and clinic cases, the expenditures are business-related expenses. Further, the Treasury Regulations allow Paolo to deduct the expenses for travel, meals, and lodging while away from home to attend this conference. Roger J. Benton College of Law of Southern Kentucky University ("Benton College of Law") has already reimbursed Paolo for her airfare; therefore, she is not entitled to deduct that amount on her taxes. *See Gardner*, 1983 Tax Ct. Memo LEXIS 245, at *17 (disallowing business deduction for transportation when employer reimbursed

---

Provides a clear explanation of the legal standard from precedent. Includes the key facts, holding, and reasoning from this case so that the reader can clearly understand how the court applies the test in a real-world scenario.

Presents affirmative argument as the only viable argument for this section.

taxpayer for such amount). In addition, Paolo must exclude certain other travel expenses from her list of deductions related to the conference. Paolo attended the conference sessions and networked with attendees for three consecutive days, but she remained in Las Vegas an additional day to tour the city. Her final day in Las Vegas is, therefore, a personal expense, not subject to deduction on her tax return. In examining the time devoted to business activities as compared to personal matters on this trip, the court will conclude that Paolo can claim three-fourths of the claimed amount for the conference but cannot deduct one-fourth of the total expenses.

Identifies how Paolo's deductions are limited under the circumstances.

2. Floral Design Workshop

The court will likely disallow the amount for the floral design workshop claimed as a business expense. Expenses made by a taxpayer for programs of study that will lead to a new trade or business are nondeductible educational expenses. Treas. Reg. § 1.162-5(b)(3). Currently, Paolo is a law professor and works with clients in the school's family law clinic. She does not have a floral design business or flower shop. Attending a floral design workshop is not directly related to her law profession, and at most, the workshop prepares her for a new trade or business as a florist. Therefore, this expenditure, which the court probably will consider a hobby or interest, cannot be deducted as a business expense.

In the absence of a case illustration where education qualifies taxpayer for a new trade or business, author uses rule-based reasoning to provide the argument for the floral design workshop.

Applies the rule from the regulation directly to the facts of this case. Provides only an affirmative argument given that there is no viable counter-argument under the circumstances.

3. Professional Association, Magazine Subscription, Refreshments for Students, and Book Editor

The court will likely conclude that Paolo may deduct the expenses related to her State Bar membership, the class refreshments, and her book editor but will disallow those for the subscription and laptop. Treasury Regulations provide that a taxpayer may claim as deductions the cost of supplies used by her in the practice of her profession, dues to professional societies, and subscriptions to professional journals. Treas. Reg. § 1.162-6; *Gardner*, 1983 Tax Ct. Memo LEXIS 245, at *9-10 (recognizing professor's supplies and materials to supplement those provided by school as deductible business expense because school expected faculty to provide some of these items and the expenses were well documented). In particular, dues and subscriptions are deductible as business expenses, provided the "expenditures have the requisite connection to any trade

Addresses the next group of expenses.

Provides the relevant law for this category.

or business" of the taxpayer. *Nehus*, 1994 Tax Ct. Memo LEXIS 645, at *19. For example, organization dues are generally deductible when the group's membership is limited to those in the relevant business field or practice area. *Gardner*, 1983 Tax. Ct. Memo LEXIS 245, at *11 (disallowing deduction when professor failed to prove associations were "professional societies" with membership limited to the field of education). For any planned deduction, the taxpayer should be able to show that her employer required the expenditure or that the expenditure is a "usual and customary" cost incurred by other similarly situated employees. *See id.* at *10.

Provides a clear explanation of the legal standard from precedent. Includes the key facts, holding, and reasoning from this case so that the reader can clearly understand how the court applies the test in a real-world scenario.

In *Nehus*, the taxpayer, an accountant, claimed deductions for subscriptions to the Los Angeles Times and the Wall Street Journal, both newspapers of general circulation. *Nehus*, 1994 Tax Ct. Memo LEXIS 645, at *19. He also claimed costs for the Prentiss Hall Federal Tax Handbook and dues for the California Society of Certified Public Accountants and California State Board of Accountancy. *Id.* The court disallowed the payments for the newspapers because they were of general circulation and no evidence was presented that the expenditures had the "requisite connection" to any specific trade or business of the taxpayer, namely his accounting profession. *Id.* However, the court permitted deductions for the tax handbook and the dues for the professional organizations because they were ordinary and necessary expenses directly tied to the taxpayer's profession. *Id.* Although not specifically stated by the court, the tax handbook and association dues evidently were customary expenses in the taxpayer's field and designed to further the development of his accounting business. *See id.*

Infers the court's reasoning.

Leads with affirmative argument.

The Commissioner will likely allow the deductions for Paolo's professional association fees, class refreshments, and book editor as business expenses but will maintain that the magazine subscription is nondeductible. Paolo's state bar membership directly relates to her profession as a law professor and director of the clinic. With her bar license, Paolo has more credibility with her students as a legitimate practicing lawyer, and the license allows her to advocate for clients of the school's family law clinic. Clearly, as with the accounting-related memberships in *Nehus*, these expenditures by Paolo have the requisite connection to her profession.

In addition, the amounts spent by Paolo on refreshments for her law school class relate to her trade. Benton College of Law did not reimburse Paolo for the pizza, cookies, and donuts that she purchased for her class over the school year, and the school does not have a policy in place for compensating professors in such a manner. However, other schools have a reimbursement policy and practice, and some schools even allocate budgets for professors to provide snacks for their students and other forms of entertainment, in an effort to improve faculty-student relations and student morale. This evidence shows that such expenditures for a class are both ordinary and necessary, as well as being customary and helpful to the teaching profession. *See Gardner*, 1983 Tax Ct. Memo LEXIS 245, at *10 (noting that the tax-payer needed to show that her employer required the expenditure or that it was usual and customary for pro-fessors at the university to provide refreshments for such open house events). Lastly, writers and educators typi-cally use the services of an editor or proofreader for their book projects. In an effort to produce a well-written prod-uct, Paolo paid an editor to review her book, a book that she plans to include on her list of scholarship for promo-tion purposes. Thus, Paolo's editing and proofreading costs further her business interests and constitute deduct-ible expenses.

> Commissioner will concede that certain expenses are deductible. Author provides the relevant analysis.

Paolo will try to argue that the magazine subscription should be a deductible expense, as the publication allowed her to keep current on investments and trends in money management. She used this information to educate her law school class on financial management matters and to illustrate how to serve their trust clients fully. Despite her attempts to relate the subscription to her profession, Paolo's argument will likely fail. She draws a rather attenuated connection between the magazine's content and her wills, trusts, and estates course. In addition, there is no suggestion that other university educators deduct similar expenses. As stated by the court in *Nehus*, the publication in this case is generally circulated, purchased by the mass public, and therefore, cannot be deducted as a business expense.

> Follows with counter-argument. Focuses on the remaining items.

4. Hotel and Laptop

Paolo also claims deductible business expenses for her new laptop and for a hotel stay to write her book. She may have some challenges seeking deductions for these items.

As mentioned, "[t]he furnishing of supplies and materials to supplement those provided by a school may constitute an important part of the duties of a university professor and can constitute an ordinary and necessary business expense." *Gardner*, 1983 Tax Ct. Memo LEXIS 245, at *9. The taxpayer must show a nexus between the expense and her trade or business. *Nehus*, 1994 Tax Ct. Memo LEXIS 645, at *19.

> **Provides a clear explanation of the legal standard from precedent. Includes the key facts, holding, and reasoning from this case so that the reader can clearly understand how the court applies the test in a real-world scenario.**

In *Langer*, the court held that several expenses claimed by the taxpayer, a piano teacher, were clearly personal and not business expenses. *Langer*, 2008 Tax Ct. Memo LEXIS 253, at *8-9. The taxpayer attempted to claim swimming pool supplies and maintenance, home and holiday decorations, a nativity set, cookbooks, and a television set but failed to explain how these items "related to the piano teaching business." *Id.* at *8. The taxpayer's arguments were "beyond belief and contrary to all reason." *Id.* For example, the taxpayer argued that the costs for pool supplies and maintenance related to the business because parents would sit and wait by the pool while their children finished their piano lessons. *Id.* Finding that the expenses were not ordinary and necessary nor business related, the court determined they were not deductible. *Id.* at *9.

> **Begins with the affirmative argument (for the Commissioner) and a clear leading thesis sentence for this section.**

The Commissioner will argue that the costs for Paolo's hotel stay and laptop are not deductible as ordinary and necessary business expenses. Like the expenditures in *Langer*, these amounts are clearly personal and not solely business expenses. Paolo had a few visitors to the hotel during her stay and even ordered two movies. In addition, Paolo used her laptop to pay bills online and access social networking sites, and she probably used the word processing program to write other items such as letters to family and friends. The only claimed business purposes were for grading and writing her book, yet, the primary uses for the computer were personal.

> **Distinguishes the precedent case to argue that Paolo should be permitted to deduct the expenses.**

Despite the noted personal activities, Paolo will attempt to show she stayed at the hotel to have a quiet place to write, without any interruptions, and she used the computer to type her manuscript. She will distinguish her situation from that of the *Langer* taxpayer, whose arguments were beyond belief and contrary to reason. In *Langer*, no nexus was established between the expenditures and the taxpayer's business. Here, both items furthered the development of Paolo's book and, in turn, helped her to fulfill the school's scholarship requirements.

Short rebuttal to Paolo's argument, followed by a conclusion for this section.

Paolo's arguments, however, will likely fail given her inability to show that the expenses were normal and customary within academia. In fact, most universities provide professors with office space and a computer to complete work-related projects. Thus, there is little need to purchase a separate computer system for business purposes. Additionally, Paolo used her laptop for personal activities such as accessing social networking sites and paying bills. Further, there is no evidence that university or law professors regularly expense separate lodging for the writing and completion of an article, book, or other publication or customarily purchase a computer or laptop for business purposes. Thus, the court likely will disallow Paolo's deductions.

5. Suits and Alterations

Includes a brief on-point case illustration with an analogy.

Specific argument and factual support as to why Paolo's suits and alterations are nondeductible.

Lastly, Paolo seeks to deduct the cost of four new suits and the related alterations, but the court will probably disallow these deductions as business expenditures. "Expenses for clothing adaptable for general use are not deductible." *Langer*, 2008 Tax Ct. Memo LEXIS 253, at *9. In *Langer*, the petitioner claimed an expense deduction for sweaters purchased by his wife, a piano teacher. *Id*. The court disallowed these deductions because no evidence showed the sweaters were not adaptable for general purposes. *Id*. Here, Paolo purchased four new designer suits, two pantsuits and two skirt suits. Each suit required alterations. Although the suits constitute professional business attire, Paolo could easily wear these outfits to a personal event or outing. The suits are not part of a unique business or work uniform, such as that worn by postal workers or police officers. Thus, like the taxpayer in *Langer*, Paolo could wear this clothing for any general use, and accordingly, the court will likely disallow the expenses for the clothing and alterations.

Ends with clear conclusion that summarizes which deductions the court likely will permit.

In summary, a court will likely find that Paolo can deduct the following expenses: part of her business travel to the conference in Las Vegas, state bar dues, class refreshments, and services for a book editor and proofreader. She, however, will be unable to deduct the costs for the personal part of her travel to Las Vegas, the floral design workshop, magazine subscription, hotel stay to write her book, her new laptop, as well as her suits and alterations. Going forward, Paolo will need to substantiate all amounts claimed as a business expense deduction by maintaining sufficient records detailing the amount, time, and place of the expenditure. *See Langer*, 2008 Tax Ct. Memo LEXIS 253, at *5.

STATUTORY ANALYSIS FOR SUCCESS

EXERCISE 82 *

SAMPLE ANSWER

Johnson's carpal tunnel syndrome probably is not a qualifying disability under the ADA, because it limits her from performing only one specific type of job, rather than the required broader class of jobs. An impairment "substantially limits" a major life activity if the individual is unable to perform, or is "significantly limited in the ability to perform," an activity compared to an "average person in the general population." 29 C.F.R. § 1630.2(j)(3)(i) (2011).

In determining whether an impairment substantially limits a major life activity, courts consider (i) "[t]he nature and severity of the impairment; (ii) the duration or expected duration of the impairment; and (iii) [t]he permanent or long term impact, the expected permanent or long term impact, or the expected permanent or long term impact of or resulting from the impairment." *Id.* § 1630.2(j)(2).

In addition, a court determining whether an impairment substantially limits the major life activity of working may also consider (A) the geographical area at issue; (B) the job from which the individual has been disqualified because of an impairment, and the number and types of jobs utilizing similar training, knowledge, skills or abilities, within that geographic area, from which the individual is also disqualified because of the impairment (class of jobs); and/or (C) the job from which the individual has been disqualified because of an impairment, and the number and types of other jobs not utilizing similar training, knowledge, skills or abilities, within that geographic area, from which the individual is also disqualified because of the impairment (broad range of jobs in various classes). *Id.* § 1630.2(j)(3). Courts also take into account the plaintiff's preparation and training for other work.

---

* This answer is based on the following case: *United Pac. Ins. Co. v. Discount Co.*, 550 P.2d 699 (Wash. Ct. App. 1976).

Provides specific examples that explain the rule's contours.

Where, for example, a Toyota manufacturing plant worker was unable to lift heavy weights or use vibrating tools due to her carpal tunnel syndrome, a court found she did not have a qualifying disability under the ADA. *McKay v. Toyota Motor Mfg.*, 878 F. Supp. 1012, 1015 (E.D. Ky. 1995). The plaintiff was working on a teaching certificate at the time, and she was twenty-four years old. *Id.* Because the plaintiff was relatively young and had other employment possibilities, the court found that the carpal tunnel syndrome did not affect the major life activity of working and was therefore not a qualifying disability under the ADA. *Id.* The court noted that she was unable to perform only a narrow class of tasks on the production line and was not barred from all production line jobs. *Id.*

Includes details from the precedent case that will assist in analyzing the present facts.

In contrast, when the worker was unable to perform any production line work at all, carpal tunnel syndrome was held to be a qualifying disability for purposes of the ADA. *Lowry v. Cabletron Sys. Inc.,* 973 F. Supp. 77 (D.N.H. 1997). The court distinguished the case from *McKay* on the grounds that McKay's carpal tunnel syndrome did not affect her prospects in a broad class of tasks, but rather a narrow subset of those tasks. *Id.* at 82. Lowry, on the other hand, was unable to perform a broad class of tasks, namely all production line work. *Id.* Lowry's carpal tunnel syndrome, as plead, affected the major life activity of working, and therefore qualified as a disability for purposes of the ADA. *Id.*

Begins the application by stating the argument's direction.

Johnson's carpal tunnel syndrome is more akin to McKay's than Lowry's, and therefore Johnson's carpal tunnel syndrome is probably not a qualifying disability under the ADA. Just as McKay was disqualified from welding but was able to perform other tasks on the production line, Johnson is unable to do just one thing—weld. She can sweep and perform general clean-up, and these tasks constitute forty percent of her job responsibilities. *McKay* and *Lowry* establish that to affect the major life activity of working, a condition must affect a broad class of tasks, and must affect an individual's employment prospects. Johnson is young and a recent high school graduate, so she likely can shift into other employment opportunities. In addition, she has secured other employment, albeit with fewer benefits.

Makes explicit comparisons between the precedent cases and the present facts.

Uses transitions to move clearly from one argument to the next.

The guidelines also call for the court to consider the plaintiff's geographical area and jobs that may be available. Johnson is in the Louisville area, which is a large city with diverse employment possibilities. This consideration too indicates that Johnson's carpal tunnel syndrome does not limit her employment prospects except with regard to the specific job of welding.

On the other hand, Johnson, a welder by trade, is unable to perform her job. Arguably, her carpal tunnel syndrome is preventing her from performing not just one task, but the main task for which she was employed. In fact, she was fired for being unable to weld, thereby confirming that welding is a key part of her tasks. This argument will likely fail, because Johnson is a young person who is new to welding, just as McKay was young and had other employment prospects. Furthermore, Johnson is able to perform a multitude of other tasks and is limited from only one very specific job—welding.

> Sets out the strongest counter-argument and rebuts it using specific facts and details of case law.

Therefore, Johnson's carpal tunnel syndrome does not limit her from a broad class of jobs and does not limit her overall employment prospects very much. Her condition does not affect the major life activity of working, and she does not have a qualifying disability under the ADA.

STATUTORY ANALYSIS FOR SUCCESS

EXERCISE 84

SAMPLE ANSWER

Starts with a clear statement of the conclusion.

The court should not grant the motion for new trial based on Smith's assertion of fraud because the MSA was prepared and signed in conformity with statutory requirements, and he can present no evidence of a misrepresentation or material omission on which he relied to his detriment.

Sets out the applicable law with citations and very brief quotations of the most relevant terms.

Section 6.602 of the Texas Family Code provides that an MSA that complies with the statutory provisions is immediately binding on the parties and "is not subject to revocation." Tex. Fam. Code Ann. § 6.602 (West 2011). An agreement that meets the statutory requirements is "more binding than a basic written contract." *Loehr v. Loehr*, No. 13-08-00380-CV, 2009 Tex. App. LEXIS 6863, at *6 (Tex. App. Aug. 28, 2009) (citing *In re Joyner*, 196 S.W.3d 883, 889 (Tex. App. 2006)).

Sets out the specific standard that the motion will have to meet.

Once a divorce decree based on an MSA is finalized, a motion for new trial based on allegations of fraud should be granted only if the opposing party was fraudulently induced into signing the MSA. *See id.* at *7-8. A claim of fraudulent inducement requires evidence of the following: (1) a material misrepresentation, (2) knowledge that the misrepresentation was false or asserted without knowledge of its truth, (3) intent that the other party act upon it, and (4) actual reliance on the misrepresentation. *Id.* at *7.

Moves cleanly to examples of the rule in action—shows how the rule is applied through case examples.

In *Ricks v. Ricks*, 169 S.W.3d 532 (Tex. App. 2005), the divorce decree was entered on the basis of an MSA. *Id.* at 524. The court affirmed denial of a motion for new trial that was filed by Janci Ricks. *Id.* Janci's motion was based in part on an allegation that her former spouse, Jon, had misrepresented the value of some shares in a medical center, and he had thereby fraudulently obtained her consent to the MSA. *Id.* at 525–27. During the mediation, the parties' experts first had determined the value of the shares to be $60,000, and then the parties' attorneys agreed on a value of $126,000 based on new information. *Id.* at 527. After the mediation, Janci learned the shares had produced dividend income of $36,000 in the previous year, which had not been disclosed, and she argued the dividends prima facie made the shares worth at least $500,000. *Id.* Even though she knew the shares had produced some dividends, she did not previously know the full amount. *Id.*

However, Janci's allegation was nothing more than a bare assertion; she presented no evidence to support the claimed value, and the record contained no evidence that Jon represented any value other than what the parties' experts and then their attorneys had agreed to. *Id.* at 527. The court, therefore, affirmed the denial of the motion for new trial. *Id.* at 525, 527.

Similarly, a motion for new trial was denied when Janet Loehr alleged that her former spouse, Roland, had misrepresented the nature of certain pieces of real property listed on the inventory attached to their MSA. *Loehr,* 2009 Tex. App. LEXIS 686309, at *1–3. The *Loehr* court likened Janet's "speculations" of Roland's fraud to the unsubstantiated claims made by Janci Ricks about the value of the clinic shares. *Id.* The *Loehr* court further reasoned that, in any event, the Loehrs had "remov[ed] their divorce from traditional settlement procedures[,]" by using the mediation process and signing an MSA. *Id.* at *8–9. Because the purpose of the mediation process under section 6.602 of the Texas Family Code is to keep the mediated divorce out of the courtroom, the court reasoned that when the parties sign an MSA, the court is bound to enforce the agreement without regard to whether the terms of the agreement were "just and right." *Id.* Admonishing that Janet should have checked the MSA's terms and conditions herself, the court declined to "reward [her] with a reprieve from the agreement merely because she failed to exercise due diligence in reviewing the terms and conditions before signing her name to the MSA." *Id.*

Just as the fraud allegations in *Ricks* and *Loehr* failed due to lack of any specific misrepresentation, the allegations here too should fail because Ortega made no misrepresentation of value. Although the medical center shares in *Ricks* arguably could have later been worth more than their value at mediation, the lack of any specific representation to the contrary in mediation meant that no new trial was warranted. *Ricks,* 169 S.W.3d at 527. In Ortega's case too, later indications of a different value for the painting do not require a new trial because Ortega made no misrepresentation of value, or indeed, any representation of value at all. Likewise, although the real property in *Loehr* was allegedly incorrectly represented on the inventory attached

Sidebar notes:

Gives the outcome of each case example, so readers can predict how the case at hand may turn out.

Transitions meaningfully to subsequent case examples so readers can see how the cases compare to one another.

Makes a clean break between case explanation and application—immediately makes a connection between precedent and the case at hand.

438

to the MSA, the former spouse had not specifically misrepresented the value, so the motion for new trial was denied. *Loehr*, 2009 Tex. App. LEXIS 6863, at *1–3. In the case at hand as well, no misrepresentation of value was made so as to call for a new trial.

Adds further arguments by transitioning clearly and adding further specific factual analysis from the fact pattern.

Moreover, just as in *Loehr*, the purportedly defrauded party should have exercised due diligence before signing an MSA. Instead of agreeing to the MSA without taking any independent steps to value the painting, Smith could have had the painting valued. He chose not to do so, and signed an agreement clearly marked as irrevocable. Just as in *Loehr*, the motion for new trial should be denied.

Smith may argue that when Ortega said the painting had only emotional value, she was making a specific statement that the painting was not worth anything in financial terms. Those statements, even if taken as a specific representation of value, do not show that Ortega knew they were false at the time or that she intended Smith to act upon them to his detriment.

Provides a credible counter-argument and then shows with specifics why the counter-argument fails.

In a similar situation, the *Loehr* court denied a motion for new trial when Janet Loehr could not show evidence that her former spouse knew his categorization of real property was false, or that he intended Janet to act upon the misrepresentation to her detriment. *Id.* Lacking similar evidence here, the court likely will deny Smith's motion for new trial.

The *Ricks* court's reasoning that a contract can be subject to rescission if one with "a duty to disclose material information . . . fails to do so, and leads the other party . . . to rely on the misrepresentation," *Ricks*, 169 S.W.3d at 526, similarly will not assist Smith. He cannot present evidence that Ortega misrepresented the value or that he relied on that misrepresentation to his detriment. He was party to the purchase of the horse painting, knew the purchase price, and fourteen months later willingly traded the painting for four landscapes.

Smith also might argue he could not pay attention to the details because he felt pressured to settle. Not only did the mediator say he would settle for sure if he were in their position, but his attorney also added to the pressure by telling him she would refer his case to a new firm if the case was not settled that day. However, Smith was represented by counsel throughout the mediation, including when the agreement was made, and the mediation took six hours, more than sufficient time for Smith to check everything. Just as the *Loehr* court declined to reward Janet Loehr for her lack of due diligence by revoking the MSA she and Roland had made, a court here probably would refuse to reward Smith "with a reprieve from the agreement. . . ." *Loehr*, 2009 Tex. App. LEXIS 6863, at *9.

Ends with a clear conclusion that briefly states why the case turns out the way it does.

The trial court should deny the motion for new trial, because Ortega made no misrepresentation of value and withheld no material information. Additionally, any failure to discover the painting's true value was due to Smith's lack of due diligence.

STATUTORY ANALYSIS FOR SUCCESS

EXERCISE 86

SAMPLE ANSWER

The State of Texas ("State") will probably fail to prove beyond reasonable doubt that Jacoby Patrick ("Patrick") unlawfully possessed Alprazolam (Xanax) in violation of the Texas Controlled Substances Act, Tex. Health & Safety Code Ann. §§ 481.001-.314 (West 2011), because several factors do not affirmatively link Patrick to the drugs found nor support a reasonable inference that he both knew of the drugs' presence and exercised control over them.

Under the Texas Controlled Substances Act, a person commits a Class A misdemeanor offense "if the person knowingly or intentionally possesses a controlled substance listed in Penalty Group 3 [in an amount under 28 grams], unless the person obtains the substance directly from a valid prescription or . . . practitioner[.]" *Id.* § 481.117(a), (b).

Alprazolam (or Xanax) constitutes a substance under "Penalty Group 3." *Id.* § 481.104(2). Possession is defined as the "actual care, custody, control, or management" of the substance at issue. *Id.* § 481.002(38). Thus, to support a conviction for unlawful possession of a controlled substance, the State must prove beyond a reasonable doubt that (1) the accused exercised care, control, or management over the contraband; and (2) the accused knew the matter possessed was contraband. *Porter v. State*, 873 S.W.2d 729, 732 (Tex. App. 1994). The accused must have both knowledge of the contraband and management or control over it. *Id.* Because knowledge is subjective, it "must always be inferred to some extent, in the absence of an admission by the accused." *McGoldrick v. State*, 682 S.W.2d 573, 578 (Tex. Crim. App. 1985).

The accused being in the presence of contraband is not enough for possession; he must have dominion and control over the substance. *Porter*, 873 S.W.2d at 732; *McGoldrick*, 682 S.W.2d at 578 (emphasizing "possession means more than just being where the action is" and quoting *Wilkes v. State*, 572 S.W.2d 538 (Tex. Crim. App. 1978)). However, control "may be shown by actual or constructive possession[.]" *McGoldrick*, 682 S.W.2d at 578.

441

Furthermore, "[p]ossession and control of drugs need not be exclusive but may be joint." *Chisum v. State*, 988 S.W.2d 244, 247 (Tex. App. 1999). If the accused's control and possession of the place in which the contraband is found is not exclusive, the accused may not be charged with knowledge of and control over the contraband unless the State proves affirmative links between the substance and the accused. *Porter*, 873 S.W.2d at 732. Those links must give rise to "a reasonable inference . . . that the accused knew of the contraband's existence and that he exercised control over it." *Id*. (quoting *Edwards v. State*, 813 S.W.2d 572, 575 (Tex. App. 1991)); *Ortiz v. State*, 930 S.W.2d 849, 853 (Tex. App. 1996) (confirming a jury may infer that the accused had actual care, control or management of a controlled substance and knew of the presence of the contraband and its forbidden nature from the presence of certain incriminating factors and citing *Deshong v. State*, 625 S.W.2d 327, 329 (Tex. Crim. App.1981) (accused owned the automobile in which contraband was found, accused operated the automobile, and the contraband was so situated that it was accessible to the accused)).

When evaluating affirmative links, the courts consider factors including whether the accused 1) was present when the search was executed; 2) was close to and had access to the contraband, 3) was under the influence of a controlled substance when arrested, 4) possessed other contraband when arrested, 5) made incriminating statements when arrested, 6) attempted to flee or made furtive gestures, 7) owned or had the right to possess the place where the drugs were found, and with respect to contraband, whether 8) there was an odor of the contraband, 9) other contraband or drug paraphernalia was present, 10) the contraband was in plain view, and 11) the place it was found in was enclosed. *Chisum*, 988 S.W.2d at 248; *see Ortiz*, 930 S.W.2d at 853. Texas courts tend to address these factors collectively in determining whether sufficient evidence exists to infer the accused's knowledge of the contraband's presence and control over it. *See Chisum*, 988 S.W.2d at 248; *Porter*, 873 S.W.2d at 732–33 (finding that affirmative links supporting accused's knowledge coupled with additional evidence permitted reasonable inference that accused exercised control over contraband).

"Although several factors have been identified, the number of factors supported by the evidence is not as

Remember factors
are to be weighed
by the court. They
are not elements
or requirements
but rather
considerations or
guidelines.

important as the 'logical force' they collectively create to
provide that a crime has been committed." *Utomi v. State*,
243 S.W.3d 75, 79 (Tex. App. 2007) (quoting *Roberson
v. State*, 80 S.W.3d 730, 735 (Tex. App. 2002)). The court will
consider the particular facts and circumstances of each
case. *Porter*, 873 S.W.2d at 729. "No set formula of facts
exists which would dictate a finding of an 'affirmative link'
sufficient to support an inference of knowing possession of
contraband." *Id.* Moreover, "[e]vidence that links the
accused to the drugs must establish a connection that is
more than fortuitous." *Utomi*, 243 S.W.3d at 79.

Identifies the best
cases from the
case list to
illustrate the
rules above. These
cases are factually
analogous to
Patrick's situation
and lay a good
foundation for the
parties'
arguments. The
first case serves as
positive authority
for Patrick. The
second case
supports the
State's position.

The *McGoldrick* court held that insufficient evidence
supported appellant John McGoldrick's ("McGoldrick's")
conviction for unlawful possession of a controlled substance. 682 S.W.2d at 580. Two deputies worked as undercover narcotic officers; Officer Pollock posed as a prospective
buyer, and Officer Bousquet set up a meeting between
Pollock and Gary Johnson ("Johnson"). *Id.* at 575. After an
initial meeting and a series of telephone calls, the parties
met at the Kroger store's parking lot at 6:00 p.m. *Id.*
Johnson arrived in the brown Malibu and Pollock gave
him the bag of money. *Id.* Johnson then took Bousquet's
green Dodge to obtain the marijuana. *Id.*

At this point, several police vehicles and a helicopter
followed Johnson, and the officers observed a series of
stops. *Id.* In particular, the driver of the Dodge (apparently defendant Johnson) stopped at a trailer where two
men were standing outside. *Id.* All three men went inside
the trailer and one went to a shed, retrieved a package,
and put it in the trunk of the Dodge. *Id.* Johnson got in the
driver's seat of the Dodge and a second man entered the
Dodge. *Id.* The third man, appellant McGoldrick, followed
the Dodge in his light beige car. *Id.* The Dodge then went
to a shopping center, and the passenger exited the Dodge
and got in a white Ford. *Id.* McGoldrick turned in a different direction and left the area. *Id.*

Details the
relevant facts
that the parties
rely on in this
case for their
arguments and
the court
identifies as key
to its decision.
Shows the
appellant's mere
presence at the
scene and his lack
of knowledge and
involvement.

Both the Dodge and the Ford were driven to another
parking lot where packages were removed from the Ford
and placed in the trunk of the Dodge. *Id.* at 576. The defendants then drove the Ford to Kroger's parking lot to meet
Pollock and then back to the parking lot were the Dodge
was located to retrieve the marijuana. *Id.* Once the Dodge's
trunk was opened, the officers arrested Johnson. *Id.* A few
minutes later, officers arrested Leland Morrow ("Morrow"),
who drove the Ford. *Id.*

Officers then arrested McGoldrick. *Id.* They found an unloaded pistol, no ammunition, a newspaper, some duct tape, white garbage bags, and a wallet with another person's identification card in his car. *Id.* No marijuana was found. *Id.* On his person, officers found some business cards and receipts. *Id.* On the back of one receipt, there were three numbers for defendant Johnson. *Id.* McGoldrick maintained that he followed Johnson to find Tommy Hansen ("Hansen"), who owed McGoldrick money. *Id.* Hansen's father said his son could be reached through Johnson and gave McGoldrick directions to Johnson's trailer and Johnson's telephone numbers. 682 S.W.2d at 576–77. The father confirmed these events. *Id.* at 577.

McGoldrick denied any knowledge or involvement with the drug transaction, and the Court agreed with him. *Id.* The State relied on the following evidence as affirmative links to show McGoldrick's knowledge and involvement: Johnson's reference to his suppliers as "they," McGoldrick's presence at the trailer when purported contraband was loaded in the car, his following Johnson, the presence of similar items in McGoldrick's car trunk to those in the Dodge's trunk, and McGoldrick's possession of Johnson's telephone numbers. *Id.* at 580.

The Court found that the State did not sustain its burden of proof that McGoldrick was a party to the offense of marijuana possession by defendants Johnson and Morrow. *Id.* The State failed to show additional facts beyond McGoldrick's mere presence at the scene where the action supposedly took place. *Id.* As McGoldrick argued, the evidence did not show that he was ever in a position to view any marijuana, he ever loaded or handled the drug, or he owned or controlled a vehicle or premises the drug was in. *Id.* Also, the officers did not find marijuana on his person or in his car, there was no odor of marijuana about him, and he was not under the influence of marijuana when arrested. *Id.* Thus, the facts and circumstances did not affirmatively link McGoldrick to the drugs in such a manner that a jury could conclude he had knowledge of the contraband or control over it. *Id.*

> Note that one could include a case illustration of *Porter* to show another example of when a reasonable inference of knowing possession of contraband could be drawn.

> For predictive writing, when available, consider setting out two cases that show what does—and does not—satisfy the charge. Transition clearly, so the reader can follow case illustrations.

In *Chisum,* in contrast, the court affirmed the judgment on the verdict that defendant was guilty of unlawful possession. 988 S.W.2d at 248. Officers searched defendant Russell Chisum's ("Chisum") home and arrested him for cocaine possession. *Id.* at 247. Chisum shared the house with a woman whom he had purportedly thrown out of his house for using cocaine. *Id.* at 248. Chisum

444

claimed the woman returned to his home and planted the drugs there because she was angry with him for throwing her out of the house. *Id.*

Because a woman's clothing was found in the house, the court could not determine Chisum had exclusive possession and control over the house and had to rely on independent facts to establish Chisum's knowledge of and control over the drugs. *Id.* at 247–28. In evaluating the evidence, the court tracked the independent facts it previously had provided for an assessment of affirmative links between Chisum and the drugs: (1) Chisum was not present when the officers first arrived to search his home, but he was brought there during the search; (2) he was not found close to the drugs; (3) he was not under the influence when the officers arrested him; (4) he had no contraband on his person; (5) he said at the time of arrest that the drugs in the boxes did not belong to him but belonged to his brother who made him sell them; (6) he did not make furtive gestures or attempt to flee. (7) he owned and had the right to possess the house; (8) he had no drug odor about him or (9) he had no evidence of other drugs or paraphernalia; (10) the drugs were not in plain view but hidden and (11) the drugs were enclosed in cigarette boxes in a closet. *Id.*

Despite the evidence that might have exonerated Chisum, the Court concluded that the overwhelming weight of the evidence supported the verdict. *Id.* Chisum owned the house and was living there; he also admitted he knew the drugs were in his house and he sold them for his brother. *Id.* The court found this evidence affirmatively linked Chisum to the drugs and was legally sufficient to support the verdict. *Id.*

> Leads with affirmative argument and analogy to precedent.

Patrick will argue that, like the accused in *McGoldrick*, he was merely present at the scene and no additional facts support an affirmative link between him and the drugs. Similar to the lack of evidence in *McGoldrick*, the evidence in this case does not show Patrick was ever in a position to have viewed the drugs or that he ever handled the drugs. Further, Patrick did not own the vehicle he was driving and did not have Alprazolam (Xanax) or other drugs on his person. He was simply present at the scene, which is insufficient to support a conviction.

Moreover, the other factors considered by the courts weigh in Patrick's favor. The pills were not in plain view but hidden and enclosed in the car's center console. In addition, the pills were not located directly in front of Patrick;

they were in the console and one had to lift the cover to access the pills. Patrick was not under the influence of drugs at the time of his arrest, and he made no incriminating statements when arrested. He did not make any furtive gestures or try to flee the scene but rather freely consented to the search of his person and the car. There are no additional facts and circumstances, beyond Patrick's mere presence at the scene, from which one could infer he knew of and exercised control over the pills located in the console.

Transitions to the counter-argument where the State analogizes to *Chisum*. Emphasizes the affirmative links between Patrick and the drugs.

However, relying on *Chisum*, the State will maintain the evidence in Patrick's case is even more compelling for unlawful possession of drugs. Like the defendant in *Chisum*, Patrick had a right to possess the place where the officers found the drugs. Patrick was driving the borrowed car in which the officers found the drugs. Also, although the drugs were hidden and enclosed in the console, Patrick was sitting right next to the drugs and could easily assess them. There was no lock on the console.

Also, the officers smelled marijuana in the car and found other drug evidence, the marijuana seeds, in the car. Patrick denied the drugs belonged to him, but he admitted he had previously taken Xanax without a prescription. Similarly, the defendant in *Chisum* admitted his familiarity with the contraband when he told officers he sold the cocaine for his brother. Lastly, Patrick's car was parked in an area known for drug activity, and the officers did not see anyone entering or leaving the car for approximately 30 minutes before their entry. *See also Porter*, 873 S.W.2d at 733 (listing several factors that support finding of unlawful possession such as close proximity and accessibility to drugs and lack of traffic entering and exiting the location).

The State will argue these independent facts and circumstances constitute overwhelming evidence affirmatively linking Patrick to the contraband, which, when weighed in the aggregate, support a finding of unlawful possession. The affirmative links absent in *Chisum* are present here and weigh in the State's favor. Because Patrick was the driver of the car and was in such close proximity to the drugs' location, and the car contained other drug evidence, a jury could reasonably infer Patrick had both knowledge of the drugs and their forbidden nature and control over them.

Patrick will distinguish his situation from the findings in *Chisum*. Unlike the convicted defendant in *Chisum*,

Patrick did not own the place where the officers found the drugs. He was merely a driver in a car loaned to him by his cousin. Moreover, unlike a house, the car that Patrick drove was easily accessible to other people, including his passenger and his cousin, who actually owned the car. Any of these people could have placed the pills in the console and known they were there. Patrick's behavior did not suggest he had any prior knowledge that the pills were in the console. In addition, unlike the defendant in *Chisum*, Patrick did not admit to selling the contraband. There is no evidence that he at any time handled the drugs in the car. He did admit to past use of Xanax, but he did not exercise dominion and control over the drugs found in the console. Thus, there is no evidence or independent facts from which a jury could infer that Patrick knew of and exercised control over the pills. His presence at the scene, alone, is insufficient to support a finding of unlawful possession under the affirmative links evaluation approved in *Chisum*, 988 S.W.2d at 248, and *Porter*, 873 S.W.2d at 733.

Because of insufficient evidence to prove affirmative links between Patrick and the Alprazolam (or Xanax), the State will likely fail to show beyond a reasonable doubt that Patrick unlawfully possessed the pills found in the car's console.

Ends with a clear conclusion.

STATUTORY ANALYSIS FOR SUCCESS

EXERCISE 88

SAMPLE ANSWER

Begins with a clear conclusion sentence predicting the likely outcome of this case in favor of the prosecution.

Corky Moore ("Moore") will likely fail to provide sufficient evidence that he had a reasonable belief in the need to defend himself against Benjamin "Hurricane" Carver ("Carver"). The California Penal Code provides that a person may use self-defense "when there is reasonable ground to apprehend a design to commit a felony or to do some great bodily injury, and imminent danger of such design being accomplished[.]" Cal. Penal Code §§ 197–199 (Deering 2011)

Starts the law section with the relevant statutory language. Provides the operative rule from the statute. Then provides the legal standard from the cases that serve to interpret or expand the understanding of the statutory provisions.

Note: This response will not address whether Moore had a valid subjective belief in the need to defend or whether he used excessive force against Carver.

"A [defendant's] bare fear of the commission" of a felony or great bodily harm against him is insufficient to justify the use of self-defense. *Id.* § 198. "[T]he circumstances must be sufficient to excite the fears of a reasonable person, and the party killing must have acted under the influence of such fears alone." *Id.*; *People v. Trevino*, 246 Cal. Rptr. 357, 360 (Ct. App. 1988). "The party killing is not precluded from feeling anger or other emotions save and except for fear; however, those other emotions cannot be causal factor in his decision to use deadly force." *Trevino*, 246 Cal. Rptr. at 360.

Provides the law for determining when the defendant has a right to self-defense (even though the amount of force used may have been excessive).

As for the requisite "reasonable grounds," the right of self-defense (apart from the reasonableness of the forced used) is satisfied as a matter of law when a reasonable person in the defendant's position would have feared for his safety or perceived the necessity of defense. *People v. Clark*, 181 Cal. Rptr. 682, 685, 687 (Ct. App. 1982) ("[A] person may be found guilty of unlawful homicide even when the evidence establishes the right of self defense if the jury finds that . . . the force used exceeded that which was reasonably necessary to repel the attack."); *see also People v. Whitfield*, 66 Cal. Rptr. 438, 440 (Ct. App. 1968) (recognizing that defendant may be entitled to use force to defend himself but still may be found to have used excessive force). Thus, the right to use self-defense is an objective test and will turn on "whether the circumstances would cause a reasonable person to perceive the necessity of defense[.]" *Clark*, 181 Cal. Rptr. at 686. Such an inquiry does not evaluate the legality of the defendant's actions from his perspective but rather examines it from the perspective of a reasonable person standing in his shoes. *Id.* at 686–87. A court will consider all the relevant surrounding circumstances, including the victim's statements and conduct at the time of killing, viewed in combination with the victim's prior threatening statements and conduct, to determine whether a reasonable person would have believed a physical attack was imminent. *See id.* at 687. Furthermore, "[j]ustification [in using self-defense] does not depend up on the existence of actual danger but rather upon appearances." *Clark*, 181 Cal. Rptr. at 685. The defendant "'may act upon such appearances with safety'" even though he was mistaken as to the need to use such force at the time. *Id.* at 685–86 (quoting People v. Collins, 11 Cal. Rptr. 504, 513 (Ct. App. 1961)).

The California Court of Appeal (Fourth District) has held a defendant did not have an objectively reasonable belief to fear for his safety. *People v. Hickman*, No. E043962, 2008 Cal. App. Unpub. LEXIS 9464, at *13 (Ct. App. Nov. 21, 2008). In *Hickman*, while returning from the store with his son Roy, the victim, Frank Martinez and his companions saw a parked SUV, and Hollands, the adopted brother of the defendant, Hickman, was walking from the SUV towards Martinez. *Id.* at *3. Both Hollands and Hickman had confronted Martinez earlier that day. *Id.* Hollands approached Martinez and began to fight with him. *Id.* at *4. Martinez's son tried to intervene, but Hickman warned him not to get involved and hit him with a stick. *Id.* Martinez then threw a piece of blacktop at Hickman, causing him to fall to the ground. *Id.* Hickman and Hollands got into their SUV and started to taunt Martinez and the others as they continued to walk home. *Id.* Roy threw a rock at the SUV, shattering the back driver's-side window. *Id.* Martinez began to throw rocks too. *Id.* Hickman then circled the field, drove toward Martinez, who fell while running away, and ran him over. *Id.* According to Hickman, he felt he was in danger and accelerated his SUV only in response to his being hit in the back of the neck by another rock. *Id.* at *5.

The court concluded that "a reasonable person in [the defendant's] position would not have believed his life was in such imminent threat of death or great bodily injury that running over [the victim] was necessary to avert that threat." *Id.* at *13. The court further emphasized there was no "evidence presented [by the defendant] that indicated there was such a reasonable threat present." *Id.* Although not explicitly stated by the court, the circumstances did

> **[Annotation, left margin:]** Provides a clear explanation of the legal standard from precedent. Includes the key facts, holding, and reasoning from this case so that the reader can clearly understand how the court applies the test in a real-world scenario.

> **[Annotation, right margin:]** Leads with case illustration that supports the author's conclusion that Moore did not reasonably fear for his safety.

not present any appearance of imminent danger or serious bodily harm to the defendant. *See id.* at *12–13. The defendant merely had rocks thrown in his direction. *See id.* at *4–6, 12. Moreover, the defendant remained at the wheel of a moving SUV while the victim and his group remained on foot. *Id.* Thus, the defendant did not reasonably believe his life was in danger. *Id.* at *13.

Similarly, the Second District court found that the defendant did not reasonably believe the victim would cause him serious injury. *People v. Bayardo*, No. B167682, 2004 Cal. App. Unpub. LEXIS 6952, at *13–14 (Ct. App. July 26, 2004). In *Bayardo*, an ongoing family feud between the Ponce and Gonzales families escalated into a brawl involving the fathers of the two families and eventually Bayardo, the defendant, who was associated with the Gonzaleses. *Id.* at *3–8. Throughout the day, different disturbances erupted, and Ponce, the victim, exchanged angry remarks with Gonzales, crossed the street, and started to fistfight with him. *Id.* at *3–4. During the fight, the victim supposedly threatened not only Gonzales but also his friends, wife, and kids. *Id.* at *6. Gonzales sustained a cut on his nose from this fight. *Id.* at *4. After the fight ended, Ponce continued to agitate the situation by taunting Gonzales's family and friends. *Id.* at *4–5. Ponce crossed the street a second time, allegedly outraged, running fast, and looking directly at Bayardo. *Id.* at *4–8. Ponce supposedly struck Bayardo on the back of the head. *Id.* at *6. Fearing for his life, Bayardo stabbed Ponce with his pocketknife. *Id.*

The court concluded there was "little evidence supporting an inference" that Bayardo's use of a knife against the victim was a reasonable act of self-defense. *Id.* at *13. In addressing the level of force used by the defendant, the court also remarked that the defendant failed to identify any facts indicating that he *reasonably believed* Ponce had a gun or could inflict serious injury with his fists. *Id.* at *13–14.

Bayardo stated that, when Ponce hit him, he did not see a knife or gun. *Id.* at *14. Bayardo also admitted he had watched the fistfight between Ponce and Gonzalez and that afterwards he did not see any serious injuries on Gonzalez. *Id.* The court observed that Bayardo had presented no evidence indicating he had a reasonable belief Ponce had a gun or could inflict serious injury with his fists, implying that the circumstances did not present a situation in which a reasonable person would have feared

Infers the court's reasoning for its decision.

Provides a second case illustration that supports the author's conclusion that Moore did not reasonably fear for his safety.

Bayardo is one of the cases on the list in which the court concluded there was sufficient evidence to show an unlawful killing. The court focused largely on the excessive use of force but the author offers it as an example of a defendant who faced a harmless situation.

In Whitfield, the court stated, without explanation, that it did not think the defendants were entitled to use force against the victim.

The author infers the court's apparent position on whether the defendant's belief was reasonable under the circumstances, using the relevant discussion about the level of force used. The court specifically noted that defendant did not reasonably fear serious harm from the victim.

serious bodily injury from the victim, and affirmed the judgment against Bayardo. *Id.* at *14, 17.

> **Describes the facts and reasoning in a case where the court reaches the opposite conclusion.**

In *Clark*, however, the Third District held that, although the amount of force used was excessive, the defendant's right of self-defense was established as a matter of law. 181 Cal. Rptr. at 688. In *Clark*, the victim, Simmons, knew his wife, Gayle, had an affair with Clark, and Simmons made a number of verbal threats and unsuccessful attempts to confront Clark. *Id.* at 684. Simmons even chased Clark in his car on two separate occasions. *Id.* Clark even began to carry a loaded gun under the seat in his car. *Id.* On the day of the killing, Simmons again had chased Clark's car, and Simmons used his truck to block Clark's driveway. *Id.* at 684–85. Clark testified that Simmons appeared "furious," and he approached Clark's car window and said, "[Y]our time is now." *Id.* at 685. Simmons reached into Clark's car window and Clark shot and killed him. *Id.*

The court held that, as a matter of law, the "defendant had the right to defend himself against the attack of the victim." *Id.* at 687. A reasonable person in the defendant's circumstances would have feared for his safety given that the "victim had indicated in no uncertain terms his intent to force a physical confrontation" with the defendant. *Id.* The court emphasized Simmons's several previous attempts to confront Clark physically and the victim's aggressive conduct on the day of the killing that gave a clear indication of an imminent assault. *Id.*

> **Infers the court's reasoning for its decision.**

The court apparently reasoned that the history between Clark and Simmons established a pattern of conduct in the mind of Clark that influenced Clark's interpretation of any future encounters. *See* 181 Cal. Rptr. at 687. The court did not examine Simmons's conduct on the final day in a vacuum but rather viewed his conduct on the final day in the context of his previous actions to find reasonable fear of imminent harm. *Id.* Thus, in light of the parties' history, the court concluded that a reasonable person would have interpreted the victim's actions on the final day as manifesting a clear intent to assault the defendant. *Id.*

> **Note the court concluded the defendant had a right to self-defense but also found that the amount of force used was excessive.**

The prosecution here will argue that Moore did not reasonably fear for his safety under the circumstances. Like the defendants in *Hickman* and *Bayardo*, nothing from the surrounding facts indicates that Moore reasonably believed that Carver would inflict a felony or serious injury upon him. As Carver approached Moore in the parking garage, Carver simply said, "Hey you!" He did not seem overly aggressive or angry. Carver did not use any name-calling or threatening words. He merely called out to Moore, hoping that he would stop so they could talk. Similar to the situation in *Hickman* when the victim only threw rocks at the defendant, Moore was in presence of an equally harmless victim. Carver stood only six inches taller than Moore did and, according to Moore, Carver seemed to be sweating profusely as he approached. He had to work hard to catch up with Moore, and Carver's flushed face likely was to the result of his running from the bar to catch up with Moore. There was no sign of anger in Carver's disposition or appearance. Furthermore, like Bayardo, who admitted he did not see the victim, Ponce, with a knife or gun, Moore did not notice any weapon in Carver's hands as he ran toward Moore that night. Moore had no reason to fear for his life or serious bodily injury. A reasonable person under such circumstances would not have believed he was facing an imminent and unlawful threat of death or great bodily harm. Therefore, Moore cannot establish the requisite objective and reasonable perception of the need to use self-defense.

On the other hand, Moore will rely on his past knowledge of and experience with Carver to support his reasonable perception of the need to use force against Carver. Moore will argue that his situation is similar to the defendant in *Clark* whose history with Simmons, coupled with Simmons's conduct on that final day supported Clark's right to self-defense. In particular, Moore will emphasize that Carver had a reputation for being a quarrelsome troublemaker and having an anger problem. Bar patrons and the bartender told Moore about the many arguments and fights involving or started by Carver. Moore knew Carver had a bad reputation and propensity to act violently. Furthermore, Carver was extremely jealous and often challenged patrons who simply talked to his girlfriend, Christy, or looked too long in her direction. Moore witnessed Carver beat up a man with his bare hands just because the man had asked Christy to dance. Carver injured the man so badly that he remained in the hospital for a week.

Moore reasonably feared the same abusive treatment from Carver. Before the night Carver chased Moore to the parking garage, Moore had last seen Carver when Moore had to hurriedly leave Mahogany because Carver headed

---

Sidebar annotations (left margin):

Begins with the affirmative argument (for the prosecution) and a clear leading thesis sentence for this section. Follows with a clear analogy to the precedent case and incorporates the legal standard in this analogy.

Incorporates a fact-on-fact analogy to the precedent case.

Next, provides Moore's counter-argument. Analogizes to the best case on the list that supports Moore's position, *Clark*.

Sidebar annotation (right margin):

Identifies specific facts supporting the prosecution's position and explains the relevance of each fact.

toward him where he was standing and talking to Christy. Carver had walked in the bar and seen Christy speaking with Moore. Carver glared at Moore, and his face became red. Moore believed Carver would have hit him at that moment, but Christy luckily distracted Carver and pulled him to the dance floor. On his next visit to the bar, the bartender told Moore Carver had been asking about him, which reasonably indicated to Moore that Carver was still angry about the Christy incident. During that final encounter, on the day when the bar reopened, Moore did not want to be another victim of Carver's explosive temper and jealously.

As Carver followed Moore out of the bar and approached him in the deserted garage, Carver's flushed-red face instantly brought back memories of Moore's narrowly escaping a beating for talking to Carver's girlfriend. Carver had never spoken to Moore before, just angrily glared in his direction. Moore did not expect this encounter to be any different, and there was no one in the garage to intervene. In addition, Carver stood a half-foot taller than Moore and weighed forty pounds more. The size difference alone was intimidating and threatening under the circumstances. Furthermore, the only exit from the garage was in the direction of Carver's oncoming path. Moore could not escape and stood trapped between the cars. Just as Simmons's behavior before and during the final encounter in *Clark* caused Clark to reasonably fear for his safety as a matter of law, Moore's history with Carver, knowledge of Carver's prior violent encounters, and Carver's approach on that final day caused Moore to reasonably fear for his safety as a matter of law.

Moore's argument, however, will likely fail. Unlike the situation in *Clark* that involved a car chase and a series of escalating events, here there was no behavior by Carver on the day of the incident that a reasonable person could characterize as anything but peaceful or inquisitive. Carver did not make any threatening gestures or statements toward Moore. Carver did not have a weapon. In addition, unlike the events in *Clark* that occurred during the months after the affair ended, Moore's most recent encounter with Carver had been one month earlier. Moore had no contact with Carver during the month in which the owner closed the bar for renovations. Moreover, Moore did not hear about any incidents involving Carver during this time. Thus, Moore had no reason to suspect that Carver still harbored any alleged ill will toward him.

> Provides a rebuttal argument as to why Moore's evidence is insufficient. Identifies key facts and the relevance of those facts to the argument.

> Distinguishes the *Clark* case.

453

Carver would have had more than enough time during this month to calm down, assuming he in fact was still angry with Moore. Lastly, and most importantly, Carver had never committed any act of violence against Moore. Moore unreasonably based his fears on second-hand accounts and Carver's disputes with other bar patrons. The situation that Moore faced was as innocuous as the ones confronted by the defendants in *Hickman* and *Bayardo*.

Ends with clear conclusion.

Thus, a court will likely find that Moore could not have reasonably felt threatened by his final encounter with Carver in the parking garage.

STATUTES WITH LEGISLATIVE HISTORY

EXERCISE 90

SAMPLE ANSWER

An initial sentence gives the conclusion for both issues.

Green was cited with two tickets under the snake statute—he can probably prevail in court regarding the ticket for his exhibition of the Green Rough snake, but not the ticket for the Black Mamba. The legislative history indicates that people must be put at serious risk or harmed before a Class C misdemeanor ticket should be issued.

References the statute's text before delving into the legislative history.

The statute's text makes it an "offense for a person to display, exhibit, handle, or use a poisonous or dangerous snake or reptile in a manner that threatens the life or health of any person." Tenn. Code Ann. 39-17-101 (2011). Thus, the statute does not apply to snakes that are neither poisonous nor dangerous.

Provides a sentence or two that explain the discussion to come.

The legislative history of the statute recognizes the educational value of snake shows; it indicates that the statute is intended to punish actual injuries or serious threats to health or safety. At the initial hearings on the possible legislation, herpetologist Mary Mastoff testified that "[s]nakes are not a show. Snakes are creatures that have much to teach us." Discussions in the legislature support the idea that it can be educational to see snake exhibitions, provided that the snakes are presented in a safe manner.

Looks to failed legislation in order to see what the legislature did *not* intend.

Thus, the statute does not prohibit snake shows, but requires that shows involving "poisonous or dangerous" snakes be conducted in a manner that does not "threaten the life or health" of any person. In fact, legislation completely banning shows with venomous snakes and requiring a six-foot barrier with other snakes failed to pass the house. This, together with testimony stressing the positive economic impact of circuses, suggests that the legislature did not intend to supress snake shows completely.

Looks at statute's text in order to determine the statute's scope; enhances the analysis with legislative history.

The statute applies only to snakes that are "poisonous or dangerous." While any snake could in some sense be considered "dangerous" because most can bite a human, Representative Chuck Johnson clarified that "dangerous" is meant to mean constricting snakes. He stated during floor debates that "[i]f a snake is poisonous or dangerous, and by dangerous we mean those snakes that squeeze people, you know, those anacondas and such, then this statute will address those snakes." Thus, non-venomous, non-constricting snakes probably should not be included within the statute's scope.

With regard to the language "in a manner that threatens the life or health of any person," the legislature appears to have intended only serious threats to be included. In his signing statement, for example, the Governor of Tennessee stated that "if there's a serious problem, then there's a penalty."

In addition, other legislators stressed that small problems and matters of snake management would be left to the expert. Senator Sylvia Malone explained, for example, that "things don't have to be perfect . . . the show just can't 'endanger the life or health' of anyone. So that's fair. If things are just a bit wrong or someone has a tiny problem, that's not a person's 'life or health' being endangered. So there's some room to maneuver and some proportionality." In addition, Representative Todd Stevens noted that the law "leaves the details to the person who knows the snakes—the snake handler." Thus, the legislative history emphasizes that serious risks to life and health are covered by the statute, whereas small slips are not considered to be offenses.

The ticket for Green's presentation of the Black Mamba is probably justified, and Green will have little success if he goes to trial. Although the Black Mamba was in a secure container, a four-year-old boy was able to open the case and release the snake. A Black Mamba is an extremely dangerous and fast snake, and the threat of a Black Mamba at large in a group of people is considerable.

The ticket for Green's presentation of the Green Rough snake will be easier to challenge. The statute only applies to snakes that are "poisonous or dangerous." The Green Rough Snake is not poisonous, but is a docile snake that rarely bites. Representative Chuck Johnson stated that "dangerous" is meant to mean constricting snakes. He stated during floor debates that "[i]f a snake is poisonous or dangerous, and by dangerous we mean those snakes that squeeze people, you know, those anacondas and such, then this statute will address those snakes." The Green Rough snake is not one of those snakes.

Moreover, the Green Rough snake was not exhibited in a manner that would threaten life or health of a person, as the statute also requires. Green kept the Green Rough

| Shifts clearly to discussion of a separate portion of the statute. |

| Uses specific language and quotations to make the argument. |

| Applies the legislative history analysis to the facts at hand. |

| Makes a clear shift to the second misdemeanor ticket. |

Uses transitions to show that this argument is a further point to support the same argument.

snake at a distance from the children—a child was only able to touch the snake when he ran toward it and grabbed the snake. Even so, there was little threat to the child's safety, because the snake is not a dangerous or venomous one. The snake let out its trademark stench, but this was not a threat to health or safety.

Thus, because the Black Mamba is a deadly snake kept in unsafe conditions, the ticket will be very difficult to challenge. The Green Rough snake, however, does not fit within the statute's scope, because it is not "poisonous or dangerous" so the ticket should be challenged.

STATUTES WITH LEGISLATIVE HISTORY

EXERCISE 92

SAMPLE ANSWER

Based on the statute's text and legislative history, the jello wrestling event will probably be considered a wrestling event for purposes of the statute, and Wall will need to report and pay taxes under New Hampshire law.

The plain text of the statute includes wrestling within the definition of "fighting sports." In addition, the definition of "fighting sports" also includes "any other form of amateur or professional sport combat in which blows are struck that reasonably may be expected to inflict injury." Athough jello wrestling is not considered to be a form of combat sport in which blows "may be expected to inflict injury," the legislative history shows that it is a form of wrestling such that Wall's events must be reported and taxed.

The statute was passed in order to monitor and slightly discourage events that can cause injury between contestants, even where the event is light-hearted or fun in nature. The statute requiring that fighting sports be taxed and reported was passed in 1979. At that time, authorities discovered that underground boxing and wrestling matches had developed and serious injuries were occurring. According to the Governor's signing statement, the reporting and taxing of these events was meant to bring them into the open, so that matches would be conducted in a safer and more legitimate manner.

During the committee deliberations, Senator Chuck Jones argued that novelty events should not be taxed, even if they do involve fighting—he specfically mentioned jello wrestling as an event that should not be reportable or taxable. Senator Jones's view, however, did not win the day, as he had urged that the bill's language be revised, while ultimately, the language remained unchanged. Representative Mary Silva urged that the broader language remain intact, with the view that the more reporting and taxing, the better.

In the floor debates after the bill left the committee, Representative Mack Richards, who sponsored the bill, explained that his children had competed in fighting sport

458

events, and that even novelty or charity events can lead to injury. He urged that the bill be passed so that such events could be tracked and taxed. Although Senator Sue Strang argued against this new tax, Representative Richards noted with approval that taxing might discourage such events.

Based on the legislative history, Wall's jello events will be included within the term "wrestling" in the statute. The rules of Wall's events indicate that no hitting or kicking can occur, thereby removing jello wrestling from the statutory language that refers to any "form of amateur or professional sport combat in which blows are struck that reasonably may be expected to inflict injury." But the jello wrestling events do seem to fall within the term "wrestling," which is separately set out in the provision. Committee members and legislators in the floor debates emphasized the breadth with which the provision should be read. Sponsoring Representative Richards emphasized that even light-hearted events could be dangerous, thereby indicating that events such as jello wrestling should be included. Even the Governor's signing statement emphasized the "varied" fighting events in the state, indicating that a wide variety of events would include jello wrestling.

Wall could argue that his events should not be taxed, and that Senator Strang voiced the opposition to these new taxes. This argument will likely fail, however, because Strang's position did not prevail, and the bill passed. The legislature made the decision to add the new tax, so if Wall's events fit within the provision, they must be taxed.

> Provides the counter-argument and explains why it will not prevail.

The statute's definition of "wrestling" seems to include jello wrestling, because the committee members and senators and representatives in the floor debates emphasized the breadth with which the definition should be read. Wall therefore will probably be required to report his events and pay taxes on his ticket sales.

STATUTES WITH LEGISLATIVE HISTORY

EXERCISE 94[*]

SAMPLE ANSWER

Starts with a clear conclusion that explains the basis for the reasoning.

The strict liability provision is not clear from its plain language because the provision's context suggests a concern with environmental harms while the strict liability provision itself addresses *all* types of harms. The legislative history indicates, however, that the provision's purpose was to address environmental concerns, indicating that the provision should not apply to the personal injury claims at issue here.

Explains that statutory analysis begins with the provision's plain text.

The words of a statute are its principal source of meaning. Where statutory language is plain on its face, there is no need to look to legislative history to determine the meaning of the words. The meaning can be guided, however, by consideration of the purpose that the legislature meant to address. Here, the strict liability provision is clear but its context lends ambiguity to the provision's meaning. That is, the statutory language states that the right-of-way holder shall be strictly liable for "damages in connection with or resulting from activities along or in the vicinity of the proposed trans-Alaskan pipeline right-of-way." 43 U.S.C. § 1653(a)(1) (2011).

Discusses the statute's plain language in detail, with references to statute's specifics.

Explains why the court may decide to look to the statute's purpose even though the language is clear.

This language is extremely broad, suggesting that all types of harms are included. The latter part of the provision, however, seems to focus specifically on environmental harms, stating that the strict liability rule applies "without regard to ownership of any affected lands, structures, fish, wildlife, or biotic or other natural resources relied upon by Alaska Natives, Native organizations, or others for subsistence or economic purposes." *Id.* If the statute were applied as the first portion is written, it would hold the right-of-way holder liable for all harms, whether related to the environment or not, which would seem to contradict the second part of the statutory provision, which discusses various types of lands.

In addition, the provision provides no reason for the right-of-way holder to be liable for such a broad range of claims without any consideration given to fault. Thus,

---

[*] This question and answer are based on *Heppner v. Alyeska Pipeline Serv. Co.*, 665 F.2d 868 (9th Cir. 1981).

because the statutory language is broad with regard to liability, but then seems to focus on environmental harms, a court may well look to the legislative history in order to determine the provision's correct interpretation.

This statute's legislative history indicates that the statute was aimed at environmental harms rather than broader strict liability that would include ordinary negligence and other claims. The only harms discussed in the legislative history are environmental harms, and the legislative history does not indicate any reason that the pipeline operators would be subject to such a heavy burden of liability with regard to general negligence.

> Provides a clear conclusion with regard to the statute's purpose as explained in the legislative history.

First, the conference report's discussion of liability repeatedly references environmental risks and harms. It does not mention other types of risk, such as ordinary negligence. H.R. Rep. No. 93-624, at 28 (1973) (Conf. Rep.). The conference report does not directly address the scope of the strict liability provision applicable here. It does, however, make specific references to environmental harms when discussing a neighboring provision applicable to oil loaded onto a vessel after traveling through the pipeline. In that provision, owners or operators are strictly liable for "discharges of oil from [a] vessel," which limits the scope of strict liability to a specific type of harm. To hold an owner or operator strictly liable for tangentially-related harms such as a truck accident seems inconsistent when compared with the narrower class of strict liability applicable in a neighboring statutory section that addresses the same oil as it flows through a pipeline and onto a vessel.

Second, a letter from the Secretary of the Interior as part of the Congressional hearings also addresses purely environmental harms. S. Rep. No. 207, 93d Cong., 1st Sess. 102 (1973), *reprinted in* 1973 U.S.C.C.A.N. 2508, 2509-10. The letter states that "[t]he environmental risks involved in the Alaska route are not insurmountable." This suggests that Congress was focused on environmental harms in its discussions leading up to the provision's enactment and that the provision should be read as applying to environmental harms rather than tangential truck accidents.

> Pieces together the legislature's intent by looking at more than one source of legislative history.

Because the provision's meaning does not make sense in context, I would look to the legislative history. The provision read in the context of its legislative history indicates that the strict liability provision was geared toward environmental harms and that other claims should be addressed using general negligence law.

STATUTES WITH LEGISLATIVE HISTORY

EXERCISE 96 *

SAMPLE ANSWER

Begins with clear statement of the conclusion; briefly states the reason for this conclusion.

The Environmental Protection Agency's regulation that includes habitat destruction within the statute's definition of "harm" will probably be upheld. Based on the legislative history, the regulation is in keeping with Congress's intentions in passing the Endangered Species Act.

As an initial matter, the dictionary definition of "harm" suggests that the meaning should be broad, because the definition includes "hurt or damage." If a creature's habitat is taken away, it does suffer some hurt or damage. Each animal or other species must have some sort of home, and without that home, it suffers harm.

Statutory interpretation starts with plain text analysis.

Uses a variety of plain-text analysis approaches before turning to legislative history.

In addition, if the word "harm" only means directly hurting an animal, then the word "harm" is surplusage that does not add anything to the word "take." Statutes are generally assumed to have meaning in each word, and words in statutes are understood not to have a purely surplus function.

Next, the legislative history indicates that Congress had a broad and urgent concern for the protection of species when it enacted the Act. For example, the Assistant Secretary of the Interior testified in the 1973 hearings that the variety of species could hold enormous and untold value to humanity: "They are keys to puzzles which we cannot solve, and may provide answers to questions which we have not yet learned to ask." In addition, Stephen R. Seater, for Defenders of Wildlife stated that species are disappearing at the pace of about one per year, and "the pace of disappearance of species" appeared to be "accelerating."

Makes a clear shift to legislative history analysis; begins with a strong topic sentence that shows the paragraph's direction.

Uses specifics from the legislative history to advance the argument.

Moreover, congressional testimony in advance of the 1973 Act indicated that the main cause of the rapid extinction was destruction of habitats. And, Congress made a finding in 1973 that destruction of habitats was a major reason for extinction, together with hunting. The Assistant Deputy Chief for the National Forest System said that the destruction of natural habitats was a more significant

---

* This problem and its answer are based on the case of *Babbit v. Sweet Home Chapter of Communities for a Great Oregon*, 515 U.S. 678 (1995).

cause of extinction than hunting. Thus, because Congress was extremely concerned with extinction of species, and a major cause of that extinction was explained to be the destruction of habitats, a definition of "harm" that includes destruction of habitats would be in keeping with Congress's concerns and purpose for enacting the Act.

Based on the testimony that Congress heard, the increasing destruction of habitats and the resulting loss of species suggests that the Act's protections would likely extend to protection of species' habitats rather than only the direct application of force to an animal.

Furthermore, the trend in the Act's development is for protection of species to increase and become more urgent as Congress receives more information about the rapid extinction of species. That is, the initial version of the Act contained only limited provisions to protect endangered species, and only those that were native to the United States. The subsequent version expanded those provisions to include protection of species threatened anywhere in the world, and provided extra protection.

In addition, the overall tenor of all the congressional testimony and findings on the Act suggest that Congress intended to preserve endangered species by all possible means. The Assistant Secretary of the Interior in 1973 explained that certain species could hold the cure to cancer or other diseases, and that destruction of habitats is a significant problem that results in the destruction of species. Given that Congress's actions were based on testimony stressing the importance of habitat preservation, a broad definition of "harm" is a reasonable interpretation of Congress's intent.

> Begins with clear topic sentence, backed up by specifics from the legislative history.

It could be argued, however, that Congress did not intend to include destruction of habitats within the definition of "harm," because a draft of the Senate version of the Act included a direct prohibition on "destruction, modification, or curtailment of [the] habitat or range" of fish or wildlife, but that language was deleted before enactment. This deletion could suggest that Congress intentionally took out the prohibition on destruction of habitats, and therefore the definition of "harm" should not be read as including destruction of habitats.

> Uses the statute's various versions and drafting history to make an argument.

This argument will likely fail. The Senate version of the Act initially included a specific prohibition on destruction of habitats, and that prohibition was later removed. The new version, however, includes the word "harm,"

> States clearly why the counter-argument fails.

which is even broader than the previous version. Thus, Congress appeared to reject specific examples of harm in favor of a catch-all term that would include every possible type of harm.

Thus, the Congressional hearings and findings suggest an intent toward a broad view of conservation. Also, the testimony and hearings specifically mention conservation of habitats. Therefore, the agency's regulation that defines "harm" as including destruction of habitats will likely be upheld.

STATUTES WITH LEGISLATIVE HISTORY

EXERCISE 98

SAMPLE ANSWER*

Indiana's Good Samaritan statute probably will not protect Dr. Smith from a lawsuit related to her care of Sandra Simmons. Dr. Smith had a pre-existing duty to Simmons, in that Dr. Smith was Simmons's physician, so her care was not "without obligation" as the statute requires. In addition, the statute applies only to care rendered to "accident" victims, and the legislative history does not indicate that the statute was intended to include victims of medical emergencies.

The statute protects from liability those who render aid at the scene of an accident or care for accident victims:

> Any person who gratuitously and without obligation renders emergency care at the scene of an accident or emergency care to the victim thereof, shall not be liable for any civil damages for any personal injury as a result of any act or omission by such person in rendering the emergency care or as a result of any act or failure to act to provide or arrange for further medical treatment or care for the injured person, except acts or omissions amounting to gross negligence or willful or wanton misconduct.

Ind. Code § 34-4-12-1 (2011). The statutory language and legislative history suggest that existing patient-physician relationships and medical emergencies are not covered by the statute.

(1) Dr. Smith's care probably was not "without obligation."

While Dr. Smith was not on call the evening of Simmons's illness, the two had a physician-patient and personal relationship such that Dr. Smith's care would probably not be considered "without obligation" as the statute requires.

---

* This answer is based upon the court's opinion in *Beckerman v. Gordon*, 614 N.E.2d 610 (Ind. App. 1993).

To be covered by the statute, a Good Samaritan's care must be "gratuitous[] and without obligation." The plain language of the text indicates that the care must be without charge and without any kind of relationship that obligates the Good Samaritan to the patient. The legislative history indicates that the Indiana legislature did not intend to affect pre-existing doctor-patient relationships. Indeed, several legislators spoke on the issue and said that emergency physicians and others who work in emergency medicine should not be immunized from liability by this statute.

In statutory interpretation, discusses the plain meaning first, before moving to legislative history.

For example, in the floor debates in advance of the passage of the current statute, Representative John Garcia expressed his strong support for physicians and others in the healthcare professions. He noted, however, that the statute's protections should not extend to physicians' pre-existing patients: "Not against their own patients, of course, but against the helpless stranger, the lost traveler, the injured person on the airplane, or the woman suddenly giving birth away from her own doctor." Indeed, the bill's sponsor, Representative Tammy Washington, pointed out that other laws had been created to address caps on medical malpractice damages and the like, and that the Good Samaritan law was not intended to be a medical malpractice law of general application.

Uses specific examples and quotations to support the writer's conclusion on the issue.

Likewise, a previous, vetoed version of this law indicates that the governor did not intend to have an overly broad law that would apply to all emergency medical personnel. The vetoed legislation that would have protected "[a]ny person who renders emergency care at the scene of a serious medical situation." This, the governor said, would effectively immunize the entire emergency room personnel from liability.

Dr. Smith's care of Simmons was gratuitous, in that she waived any fees. But to the extent that Simmons and Dr. Smith had a pre-existing doctor-patient relationship, the legislative history indicates that Dr. Smith's care is not protected as the actions of a Good Samaritan by the statute.

Entertains opposing argument and shows why it will likely fail; uses specifics to rebut, rather than conclusory statements.

On the other hand, Dr. Smith could argue that while she did have a physician-patient relationship with Simmons, Dr. Smith's actions on that particular night were not those of a personal physician, but of a friend who heard someone in pain. Because she was not on call that night and could have referred Simmons to the on-call doctor, Dr. Smith arguably had no duty to go and help Simmons at 2:00 a.m. This argument will likely fail, however, because Dr. Smith's and Simmons's relationship—one that intertwined medical care and friendship—suggests that Dr. Smith was under an "obligation," namely the obligations of both friendship and medical care. In addition, the examples given by legislators mention roadside accident victims and the like, namely people without any prior relationship.

Thus, Dr. Smith's care of Simmons probably will not be considered "without obligation" as required by the statute.

(2) Simmons's care was not due to an "accident."

While the statutory language mentions "emergency care," it states that the statute applies to emergency care given to victims of accidents. The statute does not mention emergencies in general or other medical emergencies.

> Sets out conclusion that gives the reader information as to the reasoning that supports the conclusion.

The statute's plain language suggests that medical conditions would not be included within the term "accident." Ballentine's Law Dictionary, for example, defines an accident as "[a]n occurrence by chance or not as expected . . . an occurrence which could not have been foreseen by the exercise of reasonable prudence, one which happens from the uncontrollable operations of nature alone, without human agent." *Ballentine's Law Dictionary* (3d ed. 2010).

While a heart attack such as the one suffered by Simmons could be considered an occurrence "not as expected," illness does occur in the usual course of events and is a normal part of life.

> Looks for patterns in the development of Good Samaritan legislation that would assist in the analysis.

In addition, when Indiana's Good Samaritan statute is viewed in the national context of Good Samaritan statutes, Indiana's statute appears to have been intentionally left narrow. That is, other states in the early 1990s developed statutes that would apply to "emergencies" as well as "accidents," while Indiana's subsequent amendment of its statute did not include this change. For example, the California statute previously mentioned only the terms "at the scene of an accident" to describe its scope. In 1990, however, it was amended to its current form, which calls for immunity "at the scene of an emergency." Georgia's Good Samaritan statute was amended in 1992. The previous language—"accident or calamity"—was revised so that the statute now applies to any "accident or emergency."

> Uses specific language so that the reader can see exactly how the writer reached the conclusion.

467

The Georgia statute now seems to call for a broader application that may well include medical emergencies.

Indiana's Good Samaritan statute, on the other hand, was broader in its pre-1971 version, which referred to those who render aid at "an accident, casualty, or disaster to a person injured therein." The current version, enacted in 1971, refers only to "emergency care at the scene of an accident or emergency care to the victim thereof." The Indiana legislature was well aware of the national trend in broadening Good Samaritan statutes, as the legislature heard testimony from a national expert on Good Samaritan statutes who referred to the national trend.

The Indiana legislature appears to have considered this trend and balanced it against other testimony it received, namely that of a mother who went into labor in a hospital, where a doctor delivered her baby but made costly errors. The legislature, it appears, did not wish to relieve doctors or other caregivers of liability where the caregiver has some prior relationship with or duty to the patient.

> Uses multiple approaches to make its point; does not make just one point and conclude.

Furthermore, each senator or representative who spoke on this legislation referred to accidents in which the victim would have been left without care had the Good Samaritan not rendered aid. Bill sponsor and Representative Tammy Washington, for example, outlined the bill's intended scope, which, she said, applied to situations in which an accident victim is needing help, and a caregiver may be discouraged from helping for fear of liability. She specifically said that legislation such as caps on medical malpractice damages and the like would address the medical profession's concerns with regard to existing patients rather than previously-unknown accident victims.

Likewise, Senator Susan Simone explained that the bill was meant to cover situations in which medical professionals are forced to choose between helping a fellow citizen and worry about their own potential liability: "doctors and nurses who see an accident are going to have to think first about their own liability. And that's not right." Finally, Senator Robert Giles stated that he would not support any legislation that relieved healthcare professionals of liability in a blanket form, and he did not believe the current legislation had that effect: "If we're looking to relieve all doctors and nurses of doing their jobs right, then forget it, I'm not going along with anything that does that. I don't think this language does."

Thus, the statute appears to have been left fairly narrow in its scope, so that medical emergencies that are not the result of an accident would not be included. Simmons's care was not the result of an accident, but rather of an illness that first showed itself in a dramatic and ultimately fatal manner. The Indiana statute does not appear, from its history and context, to be designed to address such a situation.

Given the legislative history of the Indiana Good Samaritan statute and the dictionary definition of "accident," the Indiana statute is unlikely to protect Dr. Smith from liability for her care of Simmons.

STATUTES WITH LEGISLATIVE HISTORY

EXERCISE 100

SAMPLE ANSWER

<table>
<tr>
<td>

Leads with clear thesis sentence identifying the likely conclusion that a court would reach on this issue.

</td>
<td>

A court likely will find that, in light of the statute's purpose and related sections, Section 3105.91 does not confer a right to receive a share of the quasi-marital property upon the guilty party in a putative marriage.* Section 3105.91 provides the following:

</td>
</tr>
</table>

> If a determination is made that a marriage is void or voidable and the court finds that *either party or both parties believed in good faith that the marriage was valid, the court shall*:
>
> (1)   Declare the party or parties to have status of a putative spouse.
>
> (2)   If the division of property is in issue, *divide*, in accordance with Section 3105.171(B) (requiring equitable division of marital property), *that property acquired during the union* which would have been marital property if the union had not been void or voidable. This property is known as "quasi-marital property."

Ohio Rev. Code Ann. § 3105.91 (LexisNexis 1986) (emphasis added).

<table>
<tr>
<td>

Provides Wang's argument first, starting with the plain meaning argument. Note: the statutory language is always the starting point, as it is the best evidence of legislative intent.

</td>
<td>

Wang will maintain that the statutory language is ambiguous as to whether it should be applied to benefit a party who is not a putative spouse or who has committed wrongdoing. The statutory language at issue provides that, "If . . . the court finds that *either party or both parties believed in good faith that the marriage was valid, the court . . .*" is required to take certain action. *Id.* (emphasis in original). As the provision is written, it is unclear how the conjunction "or" operates. Logically, it would seem that

</td>
</tr>
</table>

---

* The statute and legislative history for this exercise were adopted, in part, from the Section 2251 of the California Family Code and the California Court of Appeal decisions and briefs filed in *In re Marriage of Sun*, 112 Cal. Rptr. 3d 906 (Ct. App. 2010) and *In re Marriage of Tejeda*, 102 Cal. Rptr. 3d 361 (Ct. App. 2009).

if the court were to determine that both parties in a relationship believed in good faith their marriage was valid, the court would confer putative spouse status upon both parties and divide the marital property accordingly. This interpretation makes perfect sense given that both parties were innocent and honestly believed they were in a legitimate marriage. Therefore, the division of marital property directly attaches to both putative spouses.

In the alternative, it equally makes sense for the division of property to apply directly to a single party whom the court has identified as an innocent putative spouse. Thus, as applied, if the court were to conclude that a single party to a relationship believed in good faith that the marriage was valid, the court would declare that *particular* party a putative spouse, not both parties. Any contrary interpretation would be against the manifest purpose of the Putative Spouse Act and the legislature's intent.

However, given the unclear language, one could propose that a division of marital property rightfully takes place when the court identifies either party or both parties as a putative spouse. In such cases, the guilty spouse would reap a benefit, and the conjunction "or" in the statute not only would serve to dilute the innocent spouse's position but also would be meaningless because the division of marital property would attach to both parties in either situation. Therefore, the plain language of Section 3105.91 is ambiguous. When only one putative spouse exists, it is unclear whether the statute requires the court to grant the non-putative, or guilty, spouse a benefit in the marital property (typically, a one-half interest).

The legislative history, however, sheds light on the appropriate interpretation—one that protects the innocent spouse. The House Committee Report dated April 16, 1986, reflects the legislators' concern that the purpose of the Putative Spouse Act be realized. The report provides that the "judiciary has recognized time and time again the need to protect innocent spouses from the negative consequences of an invalid or illegal marriage that was no fault of their own," and describes two cases in which the courts had applied the putative spouse doctrine in favor of only the one party in the relationship who in good faith believed the marriage was valid. A spouse who was a bad actor was not intended to benefit under the Act. As mentioned in the report, the statute must be interpreted to "preserve the integrity and sanctity of marriage, and protect innocent spouses."

> Identifies the support for Wang's interpretation through legislative history.

> Addresses legislative history after first discussing the plain language or meaning of the words in the statute.

Additionally, the remarks made by Representative Eleanor Murray ("Murray"), the house bill's sponsor, on April 22, 1986, support Wang's interpretation. Murray explained how the Act served to reflect the current case law, and she closed by reminding her fellow legislators that "[w]hen a party believes in good faith that a valid marriage exists, that marriage should be validated." Representative Joshua Eric's statements lend further support for Wang's interpretation and confirm the legislature's purpose in drafting this Act was "to continue to protect the rights of innocent spouses." These statements all reinforce the legislature's intent to limit Section 3105.91's property division to the innocent putative spouse.

On the other hand, Landry will argue that the statutory language is clear and unambiguous and should be applied as written. Nothing in the language of the statute's property division mandate suggests that it is limited to cases in which both parties are putative spouses. Section 3105.91 requires two predicate findings: (1) that the marriage is void or voidable and (2) that either party or both parties believed in good faith that the marriage was valid. Upon making both findings, the court must do two things: (1) declare any party with the requisite good faith belief to have putative spouse status and (2) divide the quasi-marital property in accordance with property division rules under Section 3105.171(B). Thus, as clearly written, once *either* party is declared a putative spouse, the union becomes a putative marriage, and the property subject to this marriage should be divided equitably, without regard to fault.

Additionally, Landry can find support in the legislative history for his interpretation of the Putative Spouse Act. In particular, Representative Murray's statements on April 22, 1986, envision a developing putative spouse doctrine, not one that remains static and merely reflects the current state of the common law. She stated, "th[e] new Act memorializes and codifies this equitable doctrine and makes it possible *for the law to develop* from one unifying legislation." Change is to be expected. Moreover, Representative Murray's comments provide that a grant of marital property to the guilty spouse under the statute should not frustrate the innocent spouse's expectations. As she stated, "With this legislation, we should have a more consistent application of the rules and division of marital property that reflects the expectations of the parties in the relationship. In a marriage, parties arrange their economic affairs with the expectation that, if there is

Margin notes:

Addresses Landry's counter-argument and begins with a plain meaning argument.

Identifies supporting evidence from the legislative history, the floor debate.

a dissolution or end to the marriage, the marital property will be divided equally. The putative spouse doctrine embodies that expectation." Consequently, the legislators' intent in drafting the Putative Spouse Act was clearly to provide for the application of property division rules to all parties of a putative marriage, regardless of fault, guilt, wrongdoing, or perceived unfair advantage.

Furthermore, a review of other related Ohio statutes supports this interpretation. More specifically, Section 3106 concerning order for support and Section 3107 regarding attorney's fees and costs exemplify the legislature's deliberate decision to treat guilty and innocent spouses differently. Section 3106 permits an order for support for a party who has been "found to be a putative spouse." Additionally, Section 3107 allows an award of attorney's fees and costs to a party who is "found to be innocent of fraud or wrongdoing in inducing or entering into the marriage, and free from knowledge of the then existence of any prior marriage or impediment to the contracting of the marriage for which a judgment of nullity is sought." In both of these statutes, the legislature made allowances for the innocent party and specifically carved out provisions for the innocent spouse. A clear distinction was made between the guilty spouse and the innocent or putative spouse in these sections. No such distinction was made in Section 3105.91, however, and that failure to distinguish cannot be interpreted as a mistake or oversight. Under the maxim *expressio unius est exclusion alterius* (the expression of one thing in a statute necessarily means the exclusion of other things), it may be inferred that the legislature intended for the property to be divided without regard to fault.

> Uses a canon of construction to support Landry's interpretation of the statute.

Had it so intended, the legislature could have easily included applicable language, such as a new section (c) that provides, "A court shall not make the orders or declarations authorized in subdivision (a) unless the party or parties that believed in good faith that the marriage was valid requests the court to do so."** Alternatively, the court could have added a new provision (c) (similar to the one in Section 3107) that states:

> Identifies language that the legislature could have included to explicitly limit property division to the innocent spouse.

"(c) Notwithstanding the foregoing, only the party who is found to be innocent of fraud or wrongdoing in inducing or entering into the marriage, and free from knowledge of the then existence of any prior marriage

---

** This proposed language was introduced by the California Senate in SB 254 on February 10, 2011.

or impediment to the contracting of the marriage for which a judgment of nullity is sought shall be awarded property under section (a)(2)."

Landry, therefore, can assert that the legislature did not single out the innocent party or the putative spouse, either explicitly or implicitly, in drafting Section 3105.91. Thus, the legislature did not intend to limit the division of quasi-marital property to an innocent spouse.

Landry's argument will likely fail given the plain meaning of the statute, the development of related legislation, and key statements from the bill's sponsor, Murray. Specifically, Landry's construction of the plain language renders the phrase "the party or parties" meaningless if a court's determination that one party has putative spouse status results in both parties becoming putative spouses. There would be no need to include the word "party" in the statute. The statute permits the court to declare either a single party or both parties have the status of a putative spouse. By giving the court the option of deeming one or both parties a putative spouse, the legislature intended that only an innocent party can seek to be a putative spouse. Furthermore, given that the purpose of Section 3105.91 is clearly to protect innocent parties of an invalid marriage from losing marital property rights, it would be an absurd result to allow a guilty party to reap the benefits of putative spouse status, especially when the innocent spouse did not know there was a putative marriage. If Landry's interpretation were right, then a party who in bad faith conceals his or her bigamy can benefit from a putative marriage. Thus, Section 3105.91 must be interpreted to protect the innocent spouse.

SUBJECT MATTER INDEX

Agency Law

- Apparent Authority: Exercise 37

Civil Procedure Law

- Class Action Certification: Exercise 34
- Forum Clause: Exercise 58
- Jurisdiction: Exercise 70
- Motion for New Trial, After Default: Exercises 40, 51
- Motion to Strike Based on Anti-SLAPP (Strategic Lawsuit Against Public Participation) statute: Exercise 73
- Remand of Removed Case: Exercise 58
- Res Judicata: Exercise 27
- Right to Trial by Jury: Exercise 65
- Service of Process: Exercise 15
- Statute of Limitations: Exercise 87
- Stay of Case Pending Appeal: Exercise 60

Constitutional Law

- Fourth Amendment: Exercises 33, 36, 41, 64

Contract Law and Uniform Commercial Code

- Bailment: Exercise 31
- Force Majeure: Exercise 52
- Consideration: Exercise 30
- Covenant Not to Compete: Exercises 10, 17
- Illusory Promise: Exercise 16
- Implied Covenant of Good Faith and Fair Dealing: Exercise 72
- Minors
  - Disaffirmance: Exercise 45
  - Voidable Contract: Exercise 63
- Offer: Exercises 22, 23
- Statute of Frauds: Exercise 30

Criminal Law

- Act in "Furtherance of" Crime: Exercise 95
- Battery: Exercise 68
- Burglary: Exercises 13, 48
- Teeth as "Dangerous Weapon": Exercise 93
- Felony Murder: Exercise 89
- Mistake of Fact: Exercise 66
- Obstruction of Justice: Exercise 99
- Possession of Controlled Substance: Exercise 86
- Robbery: Exercise 55
- Self Defense: Exercises 79, 88
- Trespass: Exercise 76

Criminal Procedure Law

- Fourth Amendment
  - Apparent Authority to Search: Exercise 36
  - Reasonableness of Search: Exercises 33, 41
  - Standing to Contest Search: Exercise 64
- Voir Dire: Exercise 91

Education Law

- Family Educational Rights and Privacy Act (FERPA): Exercise 78

Employment Law

- Americans with Disabilities Act (ADA): Exercises 11, 82, 85
- Implied For-Cause Contract: Exercises 39, 67
- Workers' Compensation: Exercise 77

Environment Law

- Endangered Species, Habitat: Exercise 96

Evidence

- Admissibility of Line-Up Evidence: Exercise 32
- Hearsay: Exercises 25, 28
- Marital Privilege: Exercise 29

Family Law

- Common Law Marriage: Exercise 57
- Custody
  - Best Interests of Child: Exercise 83
  - Settlement Agreement, Mediation and Fraud: Exercise 84
- Divorce, Jurisdiction: Exercise 70
- Putative Spouse: Exercises 75, 100

Professional Responsibility

- Advertisements: Exercise 19

Property and Landlord-Tenant Law

- Adverse Possession: Exercise 56
- Constructive Eviction: Exercises 53, 54
- Fixtures: Exercise 71

Remedies

- Equitable Estoppel/Tolling: Exercise 50
- Statute of Limitations and Discovery Rule: Exercise 87

Tax Law

- Deductions
  - Donation: Exercise 97
  - Ordinary and Necessary Business Expense: Exercise 80
  - Substantiation of Expense: Exercise 74

Tort Law

- Assault: Exercise 18
- Battery: Exercises 42, 62
- Conversion: Exercise 44
- Defamation: Exercise 50
- False Imprisonment
  - General: Exercise 61
  - Shopkeeper's Privilege: Exercises 46, 47
- Good Samaritan Law: Exercises 14, 81

- Intentional Infliction of Emotional Distress: Exercises 21, 35
- Negligence: Exercises 24, 26
- Negligent Hiring: Exercise 38
- Negligent Infliction of Emotional Distress: Exercise 49
- Premises Liability: Exercise 12
- Tortious Interference with Business Expectancy: Exercise 59

Miscellaneous

- Open Meetings Act: Exercise 69
- Snake Exhibit: Exercise 90
- Statute's Strict Liability Provision: Exercise 94
- Wrestling Statute: Exercise 92